The Dark Well

Also by Brenda Shaw:

Seagate II
The Cold Winds of Summer

To Rich Blumm

The Dark Well

Coming of Age on a Maine Farm

by

Brenda Shaw

Brenda Shaw

Audenreed Press

First edition published 1997
Printed in the United States of America

ISBN 1-879418-89-4

Library of Congress Catalog Card Number 96-85583

Parts of chapters 43 and 44 appeared in a slightly different version in *Pacifica '95*, 1995. ©1995 Lane Literary Guild and/or the author.

Chapter 13 appeared in a slightly different version in *Diarist's Journal*, 51st Issue, 1996. Copyright retained by author.

The names of some persons in this memoir have been changed to ensure their privacy.

Cover and graphics by Susan Applegate

Printed on acid-free paper

Audenreed Press
P O Box 1305 #103
Brunswick, ME 04011
207-833-5016

To the memories of my mother

Bess Marguerite Lynde

and father

Shirley Woodman Shaw

and for my husband and sons

Timothy, James and David

The family is a nourishing and a dangerous place.

—Enid Shomer

Contents

PART SIX: Escape

EPILOGUE

Illustrations

Charts

Photographs (Inserted between pages 341-358)

Acknowledgments

Without the help, encouragement and understanding of many people, this book would never have been published. Without the residencies provided by two writers' havens—Centrum and Walden Farm—the manuscript might never have been completed. The Centrum residency was supported by a grant from the National Endowment for the Arts; the Walden residency by its sponsor, Elizabeth Udall.

Perhaps most important of all are the people who read and commented on the completed manuscript: Quinton Hallett, Vicki Nelson, Mabel Armstrong, Lee Crawley Kirk, Hannah Wilson, Alice Evans, Timothy Weakley and Lynde Russell. Members of the Toad Falls writers group listened and gave valuable comments week by week as I read sections of the manuscript.

My husband, Timothy Weakley, put up cheerfully with the trials of living with a preoccupied wife who neglects things domestic in order to write. He has given me every encouragement and guided me through many computer problems.

Quinton Hallett's meticulous proofreading of the final manuscript saved me much grief, and her advice about style and layout was invaluable. William L. Sullivan was crucial in educating me in state-of-the-art book production and distribution.

Susan Applegate designed an elegant and evocative cover, and two diagrams with which I am delighted. Kay Moore did a magical thing at the right time.

Miriam Walsh, now in her nineties, widow of my cousin Orren, told me much about my mother's side of the family and provided me with pictures of Mother and other family members. She also gave me the Lynde Family Bible that my mysterious Aunt Alta had annotated heavily with comments about family scandals.

I also wish to thank my second cousins once removed Leah May, David Pratt and Dennis Crawford—dedicated genealogists—who helped me fill in some of the missing background of my father's side of the family.

My gratitude also goes to local historians, librarians and graveyard custodians in Maine and Massachusetts, too numerous to name, who provided background material for this book with enthusiasm and good cheer.

Part One: Too Cold to Snow

Prologue

On the night of January 25, 1928, at our farm near the western boundary of Augusta, Maine, I was born in my parents' bedroom behind the kitchen. A blizzard howled outside, and the roads were impassable. The doctor who had been summoned was mired in a snowdrift. Only my father was present to attend my mother.

On the afternoon of August 14, 1928, when I was seven months old, a family tragedy determined the course of my life. For the next five years, I lived in a complicated network of lies and secrecy without consciously realizing it. Then a neighbor, angered that my family was deceiving me, gave me a fragment of the truth. This fragment was the key that sparked my search for the rest of the story.

1. First Memories

"Cogito, ergo sum," said Descartes. "I think, therefore I am." I would reverse this and say, "I am, therefore I think."

Before I could form words, I thought. Traces of these thoughts rise in my mind now as from a dark well. Being preverbal, they are not easy to express in words. They hang disembodied in the air without preliminary or sequel. But for my own enlightenment, I will try to capture these fragments in a net of language:

*   *   *   *   *

At first I am a pair of eyes, very close to the floor. Eyes in a blur of being. The blur is blue-gray and blends into the surroundings. I am also the hands and feet that emerge from the blur, formed and clear. Creatures are always near me who have hands and feet too, but theirs are larger. These creatures aren't blurry—they're all formed and clear like my hands and feet. And then one of them hands me a mirror.

*   *   *   *   *

The blood red sun stares at me over the hill with his awful eye. The shadows grow purple and long. Something has happened that can never be undone.

*   *   *   *   *

I am thumping along the carpet on my hands and knees. I am pretty fast. They laugh at me.

*   *   *   *   *

I am lying in my cot. The kitchen is yellow with sun. The stove is black and hot. The pan on it is black and hot, too. Something in the pan crackles and steams, and its smell makes me long for it. I cry and reach toward it. She knows what I want. She cuts a piece from the thing in the pan and gives it to me. I put it in my mouth and suck the juice. It is tart and salty—just what I wanted.

* * * * *

Someone in a black velvet dress has taken me on her lap. Velvet brushes my cheeks, strokes my hands—soft, still, muffling all sound, all woe. Black for sleep, for peace. Later I learn that velvet can be the color of plums, and when I first see snow I learn it can be white.

* * * * *

I wake. It's dawn. Air and snow drift in chill and sharp beneath the window sash. The light is cold and shimmers through the frost. I cannot see through the window pane: layers of silvered leaf sparkle across it. I know the snow piles deep outside—white velvet, stopping all sound.

I pull myself up on the bars of my crib and clamor for the woman I know as "Mama," who is lying asleep in the next room. I am cold. I want to go into her bed and feel the warmth of her body. She comes to get me and takes me back to bed with her.

* * * * *

Then magically it is summer. I am running from Papa's house to Aunty Grace's house through tall grass. I have words in my head and am beginning to say them. They are fun and the running is fun. I am laughing. Papa is laughing. He catches me. Then I am running again and tumble down onto my stomach, but the ground is soft and doesn't hurt me. I get up and keep running.

I can't put an age to this one: I am being weaned from the bottle to a cup, and learning to use a spoon instead of my fingers. I hate the cup. It is hard against my lips, and when I try to suck the milk it runs out of my mouth, around the edge of the cup, down my chin and onto my chest.

The spoon is clumsy, and I want to use my fingers, but in spite of the difficulty and frustration, I begin to like learning to handle the spoon. Later I have to learn to use a fork. It's clumsy at first, too, but I like stabbing things with it. I have to be careful not to bite the tines when there is food on them.

I soon get used to the cup and forget for a while the joys of the bottle. Then one day I remember how warm and comforting it was. I ask Mama if I can have a bottle again. She goes and finds one, and a nipple, and fills the bottle with fresh, warm milk. She hands it to me and I put the nipple into my mouth. It feels strange and tastes of rubber. Not as I remember it at all. I go outside into the soft sunlight and suck on the nipple, trying to bring back the pleasure I had known. It's hard work trying to get milk through that little hole. A cup is easier. I take the bottle back inside and tell Mama. She smiles, takes the nipple off the bottle, pours the milk into a cup, and I drink it. It seems easy and natural. I never ask for the bottle again.

The first memory which I can relate to a particular age, and which is more than just a disconnected, wordless impression, is of asking Richard Lee, the skinny ten-year-old boy from the farm across the road, how long a thousand days is. He laughs and his black eyes crinkle and he says "You haven't lived a thousand days yet!" It's warm that day and we are wearing summer clothing. As I had been born in January, I must have been about two and a half.

The next memory is of my third birthday party. Richard and his older sister Gracie have come over and given me a blue book with a bird on the cover. A slender bird with a red breast and a bright blue back. A bluebird, of course. But the story inside is about a robin. Robins aren't slender and don't have blue backs. I feel deceived. Then we play a hiding game. I can't remember what was hidden, but after I give up hunting, Richard produces it like magic from the cuff of his trousers.

The time between these very earliest memories and starting school was both a time of peace and a time of rage. The peace was the comfort of home and the presence of loving people. Papa, the woman I knew as Mama, and Aunt Grace—my father's sister who lived with Uncle Fred in the bungalow on the other side of the raspberry field—filled my days and nights with warmth. In spite of the Maine winters, the drafty farmhouse and the ailing furnace, they kept me warm. On cold days I was bundled up snugly and taken out into a chill that stung my face, coated my eyelashes with frost and turned my exhaled breath to crystal. Nights when blizzards howled around the farmhouse I went to sleep safe in my cot in front of the flickering flames of the dining room fireplace, before being taken upstairs to bed with Mama.

The memory of this utter peace before sleep came back to me years later, seemingly out of nowhere. I was married with two young sons, and listening to Corelli's Christmas Concerto as I got supper for my family. The slow movement of the Christmas Concerto always made me sad. I was dropping tears into the salad and wondering why such a beautiful and essentially optimistic piece of music made me cry. Then suddenly the memory came back. I was lying in my cot in the dining room at the farm. It was evening and the fire was sputtering gently in the fireplace. The room was dark except for the firelight playing on the walls and ceiling. There was a feeling of complete calm and peace, such as I have not known since.

It was homesickness, then, for a time and place that no longer existed.

At that point my son David, then aged three, came in, listened attentively to the melody and said "That's 'O Where, O Where Has My Little Dog Gone!'" In a flash I recognized the resemblance and burst out laughing. His wonderful remark did not spoil the music for me, but it took the sadness away. David has also made me listen to Handel with a new ear and wonder which came first, "The Water Music" or "Pop Goes the Weasel" and "Lavender's Blue, Dilly Dilly."

The early memories keep sorting themselves into "warm" and "cold." One is of the first time that I was fully conscious of the wonder of the sun. It was early on a summer morning and the shadows were long as I wandered off alone into the meadow. My arms were bare and the sun was warm and golden on them. The grass was chest high. I sat down, and it was over my head. The sun brought out the sweetness of the grass; the air was full of it. I listened to the tiny sounds of insects humming and buzzing all about me. They made little clicking and snapping noises as they went their way up and down the stalks of grass. The world was beautiful and I was filled with exaltation. Later when I had learned that the world was also ugly, the sun remained a symbol of warmth and strength. It could bring back the beauty of the world and with it the same sense of exaltation. This is what I assume others must mean by religious experience. It was a state of bliss.

Another cold memory: In winter the only warm room in the house was the kitchen, and even there the floor, under its worn and cracked linoleum, was cold. I remember sitting in front of the old wood-burning stove with my feet in the oven. My father said "It's twenty below out there—too cold to snow!" I remember the smell of my damp, heavy woolen stockings, still caked with snow from outdoors, steaming from the heat of the oven.

We kept short, small-diameter logs of wood in the oven all day. At night we put them into old woolen stockings and took them to bed for warmth. I remember the Granny at the Lees' farm who had legs that looked like logs of wood in stockings.

I was attracted to flowers very early. My first 'pet' was a pink geranium. Mama had planted it in a small earthenware pot and set it on the porch railing. I declared it was mine and began carrying it with me everywhere. If I fell down it might fly out of its pot, but I'd tuck it back in and keep going. It never seemed to come to any harm. I even took it into the bathtub with me so it could have a drink. I had a scruffy yellow cloth dog with fake fur about the same time which vied for attention with the geranium.

But, as I said, this time of peace was also a time of rage. And sometimes of fear. The woodwork in the farmhouse, except in the kitchen, was white. All the skirting boards, door frames and doors were white. Most of the doorknobs on the doors were white, but a few were black. I was terrified of the black doorknobs. I would scream when I saw them and could not be comforted. Mama solved this problem by making hoods for the doorknobs out of circles of white cloth held in place with twine or a rubber band.

My father's bedroom closet was another source of trouble. If the door to the closet was shut, all was well. But if it was open it sloped back into the darkness and all I could see was a yawning black hole. Sometimes sounds came from the closet, and if I glanced quickly at the open door I thought I could see, just for a flash, something white moving in there. My father laughed and said the sounds were mice.

I don't know why I was afraid. I don't know why I was angry, either, but I both remember, and was told later—interminably—what a terrible child I had been. I would lie on the floor kicking, calling people "black panthers" because it was the worst epithet I could think of (shades of Jungle Jim in the comics). I would rub my feet together in rage till the skin came off. I remember pushing people down—big people who were leaning over and didn't expect to be attacked from behind by a small child. To my enduring chagrin I've been told I even pushed Gracie Lee down. She'd had polio and was unsteady on her feet.

If Mama was at the sewing machine I would come and give the material a pull, just to disrupt things. I purposely peed on her best rug because it brought shouts of dismay. I took savage delight in throwing rocks through windows and hearing the tinkle of broken glass. I hit people with my fists or with whatever came to hand. An elderly friend of Mama's reproved me once, saying "You mustn't hit your Aunty or your Mama or anyone else. Don't you know that can cause cancer, and cancer kills people? If that happened it would be your fault!"

Although most of these attacks were motivated by malicious anger, one was purely experimental in nature. In the Sunday comics people in the Dick Tracy cartoon were always knocking each other out by a blow on the head. I thought that it would be interesting to see Pa get knocked out. So I sneaked up behind him when he was squatting down to weed the vegetables and hit him on the head with the toy wooden wheelbarrow he had made for me. It did not have the intended effect, however, and he leaped up roaring. I took off at speed with him after me, and was soon captured.

"Why did you do that?" he cried.

"I wanted to see how you'd look knocked out," I said.

Instead of giving me the deserved spanking, he doubled up with laughter and carried me back into the house.

Types of punishment were few, but persistently administered with no improvement in my behavior. I don't recall Papa or Aunt Grace punishing me, but Mama kept a willow switch high up behind the kitchen mirror where I couldn't reach it. Its sting on my legs was excruciating. She also had a yardstick she applied with vigor to my backside. That was a more muted sort of pain. Uncle Fred's remedy was to tie my hands behind my back, or better still, tie me into a heavy chair I could not tip over. The worst humiliation I recall in my childhood was being seen through the window, tied to a chair, by Richard Lee. The next worst one was being seen by him when my cheeks were out like a chipmunk's with the mumps.

I can't recall what brought on the earliest tantrums, but I do recall vividly what happened with the insurance salesman. It was April. The water from the melting snow ran down the ruts in the long farm driveway to the state road. There the water lay in pools in the ditches, and the dead grass poked its fingers through the snow. The sun was warm and the surrounding fields wore a low pall of steam.

I had on a woolen cap, and a sweater covered the top half of my short dress. My legs in thick woolen stockings plunged down into four-buckle rubber overshoes. I wielded a hoe deftly and to effect. I was hoeing mud into dams across the ruts in the driveway. The water backed up behind my embankments to form shallow ponds. The hoe went squish squish in the mud. The mud's water-laden surface gleamed in the sun. I wished my feet were bare so I could feel it between my toes. My concentration was total. Blue space reflected in the pools I had created.

"You'll get your dress dirty doing that," the man said. He wore a crisp light-colored spring suit and carried a briefcase.

"Thought little girls like you would be in the kitchen helping your mother. It's about lunch time, isn't it? Is your father home? I gotta see him about his fire insurance."

I looked at the man. He towered above me. The creases in his trousers were precise. His briefcase was polished and shone in the sun. His smile lay like a snake across his face. I picked up a hoeful of mud and flung it at him. And another. And another.

Years later Mrs. Lee asked me if I remembered throwing mud at the insurance salesman.

"Yes," I said.

"It cost your Pa a lot of money to have his suit cleaned. Can you remember why you threw the mud?"

I tried to think, but the reason was gone. It wouldn't come back to me.

Why I was so filled with ferocity during this early period I didn't know, nor could anyone else explain it. I oscillated between a timeless, innocent peace and a hate-filled rage. I now suspect, in the light of what I've learned since, that I sensed all was not as it should be, that something had happened which I could no longer remember, and that my people were not being honest with me. That, certainly, proved later to be the case.

2. The Trolley Line

The woodcutter, a lean man thin of face and sharp of feature, paused, resting on his axe. Something was different. Something he should be paying attention to. He'd heard no sound but the drip of melting snow. The clouds were yellow-grey and the air smelled of spring. He knew the sap in the maples

21

had begun to rise. He'd tap them soon for the sugaring-off. But what had made him stop to listen? Sap makes no sound.

He looked around him. There was nothing. He shrugged and bent again to his labor. The wind was coming from the northeast, and he could hear the trolley jangling its bell at Morang's Crossing, a quarter mile away. It would soon pass within twenty yards of him on its way through the forest to Granite Hill.

The trolley line marked the boundary of his farm. He'd go and watch it pass. Likely he'd know everyone on board. He stuck his axe into a stump and started off through the snow.

"Papa, Papa, wait for me!"

The man whirled in his tracks. That was what he'd sensed was wrong. The child had followed him into the forest. She was wading through the snow up to her waist.

"For the love of Mike, what are you doing here?" he exclaimed.

"Wanted to come to the woods with Papa."

"Is Mama with you?"

"No. Mama's in the kitchen."

"Jesus, it's a half mile through deep snow up here, and you hardly walking! What if you'd got lost?"

"Followed your tracks."

"If you'd missed me and gone another twenty yards you could have been killed. Quick, I'll put you on my shoulders and show you why."

He lifted the child up and headed for the trolley line. Already he could hear the trolley's clanking approach. They reached the embankment just in time. They looked up and saw the engine and its single coach towering above them, creaking and swaying on the rails. It was red and green and the poles at the doors were made of brass which shone in the weak sun filtering through the clouds. The trolleyman rang his bell and the passengers waved and cheered at the woodcutter and his child, and they waved back.

"I wanted you to see," said the woodcutter. "If you'd got onto the trolley track the driver might not have seen you, you're so small. The trolley could have hit you. It's dangerous, like the road in front of the farmhouse. You must never come near the trolley track alone. You must never follow me into the woods. There are other dangers—water holes, bogs, wildcats, bears, and sometimes moose."

She regarded him with an attentive, serious stare. Was she frightened by his words, he wondered, or just thoughtful?

"I want you to love the woods as I do," he explained, "but till you're older you must come only with me. Do you understand?"

She nodded her head, but said not a word. She understood, but had not promised to obey.

3. Winter Pool

In March I went with Papa to the woods. By now I usually called him just "Pa," and also shortened Mama to "Ma." I don't know why, perhaps it was just easier to say.

The melting snow was not as deep as usual, and we went to a part of the forest I hadn't seen before. There we found a magical thing—a broad sheet of water shining in the shifty sunlight, reflecting the thin trees around its edge.

I clung to Pa's leg; my shoulder came to his knee. "Wading? Wading?" I asked.

Pa laughed. "Too cold," he said. "No wading till summer."

In June, with the sun tacking the clothes to my body with sweat, I remembered the pool. Ignoring Pa's orders about going into the woods alone, I went to find it. I knew that Pa and I had entered the forest near Maude's brook. There was no path, but my sense of direction told me where to go. After a while I found the thin trees. They stood solid and dark on the dry forest floor. Where was the water? Had I found the wrong grove of trees?

I went back home and found Pa in the woodshed, chopping kindling. "Take me to the pool, please, Pa."

"What pool?" he asked.

"The wading pool we found in the winter. You said we'd wade in the summer."

Pa remembered, laughed. "I guess it's not there, now that you need it," he said. "It just collected in that hollow from the melting snow."

I looked up at him in surprise. "But where did the water go, Pa? How could it just go away?"

Pa's face changed and his smile stopped. "Lots of things you think are there forever go away. Things—and people, too," he said.

How could something so beautiful, so magical, so seemingly permanent, be there with its promise in the winter and by summer vanish without trace? And could people really do that too?

4. Lynde

I've always known my brother Lynde. He lived on the farm with us when I was born, but then he went away, so I don't remember him until later when he came back for visits.

Sometimes when I got up in the morning Ma would say to me "Lyndie's here," and I would run quickly to the room I knew he slept in. He'd be lying there asleep, the bedclothes half off him. His dark head would be flat on the bed, the pillow he never used on the floor beside him.

Lynde wasn't little like me. He was lean and strong and almost as tall as Pa. He was warm and handsome with hazel eyes, long lashes and a quick grin. I'd jump on the bed and wake him. Then we'd sit there together and talk, and he'd laugh and laugh at the things I told him. He laughed like a donkey, a braying sound when he breathed in that sent me into paroxysms of delight.

Then he'd get up and take me down into the warm farm kitchen to Ma and go back upstairs to get dressed. He'd stay a few days and then go away again.

Most times he came alone, but once in the summer he came with a friend called "Junie." Lynde told me "Junie" was short for "Junior," which meant he had the same first names as his father.

Junie had a little black car with places for two people to sit in the front and a rumble seat at the back. They took me for a ride up Pelton's Hill which was just past our farm on the road to Manchester. I sat in the rumble seat with Lynde while Junie drove. The warm wind blew our hair, and the sun shone hot upon us. When I looked toward the side of the road, everything was flying by us very fast, but when I looked ahead the hill was like a mountain and seemed so steep we'd never get to the top. We were crawling up its surface. Then I'd look to the side again and things were whizzing by. How could things be both ways at once like that? It was the first time I remember being in a car. It was pure joy.

When I asked Ma why Lynde didn't live with us she told me he was going to school in Boston and lived with friends there. "What's Boston?" I asked. It was a word I hadn't heard before. "It's a place where people live," Ma said. I had no idea then what an important role Boston would have in my life.

In the half-light of my brain, I can just glimpse another memory trace about a car, but cannot place it chronologically. Ma and Pa and I are in Uncle Fred's car going toward Augusta. Ahead of us two cars hit each other. Glass and water are all over the road, and the cars are at funny angles. A little boy and a man and woman get out of one car. We take them back home with us and they stay for a few days until they are recovered enough to go on. The woman's name is Fay and the little boy is Lawrence, but I can't remember the man's name.

Once, later, they come to see us and thank us for helping them. Still later the man comes alone and tells us that Fay has died.

5. The Halletts

The summer I was three, a family lived in a tent on our farm. Vance Hallett had lost his job because he broke his leg. There was no Social Security then, and he couldn't pay his rent, so he and his wife and three-year-old child Kathleen were evicted.

It was a common story, happening to many during the Depression. Homelessness is not new in rich America. In fact, I never knew that America was rich until I grew up and went to Europe and heard all about it.

The Halletts set up their tent in a grove of trees that separated our front and back fields. Using scrap lumber, my father and Hallett built a little house in one of the trees for me and Kathleen to play in. The grove was shady and cool and the back field warm and sweet and full of the smell of wild strawberries. At the far side of it lay the deep woods where we were forbidden to go alone. We romped in the meadow, listened to the buzzing of the insects and calls of the birds, and drank the cold home-made lemonade Ma brought up in the afternoon.

The front and side fields were planted with vegetables and raspberries. We sold the produce to shops in town. The Halletts helped us gather the vegetables and berries; in exchange they could take whatever they needed for themselves. They ate from our garden all summer, and got their water from our deep cold well.

By September when the chill began in earnest, Vance Hallett's leg had healed and he found another job, working in a granite quarry in the village of Granite Hill. This village was about three miles away, at the far side of the deep woods. They found a house there to rent.

Ma and I could visit the Halletts by walking along the logging road till it crossed the trolley line. There we could flag down the trolley. It took us to the Granite Hill terminus which was near the Hallett's house, and Kathleen and I played while our elders talked. In the winter after severe blizzards when the trolley line was impassable, Ma would snowshoe the three miles to Granite

Hill to check on an elderly friend there, and also to make sure all was well with the Halletts. Mrs. Hallett, though only in her late thirties, had already begun to suffer from rheumatoid arthritis and had difficulty walking and doing her housework.

The friendship between our families continued until Hallett got a job in Hallowell, eleven miles away, and then we gradually lost touch.

6. My People

By the time I was three I was becoming aware of the people around me as individuals. I had always known them, but I'd never really thought about them. Now I realized they were each unique and quite different from one another.

Uncle Fred was tall, lean, craggy and stooped. Everything about him seemed knobbly. His loose bib overalls hung down over his bumpy knees. His long face seemed too heavy for his skinny body, and deep furrows ran down his cheeks. His nose was long too, but broad and lumpy at the end. He covered his thin white hair with a cloth cap in winter and a straw sun hat in summer. His wide jaw hung loose and seemed to flap.

I can barely remember when the big steam shovel came to dig up and widen the dirt road in front of the farm. The steam shovel roared and grunted and picked up mouthfuls of dirt and rocks. Then its lower jaw opened and the dirt fell out into the truck. After that, the steam shovel's jaw would flap back and forth like Uncle Fred's.

I heard Richard's father, Merrill Lee, say once that Uncle Fred was as ugly as Abe Lincoln.

Pa was long and lean too, but quite different from Uncle Fred. Pa wasn't ugly and he wasn't knobbly, just thin. His narrow nose was cleanly shaped, except for a small bump on one side; his dark grey hair straight and thicker than Fred's. Ma said it used to be tightly curled, but Pa hated that, and kept plastering it flat under his cap until it straightened out. Pa's eyes were a strong blue, not watery blue like Fred's, and he had a dimple in his chin.

Fred and Pa smoked cigarettes they rolled themselves. They kept packs of thin light-brown cigarette papers in their pockets. When they wanted to smoke they'd lay out one of the papers on the kitchen table, get the can of Prince Albert tobacco and pinch some out. They'd spread this carefully down the length of the paper and roll the paper up around it. Holding the resulting cylinder in their fingers, they'd tap one end against the table to pack the tobacco firmly in place. Then they'd lick the thin line of adhesive on the long edge of the paper and press it closed.

Sometimes they'd have a pack of Camel cigarettes, but mostly it was roll-your-own. Ma and Aunt Grace didn't smoke. Women never smoked, they said.

Aunt Grace was plump, soft to touch and shorter than Ma. Her round face looked happy, and she always had a smile for me. Unlike Fred, she had hardly any wrinkles. Ma said that was because she was fifteen years younger than Fred. Grace's eyes were blue like Pa's. Her silky grey hair curled loosely around her face, but she drew the rest up into a bun or "pug" on top of her head.

In summer Grace sometimes wore low-cut dresses, and when she leaned over I could see the cleavage of her breasts. When I asked what it was, she flushed and laughed. "That's just my fatness," she said.

Ma was almost as tall as Pa, and had the same skinny body and blue eyes. Her cheeks were broad and high, and her nose was broad too. The first time I saw a picture of an Indian chief I thought Ma looked like him. "You think I'm descended from Sitting Bull, do you?" she asked, laughing.

Ma had pale, wrinkly skin, and like Grace she pulled her grey hair up into a pug. Both women wore dresses that came almost to their ankles, though other women who came to the farm often wore theirs just below the knee.

On Sundays, Grace and Fred always ate dinner with us. As with all farm families, dinner was at noon. We'd sit around the table in the big farm kitchen. On the Fourth of July and Thanksgiving and Christmas, however, we'd eat in the dining room and use the silver with the monogram S cut into it.

Uncle Fred was always cross when I was around. He didn't like children. Of course that meant I didn't like him, either. Uncle Fred had a funny stomach. He couldn't eat cucumbers, and kept saying to Ma that I shouldn't eat them either because they'd make me sick. Especially I shouldn't drink milk with them because that would make it even worse. I loved cucumbers and I loved milk, so when Fred ate with us I'd always try to eat both at the same time just to see the disgust on his face. I never got sick.

7. Gender, the Funny Papers and Janet the Pig

Back on the edges of memory I can see myself belly-flat on the sitting room floor with the Sunday "funny papers" spread before me. Pa was belly-flat beside me and was reading to me about Maggie and Jiggs, Tilly the Toiler, Tarzan, Dick Tracy, the Katzenjammer Kids, Li'l Abner and Boob McNutt.

We'd just returned from Hunter's store at the Manchester Forks where Uncle Fred drove us every Sunday morning to get groceries and the papers and to fill up his car with gasoline. The Manchester Forks was so called because at the village of Manchester the Winthrop Road, the Pond Road and the Readfield Road met. Alton Hunter, the proprietor of Hunter's store, was a big man with wild dark brown hair who always wore sandals. His sister, Marguerite, who also worked in the store, was dark too, with a faint mustache on her upper lip and masses of black hair on her legs.

Alton Hunter lived on a farm that lay about half way between our farm and his store at the Forks. He had an enormous mountain of sawdust in the farmyard in which he buried blocks of ice he cut from the lake in the winter. The sawdust kept the ice from melting, and in the summer we went and fetched our ice from under Sawdust Mountain.

I can't imagine how Alton managed his store, his farm and his ice business, unless he had a fleet of relatives behind the scenes to help him. He had two children and, I learned later, a mail-order wife. Alton hadn't found anyone he wanted among the local talent, so he subscribed to an outfit that provided brides to order. The one he got, in turn, provided him with two sons and then swanned off.

I don't know how Alton arranged his child care, along with all his other commitments, after she'd gone. When I was reading the comics, his boys were the same age as the Katzenjammer Kids, and they looked and acted like them too. I thought that was why Alton sold funny papers—because his kids were in them.

Of all the characters in the comics, Boob McNutt most impressed me at first. (Later, Flash Gordon became my god.) Boob McNutt had a big red nose and flaming red hair that stuck straight out from his head. I can't remember what he did in the comics, but I used to spin fantasies about him in my own head which I didn't reveal to anyone.

In some of my fantasies Boob was stark naked. I mention this because, though I knew he was a man, I didn't know that men looked different naked than women did, so I visualized him as looking like me. I'd never seen anyone naked but myself. Everyone else carefully kept their clothes on. I didn't think of nudity as wrong. In fact, I didn't think about it one way or the other—or think it was strange, at that time, that I was the only one who was ever naked.

The necessary revelation came through Janet the pig. Janet arrived as a tiny piglet and grew up in a sty out near the chicken house. Ma and I made a pet of her, of course, and Janet quickly learned to crave our attention. She let us know her desires by squealing o-o-o-o-o-r-e-e-e-e-e, o-o-o-o-o-r-e-e-e-e-e over and over until we came out to her sty. What she wanted was her back scratched, said Ma. We kept a board leaning against the sty to be used as a pig-scratcher. We would reach over the wall of the sty and rub her back with the edge of the board. The o-o-o-o-o-r-e-e-e-e-e's would subside into delighted grunts as she leaned into the board.

Albert Carter, a farmer who lived down past the country school on the Leighton Road, came by one day to see Pa. He had his four-year-old boy Kenneth with him. Janet was sounding off, and I took Kenneth out to the sty and showed him how to scratch her back. After pleasuring her with the board, Kenneth unbuttoned the front of his trousers, drew out a small pink spigot, and peed on her back. I was astounded. How did he do that? I couldn't do that with my equipment. It didn't occur to me to ask Kenneth how he did it, I just assumed I could figure it out myself.

After he left, I experimented, but nothing would induce my stubborn flesh to form itself into a spigot. I approached Ma on this subject. She smiled and said, "Boys are made differently from girls—that's why they're called boys."

So it wasn't just the clothes they wore or the way they cut their hair! I was cross that boys had such a convenient tool and I hadn't. They would never have to suffer the indignity of peeing into their shoes.

8. The Lay of the Land and the Saturday Night Bath

Our farmhouse was big and airy with high ceilings and light-colored, papered walls. In the front and the back it was only one room wide. The sitting room was in front facing the road and Lees' farm, and the kitchen was in back. Between them, Pa's bedroom and the dining room sat side by side.

We mostly lived in the kitchen. Its yellow painted walls and big windows made it light and cheerful, and the big black stove, raised up off the floor on its fancy wrought-iron legs so it wouldn't set the house on fire, kept us warm in winter.

Pa's rocker sat next to the window nearest the stove where the light was best and he could keep warm in winter. He'd read the paper there, or nap.

The big, square, all-purpose table took up the middle of the room. We ate there, shelled peas and beans, hulled strawberries or shucked corn on it, and talked round it when people dropped in. The "new" second-hand refrigerator that had replaced our ice box was next to the dining room door, and we kept the phone on top to be out of the way. When it rang, we'd lift the phone down to talk. It was like a big black daffodil: a long stem set into a base and a round blossom at the top of the stem with a little speaker coming out at the front. A hook on the stem held the receiver, which we lifted to listen. We kept one of the kitchen chairs beside the refrigerator so we could talk sitting down. When Aunt Edith came to see us, she'd always sit in that chair with the cat in her lap and talk to Ma while Ma worked. Once in a thunder storm the lightning came in on the phone line and knocked the phone off the fridge onto Edith's head.

Sometimes lightning would come in on the water pipes too, and jump back and forth between the faucets at the sink. We had lightning rods on all the farm buildings to ground the lightning so it wouldn't start a fire.

The dining room had a big bay window full of plants and a cage with two canaries. It faced the raspberry patch that separated our house from Grace and Fred's bungalow. A sliding screen partition across the bay window allowed us to tend the plants and birds, but kept the cat out.

The fireplace, in front of which I was allowed to fall asleep in my cot on winter evenings, was set into the wall opposite the bay window. Its rich blue and brown marbled tiles glowed softly, both in firelight and in daylight. The sitting and dining rooms were joined by a large five-foot-wide doorway, which was usually left open but could be closed by doors that rolled out from spaces between the walls on each side of the doorway.

The sitting room was large and full of light from windows all along the front. A window on the side overlooked a strip of lawn and the raspberries beyond. Along the wall opposite that window, Ma kept her chaise longue, and she'd nap there sometimes in the afternoon.

In the front corners of the sitting room stood Ma's knick-knack stands, one on each side. On these she kept fresh flowers, bits of china and glassware, photographs, shells, colorful rocks and decorative seed pods and cones she'd found in the woods.

At the front of the house, a large veranda wrapped around three sides of the sitting room. An orange hammock with green stripes hung on the side next to the driveway. The hammock had a seat with a back, and you could either sit on it and swing, or sleep on it

The veranda served as a convenient race track, first for my scooter and later for my tricycle, as long as I was careful not to go too close to the porch steps. I'd get going very fast and loved the rumbling sound of the wheels on the wooden floor.

Our house, the stable and the barn were all connected together by three sheds and a henhouse, so nobody had to go outside in the cold to get to them in winter.

The long driveway, which was a dirt track with grass growing in the middle, came up from the State road, ran along the side of the house and stable, then looped to the left in a gentle curve. Then it plunged down past Grace's bungalow to the road again.

You didn't have to walk up around the driveway to get to the bungalow, however, because "Bean Lane" ran directly across the raspberry patch between the two houses. Bean Lane was a path Pa had built of bricks set in squares and was so called because every summer he planted scarlet runner

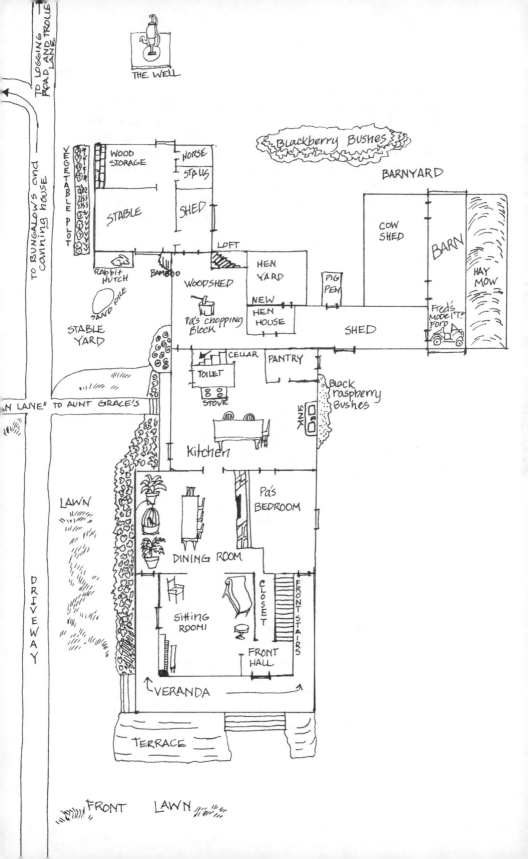

pole beans along it. These formed a leafy corridor decorated first with scarlet bean blossoms and later with long slender bean pods.

Our water supply was out behind the stable. The farm's former owner had drilled a fine deep well there from which the water came up cold and pure.

A big black iron hand pump was set into a concrete curbing directly over the well. The curbing was the favorite sunning place for a family of large, friendly brown snakes with yellow bellies. As she did with all animals, Ma had made pets of the snakes and encouraged me to stroke their warm, satiny backs.

Another, smaller, hand pump was located in the cellar at the foot of the stairs to the kitchen, and a third graced one end of our grey slate kitchen sink.

In the beginning, when I was tiny, that kitchen sink was my bathtub. Pa pumped water from the well into large pans which he placed on the kitchen stove to heat. Then he'd put the plug in the sink, add the hot water and adjust its temperature with bursts from the pump. Then Ma would bathe me.

In summer when it was hot and I was old enough to run around barefoot outdoors, Ma or Pa would bring me in, set me down on the end of the sink, and pump refreshing cold water over my legs and feet to remove the sand and mud.

When I was too big for the sink, the era of the galvanized metal tub on the kitchen floor commenced. Pa heated the water as usual, filled the tub and adjusted the temperature. Then, behind a screen of blanket-covered chairs, I soaked in privacy until the water cooled. Saturday night was bath night, and I loved this new weekly ritual. I had no interest in dolls, so I took my rubber rats into the tub to play with. Pa had bought them for me in Woolworth's. They were made of hollow rubber and had a metal "squeaker" in their bellies so they would squeak when squeezed. I had two grey ones and two white ones.

The tin tub routine was not because our farmhouse had no proper bathroom or indoor plumbing. Unlike many of our neighbors, we had both. Superimposed on our system of hand pumps was an ancient, wheezing electric pump at the foot of the cellar stairs. It was supposed to pump hot and cold water up to two faucets Pa had installed on the kitchen sink, one on either side of the hand pump. The electric pump was also supposed to get water to our downstairs toilet and to the upstairs bathroom. This electrically powered system sometimes worked, but more often did not. Pa was always in the cellar tinkering with it. We kept a pail of water in the downstairs toilet room for flushing, in case the pump gave out.

The large, rather elegant Victorian bathroom upstairs lay behind the back bedroom where Ma and I slept. It was panelled in natural wood and contained a long, slender cast-iron bathtub with dragon's-claw feet and a matching hand basin. The bathroom was beautiful but useless. In winter the water was cut off for fear the pipes would freeze and burst. In summer, it was also mostly unusable, though I never found out why. The few times I tried to use it, the puny amount of hot water available wasn't worth the effort.

I suspect something had gone wrong with the system and Pa couldn't afford to fix it. Although Pa was a farmer, he also had a plumber's license, but he said he never did plumbing for anyone else unless he ran out of money and had to.

There's a saying in Maine that the plumber's own plumbing never works, and it was certainly true in our case.

9. Learning Grown-up Things

The winter after the Halletts lived in our back field, I turned four. That year, 1932, I began to learn grown-up things. On a farm plenty of hard work has to be done, and children are taught young. I was eager to learn.

Ma showed me how to make butter, which we only made in small amounts for our own use. We didn't use our churn, just whipped up what we needed with an eggbeater. The day before my lesson, Ma had poured rich, fresh milk into a pan and set it on the pantry shelf to let the cream rise. By the time we were ready for the butter making, the cream was a heavy, thick layer on top of the pan. Ma skimmed it off with a flat metal skimmer and put it in a bowl. I already knew how to use the old hand-held egg beater. "Just keep beating the cream till the butter 'comes,'" she said. "Watch carefully so you'll see it when it first appears. It will separate out from the cream, and what is left will be buttermilk."

It took a long time and my arms were tired, but I kept at it. At first, tiny yellow specks could be seen coalescing in the cream. Then the cream separated into clumps of butter surrounded by bluish-white buttermilk. Ma showed me how to pat the clumps together into one large ball with a wooden butter paddle and press it and press it till all the buttermilk was worked out. Then she poured the buttermilk off into a pitcher.

She brought out a little wooden box about six inches square with a lid that lifted off. On the bottom of the box someone had carved a design. Two incised lines crossed each other, forming four small squares. Inside each square was a carving.

"This is a butter mold," Ma explained. "Those carvings on the bottom are the designs you see on playing cards: a Heart, a Spade, a Diamond and a Club. Fill the mold with butter, pressing it in with this wooden spoon."

I did so, making sure all the corners were filled and the middle pressed hard enough to get the butter into the designs on the bottom.

"Now, put the lid on and take the mold out to the ice box to harden," Ma directed. "When it's cold, the mold will come off cleanly, and you'll have a pound of butter that can be cut into four quarters."

Aunt Grace taught me to roll out pastry with a rolling pin and to make "turnovers" by filling flat rounds of pie crust with home-made jam, folding them over and thumbing the edges together. She showed me how to make designs on the pie crust with a knife by making little cuts so the steam could escape.

She demonstrated how to mix eggs, milk, sugar, nutmeg and cinnamon and pour the result into brown pottery custard cups to bake in the oven. She divulged the art of making French omelettes with eggs beaten full of air. These were baked in the oven and came out golden brown and marvellously light, unlike the heavy unbeaten ones fried in bacon fat in the black iron skillet.

Aunt Grace's cooking lessons took place in Ma's canning house, which was next to the bungalow and convenient to the raspberry field. Pa had built the canning house for Ma out of lath and plaster covered with paperboard. It measured about fifteen by twenty feet, and had a lot of shelves and work tables around the edge. In the middle sat an old black stove with a metal stovepipe to a vent in the roof.

Everyone said Ma made the best jellies and jams anywhere in the area. The jelly was clear, the color of rubies, full of flavor and always jelled to perfection. During the fruit season, she was out in the canning house every day, and people came from miles around to buy not only her jelly and jam but also our freshly picked raspberries, corn and other vegetables straight from the fields. Aunt Grace cooked in the canning house when Ma wasn't using it. It was roomier, cooler and more convenient than the kitchen in her bungalow.

I wanted Ma to teach me how to make jelly, but she wouldn't do it. It was too dangerous. Boiling pans of juice were not to be interfered with by four-year-olds, and I was warned to keep out of the way.

Ma did, however, show me how to use a needle. She had been a tailoress, and still made clothes for me and Aunt Grace. A tailoress was what we called a woman who made men's suits. Men who couldn't afford a tailor went to a tailoress, because she didn't charge as much.

Ma taught me to cut cloth for dolls' clothes with care and save the bits. Then she showed me how to turn the bits into designs for quilt making. She started doing this after I had stolen two large pieces of cloth—a browny-gold one and a deep red one. I had taken the cloth and the shears, a spool of thread, and a needle out in the back shed and made myself a "dress."

I had watched Ma lay out patterns, cut the cloth to match the shapes, and then pin the shapes on me or on Aunt Grace to see if the garment would fit. I don't know what she had planned to use the pieces of cloth for, but I decided to make something for myself. I had no pattern, so I cut the pieces by eye. I felt excited and free and joyful and worked very fast. I'd seen someone wearing a skirt and bolero of one color and a blouse of another, so I cut the browny-gold cloth into two shapes, one that would go around my waist and come to my knees. The other I folded in half and cut armholes and a neck hole in it. Then I slit it down the front to form the bolero. I did the same to the red piece, but didn't cut it down the front, so it could be used as a blouse.

I sewed these pieces up with long basting stitches as I'd seen Ma do, and put them on. Then I went back to the farmhouse and found Ma in the sitting room talking with someone who had stopped by. I remember their shocked faces and a jumble of words. One phrase, ". . . but it fits her!" stood out from the rest.

To my surprise I wasn't punished for cutting up the cloth. After letting me wear my creation around till I got tired of it, Ma kept it as a souvenir. She showed it to me many years later.

Ma also tried to show me how to knit. I'd been watching her intently as she knit a sock, so she took four more needles, cast on the first row, knit another row on top of that, and then handed the needles to me. She began to explain how to make the stitches, but I couldn't get it straight. What she said didn't seem to be what she did herself. Ma was a patient woman, but I was not a patient child. "I'll do it myself!" I snapped, and walked out the door with my knitting. Wisely, Ma let me go without comment. I sat down on the back porch and concentrated hard.

I don't remember how long it took me, but suddenly what I'd seen and what I'd been told fell into place and I understood what to do.

It was autumn then, and that Christmas I gave Richard Lee the results of this first attempt at knitting—a pair of wristers to fill the gap between his gloves and the sleeves of his too- short jacket when he delivered milk on cold mornings.

I learned a lot in the house, but what I liked doing best was following Pa about wherever he went. Summer and winter I dogged his footsteps whenever he would let me. He seldom spoke, but we seemed to understand each other without words.

He gave me a tiny plot at one corner of the vegetable garden and showed me how to plant vegetable seeds in the ground. All summer I tended them, watched them sprout into seedlings and grow into plants. He told me to let some of the strongest plants go to seed, then demonstrated how to collect and save the seed to plant next year. Ma also gave me a tiny plot in one of her flower borders in which to plant flower seeds.

Often Pa took me up through the back field and into the woods, which I loved. In summer, he showed me how to find and pick wild strawberries, and told me the names of the golden rod, hawkweed, daisies and Queen Anne's lace that filled the fields. The woods were perfumed by the smell of pine and fir, maple and beech, ash and poplar. Jays, chicadees, orioles, and blackbirds called in the trees. Woodpeckers rang out their machine-gun tattoos. Sometimes a partridge would start up, the thunder of its wings beating the air. Shade-loving trilliums, lilies of the valley, Stinking Benjamins, Jacks-in-the Pulpit, puff-balls and ferns were scattered over the forest floor. Pa would collect the "fiddle-heads" from the ferns to take back for Ma to cook. Sometimes we found lady's slippers, but never picked them because they were rare and "must be left for others to see."

In winter, the woods were different but equally wonderful, with snow deep on the ground and the trees burdened with it. Pa would put on snow shoes and carry me on his shoulders. Later he made me skis out of barrel staves to keep me from sinking into the snow.

In March when the sap in the maples began to run, he showed me how to tap the trees and collect it. We went to the woods in the morning and located a maple grove. With a hand drill Pa made a hole about three inches deep in several of the trees. Into each hole he hammered a tap.

The kind of tap Pa used was a tubular piece of metal wider at the open end and tapering down to a closed end. The closed end had been cut crosswise so maple sap could seep through the cuts into the tap. The taps had a hook underneath at the front where Pa hung a glass jar for the sap to run into. It seeped out drop by drop.

"We'll come back this afternoon and the jars will be nearly full," he said.

We returned with a sled on which Pa had secured a large pot. We emptied the sap into it, then replaced the jars on the taps.

When we got back home, Ma put the pot on the stove and got the sap boiling. Water boiled off as steam, and as the sap became more concentrated the kitchen began filling with the sweet aroma of maple syrup. When it was the proper thickness, Ma removed the pan to cool, but put some of the syrup into a smaller pan to continue boiling.

"We'll have to watch it carefully now so it doesn't burn. It will soon turn into maple sugar. Just before it sets hard, we'll put it into these little leaf-shaped molds, and when it's cool it will be maple sugar candy."

It was the best candy I'd ever tasted.

Of course learning didn't stop when I turned five, but much of it was of a different sort. When I started school, my world expanded beyond belief—in ways both good and evil. But the year I was four laid down the homely bases of survival: cooperation, the enjoyment of hard work, delight in craftsmanship, and understanding of the cycles of nature.

10. The Chick

The chicks were fluffy and golden. I cupped two gently in my hands, careful not to squeeze them. I was five now, and had been taught to handle small, delicate creatures with care.

Pa had bought the chicks—twenty-five of them, a day old—the week before. He'd given them to me. I would be their mother until they were old enough to join the other hens.

It was April. The chicks lived in a box in the kitchen, with a preserving jar full of warm water at the center for them to cuddle around. The jar was covered with the soft remains of an old angora sweater.

If the chicks' chirping was contented, all was well. If one by one they started a chorus of "Yip, yip, yip" it meant the bottle was cooling off. I'd refill it, and as they crowded around its renewed warmth I'd make the "h-r-r-r" sound with my tongue that a mother hen would make to calm them. The yipping would cease, and a contented sleepy tweeting would follow.

Today it was warm in the kitchen. The sun shone into the box and onto the kitchen linoleum. I set several chicks onto a sunlit patch on the floor. They teetered on toothpick legs. I touched their honey-colored down gently. They pressed themselves to the warmth of my hands. "You play in the sun. I'll fill up your bottle," I said.

While I was at the sink Pa came in from the woodshed, not expecting chickens on the floor. His big foot barely missed one, trod squarely on another. When he raised his foot at my shriek the chick was totally flattened, though still in one piece.

Pa said, "Oh Christ, the poor little thing. It shouldn't have been out of the box." Quickly he put the remaining chicks back with the others. I touched the flattened shape.

"It's dead," said Pa.

"What's 'dead'"? I asked.

"It's been hurt so bad it's not alive anymore. It'll never breathe again."

I sat by the body and watched. I touched it gingerly, but it would not respond.

"It's dead," Pa said again.

"No, it's not. Look. It's not flat any more, Pa. It's swelling up again. It's not dead."

Sadly, Pa took the chick in his two hands. "No," he said. "When I flattened it, it broke inside. Now the insides are getting their shape back a little, but they're too broken to work any more. Come. We'll go and bury it. That way it will dissolve into the ground and help the flowers to grow."

A dead chicken make the flowers grow? How could this be? I went out with Pa to go and see.

11. The Lees and the "Near Miss"

From the earliest times I had been told never to cross the road to the Lee farm unless someone was with me. Cars coming from the direction of Manchester Forks disappeared into a dip at the bottom of Pelton's Hill, rose up again shortly afterwards, and passed our farm. Ma, Pa and Aunt Grace had all told me I must STOP and look hard at the hill and then at the place where the dip was, to make sure nothing was in sight. Then I had to WAIT to make sure no car had disappeared into the dip just before I'd looked. Otherwise one could pop up out of the dip, run over me and kill me.

I was also told I must never go to the Lees without a good reason. They were busy people and all worked very hard—even Richard, who was the youngest. They must not be disturbed by young children wanting to be played with.

I listened to all this carefully. I understood that the Lees were busy, and that being run over by a car was dangerous and could kill me (whatever that meant), but the lure of the Lees was sometimes too strong. Even though they did not live on our farm and the road separated us, they seemed like my own people.

The Lees' kitchen was the hub of their universe, and everyone seemed to be in it or passing through it. Richard and Mr. Lee came in and out with milk pails or fruit and vegetables from the garden, or to warm themselves at the stove in winter when the clothes rack steamed by the stove. Gracie was there before or after school, and her older sister Harriet was too, when she came home on vacation from Gorham Normal School where she was learning to be a teacher. The oldest Lee boy, Bob, had gone off to West Point in 1927, before I was born, to train for the Army Air Corps. Bob Lee wasn't even a face to me. He was an aeroplane flying so low overhead that he shook the houses. Everyone in the neighborhood would run outdoors when that great vrooming monster passed over. They would wave and wave at the underbelly of Bob's plane as it continued on to land at the Augusta Airport. The Lees would dash off in the milk van to meet him, and he'd stay a few hours and then continue on his mission.

Unlike us, the Lees were a brown-eyed family, except for Mrs. Lee who had hazel eyes. She wore knee-length cotton housedresses covered in front by an apron which went from her neck to her knees and tied in the back. Her legs were thin and wiry and strong and never still. She was always on the go from sink to stove to pantry to milkroom and back. She was like a bird, bright-eyed and quick, darting everywhere, and always cheerful, interested, taking everything in with a laugh or a smile or some lively comment. Openness and love of life seemed to flow from her.

Nan Townsend, Mrs. Lee's mother, lived with them. She was a thin, large-boned woman, taller than Mrs. Lee, and must have been very strong and impressive when young. Now she moved slowly as if her legs hurt, and mostly worked sitting down at the kitchen table. There she shelled peas, husked corn, peeled vegetables, knit, sewed, darned or did whatever else had to be done. Her bumpy hands were never idle. She was kind to me, but could be sharp-tongued if I did not behave myself. So could Mrs. Lee. None of the Lees took any nonsense, but they let me know where the boundaries were in a clear but kind way. I never felt strange or afraid or upset when I was with them.

I had one near miss with a car when I sneaked across the road to see the Lees one day. I did stop and look to see if the road was clear, but didn't bother to wait to make sure no car was hidden in the dip. I shot onto the road, running as fast as I could. The enormous square radiator of a car appeared from nowhere, coming right at me, but only for a flash, as my speed carried me out of its way. I didn't think anyone would find out about this, and told no one.

Next day Gracie came over and took me back to their kitchen. No one else was in it, for once. Gracie looked at me severely and said, "You almost got run over yesterday!"

I looked up at her in surprise. "How did you know?"

"Mrs. Luce came in and told Mother 'I almost killed that child—she ran straight out in front of me, and I missed her by an inch!' She said she didn't stop shaking for an hour afterwards!"

Mrs. Lee, who was in the milkroom and heard us talking, came into the kitchen and joined us. "You mustn't do that to people, Brenda. Mrs. Luce was very upset. And what do you think your Mama and Papa would do if you got killed?"

I just looked down and said nothing, but the shock of seeing that car radiator at my shoulder had gone from head to toe, and now my embarrassment at learning that the Lees knew all about it was acute. Next time I crossed the road against orders, I stopped and waited.

No one spoke of the near miss at home. Did they not find out? Or is it just a hole in my memory that I'd rather leave blank?

Or were the Lees appointed by mutual consent to get the point across?

12. Barton, Edith, and the Magic of Reading, Writing and Music

When I was four, another uncle was added to the farm. His name was Barton, though everyone called him Bart. Before that, just on the edge of memory, I'd gone with Ma and Pa and Aunt Grace in Uncle Fred's car to Boothbay Harbor, a town on the coast forty miles away, to visit Barton and his wife Edith. Of that trip I remember only being in the car, the names "Boothbay Harbor," "Barton," and "Edith," and sitting around in the kitchen of their small apartment. The apartment was and clean and tight and like no place I'd ever seen.

The kitchen stove, square and cream-colored instead of black iron, didn't have a smoke pipe. Instead of burning wood, it lit up in four places on the top when Edith struck a match; then it smelled sharp and sour. In the corner beside the stove stood something called a "Frigidaire"—tall and white with a door that opened in front. On top sat a round white thing with holes in it that Pa said made the inside cold. The only ice inside was a tray of little square ice cubes, but it was certainly cold! We hadn't got our electric refrigerator yet, and I thought it was funny they didn't have an ice box out in a shed like we did.

That summer Barton and Edith came to the farm and stayed with us while Fred, Pa and Barton built a house for them in the field on the far side of Grace and Fred's bungalow. I remember the house going up. They dug an enormous hole in the ground called a cellar and drove wooden posts down into it. Under the magic of their hammers a frame rose up out of the cellar and took the shape of a house. With sharp, accurate zaps of their hammers they nailed many boards to the frame. The men never missed a nail when they struck. When I tried it, I only struck my thumb. I was told, "Let the men drive the nails. Little girls don't do that." I was furious.

The house was up in two weeks and the men working inside it. By the end of the summer Barton and Edith were living in it.

Right from the beginning I was afraid of Uncle Barton. He was big and broad with a square face and terrible eyes that stuck out and glared at me. They were black and reminded me of the black doorknobs in the farmhouse that Ma had to cover up for me. Everyone else in the family had blue eyes, except for Lynde, whose eyes were hazel.

I kept out of Bart's way because I sensed it wouldn't take much to put him out of control. So I had two uncles who didn't like me. Fred never had, with good enough reason, but Aunt Grace made up for Fred. Aunt Edith couldn't make up for Barton, however. She seemed to have no personality at all. I never recall her talking when she stayed with us. She just sat stroking the cat and listening to the others, or was in her room reading while she pretended to be having a nap. I know. I went in one time unannounced and caught her at it. She was very cross about that. "You shouldn't be in here, Brenda! My room is private. You must never ever come in when my door is closed."

I'd always had the run of the house. It was the first time I'd heard the word "private." I asked Ma about it, and she explained that privacy was something people needed sometimes.

Edith wasn't a bad woman, I didn't dislike her and I didn't fear her. She had a long, horsey face and short, tightly waved grey hair that sat close to her head. She had no eyebrows or eyelashes and used to paint them on. Since she couldn't do it with her glasses on and couldn't see with them off, the results were bizarre.

I never remember Edith helping the busy Ma and Aunt Grace. Bart didn't do much either, once the house was built. He was supposed to be helping Pa and Fred run the farm, but he was seldom out there with overalls on. Instead, he lounged about their house in a loose beige cardigan and brown pants and always seemed to be wearing slippers. Often he wasn't around at all. I didn't know where he went or what he did, or how he got there. Like my father, Barton couldn't drive and had no car. But Aunt Edith was always at home. After the house was finished inside she kept it spotless, but I never saw her do any housework. She was always just sitting there reading. But done the housework must have been, for there was never anything out of place. I'd never seen a house that clean before.

Ma and Aunt Grace never sat and read to themselves. They never had time, though whenever they could, they read to me. So did Pa. He read to me every evening and then chased me around the house till I was tired enough to "scooter" off to bed on my red scooter. This ritual was referred to as "Read It, Run It and Scooter It".

Aunt Grace loved to sing, and she taught me many of the songs in *The Community Songbook*. She also told me stories as she worked. I told her stories, too—long involved sagas about my pet chickens, whom I considered my equals.

But my constant demands for attention were wearing everyone down. To give Ma and Aunt Grace some relief, Ma arranged that I go for an hour or so in the afternoons to the Lees. Gracie Lee was in high school and got home on the bus about half past two. She agreed to teach me the letters of the alphabet and numbers. She cut all 26 letters and the numbers one through ten out of left-over scraps of wallpaper, and used these to decorate the little room where we worked. She pinned them up on the wall in the proper order so I could see them. Because they'd been cut from wallpaper scraps they were all different colors. Some had light and dark beige swirls on them, others had cherries or green leaves or flowers or birds.

Gracie would tell me the names of each letter and then the different sounds each letter could make. A made the sound of its name sometimes, but

41

sometimes it was "ah" like car or "ah" like cat. B sounded like the beginning of its name, which was like the beginning of my name. B only made that one sound instead of three sounds like A.

Gracie showed me how to hold a pencil and try to draw the shape of each letter. We would do a few letters and a few numbers each day. I was fascinated by the sounds of the letters and by the feel of my hand trying to make the shapes with my pencil. It was hard work, but I wanted to do it.

Some time later that year Aunt Grace, driven frantic by my constant demands to be read to, said: "I haven't time to read to you, but I shall teach you to read so you can do it for yourself!" I was ecstatic. She sat me down and gave me a crash course in how to sound out words. It was exactly the right time to do it. Gracie Lee's work with the letters of the alphabet had prepared the ground and planted the seed. It seems to me now that it only took a couple of weeks to get to reading on my own, but common sense tells me that can't be so. I was in a state of bliss and off everyone's back after that.

The Community Songbook, which Aunt Grace had introduced to me, also paid off. I spent hours singing to myself and listening to music.

We had an ancient "graphophone," and its big cabinet under the turntable was full of records. The graphophone was taller than I and had a winding crank near the top. I had to stand on a chair to crank it. Its metal needles had to be replaced every few playings. Some of the records were warped so they and the graphophone head went up and down as well as round and round. I played the records over and over and knew all the songs by heart: "My Darling Clementine," "The Anvil Chorus," "The Forge in the Forest," "The Church in the Wildwood," "La Golandrina," "Santa Lucia," "I'll Take You Home Again, Kathleen." Geraldine Farrar sang a whole record full, and there were lots of Stephen Foster: "Carry me Back to Old Virginny," "My Darling Nelly Gray," "Old Black Joe."

Harry Lauder sang Scottish songs, such as "A Wee Deochandorus." On the radio I heard cowboy songs, which Pa sometimes sang too: "Home on the Range," "Red River Valley," "The Streets of Laredo." He also sang other songs: "Pop Goes the Weasel," "The Arkansas Traveler," "Turkey In the Straw," "How Much Wood Can a Woodchuck Chuck" and "Oh they cut down the old pine tree/and they hauled it away to the mill/to make a cradle of pine/for that baby of mine/when they cut down the old pine tree."

Something very unpleasant must have happened when I was listening to "La Golandrina," which was one of my favorites. I can't remember what it was, but I began feeling sick when I heard the record. If anyone played it, I would begin to cry and scream and tell them to turn it off. Later I forgot my fear of that song and began playing it again. When Ma reminded me that for a long time I didn't want to listen to "La Golandrina" this surprised me, as I could remember nothing about it. Yet today, I can look back and recall both the sick feeling and my surprise when I was later told about it. Some odd kind of double repression seems to have been at work.

13. Picking the Bones

I wake at dawn, a dream slipping from my grasp. I can't remember the dream, but as I lie there in the half-light, letting my mind free-wheel, a scene from decades ago, in the farmhouse of my childhood, floats into it.

Ma is teaching me how to pick the remaining bits of meat from a cooked chicken carcass. "Look," she says, "see the neck. It's curved and the grain of the meat follows the curve. To get it off, bend the neck back against the curve."

I bend the neck. The flesh at the cut ends springs back away from the bones.

"Now just peel it off."

It comes easily away in my fingers. I eat the long bands of muscle.

"That's all you need to do with the neck," Ma says. "The flesh comes off quite cleanly. The back will take you longer. See those two ivory colored rings? Those are the rims of bony depressions. Inside the depressions is dark meat. You can dig it out with your thumb."

I dig. The thumb-sized pieces slip out whole. They are tender, rich and delicious.

"The smaller depressions over here are too small for thumbs. Pick up the back and use your front teeth. They'll fit into the depressions."

They did.

"Now turn the back over. See all the little pockets in the bone? The meat will come out of them the same way."

Beige, to ivory, to cream, to umber-colored shapes of flesh in various sizes come out, each with its own taste and texture. Soon only two larger dark masses are left, one on each side of the midline.

"What are those?" I ask.

"Just meat," she says. "Eat them, they're good."

They were.

Later, when I took comparative anatomy at the University, I learned that those dark masses were the chicken's kidneys, and the little cocked hats on top of them the adrenals. In the smaller pockets were lymph nodes and glands. I'd known their taste, now I knew their names.

Ma was a product of hard times, and my childhood was no exception. She taught me young the arts of survival: Day One: the roasted fowl. Days Two and Three: the cold meat. Day Four: the carcass, stripped of every bit of flesh as our reward before the bones went into the pot to be boiled. With them went the inedible parts of vegetables which, though unchewable, would yield a nourishing brew. The resultant stock, when strained and chilled, was a protein gel. With the fat removed it would be mixed with sliced vegetables to form two days' worth of soup.

I cannot to this day bear to see anyone throw out a chicken carcass unless it has been carried through to this stage. To do less with it is sin.

14. The Revelation

The second event that changed my life happened in the summer of the year I turned five. (The first event occurred before I could remember it, something I would not learn about for many years yet.)

I was "helping" Ma make an angel cake for Aunt Grace's birthday, and Ma didn't have enough eggs. We only kept about a dozen hens, and at that time most of them were "brooding": sitting on a clutch of fertile eggs. They wouldn't lay again till after the chicks had hatched.

Ma dug into her purse and handed me some money. "Here, take this over to the Lees and ask if they can let us have a dozen eggs. Be sure to stop and look both ways for cars," she shouted after me as I streaked off. I did as I was told. Since the road past the farm had been transformed from dirt to tar, the traffic had increased in both volume and speed. I'd been well trained, and the "near miss" I'd had reinforced it.

I found Mrs. Lee in the milkroom sterilizing bottles which would be filled with milk and delivered to customers on the milk route.

"Ma wants to know if she can have a dozen eggs," I said.

Mrs. Lee turned and gave me a kind of look I'd never seen before. Had I done something wrong?

"She's *not* your mother, she's your grandmother," she said.

"She is not!" I cried. "She's my *Mama.*"

"No," Mrs. Lee said firmly, "she's your grandmother. Your *father's* mother."

I stared at her. Her usually kind and smiling face looked hard, angry, impatient. It couldn't be true. She must be lying. But Mrs. Lee didn't lie. I didn't know anyone who did. I was the only person who lied—until Ma and Pa told me it was wrong. Everyone else knew it was wrong and didn't lie.

I turned and fled from the house, across the road toward home, not even bothering to look for cars. When I reached the farmhouse, I stopped cold. I didn't dare tell Ma what Mrs. Lee had said. How could I even say it? I turned and headed along the path through the raspberry field that led to Aunt Grace's. She was at the kitchen sink scrubbing Uncle Fred's dirty handkerchiefs on a washboard. She looked up and smiled, then stopped smiling when she saw my face. I just looked at her for a moment, then:

"Is Ma my mother or my grandmother?"

She looked as if someone had struck her. She didn't say anything for a minute. Then slowly, distinctly, pausing between words she said "She's. . . your. . . grandmother."

"Who is my mother?" I whispered, hardly able to speak.

Again she paused, so long I wondered if she would answer at all. Then I suddenly remembered about "Florence," a name often mentioned—the woman Ma said had been my father's wife, who had died. "Was Florence my mother?" I asked.

"No." she answered.

"Then who is my mother?" I shouted at her, the frustration unbearable.

Her answer was one word only: "Bess."

"Where is she?"

"Dead," she spat out.

I drew back in shock. I'd never seen Grace angry before. She turned abruptly back to the washboard and resumed scrubbing. It was clear from her face and voice that she would tell me nothing more. Perhaps none of them would tell me—not the woman I had called "Mama," not Pa, not the seldom-seen Lynde. I didn't dare ask again, but I never forgave them—and I never stopped looking for my mother.

15. The Neighbors

It may seem strange I had never questioned that Ma was my mother, but my experience was very limited. I was not versed in the normal social and family relationships of the world outside. My life was contained within the distance I could walk. The people in it were the only ones I really knew, and I had known them all my life.

I had seen other children and their parents only in passing. The Lees didn't count. They weren't "children." Gracie was nearly through high school and a "grown-up" as far as I was concerned. Harriet and Robert had already left home. And Richard? He was thirteen—eight years older than I—and not a child either. He didn't "play" and never had. Life was serious business for the

Lees, all of them had always worked. Pre-teen and teen culture didn't exist yet, at least not in rural Maine.

Before I went to school, my world consisted mostly of our farm, with its three houses and outbuildings, and four neighboring houses. My father had never learned to drive, nor could he have afforded to run a car if he had. Uncle Bart didn't drive either.

Uncle Fred had a second-hand Studebaker that got him to and from his work at the shoe shop in Augusta, and got the vegetables to market. The trolley cars, which impressed me so vividly as a toddler, no longer ran by the time I went to school, and the only public transport to Augusta three miles away was an occasional bus. The bus served to get Pa to the plumbing jobs he did in the winter to supplement the meagre income from farming. By then the Depression was biting hard, and most people had two jobs to keep afloat. Uncle Fred worked five days a week at the shoeshop, winter and summer, and helped Pa on the farm evenings and weekends.

Aside from our immediate neighbors and people who came to buy vegetables, berries and jelly, few outsiders entered my world:

Mr. Wilson, the fish man, a grey and colorless soul, came on Tuesdays and supplied us with mackerel, trout, clams, lobsters, oysters and finnan haddie. Clam chowder, oyster stew and boiled lobster, which we took completely for granted, now seem to me to be some of the finest things in New England life. Or any life.

Charlie Fifield, the meat man, came on Wednesdays. He was skinny and sunken-faced with only the stumps of a few rotten teeth showing in his perpetual grin. He had a wracking cough and smoked like a damp chimney. He liked children.

Alton Hunter ran a delivery service from his all-purpose store at the Manchester Forks, and his delivery van came to the farm when we phoned in an order.

The Lees' house was directly across the street from us, but if I crossed the road and walked left toward Pelton's Hill, the only other house I would get to was just on the other side of Maude's brook. The brook was so-called because Maude Whitman lived beside it. She was a dwarf with a large, heavy head, no neck and short legs hidden beneath her ankle-length dresses. By the time I was eight, I was taller than she was. She lived with Joe, a shadowy figure I don't really remember. Later Richard told me Joe used to beat Maude.

I never went to Maude's house alone, but often went with Ma or Aunt Grace. They took Maude fruits and vegetables and flowers because she was very poor and couldn't afford much to eat.

If I walked along the road to the right, there was only our farm on our side and the Lee's orchard and hayfield on the other. I never went further than the end of our property, which was at Morang's Crossing where the trolley line cut across the road and went up the eastern boundary of our woods. The

46

crossing was known as Morang's because the people who built our house in late Victorian times and lived there for years were named Morang.

Diagonally over the Crossing was the Connors farm where Laura and Chester and their teenage children Harry and Helen lived. Laura and Helen were the fattest people I had ever seen. Between them they must have weighed a third of a ton. They waddled when they walked, and made squishing noises when they sat down. Helen would have had a pretty face if her eyes had not been obscured by fat. Laura's eye teeth protruded forward, giving her face the look of a tusked boar. Tufts of hair sprouted from her nostrils.

Ma told me that she once saw Laura and Helen downtown in Woolworths. They were walking side by side down the wide middle aisle, and were brushing merchandise off the counters on both sides.

Chester and Harry, in contrast, were lean and angular. They looked so much alike they could have been twins except for the difference in age. They were always dressed in dung-stained overalls, and seemed to spend a lot of time shovelling manure. Chester had the only bull in the area, and I often saw Richard's father, Merrill Lee, "taking a cow for a walk" down to Chester's. When we had a cow, which we did on and off, Pa used to take her for a walk too. No one explained why, and I just assumed that cows, like dogs, enjoyed taking walks.

The Connors' house smelled unlike any other I'd been in. The Lees' house smelled of things like fresh warm milk, hot cookies, apple cider and the dog. Maude's house smelled like work clothes and Joe's dirty socks. Our house smelled of wood fires, whatever was in the oven, and Prince Albert tobacco. But what the Connors' house smelled of, it took me some time to learn. It was cluttered, but so was our house. Everyone was too busy coaxing a living out of the ground to be house-proud. I finally realized that the Connors' house was not just cluttered, it was filthy. The cats were given the run of it and never house trained. Richard told me he was in their kitchen once when a piece of cooked meat fell onto the floor beside a cat's mess and Laura just picked it up and put it back on the plate without a word.

As bad as the cat smell, but quite different, was the human smell. The Connors had no bathroom, and they apparently lived up to the old farm practice of "one bath in summer and not quite so many in the winter." It was the first place where I had encountered the full-strength pong of unwashed human flesh.

Just along from the Connors' was a Shell filling station and a small restaurant called McAuley's. The McAuleys lived above it. McAuley was a huge black man who ran the canteen at the State House in Augusta while his beautiful mulatto wife tended the restaurant and looked after the three children. I thought that, after Harriet Lee, Mrs. McAuley was the most beautiful woman I had ever seen. Later when I saw photographs of Lena Horne I recognized a resemblance.

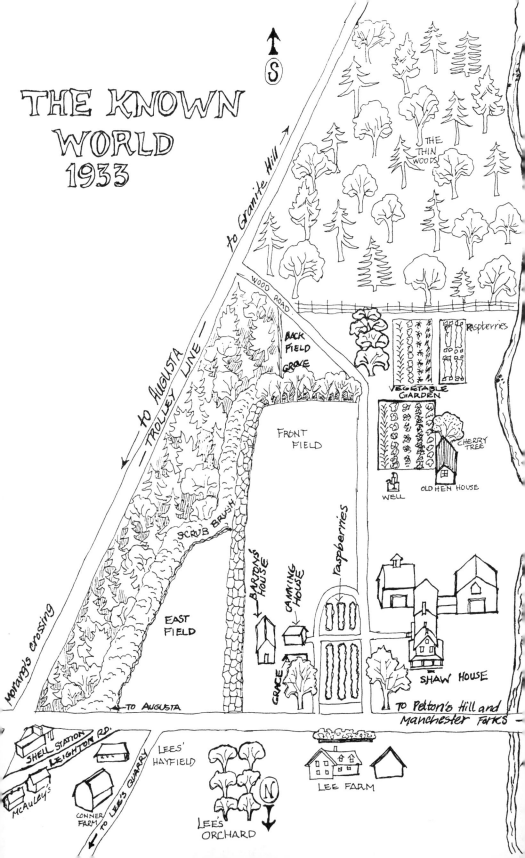

Having seen the McAuleys' black skins ever since I could remember, I thought nothing of it. They were just neighbors like the others.

Pa used to walk me down to McAuley's for a hot dog or a hamburger or an ice cream cone sometimes as a special treat. They each cost a nickel.

All this background is to show the limits of my experience. In every house I knew, a man and woman lived together, with or without children. I'd heard the word "married" but wasn't sure what it meant or to whom it applied. Uncle Fred's step-daughter Myrtle, from his first marriage, used to visit him from time to time and always came with a woman friend named Chloe.

"Are Myrtle and Chloe married?" I asked Richard after one of their visits.

"No, you goose," he laughed, "Women don't marry women and men don't marry men. Men and women marry each other."

I knew that Aunt Grace was Pa's sister and that Uncle Barton was his brother, but hadn't realized that meant Ma couldn't be my mother. The age difference between Ma and Pa didn't alert me either. To me, Ma and Pa and my aunts and uncles were all "old." Ma didn't look any older than the rest, and people often mistook her for Aunt Grace's sister. They both had grey hair swirled up on top of their heads. They both had lines around their eyes, and their necks were flabby. No one ever said Ma and Pa were either married or not married, and it never occurred to me to ask. They were just Ma and Pa.

And Florence? She was just a name I had heard—someone who had lived on the farm and who had died from a terrible illness. When I had asked about her, Ma said she had been my father's wife. No one said she was my mother, and the possibility had never occurred to me until Mrs. Lee had dropped her bombshell.

Before Mrs. Lee's revelation, I had just taken my life for granted. Now all my senses were alerted, my eyes and ears were open and I was furious at being deceived. They had all lied to me. I began listening intently to the conversations that went on around me, and to anything casual callers to the farm had to say. I lurked quietly in adjoining rooms to hear things that they would never say in front of me. My ears were sharp and I became expert at pressing them against doors. Callers and the occasional overnight guest proved to be richer sources than expected about what went on in the neighborhood, but none of these conversations told me anything about my real mother.

It was a while before Ma and Pa realized what I was doing. "People who spy hear no good of themselves," Ma told me sharply. This didn't stop me, I just became more sneaky and careful.

16. Old Photographs

Since the revelation about my mother, I'd not only been keeping my ears open but also my eyes. I began to see and wonder about things I'd hardly noticed before. Like the pictures on the wall. Some were of people I didn't know. Who were they?

I knew the one in the living room above the corner knick-knack stand must be Ma. The woman who looked out from the frame at me was much younger, but the high cheekbones, strong nose, swept-up hair and alert expression in her eyes were unmistakable.

Beneath Ma's picture, however, was one of a slender, handsome young man with tightly curled hair. He was holding two cats in his arms and smiling down on them. The face looked familiar, but I didn't know why. I asked Ma who he was.

"That's your father, my child," she enlightened me. "In his twenties, holding his pet cats."

She'd told me before that Pa used to have curly hair. Now I could believe that, at least.

Also in the living room, over the chaise longue near the door to the front hall, hung a picture of a child of about three with a round, happy face and hair cut short and straight across the forehead. The child was standing, wearing a white dress with a wide sash at the waist, and smiling for the camera. No one had ever told me who it was.

"Ma, is that a picture of me?" I asked.

Ma chuckled. "No, that's not you. That's your brother Lynde."

I thought she was joking. "Ma—she's got a dress on. That's not Lynde."

"Oh, yes it is. Early this century little boys still wore dresses until they were about five, as they did in Victorian times. And when Lynde was little, the Dutch Boy haircut was popular. Those fashions didn't go out till after the World War."

I didn't know whether to believe her or not. How could I ever be sure now whether she was telling me the truth?

I asked Lynde about the picture when he next came to visit. He laughed his donkey laugh. "Yeah, that's me," he admitted. "That's what they did then. I guess it didn't do me any harm."

Another picture I asked Ma about hung in the dining room near the fireplace. A large head-and-shoulders view of a woman with a strong, high-boned face and broad nose like Ma's peered from an oval frame of dark wood.

50

Her hair was parted in the middle and pulled back tightly from her face. Her mouth was set into a straight, severe line, no hint of a smile. She wore a cameo brooch at the throat of her high-necked dress.

"That's a picture of my mother," Ma said. "My mother Eliza. She was your great-grandmother."

"She looks cross," I noted.

"She had a hard life. There wasn't much to smile about." She did not elaborate.

Nowhere on the walls did I find anyone who could possibly have been my mother. Why were there no pictures of her? Of her holding me, perhaps? Or with Pa?

A few months later when I was pulling books out of Ma's little bookcase in the living room to see what they were about, I found, tucked behind the other books, a small leather-bound one with a brass clasp to keep it from falling open. The leather was old, worn and starting to crumble at the corners. I pushed the little button on the clasp and opened the book.

Surprised, I realized it was an album. In it were pictures of people in old-fashioned dress—men, women and children, singly or in groups. None of the pictures were identified, and none of them looked like anyone I'd ever seen. As I touched one of the photographs, I was startled to realize it was made of metal, not paper like the other pictures I'd seen. The light parts of the pictures were an odd pale greyish tan. The people's faces were all that color except for their cheeks, which were pink.

After looking to make sure none of the pictures had names on the back, I took the album to the kitchen, where Ma and Pa were talking. I interrupted them with my discovery.

"Where did you find that?" Ma asked sharply. "What are you doing with it?"

"It was in the bookcase," I said.

"What were you looking for in the bookcase?"

"Just seeing what was there."

"There are no children's books there. They're all my books. I'd rather you didn't handle them until you're old enough to read and understand them."

"I'm old enough to look at pictures, Ma. Who are the people in here? Why are the pictures that funny color?"

She hesitated, then took the album out of my hands.

"They're people I used to know many years ago. No one you've ever seen, no one you'd have any interest in. They're all dead now. I'll go and put this away."

She left the room and headed upstairs.

I looked at Pa. He smiled. "She's right, there's no one in that album that you'd be the least interested in. Ma just wants to be sure the album doesn't accidentally get damaged. The pictures are that funny color because they're tintypes, which are very old and always look like that. They don't make 'em any more."

"Are any of them pictures of my mother?" I asked.

He stopped smiling. "No," he said in a changed voice. "There's none of your mother there."

I still wasn't sure, but I trusted Pa more than I did Ma. I'd never caught Pa lying to me—except about Santa Claus. He usually just said nothing at all.

17. Visitors

Although I was cut off from the world, our farm was not. Pa and Ma and Fred and Grace all had connections with the outside. Besides the locals who came to buy produce or attend to farming matters with Pa and Fred, visitors came from far away. Not many, and not often, but they came. Some were one-timers, and I never saw them again. Others came sporadically and were mentioned often in between.

One visitor came either before my birth or when I was too young to remember him. He was a friend of my father's, and though I heard his story I don't recall his name.

He arrived late at night after everyone was in bed. (Late being after nine o'clock, since we arose at five in summer.) Doors on the farm were never locked. There probably wasn't a functional lock on the property, except for the tiny, delicate golden padlock on Ma's silk-lined cedar jewelry box. I never recall seeing a key in all the time I lived on the farm. We were never away overnight, and there was always someone home during the day except on the rare Sunday when Fred took us to a lake or to the coast.

Pa's friend knew the layout of the farmhouse and came in quietly, so as to disturb no one. He undressed in the kitchen and went through to Pa's bedroom which was directly behind it. Pa slept on the side of the bed nearest the door, so the man went around to the other side and crawled in. Pa didn't know he was there till he woke as usual at five.

The earliest visitor I can remember was "Aunty" Wyer. She was one of the only two I recall who were not relatives. I must have been about three at the time. She was a friend of Ma's, and I don't remember anything about her except that she was very old, wore long black dresses and didn't like worms. Many years later I wrote this poem about her:

AUNTY WYER

They were my friends, the worms.
I lined my pockets with earth
and tucked them into it.
I liked to feel the burrowing
living things always with me.
I thought everybody liked worms.

When Aunty Wyer came to visit
I thought she'd like to share my worms.
I brought out a handful
and put them on her lap.
She didn't thank me, she just screamed.

Ma took me and the worms outside.
The way her mouth wiggled
I could tell she wanted to laugh.

Another visitor from about the same period was a mysterious young man who came only once. He had been to South America and brought us a large wall hanging made by Indians from the bark of a tree in Peru. It was a mottled pale brown, and dramatic dark brown designs had been drawn on it with dyes extracted from some exotic plant. I remember neither the young man's name nor his relationship to us, but I suspect now that he was from the California Hardison branch of the family. They were the ones who did exciting things.

The other visitors who came were mostly relatives on my father's side. More precisely, on Ma's side, for no one named Shaw or related to Shaw ever came. And no relative from my mother's side came except Lynde. I didn't question all this at the time. They were just the people who visited.

The relationships of these people to us and to one another are still not entirely clear as I try to fit this all together decades later. Let me make a skeleton on which to hang the names (See table, p. 54) "Skeleton" seems an appropriate word. We had many in our closets, and my knowledge about them is skeletal. All the visitors on my father's side are dead now. I can only depend on living memory—mine, which alone remains. What the dead did not tell me went with them, but their bones still rattle.

Just before a blind wall of shadow disappears into the past, there are two family names: Ridley and Pratt. My great-grandmother was Eliza Ridley, and she married a Pratt. His first name is gone. They were born long enough

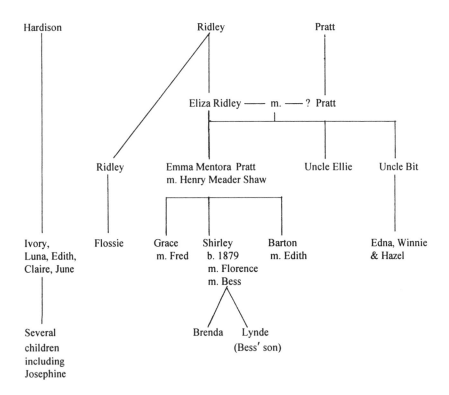

Hardison   Ridley   Pratt

Eliza Ridley —— m. —— ? Pratt

Ridley   Emma Mentora Pratt   Uncle Ellie   Uncle Bit
               m. Henry Meader Shaw

Ivory,   Flossie   Grace   Shirley   Barton   Edna, Winnie
Luna, Edith,   m. Fred   b. 1879   m. Edith   & Hazel
Claire, June   m. Florence
                           m. Bess

Several   Brenda   Lynde
children   (Bess' son)
including
Josephine

before the Civil war for Pratt to be in it. He volunteered for the Union Army, was taken prisoner, and died of scurvy and pneumonia in a southern prison.

Before he went to war, however, Pratt and Eliza had six children, which she was left to support. She appears to have been helped by a mysterious man named Stover who Ma mentioned often but never explained. Was he Eliza's lover? Second husband? Platonic dear friend? No one is alive to tell me.

Eliza's daughter Mentora became my grandmother, whom I called "Ma." She married Henry Meader Shaw when she was twenty. Shaw the black sheep. Shaw the adulterer. Shaw the drunkard. Shaw who left Ma and ran away with the hired girl, leaving her to support three children.

Those children, Grace, Shirley and Barton, are main characters in my story. Shirley, born in 1879, became my father, in spite of his name. He is the man in my life I know best—and the one I know least. Mentora and Aunt Grace were my "mothers"; Barton my mistrusted and feared uncle.

Other names lie along the edge of the story and interact with it. The only Ridley who ever visited us was Flossie from Livermore Falls, presumably the granddaughter of one of Eliza's brothers. She was in her forties, energetic, enthusiastic, and the only one in the family interested in genealogy. She went on and on about the Ridley's Scottish past. Why didn't I have the wit to listen?

The others who came were Pratts or Hardisons. Two of Eliza Ridley Pratt's other children were Elbridge ("Ellie") and "Bit" (only his nickname survives). He was never referred to as anything but "Uncle Bit" in my hearing, because he was a small man—"just a little bit"—and my grandmother, at five foot eight, was taller than he. She had a picture of them standing together—he short, paunchy and middle-aged, dressed in a three-piece suit; she the tall, strong farm woman, erect and straight, towering beside him.

Bit had three daughters: Edna and Winnie, who were twins, and Hazel. They lived first in Caribou, then in Orono, but Hazel as an adult moved to Boston. Edna came to see us only once, Winnie several times. They were both dumpy and slow and I couldn't tell them apart except Edna's hair was white and Winnie's grey. Hazel came fairly often. She was the liveliest and most interesting of the three: younger than the others, plump, beaver-toothed and cheerful.

Bit went to Alaska as a young man to prospect for gold, but came back with only a small sack of nuggets. One of these was made into a ring. When Bit died of diabetes in middle age, before I was born, the ring went to Ma, and she gave it to me when I was ten. I managed to lose it down the plug hole of the bathtub during one of the few periods the tub was functional.

One or more of the Hardison clan went to California following the scent of gold, and Uncle Fred also had his "go" at Alaskan gold—thus gold wove itself into my past in several separate threads.

When New England men came back from gold rushes in California or Alaska, usually poorer than when they left, they sometimes turned their few nuggets into beads for their wives, sweethearts or daughters. The necklaces I saw were choker-length, made of small, uniform gold beads about the size of pearls. Mrs. Lee had one, and when she had a goitre removed it neatly covered the white hairline scar across her throat.

A mysterious someone else, whose face I cannot now remember, also had one of the necklaces. I have an odd visual and auditory memory involving her, the gold beads, a china plate with irises on it, and the word "malice." When I hear the word malice I see the mysterious someone holding the necklace in her hand. It swings in her fingers and strikes the China plate.

Where did this image come from?

The plate with the irises was a real plate that stood on edge at the back of our glass-fronted china cabinet in the dining room. Ma would bring it out with great care on special occasions. It was hand painted. The iris blooms were large and in shades of blue and violet on a background subtly shaded with the faintest of blues and the palest of yellows. The plate had a gold rim, and was the most beautiful one I had ever seen.

Could I have associated "malice" with "mallet"? With a mallet striking the plate? That doesn't seem to fit. There is no association with breaking, or fear that the plate will be destroyed. It is only the song of the gold ringing out against the violets and blues.

Who was the someone? Was she my mother?

Most of our visitors did not stay overnight. They would typically arrive early in the afternoon, and then we would all sit in a circle in the living room with them, drinking tea and talking about people I didn't know and things that had happened in the past that meant nothing to me. It was all very boring. I usually slipped off to play with my chickens or rubber rats. The guests would leave late in the afternoon, and life would go back to normal.

A more exciting visit was that of the California Hardisons. They came in the summer, probably in 1934 when I was six. They appeared late in the afternoon in an enormous, elderly Ford touring car piled high with camping equipment and suitcases. I can't imagine how they got all those people and all that equipment into one car, much less how they drove from California to Maine with it.

They set up their tent in our back field and stayed several days. Ivory Hardison had brought his spinster sister Edith and several of his teenage children, whose names I forget. I don't remember his wife being present. I'm not sure whether Ivory left her at home in California, or if she had died.

Ivory was a big, muscular man with strong features and enormous hands. He is the first man I can recall who had a physical impact on me of a positive nature. I felt an immediate attraction, which surprised me and made me shy with him. He must have felt it too, for he was as shy with me as I was with him. It was my first experience of what I now know was lust.

Ma's brother Elbridge came to stay for a week when I was about nine. He was tall, thin, grey and stooped and looked like Ma. I tried to amuse him by playing the piano and also the violin, which I had by then taken up. Uncle Ellie was polite and praised me, but I don't think he was much interested.

He had a great gaping sore on his neck. It was covered by a gauze dressing which Ma changed for him every day. When she did, I could see the hole in his neck, which seemed to go in a very long way. Ma said it was skin cancer. He died not long afterwards. I think the purpose of his visit was to see Ma one last time.

There remains one other visitor whom I have not mentioned. Aunt Rita. I remember her from the earliest times, and she came fairly often. Not just to see Ma and Pa, but specifically to see me. She always brought me presents, and at Christmas and birthdays a gift from her would arrive in the mail. Ma said Rita was "a friend of the family."

Rita lived in Melrose, Massachusetts, just north of Boston, which was the town where Lynde was living with friends. She also had a cottage on Lake Megunticook in Camden, Maine, so she came to see us on her way to or from it.

Rita wasn't my real aunt, but I was someone special to her. No one told me who she was or why she came to see me, I just took her for granted. She was tall and slender with a long pleasant face and a warm smile. She had a nervous tic on her forehead. When it "ticked," her white hair rode back and forth on her head. Lynde told me that Rita's hair had fallen out with a fever, and she was bald. She wore a wig. That's why it was so thick and white and glossy and moved about when her forehead twitched.

Of all the visitors who came, Rita was the most important, but I didn't know it then. She was the only one, except Lynde, who had a direct connection with our mother.

Part Two: The Country School

18. The First Year of Hell

Ever since I could remember, I'd seen the children from Pelton's Hill walk past our farm on the way to the one-room country school on the Leighton Road. They were all Peltons. That's why the hill was called Pelton's Hill. Ned Pelton, an only child, lived with his parents at the very top. He didn't go to the country school, but was driven to a school in town by his father.

Half way down the hill, however, Ned's cousins lived: a large brood of all sizes. Beginning with the school year in September, some of them walked past our farm about 8:30 in the morning. In the warm fall and spring their skinny arms and legs stuck out of their clothing, which was always too small for them. They carried metal lunch boxes. In winter they wore heavy woolen clothes and black four-buckle rubber overshoes and trudged past earlier to get through the heavy snow. I'd never met any of these children. I would meet them when I went to the Leighton School, Ma said.

From the moment I saw the Peltons I wanted to join them. The summer I was five all I could talk about was going to school. I could already read, and I was eager to start learning other things.

For several months I'd been letting my hair grow. This was Ma's idea. If I was old enough for school, I should wear my hair in braids. That would keep it neat and prevent it becoming tangled. By September my "short shingle" had given way to shoulder-length, fine, flyaway hair that always seemed to be getting in my eyes and mouth. I hated it.

Ma showed me how to part it in the middle from crown to forehead, then from the crown down the back of my head to the hairline. She demonstrated how to scoop each half to the side, braid it neatly, and keep it from unravelling with a rubber band. This seemed very clumsy at first, but I soon got the hang

58

of it. I thought it made my face look funny to have my hair pulled back so tight, but at least it was out of my eyes and mouth.

On the first day of school, I skipped beside Aunt Grace, who was walking with me on the half mile to the schoolhouse. I was swinging my brand-new lunch box and singing, "I'm going to schoo-ul I'm going to schoo-ul" over and over. The Peltons hadn't come by yet. We walked down to Morang's Crossing. Here the old dirt country road split off from the tarred one. This took us down over Leighton's Hill. At the bottom was a junction with another country road, and we went left toward the school. A few hundred yards more, and I could see it in the distance—a tiny white building no bigger than a small house. We were early. Only a few children had arrived in the school yard when we got there. Aunt Grace took me inside the schoolhouse, introduced me to the teacher, Miss Murphy, and left. I was so eager to see the schoolroom that I hardly noticed her go.

I ran around in delight looking at the desks and seats which were screwed to the floor in rows, and at the fat little pot-bellied stove in the middle of the school's only room. Miss Murphy was plump and rounded and dressed in green. She took me by the hand and led me over to one side of the room. There were two doors side by side in the wall. One was marked "Boys" and the other "Girls." She opened the door marked "Girls" and showed me inside. It was a small closet which had been built onto the outside of the schoolhouse. It had a bench at the back with two holes in it. It was like the Lees' outhouse, and like the old "two-holer" out in our back shed which wasn't used any more. "This is the girls' toilet," she said. "If you need to go during the day, raise your hand and say, 'Miss Murphy, please may I go to the toilet?'"

Then she went to her desk, picked up a large metal bell with a black handle on it, stood in the doorway and rang it with vigor. The other children poured in from the school yard. "Please be seated," she said to them. The older children all knew where to sit and did as they were told. Miss Murphy led me to the third seat up in the row next to the windows. Then she conducted two other small girls to the two seats in front of me. Miss Murphy said she would now call the roll, and when our names were called we were to raise our hands to show that we were present.

"Sub-primary," she began. "Sylvia Palmer?"

The girl in the front seat of my row raised her hand. "Dorothy Simpson?" The girl in the second seat raised her hand. "Brenda Shaw?" I raised my hand. Then she said "First Grade. Robert Pelton?" Robert, whom I had already recognized as a Pelton, sat behind me. He raised his hand.

And on around the room and up the grades. There must have been about fifteen other children there. The big boys in the eighth grade sat on the far side next to the two toilets.

I don't remember much about what we did that first day except for morning recess and the lunch hour. We went outdoors then. The school yard was small and surrounded by a wire link fence beyond which was a pine forest. We were allowed into the edge of the forest, and also across the dirt road to the pasture where cows from a neighboring farm grazed. The pasture contained a small hill, which seemed enormous at the time.

By lunch time I had fallen in love with Toby Nelson. He was a slender, black-haired boy of about ten with a lean face, pale skin and a long, elegant nose. He was the most beautiful boy I had ever seen. I began following him around, my love plain for all to see. This did not please him. The other boys began to point and snicker; and Toby, in a fury of embarrassment, ordered me to go away. No one else seemed disposed to be friendly, either.

Miss Murphy was kind to me; the children were not. It took a few days for it to sink in how much they disliked me. The boys were the worst, except for Dorothy Simpson. I must have appeared very peculiar to them, having been raised alone by an aging parent and grandparent without experience of other children. The braids, which Ma had insisted upon, were out of fashion and laughed at. "Look at those stupid pig's tails stickin' out!" giggled Dorothy. The "short shingle" was the style in the early 1930s. Also, I already knew how to read, which put everyone's back up.

I was the next-to-smallest child in the school. Dorothy Simpson was smaller, but she was tough and wiry and as dirty a fighter as I have ever met. She hated me on sight. Just how much became clear a few days later when she told me she had something nice for me. "Put out your hand," she said. I did so, and she spat in it.

My initial enthusiasm about going to school turned to terror. I was taunted and laughed at daily during recess periods and at lunch time, and only saved from worse trouble on the way home because Aunt Grace came to meet me.

For the second time I felt betrayed. The first time was when I found out Ma wasn't my mother. Now school, which everyone had said I would enjoy, and which I'd looked forward to so avidly, had turned out to be horrible. I told Ma I never wanted to go back there, but she said it was the law that I must go. "If you don't, the Truant Officer will come and take you there."

The autumn was unusually warm, and it did not take more than a week or so for the two outhouses attached to the school house to begin to reek. I could smell them long before I reached the school yard.

There was no running water at the school, but a large container with a spigot and a supply of paper cups was available for drinking purposes. There was no sink or basin for washing hands. One day in particular this caused a bit of a problem. It was morning recess and most of us had gone across the road to the pasture. I climbed up the steep hill right to the top. The day was sunny and warm, and in spite of my apprehensions about the other children I was suddenly filled with jubilation. I turned and started to run down the hill as fast as I could, my braids flying behind me in the sweet-smelling air. But in this case joy came before a fall, and I went headlong—face first into a cowflap. I sat up screaming, cowshit in my eyes, nose and mouth. There was a roar of mirth, and when I got my eyes open I found myself surrounded by a ring of children laughing themselves into hysteria at my plight. One of the older girls stopped laughing long enough to lead me back to the school house, and she and Miss Murphy sponged me off with paper cups full of water from the water container.

Things at school did not improve. I did not know the school's reputation then, but I found out about it later. It was a favorite testing ground for new teachers. The sixteen pupils attending ranged in age from five to sixteen. The older ones should have left at fourteen to go on to high school, but the general level of intelligence was low, and a number of boys were sitting it out in the rural school until they could legally leave at sixteen.

If a new teacher could cope with nine grades which included retarded and unmanageable sixteen-year-olds, she was promoted to a better school in the town. Or she quit teaching. Miss Murphy, an older woman with considerable experience, was there during my first year only because the last young teacher had quit without notice and could not be replaced.

I suffered through the mild September and October. For those first weeks there seemed to be no escape. Anything I learned that autumn was gleaned from listening to what Miss Murphy was teaching classes higher than my own, when I was supposed to be doing something else.

That's not quite true. My vocabulary enlarged, but not in an expected direction. I hadn't been there a week when the new words began to register. "Shit." "Piss." And what I misheard as "fut." The latter was Dorothy's favorite. When I asked her what "fut" meant, she leered at me and put out the forefinger of her left hand. She rubbed the forefinger of the other hand along it repeatedly in one direction. "Shame, shame," she cried. "That's a dirty word like shit and piss and you must never say it!"

Then she doubled up with a burst of the dirtiest laughter I'd ever heard.

I sensed that I'd better not ask Miss Murphy what the words meant, so I asked Ma when I got home. Her face went grim and I could see she was angry.

"Those are vulgar words," she said. "You must never use them."

She had answered my question about three words I didn't know with another word I didn't know.

"Why not? What does 'vulgar' mean?"

"Vulgar words are rude words which only vulgar people who don't know any better use. They are words which are about things you do when you go to the toilet. Nice people don't say them. You must never say them."

Then, as usual when a subject was closed, she turned away. Again I was left to figure things out for myself, and I did eventually. I learned that second language which described another sort of life that went on with everybody but which only people who weren't nice ever acknowledged. It was the beginning of understanding the many double standards that people use to get through their lives and the dishonesty bred of fear and embarrassment.

I soon noticed that all the way up the grades the girls were quicker to learn than the boys. In my sub-primary class I sat and listened while children who would never be more than semi-literate were being taught the alphabet. Several boys who were nominally in the first to third grades, but still could not read, joined Sylvia and Dorothy and me to work on the alphabet.

Sylvia was a sturdy little girl with a quick smile. Her hair was dark and straight, cut short and square, and a bit of it was tied back with a ribbon. Her face was chubby, her nose upturned and well formed, her hazel eyes large. She was a bright child, and her reading progressed rapidly. I think Dorothy was reasonably smart too, but memories of her hatefulness have blocked out other details. The things I remember are her hard, thin, pale little face, sly grey eyes, and obscene giggle.

The temperature dropped toward the end of October, and winter came with a blizzard in mid-November. Everyone continued to walk to school, no matter what the weather. We were dressed for it: long woolen underwear, thick brown woollen stockings, heavy, lined woolen snow pants and four-buckle rubber overshoes. We never took our outdoor clothing off during school hours in the winter. We arrived after wading through drifts with snow clinging to us in frozen lumps. Gradually it would melt in the heat from the pot-bellied stove, leaving puddles on the floor while our clothes steamed. The air was heavy with the smell of wet wool.

As the weather worsened, I registered the fact that occasionally children were absent from school because of illness. It did not take me long to notice what sort of symptoms caused children to be sent home and told not to come back for a few days. I developed as many of these as I could manage, but sore throats seemed to be the most effective. I fanned myself with cold air every night at the bedroom window hoping to encourage one.

Not long after school began I had started having headaches—real headaches—that I'd never had before. I know now that they were due to fear and tension, but no one seemed to realize it then. I also developed a queasy stomach and lost my former voracious appetite. To these two real symptoms I now added as many sore throats as I could get away with. This worked with gratifying frequency, and produced exactly what I wanted. It was sheer heaven to be allowed to remain tucked up in bed at home while Ma fed me toast with butter, cream and salt on it to "make the sore throat go away."

My people were worried about me. Though they knew I hated school and feared the other children they did not seem to link my headaches and sick stomach to this, nor to suspect that my sore throats were sheer malingering. I malingered so well, in fact, that in the end I was taken to an ear, nose and throat doctor. He agreed that my throat was "bad" and I was miraculously allowed to spend most of the winter at home, with Aunt Grace teaching me. She got geography and American history books from the library in addition to the useless school texts which the teacher sent home, and I went ahead like a hare.

At the end of the school year, however, I had been absent from school for more than the legal number of days, so Pa was informed that I must repeat the sub-primary the following year. No matter that I had done all the work and knew more than required. I had lost ground, not gained.

I don't know what Ma and Pa's reaction to this was. I can't recall when or if they explained to me what had happened, or if I didn't realize my fate till I got back in the fall. Probably the latter. Anyway, in June fall seemed a long way off and I was prepared to enjoy the school-free summer. In my innocence I thought if I could get out of going to school one year, I could probably do so the next.

Another more immediate shock was in store for me, however— one for which I had in no way been prepared. No sooner was school over for the the summer than I was told I was going to visit a hospital. I was thrilled. I knew that hospitals were where sick people went to be made better, and I was eager to see what one was like.

Uncle Fred drove Ma and me to the hospital and dropped us off. When we arrived, the nurses made a great fuss over me and took us to a room where I was told I was going to dress up in hospital clothes. Ma helped me into the costume, and then I was allowed to ride in a wheelchair. That was great fun. We came into a room where there was a metal table with lights over it. Several people in white costumes and masks were there, and I was told I could climb up on the table and lie down. I thought it was a game. When I was lying down someone said, "Now we'll give you your mask to put on." Suddenly something was clapped over my face and an evil smell was choking me. I kicked and fought, but soon lost consciousness. Later I learned I'd kicked the ear-nose-and-throat surgeon in the stomach, and was glad.

I awoke vomiting blood. Ma was sitting beside me and told me I'd had my tonsils and adenoids out. I didn't know what that meant, and she explained they were what had made my throat sore. I was given ice cream to eat and allowed home the same day.

This was the third time Ma had betrayed me. I was devastated, but my throat was so sore I couldn't even talk with her about it. In answer to my agonized "Why didn't you tell me?" she said she hadn't wanted me to worry about it beforehand.

When my resentment had subsided a bit I realized that she was telling me the truth. I knew in my heart that Ma was good and loved me and wanted only the best for me. What she had failed to understand, however, was the worry that would project itself forward from this incident. What unpleasant medicine might be arranged for me next which I would know nothing about? If I got into Fred's car to go on another visit, in what ghastly circumstances was I likely to end up? I'm sure it is no coincidence that my tendency toward carsickness became evident about this time. Whom could I trust? Ma and Pa and Aunt Grace loved me, but they had all deceived me. Uncle Fred clearly did not love me, nor did Uncle Barton. What would they do to me if they got the chance?

19. Mrs. Cony and the Piano

Shortly after the tonsil episode, Lynde appeared. This was fortunate, as it took my mind off my throat. If Ma and Pa knew he was coming, they didn't tell me. As usual, I learned of his presence next morning when they said he was in his bed. He told me he had just graduated from Northeastern and would be going to Honduras to work as a civil engineer for United Fruit Company.

I'd never heard of Honduras, but Lynde had brought a map and showed me where it sat on the skinny arm of land between North and South America. He also brought me a bracelet. It was broad and shiny black with the silver shield of Northeastern on the front. The inside was silver. It was too big to wear on my wrist, but I pushed it up my arm till it fit. Lynde stayed two days and then left, not knowing when he'd be back.

A few days after Lynde's departure, I got a piano from Mrs. Cony. Mrs. Cony was a woman who sometimes came to see Ma. Ever since I could remember she had appeared at irregular intervals, driving a turquoise Terraplane coupé and accompanied by a large, tan, short-haired Labrador named Pete.

She usually brought magazines for Ma and Aunt Grace: *Women's Home Companion, Good Housekeeping, Better Homes and Gardens, McCalls, Harpers Bazaar, The Delineator.* They were ones other people had read, and she was passing them on. Sometimes she brought me books which other children had finished with, or clothes which they had outgrown but were still in good condition.

Now that I could read, I spent hours looking through the magazines, which I found were often more interesting than the books. I asked Ma and Aunt Grace questions about some of the advertisements: What was this mysterious "Kotex" which "gives women freedom never before dreamed of?"—which "assures no more discomfort at the bridge table?"—which "stays soft and dry at the edges?"—and that "allows the modern girl to enjoy sports without discomfort?"

What was feminine hygiene, which had "made women choose between poisonous antiseptics and nothing at all until Zonite came along"?

Why did married women need Lydia E. Pinkham's Vegetable Compound for their "nervousness, headaches, constipation and chronic fatigue"? It sounded like marriage wasn't very good for women's health.

To all these questions, Ma and Aunt Grace reacted with embarrassment and an exchange of looks. "You'll know all about it when you're older," was the standard reply.

This infuriated me, and made that kind of ad become a focus of interest. I tried in vain to put together the jarring, incomprehensible bits of information, but they refused to fit any logical pattern. The future looked ominous. I wasn't allowed to know anything about my mother, and the ads made clear that the lot of girls and married women was full of hurdles, handicaps and ill health.

Then one day, instead of magazines or clothes, Mrs. Cony brought me a piano. Or rather her blue Terraplane arrived just ahead of the truck which brought it. Why she had brought me a piano I wasn't told, but because she always brought something for me when she came, I just assumed that giving away pianos was not unusual.

The men in the truck unloaded it and carried it into the living room. Of course I was all over it. I'd met a piano before at the Lees, and knew that it was not meant to be banged upon. It was for playing tunes on. When the tune went up, your fingers went in one direction on the keys, and when it went down, they went the other way. Gracie Lee had shown me how to play "Chopsticks" with two fingers, and "Scotland's Burning" with one. Gracie, her mother and grandmother all played. I used to listen enraptured when Gracie sang. She had a clear, sweet voice. Sometimes I would hear her playing the piano and singing on warm summer evenings when all the windows were open. I would sneak out onto the lawn when Ma thought I was in bed, and sit under the trees by the road and listen to Gracie.

It had never occurred to me that some day I might have a piano. But now as if by magic I had one. I couldn't believe it.

The piano put Eva Fuller into an entirely different perspective for me. Eva was a woman who had begun coming by lately to see Ma. She was friendly and I liked her. Now I found that she could play the piano. She, like Gracie, had a beautiful voice, but it had a different quality. It was warm, throaty and heavy as perfume instead of light and sweet like Gracie's. She was plump with a thick neck, and I thought perhaps that was the reason for the difference. She sang hymn tunes, folk songs and cowboy songs, many of which I hadn't heard before. Each time she came I begged and begged until she sat down and played for me. Luckily she seemed to enjoy doing this, and by listening to her sing I learned the words to the songs. When she saw how enthusiastic I was, she lent me a book of folk songs and a hymnal so I could learn all the verses. She also sang songs for me that she had made up herself. She said one had won a prize and been published and sung on the radio.

As Eva played, I watched her fingers on the keys, and began to see a relationship between the sounds and the way she placed her hands on the keys. The tune was easy—it could be played with just one finger. I could do that myself after Eva had gone.

The left hand was more complicated. It hit many notes at a time, with spaces in between the fingers in different patterns. After Eva's visits I would go to the piano and try to do what she had been doing. I found that if my left hand hit notes with the same spaces in between that Eva had left, it sounded nice. If I started the tune on the correct note with my right hand, the tune would fit into the pattern of sound made by the left hand. If I didn't start at the right note it sounded terrible, but by process of elimination I could eventually find the right one.

Ma and Pa and Aunt Grace noticed that I had a "good ear" and decided it was time I had lessons. Ma arranged for one of the local farmer's wives who was said to play well to come to the farm and teach me. Mrs. Tibbetts was big and blonde and kind, but spent most of her time gossiping with Ma. She was supposed to teach me how to play by note, and was under the impression that that was what she was doing.

"She's good at it," I heard her tell Ma. "She's learning the notes very quickly."

She was wrong. I wasn't learning the notes at all. I was watching her fingers as I had Eva's and listening acutely to the results. I simply mimicked what she was doing. It didn't take me long to realize that there were three basic finger patterns which could be used successively to accompany any note in an 8-tone scale. It didn't matter which scale was used. The same three patterns worked whether you were in the key of C or in G, or in F, or any other, as long as your ear told you when to use black keys instead of white ones.

I also noticed a strange thing about the various keys. They had different colors and temperatures. The key of C was blue and cold. G was warmer and green. A was a dull, glowing orange, but not as warm as E, which was yellow-bright and hot. I loved the sound-color and feeling of A and E, but mostly played in G, because it had only one sharp and was easier. I felt comfortable in it.

I didn't like the flat keys as much and never bothered to go beyond F, which had one flat. It was reddish purple, about the color of blood.

Other inscrutable associations happened in my head, too, involving shapes and forms and music and direction. One concerned the theme song of a radio program Grace used to listen to. I know it now as "Clair de Lune." It was played on a piano, and the notes were like masses of separate golden spheres all flowing in one direction. Then one day the theme was played on an organ, and fine red lines connected all the golden spheres as they flowed along.

Everyone was pleased with my musical progress. After a few weeks Ma declared that since I could now play everything Mrs. Tibbetts had assigned me and also any other tune I wanted, there was no more need for piano lessons. That suited me fine: I thought I'd learned it all. I was perfectly content to play by the hour with our yellow tomcat, Sandy, or my favorite pet chicken, Nimerella, perched upon my lap.

Nimerella was a bantam hen with a deformed neck. She appeared to have a good ear for music, for she sometimes attempted to sing with me.

I began to make up tunes. For a while I named them. The first one I called "Tulip." The next one was "Second Tulip." But I soon ran out of names and just played whatever came into my head. It was an activity I never tired of.

20. The Hired Man

About this time I had my first run-in with Jack Lefevre. He had recently become the Lees' hired man, and was living on their farm in a room over one of the sheds. He was a burly, deeply tanned French-Canadian in his early thirties. He was part Micmac Indian, and had blue-black hair and black eyes. When he was shirtless, I could see thick fleshy lines on the smooth skin of his back. I asked Mrs. Lee what they were. She told me they were scars. When he was a boy his stepfather had lashed him with a whip. Jack ran away, and never went home again.

One day I wandered out into our barn and was playing in the defunct body of Uncle Fred's old Model T Ford, which lay on the barn floor. I heard a noise and looked up to find Jack standing behind me. He squatted down, put one arm around my shoulders and his other hand in my panties and began feeling around.

No one had ever touched me like that before, or suggested that anyone ever would. Although the physical sensation it gave me was oddly exciting, I knew instinctively that it was wrong. Surely Ma would not approve. She had told me I should not touch myself between the legs except when I went to the toilet, and surely Jack had no business doing it. I pulled away and ran. Jack did not pursue me, and I was not frightened—just angry. I didn't like Jack.

My bladder was full so I went to the toilet, but found I couldn't pee. That frightened me, so I went and told Ma what had happened. She wasn't cross with me because I hadn't done anything wrong. She said I was all right and would be able to "make water" in a few minutes. Jack was a bad man and shouldn't do that to little girls. I was to keep away from him.

She didn't seem particularly upset or make a big thing of it. I don't know if she told the Lees, but Jack continued to work across the street and I heard no more about it.

Some time during the summer Ma got the idea that if I could make friends with Dorothy Simpson, the principal antagonist of my own size at school, it might make it easier when I went back in the fall. She arranged with Dorothy's mother for Dorothy to come up and play for an afternoon.

I didn't think much of this idea. Dorothy had given me a routinely bad time at school whenever the opportunity had arisen. I couldn't trust her, and I didn't want to be her friend. But Ma insisted: "Offer the olive branch—do as you would be done by."

To my surprise, Ma's plan appeared to be working at first. At our home, with no other children to show off for, Dorothy started off being friendly. We played around the farm outbuildings for a while, then Dorothy asked if we could go over to the Lees and see their horses. I agreed, and we went off to their stable.

Jack Lefevre was there, and he let us stroke the horses' noses. When we had tired of that, he came over and hunkered down beside us. He gathered us to him, one girl on each arm, chatting to us in a friendly manner. As he chatted, his hands began to play with our nipples and then tried to go lower.

Obviously Dorothy was an old hand at this sort of caper, because she laughed her obscene laugh and pointed to Jack's crotch. "Look at his buck," she giggled. I noted the swelling and instinctively knew that "buck" meant his male organ. It was certainly bigger than Roland's was when he peed on the pig!

I was incensed that Jack would try this sort of thing again, and in a fury I turned and bit him hard on the cheek. It drew blood and he swore and loosened his grip. We broke away and ran, Dorothy laughing like a hyena. Again Jack did not pursue us. This time I didn't tell Ma. Telling her before had done nothing to stop him.

We returned to the farmhouse and Dorothy decided she wanted to ride my large and rather impressive tricycle. We took it up on the big veranda that ran around the front and sides of the farmhouse, and she began riding it around and around at top speed. We were supposed to share the tricycle, but she showed no sign of giving it up. I told her that it was my turn now. She just laughed. When I reminded her again she said, "You can't have it. I'm company. I can ride it all the time."

"That's not fair," I shouted.

"Nyah, nyah, nyah, what are you going to do about it?" she sneered.

That was too much. This girl whom I detested had invaded my territory against my will and usurped my tricycle and said I could do nothing about it. I waited till Dorothy and the tricycle were opposite the top of the veranda steps, and rushed her. Off Dorothy and the tricycle went down the steps, arms, legs and wheels flying. I hoped she'd end up in pieces, but unfortunately nothing was damaged but her pride.

Needless to say that was the first and last time Dorothy came to the farm, and when I went back to school that fall she paid me back several times over.

As for Jack Lefevre, he didn't last much longer at the Lees. Not long after that second encounter, Jack tried to rob the Shell filling station near the Conners farm, and was caught and sent to jail. I wouldn't have known if Mrs. Lee hadn't told me. My family never told me anything.

Jack wasn't in jail long and came back to the Lees afterward. They felt sorry for him because of his terrible childhood and kept him on until he decided to return to Canada a few months later. There he apparently made good, for the next I heard of him was when he sent the Lees a wedding picture. His bride was dark and pretty and dressed in silk. Jack was wearing a dark suit and a monocle. He was quite unrecognizable.

21. The Second Year of Hell

As time spun down to the last week of summer, I tried to come to terms with going back to Leighton School. My apprehensions rose, and my appetite began to fade.

Although my stomach felt sick during the whole of the next school year, I never dared tell anyone for fear someone would cut me open and take it out. But I couldn't eat. The school nurse, who visited twice a year, complained each time that I was twenty pounds underweight and undernourished, and sent home notes to Pa. He and Ma tried their best to tempt me to eat, but as long as I went to that school fear was a great stone sitting in my belly.

A new teacher, Myrtle Standish, came that fall. She was just out of normal school, handsome, chestnut-haired, well-formed and strong. Leighton was her first teaching post, but she didn't look like she'd stand any nonsense.

Unlike Miss Murphy, who had puttered about like a kindly hen, Miss Standish strode: back and forth across the front of the classroom when she was talking, around the room observing everyone when we were supposed to be writing. When she wasn't striding she was either sitting behind her desk at the front of the room correcting papers, glancing up frequently to make sure there was no impending trouble, or sitting in another chair listening to one of the classes recite.

She divided her attention equally between the nine grades, from the sub-primary on one side of the single room (with only me in it now) to the hulking eighth graders on the other side.

The dramatis personae in the school's one room had not changed from the year before. No younger child had been added at the lower end, nor had anyone at the top left. The eighth grade had simply become heavier because Larry Palmer, Sylvia's older brother, and Byron Pelletier had moved up from the seventh grade. Dorothy and Sylvia became first graders, and I was alone in the sub primary. The others were scattered through the remaining grades.

Miss Standish was not kind to me as Miss Murphy had been, but she soon realized I did not belong in the sub-primary. After two weeks she advanced me to the first grade. After two weeks more I was put in second grade. Another two weeks and I was in the third grade with reading in the fourth. There I stayed for the rest of the year. This time I knew how many days I had to go to school in order to meet the legal requirement, and made sure I was there that many. When I was "ill," it was not with the same complaint too often.

In the fine autumn weather Miss Standish spent recess in the school yard, usually chatting with the other girls. It soon became clear that she had "pets" and "hates". Dorothy was the former, I was the latter. After Dorothy, eighth-grader Byron Pelletier's three sisters, Marie, Frances and Madeleine, were Miss Standish's favorites. Marie was the oldest, in seventh grade, with hair of gold ocher and a pale olive skin. Frances, in sixth grade, was dark, with rose-and-cream skin. Madeleine, in fourth grade, had brown hair with a hint of Marie's gold ocher. They were French-Canadian and spoke both French and English well. Their clothes were clean, attractive, and well kept. They were not forward, but they talked easily with Miss Standish and she obviously enjoyed them. They had fine, clear singing voices. Later, in high school, they used to sing on the local radio.

The remaining three girls—Sylvia Palmer, Theresa Boudreau and Della Adams—were quiet, shy, and totally eclipsed by the Pelletier girls. Theresa was Leroy Boudreau's older sister. They were also French-Canadian, and spoke English badly. Della was tall and shy, wore glasses, and her hair was tightly drawn back from her face.

I was right at the bottom of the heap, cold-shouldered by Standish and ignored by the other girls, except for Dorothy who was seeking vengeance for the tricycle episode.

The boys didn't fit into Standish's hierarchy of pets and hates. While she was present in the playground they paid no attention to her, and she ignored them. They got on with their own affairs, mostly in the pasture or over the fence in the edge of the woods.

While Miss Standish was present in the playground there was no bullying, but when the weather turned cold she remained inside, correcting papers. The older girls, although they largely ignored me, were not actively hostile. Sylvia was pleasantly neutral. But Dorothy was out for blood.

It did not take Dorothy long to realize that she could do no wrong in the eyes of Standish, and that I could do no right. In the schoolroom when Standish was not looking, Dorothy would grab something I needed to use (ruler, pencil, crayons) off my desk. I would get up to retrieve my property and get shaken till my teeth rattled in my head by Standish for leaving my seat. Telling her what had happened made no difference. Dorothy simply denied it, and smiled like an angel.

I was not the only child at the country school to be given a hard time. Another was Patrick Nichol. He was a couple of years older than I but small for his age. He lived alone with his father not far from the school in a hovel which must have been almost totally derelict. No water was piped into the house, and I'm not sure whether they even had a well. The house was located by a stream, from which they may have taken their water.

I don't know whether Patrick's mother had died or left. He came to school in torn, ragged and filthy clothing, and everyone made fun of him. I felt sorry for him, but it never occurred to me to try and make common cause with him. I was too busy defending myself to pay much attention to him. He sat two rows from me, so there had been no occasion to interact with him.

One day when I arrived at the school, a group of older boys were waiting for me. Instead of looking hostile, they were smiling, and motioned me over.

"We want you to do something for us," Larry Palmer said.

"What?" I asked, suspicious.

"Poor Patrick's feeling unhappy," said Byron Pelletier. "We thought it might help if you kissed him."

I was naive enough to think this was a good idea. Patrick was standing by himself over by the fence, out of hearing range, looking miserable.

"All right," I said, and went over to him. I'd never been closer to him than two rows away before, and didn't realize how badly he smelled or how dirty his face was till I planted the kiss on his cheek.

Immediately a roar of glee went up from the other children, followed by: "Brenda loves Patrick, stink, stink, stink. She doesn't know about his dink, dink, dink."

Patrick turned bright red, furious that I had made him the butt of further attention and cruelty. He lashed out at me with his fists. I dodged and ran. We were both hounded about the matter for days until someone thought up something else nasty to do.

Another victim was Della Adams. She was tall for her age, clean, well dressed and well spoken. I had never seen her be unkind to anyone, and though she paid me no attention she seemed like a nice girl. She was known as "Glasses" because she was the only one in the school who wore them. Every so often I would hear the chant "Glasses, Glasses, Glasses" begin in the playground and know that Della was in for it again.

One day she was called upon to recite a poem at the front of the room. The seventh grade had been told to learn this poem by heart. Della was usually good at her lessons, but that day something went wrong. She got part way through the poem and got stuck. I think one of the boys had done something to startle or shock her. I saw a flash of something out of the corner of my eye just before she forgot her lines. Then what must have been a pre-orchestrated chant of "You need Glasses, Glasses, Glasses" started up. Standish did not intervene. Della glanced at her in a panic, hoping for succor, but Standish's face remained impassive and the chant got louder. Della burst into tears, snatched the glasses from her face, threw them on the floor, stomped on them and ran out of the school.

The room went dead quiet and Standish, finally shocked into action, sped out the schoolhouse door after Della. When Standish came back in, Della was not with her. Standish retrieved the smashed glasses from the floor, placed them on her desk, sat down, and read the riot act to the silent faces before her.

I have no idea what happened after that, but I never saw Della again. If anyone was punished I never heard about it. But who would tell me, anyway? I'll never know whether Standish's failure to stop the boys chanting was due to her inability to cope with the situation, or if she was deliberately leaving Della to cope on her own, sink or swim. Or did whatever the boy had done to make Della forget her poem also shock Standish into inaction?

Later that year, I noticed a peculiar phenomenon. I had a tickle in my left eye and put my hand up to rub it. I happened to glance up at the light while my hand covered my left eye, and was still looking at it when I removed my hand. The light jumped suddenly to the right. Surprised, I tried covering and uncovering the eye again. The same thing happened.

I called Ma over and showed her. She was already worried about my incessant headaches. Instead of trying the light experiment for herself, she immediately declared, "There's something wrong with your eyes! We'd better take you to the oculist!"

I was horrified. I couldn't wear glasses to school—I just couldn't! "There's nothing wrong with my eyes. It only happens when I cover one of them. I can see perfectly. Everything on the board at school. Everything across the road. Everything a mile away."

This was quite true, but Ma wouldn't listen. To the oculist I went. Either failing to recall what he had learned in optical physics about stereoscopic vision—or more likely smelling the delicious scent of unearned profit, he proclaimed, "The girl needs glasses."

My protests were unavailing.

The glasses, when they arrived, were plain glass. They did nothing. I could see equally well with or without them, and the light still jumped whether they were on or off.

Needless to say, I never wore them at school. They went into my schoolbag as soon as I was out of sight of the house and didn't go back on my face till I got home.

Aunt Grace was not well that year and no longer came to meet me. I tried always to be the first one out the door when the final bell rang and ran off as fast as I could. The closer I could get to the junction in the road where the nastier children turned off, the less chance I had of getting hurt.

I remember the relief when I got home on a Friday with the weekend ahead of me, and I remember the searing headaches that overtook me every Sunday afternoon in dread of the week to come. Rather than go upstairs alone, I'd lie on Pa's bed just off the kitchen, holding ice wrapped in a cloth to my head.

My greatest consolation that winter was my deformed pet hen, Nimerella of the good musical ear. I had set some Bantam eggs under one of our hens, and three beautiful Bantam roosters resulted. When they feathered out, their iridescent blue-green hackles flared over their shining orange-red backs, and the indigo tail feathers plumed up behind. I wanted a bantam hen, too, so asked Harry Connors, from whom I'd gotten the eggs, if he would trade me a hen for one of the roosters. It never occurred to me that such a beautiful creature as the rooster was not an economically fair trade for a hen. Still, Harry agreed. It was not till I got her home that I noticed that her neck seemed a bit peculiar. He'd passed off a deformed bird on me.

Hens, like people, are always quick to find weaknesses in one of their own, and when they do, they attack. Nimerella's plight was so like my own situation at school, I could hardly miss the parallel. I knew Nimerella wouldn't last a day in the hen house with the others, so I took her into the house and trained her to use a box so as not to mess the floor. She slept in a basket beside my bed and followed me everywhere. Every other day she laid me a tiny brown egg, the only thing I could bring myself to eat for breakfast.

Gradually her neck got worse. Mrs. Lee said it was "wryneck" and no one knew how to cure it. By spring it had twisted so that her head was hanging upside down and I had to feed her by hand. I knew she would soon die, and it was breaking my heart. Each day I ran home from school to tend her.

One day in the spring Ma met me and said Nimerella was dead, and had been laid in the woodshed. I ran out and found the cold, stiff body. But when I called her name and touched her she opened her eyes and gave out a faint, musical reply. I took her back to her basket and warmed her with heated cloths. I gave her water by medicine dropper which she gratefully drank, but she refused the grains of corn. I sat stroking her and talking to her far into the night. By morning she was dead.

Ma dug a hole in the garden and I put her in. Ma gave her a push with the spade to make sure she was well into the hole.

"Oh, don't, don't," I sobbed, grabbing at the spade. We both stood and wept. Finally I covered her gently with handfuls of earth and put a large stone over her on which I painted her name.

It was one of the saddest hours of my childhood, and as I write about it now I find myself again in tears.

Cruelty to animals was a recurrent theme at the country school. Odd for a school in a farming community. Some of the songs we sang were Western ballads with words like "They feed in the coulees, they water in the draw, their tails are all matted, their backs are all raw." These lines were always sung with a gusto which I could not understand. At home we loved and protected our animals.

Not long after school commenced in the autumn, Miss Standish read us a particularly brutal story about a dog named Bing who fought with a wolf. Every bit of flayed skin and torn gut was described in detail, and although by the end, Bing, torn and bleeding, had won the fight, I knew I was going to be sick. After fainting and vomiting, during which I was conscious of sniggers and remarks like "She can't take it," I was told I could sit outside on the steps in the fresh air until I felt better.

As soon as the schoolhouse door had closed behind Standish I was off over the fence. I could stand it no longer. I cut through the pasture and into the woods, desperate to get out of sight before my absence was discovered. I made my way in the general direction of home and finally came out of the woods into a meadow of tall Indian corn. The meadow belonged to Chester Connors, and was about a quarter mile from home. I couldn't go home yet, they'd only send me back to school. I settled down in the deep corn, which was well over my head, to wait until the sun told me it was half past three. I still felt like vomiting, but nothing came up but froth.

I don't know how long I had been there when I heard the sound of a heavy man trampling through the corn. Terrified, I tried to estimate where he was and get out of his way. No use. In my panic I ran straight into him. It was Uncle Barton, his black eyes bulging with anger. He said nothing, but picked me up and whaled me harder than I'd ever been beaten before. I didn't cry. Tears never came when I was injured, only when I felt sad. He dragged me home to a worried Ma and Pa. They didn't say anything when I told them what had happened, but I knew they understood why I'd run away. They loved animals, too.

Externally not much changed during that second year at the school. But slowly, under my terror, something else had begun to emerge. As the summer approached I was no longer willing to be the meek and frightened recipient of indignity. I began to fight back. Some of the slightly bigger children began to learn it wasn't wise to tackle me unless there were two of them. I never learned to best Dorothy. Though smaller, she was quick as a snake and I never knew when or where she would strike. But, in short, hate was beginning to temper terror.

During one lunch break Byron, one of the eighth grade boys, tripped me in the school yard just as the bell rang. By the time I'd gained my feet he'd gone inside. My leg was bleeding and I wanted revenge.

Since the eighth graders sat on the far side where the two doors opened into the outhouses, I raised my hand and asked to go to the toilet. The teacher, who was sitting in front of the room, nodded. I had to pass in front of her chair to get to the other side. After emerging from the outhouse I passed Byron's seat and, thinking I was unobserved, hit him a sharp blow on the upper arm with my fist. Unfortunately, Standish saw me do it. As I passed her chair, she reached out and struck me a sharp blow on my upper arm with her fist. I turned and glared at her.

"That didn't hurt," I said through clenched teeth.

"Then come back here and I'll give you something that will."

I went back and she administered another blow.

"That still didn't hurt."

She hit me again. My eyes never left hers. "That did not hurt."

After the third blow it must have come to her that either her fist or my arm was going to break, and if it were the latter there might be trouble.

"All right, you've had enough," she snapped. "Go back to your seat."

I sat down. Standish was red in the face and the room was deathly quiet. The little coward who ran like a rabbit to avoid trouble had faced down Standish and won. My arm was sore and discoloured for days, but it had been worth it. It was my first triumph at the country school. Soon afterwards I had the second and last one.

Shortly before the summer vacation, Standish announced a doll competition for the girls. We were each to bring a doll to school, dressed in her very best. The best-dressed doll would get a blue ribbon.

Since I hated dolls, I brought two of my rats to school in a paper bag on the day of the competition. I'd dressed them as King and Queen. I'd raided Ma's ragbag and come up with two pieces of velvet of different colors, some bits of lace and a length of white fur trim. I fashioned the velvet into robes with fancy lace collars visible beneath them. I painted black dots on the white fur trim to make it look like ermine, which The Little King wore in the comics, and trimmed the robes with it. On their heads I placed golden crowns cut from cardboard and painted with metal paint I found in an old can in the shed.

The other girls brought their dolls dressed either in the clothes they came in from the store or in outfits that their mothers had made for them. Most of the dolls were babies, and fat, and I thought they were disgusting. Some were like little girls with plump, dimpled cheeks and curly hair and eyes that opened and closed.

When the girls arrived, the boys snickered and whispered and pointed to show their contempt for such things, but Standish put her foot down and demanded a little respect.

After the other girls had set their dolls on the table at the front, I brought up my paper bag, carefully removed my rats, and placed them side by side as far from the other dolls as I could get them.

Expectation erupted into consternation. Everyone, even the boys, came up to look at the rats. No one had seen anything like this before, and the boys, for once, were speechless.

My rats were awarded the blue ribbon, to be shared between them. Standish congratulated me, but I heard later a story circulated, presumably originating from her, saying there was concern that I was a disturbed child because of my lack of interest in dolls.

The next year I went, by special arrangement, to one of the schools in town. I left the country school behind, but certain things which happened there have never faded from my memory nor, it seems, from the minds of the witnesses. In my late teens, when I had in some measure learned to deal with deliberate unkindness, I received an anonymous phone call. I didn't recognize the voice, for it had changed and deepened.

"How's Bing?" the voice asked.

I knew instantly what he meant, but said "What?" in a puzzled manner.

"Bing. How's Bing?"

"Bing who? Do you mean Bing Crosby?"

"No. The dog Bing."

"I don't know what you're talking about."

He went into minute detail, which I denied recalling. I finally said, "Well, if you think I can remember everything that happened to me when I was seven you credit me with a remarkable memory. Obviously it made very little impression on me."

Defeated, he hung up. I'd given him no satisfaction and he didn't try again.

But the call was important. It told me something about human nature: Here was a boy, now a man, who had so relished my discomfort that he still remembered it with pleasure after ten years. It was important enough to him to try and remind me of it.

This was a category of human relationship I had not encountered before. I had not done this boy an injury, yet his hatred and contempt for me reached across a decade. I wondered what he felt about the other people in his life. Presumably he had parents, probably brothers and sisters and now, perhaps, a girlfriend. What was he like with them? Did he love them? Was I his only hate? If so, why?

In spite of the propaganda we got in school about loving one's enemies, I hated people who had been cruel to me. Receiving deliberate cruelty seemed to me a completely valid reason for hating and mistrusting the giver. But I hated no one else.

Why should someone I had never injured hate me? I still don't know the answer, but I suspect that hostility is bred in the genes of the human race, and we're stuck with it. I had a few hostile genes myself. After all, I'd slung mud at a relatively innocent traveling salesman, hadn't I? I didn't hate him. I didn't know him at all. I just felt like throwing mud at him. But it wouldn't have occurred to me to phone him ten years later to ask if he remembered it— unless I wanted to apologize.

22. Victims

There have been many accounts of victimization in school written by victims, and there will no doubt be many more. I have not encountered any accounts by the bullies, though perhaps this simply reflects my taste in reading.

Perhaps the victims are more articulate than their persecutors, and have learned that the best way to reduce the after-effects of trauma is to express it and analyze it.

If there are any personal accounts written by the bullies in which they explore their motivations and discuss the rewards and benefits they sought and gained by their behavior, I'd like to read them. Did their actions have any negative effects on their later life? Or did that way of treating people always give them what they were looking for? Would they choose to repeat that behavior if they could? Have they, consciously or unconsciously, taught their children to be bullies in their turn, and are they proud of them for it? Do they feel that bullying is the natural way for the strong to treat the weak, as normal as eating and sleeping?

Once a bully, always a bully? Or is there sometimes a change of heart?

I am not speaking here of the criminal element, of those in prison for violent crime, the mass murderers, or the despots on the global scene whose power grabs have obvious rewards for themselves if successful. I'm talking about ordinary people, in ordinary communities, who are cruel only to the extent they can get away with it, and who grow up to lead relatively unremarkable lives—working, marrying, begetting children, growing old, having grandchildren and coming, usually, to a non-violent end.

While writing this account of my two years at the country school, I fell asleep one night while considering these matters. I awoke next morning with a pattern of relationships between the children at Leighton School emerging into consciousness. I realized that in trying to record events, I had written things down in the same order as they first came to mind. The first memories to emerge were of cruelty to myself. Next came memories of cruelty to others. In both instances, the torturers whose names appeared were all male but one. That one was Dorothy Simpson.

Sylvia Palmer's name had emerged early too, but for a different reason. Dorothy and Sylvia were the first children I got to know at the country school because they were with me in the sub-primary class. I thought, initially, that they would be my friends. Dorothy had quickly made it clear that friendship was impossible, but I'd still had hopes for Sylvia. She was never my enemy, but she never became my friend either—because, as I now realized, she was a member of the Palmer clan, and all her loyalties lay there.

The next names to emerge were those of the other victims: Della Adams and Patrick Nichol. They shared my pariah status, but I'd not realized this for a while.

Then came Byron Pelletier's three younger sisters: Marie, Frances and Madeleine. They were not unkind—never did me harm or seemed to wish me evil, but they had offered me no protection.

The last name to surface was Theresa Boudreau, the older sister of Leroy. I had almost completely forgotten her. It was only because I knew there were fifteen children besides myself at the school that I kept dredging my memory until she appeared. Even then, I only managed to retrieve an impression of a pale, thin girl who was very quiet.

Now that the dramatis personae had all appeared, I began sorting them out, trying to define their relationship to one another. They sorted as follows:

The Bullies: All but two of the boys. The older they were, the more savage. The only female bully was Dorothy.
The Bullied: Patrick Nichol, Della Adams and me.
The Neutrals: Leroy Boudreau, and all the girls except Dorothy.

I then set up a structure based on family relationships. First, those with siblings at school:

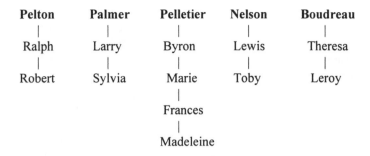

Pelton	Palmer	Pelletier	Nelson	Boudreau
Ralph	Larry	Byron	Lewis	Theresa
Robert	Sylvia	Marie	Toby	Leroy
		Frances		
		Madeleine		

Of these, the parents of the Peltons, Palmers and Pelletiers had also attended the school. Since the school, by, law had to have at least thirteen children attending in order to remain open, Martha Palmer, the matriarch of that clan, was said to have kept the school open for years by the annual birthing of yet another child.

Then there were the "only children":

Brenda Shaw   Dorothy Simpson   Patrick Nichol   Della Adams

I noted that the Palmer, Pelton, Pelletier and Nelson clans were all headed by older boys of the bullying class. If these boys had younger brothers, they were bullies too. The Palmer, Pelletier and Boudreau girls were protected from bullying by the existence of their brothers. Leroy Boudreau was younger than his sister and not a bully, but at least there were two of them. The protection was probably mutual in this case.

Della, Patrick and I were only children, alone and without protection, and therefore considered fair game.

But what about Dorothy? She was an only child, but she had everybody's number and knew how to manipulate it. She had risen to the status of teacher's pet and could get away with anything she pleased without reprimand. How had she managed this?

After a moment's thought it became clear. Of course! She was under the protection of the Palmer clan. She and Sylvia were age mates and had lived across the road from one another all their lives. They were practically litter mates. The Simpsons and the Palmers got along well. One big family.

Not only were Della and I vulnerable due to our status as only children, but we had both committed the sin of being smarter than the boys. The Pelletier girls were smart too, but they had Byron, who was the biggest and strongest male in the school, to defend them. Poor Patrick had committed the sin of being downtrodden without hope of rescue, and torturing Patrick could have no repercussions from any direction.

Is this picture of the dynamics at the Leighton School during the two years I was there typical of human relationships in the world at large? Does it reflect us all in some degree or another? I have found nothing in my later life to contradict this possibility. The same threads have run through all the larger groups of people that I have been numbered among since: high school, university, and the scientific community. The threads are more subtly woven into the fabric, but they are still there.

Luckily in those capacities I have usually (increasingly so in recent years) been able to find subgroups with the same interests as mine that have accepted me and allowed me to function and develop without the need of constant self-defense.

I have often had to stand alone, and have learned to defend myself successfully in these instances almost without exception. For this, I credit my two years at Leighton school. By the end of that second year I had controlled my fear and harnessed my anger. Not many people tangled with me more than once after that. If cornered, I will fight.

I have yet to completely conquor the shyness and wariness born of my experiences in that school, but I have learned to cover these and not let them harm my relationships.

23. The Cool Million

The spring before I left the country school, Uncle Fred decided he was going to make a Cool Million. Or rather he and Paul Griffin were going to make it—and after all, a million split two ways was not to be grumbled about. Especially in the thirties, in the depths of the Depression. According to Pa, Fred and Griffin were lucky to have jobs at all. They worked side by side at the shoe factory in Hallowell, putting high heels on ladies' shoes.

The heels were made of wood, and the wood kept splitting. Maddening and wasteful. So Fred and Griffin decided to do something about it, and earn a million dollars for their cleverness. I used to hear Fred going on and on to Pa about the Cool Million he was going to make with Paul Griffin:

"There's got to be a better material than wood for high heels," said Fred. "Wood keeps splitting along the grain. What we need is something cheap and easily available that has no grain, is not brittle, and can be poured into a mold."

"What about Celluloid?" suggested Pa.

"Wouldn't work—not strong enough. But I hear there's a lot being done both in this country and in Europe on other materials—plastics they call 'em— that some day are going to replace wood and metal and plant fibers and cause a real revolution in the way we live."

"Oh, yeah?" said Pa, dragging on his cigarette.

"Darn right. Things are moving, you know. The world is changing. In twenty years you won't know the place. There's going to be big double roads all across the country, two lanes in each direction, with grass strips down the middle to separate the traffic. They'll allow speeds of a hundred miles an hour on 'em. And in the living room everyone'll have a big box with a screen in front that will bring moving pictures right into your home."

"Oh, yeah?" said Pa.

Most people scoffed at Fred's ideas, but Fred and Griffin considered themselves advanced thinkers who kept up with the times. If someone someday was going to make a fortune on artificial heels, why not them? And why not right now?

Everyone smiled when they heard about this. Fred Gordon and Paul Griffin inventors? They were old men in their sixties with no special training—hadn't got further than primary school, either of them. Been jacks-of-all-trades all their lives, never made a decent living at anything they tried.

Ignoring the general derision, Fred and Griffin soon came up with a recipe they claimed would result in non-splitting heels of light weight and infinite durability. It was never clear how they arrived at this recipe, what their sources of information were, or which of them was the brains behind the process. They weren't talking about that. I heard Aunt Edith say to Ma that, after all, there was only one brain between the two of them anyway, so it really didn't matter.

"Listen, Shirley," I heard Fred say to Pa, "This process is gonna make our fortunes. It's based on old newspapers and resin from pine trees. What could be cheaper than that? Millions of newspapers get thrown out every day, and the woods are full of pine trees. If newspaper is shredded up and soaked in melted resin and then poured into a mold and cooled, it should be strong, durable and have no grain to split along."

"Might be worth a try," said Pa.

A few trial experiments showed that the resin was too thick to penetrate the paper, even when heated. But somewhere Fred and Griffin had heard that gasoline could be used to dilute resin, and that mixing the gasoline with kerosene would keep it from exploding.

"Those idiots will blow themselves to Kingdom Come," said Ma to Pa.

"You think it's a crazy idea? Well, it is," said Pa, "but sometimes crazy ideas work. I've heard that some big companies with millions of bucks are trying to make plastics out of coal, air and water. Is that any less crazy than newspapers, gasoline and resin? Coal comes from trees, and so do newspapers and resin."

Numerous outbuildings surrounded our farm, and the stable, which was currently unused, seemed to Fred and Griffin the ideal place to experiment. There was a good-sized room in which grain used to be stored where they could set up their equipment. So the lure of the million bucks brought Griffin out to our property with increasing frequency as the two men worked to perfect their process.

I can't imagine what Pa thought of it all. He took care to remain uninvolved. "Fred's business is Fred's business," he said.

I often saw Griffin coming and going, but at first paid little attention to him. He was just a dull elderly man in whom I had no interest. But then I began to notice his funny eyes. They made me nervous if he looked at me. He didn't seem to like children, and I was a brat.

If Griffin saw me anywhere near the stable, he glared at me with his little piggy eyes and muttered under his breath. "This is no place for children," he snarled at me one day as I paused at the stable door and looked in.

A few days later, he came across me in the vegetable plot behind the house where I was pulling up carrots for my pet rabbits.

"You're a real little farm girl, ain't ya?" he said, and grinned in a peculiar, sneering way. He leaned over and ran his hand over my chest, then went under my skirt and tried to get his fingers into my panties.

Just like Jack Lefevre last year. This man meant me no good, and I bit his hand as hard as I could. "Little Bitch!" he snarled and lunged at me, but I dodged him and ran for the house. He didn't try to follow. After that, I tried to make sure I was never on my own when he was around.

The resin experiments went on for weeks. I was too young to have any idea what they involved, but I heard Fred telling Pa about their efforts to get the amounts of shredded paper and resin right. There was also the tricky business of how much gasoline and kerosene to add to the resin. If the resin was too thick, it wouldn't soak into the paper. But when it was diluted enough to soak in, it wouldn't harden when cooled. "What we'll have to do is try boiling off the liquid until the stuff will set," said Fred.

They brewed up their concoctions on an old stove that worked on bottled gas. I was never allowed into the stable while they were working. Because I was kept out, my curiosity became unendurable. When the men weren't there I'd sneak in to see what was going on.

Griffin came in unexpectedly and caught me there one day. He came at me with a roar. "Children are never allowed near that bench. If I catch you pawing over our stuff again, I'll whale the hell out of you!" His face was purple and his funny eyes wild. He was breathing hard and I could smell the sweetish, foul odor of his breath. I got out fast.

The men finally reached the point where saucepans full of their million-maker were cooling to a uniform mass that did not fracture when struck with a hammer. It was time to get the heel molds ready and do the first big cook-up of their witches' brew in an old wash-boiler.

Pa became increasingly nervous about experiments involving gasoline being carried out in the stable, which was connected by a series of sheds to the farmhouse. If the stable went up in flames he would lose everything. So the stove was moved out into an unused chicken house some distance from the rest of the farm buildings.

The following Sunday, Griffin arrived early. He and Fred mixed the shredded paper, resin, gasoline and kerosene in the wash-boiler, lit the stove, and waited to make sure the boil-up was going well. Then I saw Fred go off to his bungalow where Aunt Grace was making coffee. Griffin apparently was still in the chicken house. Otherwise I would have gone there at once to see what was going on.

I heard the explosion, and by the time we had all dashed out, the chicken house was totally invisible in a wall of flame. "Griffin's burning!" I thought with a jolt of horror—but the source of my horror was the realization of what would have happened to me if his presence in the chicken house hadn't kept me from going there.

Aunt Grace had the vapors about what would have become of Fred if the explosion had happened five minutes earlier. Ma muttered about angels looking after fools and drunks. Pa said nothing. Fred just stood numb for a few minutes and watched the flames. Then he said "Thank God Griffin is religious! If he hadn't left to go to mass he'd be nothing but ashes now."

A confusing mixture of relief and disappointment buzzed in my head.

Griffin appeared after mass and contemplated the smoking ruin with Fred. He never, to my knowledge, appeared at the farm again after that day. And never again was anything said, in my hearing at least, about shredded paper, gasoline, kerosene, resin or ladies' heels—and certainly nothing about the Cool Million.

24. The Summer Between

When the country school recessed for the summer following my second year there, I had passed the third grade and was to have gone into the fourth grade in the autumn, with reading in the fifth. Just before the summer vacation began, however, Ma received a visit from Miss Buker, the District Superintendent of Schools. I was told to go away and play.

I sneaked up the back stairs and down the front, trying to get close enough to the living room to hear what was going on. I only caught a few fragments, one being from Ma: "They all say things like 'shit' and 'piss' every other word." Till then, I'd never heard those words pass Ma's lips.

After Miss Buker had gone, Ma called me to her.

"Miss Buker is arranging for you to go to school in town this fall," she said. "They don't have room in any of the fourth grades, but they will take you into the third grade at the Nash School."

"Have I got to stay back in the third grade?" I asked, appalled.

Ma put her hand gently on my shoulder. "Miss Buker says the teaching there is quite different so you won't be repeating the same thing, and anyway the third grade is where you would be if you hadn't stayed back a grade and then skipped two. The third is the highest grade at the Nash, so all the children will be your own age or younger. I think you'll be happier there. Then the next year you can go into the fourth grade at the Lincoln School, which takes over the pupils from the Nash."

I listened with interest, but by now I knew enough not to form any false illusions about life at a new school. I only hoped that what I was going to would be no worse than what I was coming from.

Early that summer, Uncle Bart died. The last time I saw him, he was swaying at the top of the back steps to the farmhouse. He swayed forward, then back, then further forward, then further back, then he pitched face downward onto the grass. Ma ran out and tried to help him up. He pushed her away, staggered to his feet, and described a spiral path back to his bungalow.

I don't know what led up to this scene, nor did I find out later. And I don't know how soon afterwards he died. I wasn't told when it happened and learned of it some time later. Marguerite Hunter, Alton's sister, came by to give Ma her condolences.

"I was shocked to hear of Barton's death," I heard her say.

The impact of her words ran from the top of my head down my spine and out my toes. I'd never known personally anyone who had died. Pets, yes, but not people.

After Marguerite left, I asked Ma, in disbelief, "Is Barton dead?"

"Yes," she replied.

"Why didn't you tell me?"

She turned her head away and didn't answer. I was furious at again not being told, at always being kept outside. It was one more betrayal—one more reason why I could not trust the people I loved.

Although I was shaken, I was also relieved. Barton never again would breathe at me with his sticky breath or skewer me with his black and terrible eyes.

I think I must have been very close to paranoia that summer. Although my family was honest with everyone else, they had all, at one time or another, deceived me. I had been deceived about my mother, about school, about the tonsils, and now about Barton's death. I was sure I was being deceived about other things as well. The world seemed to hold fearful secrets that everyone knew but me. Conversations stopped when I came into the room. I spied as much as I could, but heard only enough to glean hints of terrible family trouble I wasn't supposed to know about.

The whole world was beginning to seem like a conspiracy. Even the radio commentators were in on it. They said big words I couldn't understand and when I demanded what the words meant, my elders would say, "Be quiet, I'm trying to listen." The radio was old and staticky and had no aerial. It was hard enough to hear anything without a child clamoring for information.

In an attempt to puzzle out what was going on around me I had, some time before Barton's death, begun the practice of asking the same question to everyone I knew and then comparing the answers. I found this enlightening, though hardly reassuring. Many of the answers did not agree with one another. My people and the neighbors could not even agree on how best to evade my questions.

One question I had asked was "What happens to people when they die?"

Ma and Aunt Grace averred, "They go to the stars." Edith said they went to Heaven.

Barton, overhearing my question to Edith and her answer, nailed me with his searing eyes and declared, "The good people go to Heaven. The bad ones writhe in agony in the fires of Hell and the worms get what's left." There was no doubt in my mind that he considered me a bad one.

When I told Ma what he had said, she reversed her position on "going to the stars" and assured me that everyone, good and bad, went to Heaven because God pardonned sinners when they repented.

When I asked Pa, he said approximately what he had told me about my dead chicken: "The dead go into the ground to nourish the earth and make the vegetables and flowers and trees grow."

I liked Pa's answer best. It seemed a natural thing to happen.

And Barton's answer about the fires of hell? He was dead now. Where had he thought he was going?

By the end of the summer Edith had sold the house, found an apartment in town, and began building a new life. Ma told me Edith had a very good "young lady's education," knew Greek and Latin and was a talented piano player. This surprised me, since she had never shown any interest in music when she lived at the farm—never touched my piano and did not have one of her own. Once free from what must have been a deadly burden, however, she joined the Manchester Grange and a couple of clubs in town. We heard she was in great demand because of her expertise on the piano.

Did she feel as relieved as I that Bart was dead?

Occasionally, on a Sunday, Edith took the bus out to the farm to see us, and spent the day, as usual, stroking the cat and saying little. She told Ma she was enjoying her new life.

85

I had much earlier inferred that there was something secret and shameful about people's bodies: something that had to be kept covered up and whispered about, but no one would tell me what it was. Was something wrong with everyone's body, or just our family's bodies? I was wild with curiosity, anger and frustration.

When a major plumbing crisis occurred at Aunt Grace's bungalow that summer, it happened to be at one of the few times our bathroom was functional. Therefore, for a week or so, Grace came over daily to use ours. I thought this might be an opportunity to expand my knowledge of anatomy.

When the bathroom was empty and everyone too far away to hear what I was doing, I went the length of boring a hole almost through the bathroom door. I didn't bore all the way through, for fear someone would notice the hole before I had a chance to use it.

The next time Grace came to bathe, I quietly positioned myself outside the door, gave her enough time to get stripped, then made the final turn of the drill to produce the peephole.

Unfortunately, by the time I got my eye to the hole, Grace had mostly covered herself with a towel and was screaming at full volume. I fled down the back stairs, but was intercepted at the bottom by Pa, who handed me over to Ma. I couldn't tell from his expression whether he was angry or just trying not to laugh.

Ma was certainly not laughing, nor was Grace. "What you have done is very wicked," she told me grimly when she heard what had happened. "Aunty is very upset, and just at a time when she's not feeling well. You must never do such a thing again!"

She wouldn't tell me why.

Not long after this, Grace, ailing since the preceding winter, began taking more and more to her bed. No one knew what was wrong. Three doctors consulted and couldn't agree. I went to see her on days when she was feeling better and we told each other stories and sang songs. But the days she felt better grew fewer and fewer.

The rest of the time, when not helping to weed the vegetable and flower gardens or pick the vast crop of raspberries, I spent with my beloved chickens and my rubber rats. The rats were rulers of my sand pit, and I built them palaces of sand and laid out elaborate gardens for them with flowers pilfered from Ma's flower beds. All the chickens were named and had personalities of their own. I made up complicated stories about them to tell to Grace.

I also had a secret friend that summer. Her name was Sylvia. Sylvia was a popular name in the thirties, and I liked it. Perhaps I chose it because I wished that Sylvia Palmer had become my friend. My Sylvia had curly blond hair and a beautiful face and was always fun. She went everywhere with me, watering the chickens, gathering daisies in the fields, running and laughing with me in the rain. She sang with me when I played the piano and told me funny stories that made me laugh. She was always delighted with the stories that I told her back. I suppose to some extent I was trying through Sylvia to make up for the growing distance between Grace and me.

I never told anyone about Sylvia. I knew she was only make-believe and they would laugh. But she was someone to talk to.

My people had never been talkers, and now after Barton's death and the onset of Grace's illness they talked less than ever. My father seldom spoke at all. Our relationship was almost completely non-verbal, but there had always been a bond between us that did not need expression in words. We were content to work together in the fields in silence.

Pa was a gentle, shy man who, I knew from the photograph of him with his cats, had been handsome when young. Ma told me he'd been ashamed of his tightly curled hair, and of his name, Shirley, which in America is a girl's name. By the time I knew him, he had succeeded in completely flattening out his tight curls, but he hadn't changed his name. Mail frequently arrived for him addressed "Miss Shirley Shaw."

Pa had gotten his name in an odd way. Ma told me that when he was born in the recently settled Aroostook town of Woodland in 1879, no birth records were yet being kept there, so there was no pressure on parents to act quickly. Pa lay unnamed in his cot for weeks because no one could decide what to call him. Then one day Ma read a story about an Englishman named Shirley. Shirley is a common surname in England, and is sometimes used there as a masculine first name. Ma had never heard it before, and thought it would be just right for the baby. So Pa was stuck with it.

Aunt Grace, Ma's first-born, got her name in an unusual way also. Ma had planned to name her Mildred, but the postman changed that. His baby girl, Grace, had recently died of a fever. When he saw Ma's baby, he took her in his arms and burst into tears, "Call her Gracie," he said to Ma. "Please call her Gracie." Ma didn't like the name Grace but could not refuse this plea made in grief, so my aunt became Grace Mildred. Sometimes Ma called her Millie.

I asked Pa how old he was when I was born, and he told me forty-nine. So that summer he would have been fifty-seven. He'd worked hard all his life, and still got up at five in the summer, even though by then we had only one cow to milk, and one pig and the chickens to feed. Breakfast was at seven: fruit, bacon, eggs, cereal, toast. Pa said that in the old days before the Depression the traditional farm breakfast was steak and hot mince pie.

Dinner was at twelve noon when we came in from the fields. Often it was "New England Boiled Dinner," which meant corned beef, potatoes, carrots, onions, turnips and beets, all boiled in the same pot. Next day we would get the remains, chopped and fried as "Red Flannel Hash." Then back to the fields until supper, which was a light meal at five o'clock. Bedtime was between 8 and 9 for everybody. That gave the needed eight hours before 5 a.m., and no one had any trouble sleeping.

I can't remember seeing a cookbook either in our kitchen, in Grace's, or at the Lees. The knowledge of how to prepare the raised breads, rolls, johnny cake, bran muffins, soups, stews, roasts, fricassees and other delights seemed to be within these women, and could be called up at will.

In summer the food was wonderful: fresh corn, tomatoes, cucumbers and peas from the garden, and strawberry shortcake made from wild strawberries of incredible flavor. Fourth of July dinner was always roast ham, peas, corn and sweet potatoes. Without the torture of school hanging over me, my appetite returned and I made up in three months the weight what I had lost in nine.

In August was the tomato harvest, when the huge, sun-ripened red fruits were laid out on tables in the shed. The air was redolent with their pungent sweetness. We gorged ourselves with them and then canned or pickled the rest. I loved the acrid, mouth-watering tang of green tomato pickles simmering in vinegar and spices on the old cast iron stove. It was so sharp that sweat would break out on my forehead when I smelled it.

In October, the apple harvest came in. We had only two Northern Spy trees in our west field and a crabapple and a russet near the burned-out chicken house. Their fruit didn't have the flavor or lucious juiciness of the Lees' McIntoshes. The Lees had a proper orchard: a whole acre of apple trees. The smell of their McIntosh Reds hanging on the trees in the bright October sun put all perfumes I knew to shame—except perhaps the nutmeggy smell of hot spiced pumpkin pie coming from the oven when the pumpkin harvest came in.

Because of her age (she was 80 when I was eight) Ma's contribution to the farm economy had been reduced to home canning farm produce to be eaten in winter, making raspberry jam and jelly to sell, preparing the meals, cleaning the house, making cheese and butter, and tending her flower beds. She made our farm a showplace, with flowering shrubs and borders of hardy perennials. It was perhaps the only outlet for this stern and humorless woman who loved beauty, but who had had little enough of it in her life.

I write of farm life as it was during that summer and autumn because it was the last one before the combined effects of the Great Depression, death, illness and a slowly pervading hopelessness began to tear that world apart.

Part Three: The City Schools

25. The Second Death

Before I entered third grade at the Nash School in 1936, I changed my name. I'd come to hate the name Brenda. I wanted to be somebody else. I'm not sure when I began to hate it, probably shortly after I started at the country school. It was a hard name and unyielding, and people who didn't like me said it harshly and with a sneer. The summer after leaving the country school forever, I communicated my feelings to Ma:

"Brenda sounds like 'barn door.' And my middle name—Betsy! That's what people call cows. Betsy the cow. Brenda Betsy. It sounds so stupid!"

"What would you like to be called?" Ma asked mildly.

"I don't care, as long as it's not that awful name!"

"How about 'Peggy'?"

I looked up in surprise. Peggy. It was nice. It was friendly. I liked the way Ma said it. "Yes," I said. "Yes, that'll be fine."

So when I went to the Nash School I was no longer Brenda. I was Peggy, a new person with a new name and a new start. I kept that name all through grade school and high school.

By coincidence, Richard Lee also had a name change about this time. He decided he wanted to be called "Dick." When I asked him why he hated his name, he laughed.

"I don't hate my name," he said. "Richard is fine and I'll always keep it, but the nickname for Richard is 'Dick,' so most people have started calling me that."

It took as long for me to get used to calling Richard "Dick," as it did for him to remember that I was now "Peggy."

89

Fortunately Aunt Edith's newly acquired three-room apartment was only a few streets away from the school. It was arranged that Uncle Fred would take me to Edith's just before 8 a.m. on his way to the shoe factory. I would stay there till time for school, which began at 9:00. I would have lunch with Edith, and return there following the afternoon session to wait until Fred picked me up on his way from the shoe factory just after five.

Before the first day I had many misgivings, and not merely about school. I wasn't sure of Edith. That strange, silent woman had never gained either my affection or my trust. In the years she lived on the farm I never got to know her. In fact, I never did afterwards either.

I had not feared Edith before but now, facing this new transition into the unknown, I found myself wondering what awaited me. An innocent-sounding trip to visit a hospital had turned nasty before—did something like the tonsil episode lurk at Edith's?   Did she keep something horrible in her closet with which to frighten children? Or would she tie me up and leave me to starve and tell my father that I just hadn't come back from school?

And the school—surely children were the same everywhere?

The first day, then, came as an unexpectedly pleasant surprise. Edith took me early and introduced me to Miss Joy, who lived up to her name in every way. She chatted with me for a while and then told me to sit in a certain seat till all the other children had come and the bell had rung. Soon afterwards a little blonde girl with dimpled cheeks (looking remarkably like my fantasy Sylvia) came up to me and said "You're sitting in my seat."

"I'm sorry," I said, terrified, "the teacher told me to sit here."

She gave me a big smile and said, "That's all right," and went skipping off to Miss Joy who assigned her another seat.

At recess everyone was friendly, telling me their names and wanting to know where I was from. At lunch time several of the children went in the direction of Edith's house so they walked along with me, explaining where they lived and hoping I'd come and play. I couldn't believe it.

The first day also dispelled my doubts about Edith, who had a good lunch ready for me and who read to me till it was time to return to school. After school she read to me until Fred came to pick me up.

In retrospect, her choice of reading material was appalling. As I recall, during the whole school year she read me only the mystery stories which were her staple fare—blood, guts and all. Once I had to excuse myself to go to the toilet during a particularly gruesome scene for fear I would be sick. To my relief when I returned a friend of Edith's had dropped by and I was spared further details. Next day when Edith said "Shall we finish that story?" I said "I don't like that one much, can we try another?"

Considering her Greek and Latin "young lady's education" I can only marvel at her taste in literature.

As I made friends, many of the after-school waits for Uncle Fred were spent at the homes of nearby children. I always had to be careful to be back at Edith's by five to meet Fred. No one showed me any sign of hostility, and I rapidly lost my fear. My appetite was no longer a problem, and the blinding headaches did not recur.

In late September of 1936, after I'd started at Nash School, Lynde got married.

He hadn't liked his engineering job in the tropics. The heat of Honduras was oppressive, the living conditions primitive, and he missed his girlfriend Marge. After sixteen months he returned to Melrose to ask her to marry him, and to look for other work. His references were excellent, and he soon had a job offer from Tidewater Construction Company, to begin the following December. Tidewater was a large and reputable firm in Norfolk, Virginia, and it was with that company that Lynde would spend most of his working life.

He brought Marge, who was now his fiancée, to the farm to visit us at least twice during the months before their wedding. She was kind and warm and pretty, and her light brown hair curled softly around her gentle face. She and Lynde played games with me and took me to get ice cream in Lynde's second-hand Chevy that he said he'd paid $75 for. They were always happy and laughing, and I was delighted with Marge.

On their last visit before their wedding, they picked me up at Edith's after school so I wouldn't have to wait until 5:00 for Fred.

Ma and Pa must have known the date they planned to marry, but I knew nothing about it until I got a letter from Lynde with a wedding photograph enclosed. Lynde was trim and handsome in a smart-looking suit and stood beside Marge on a lawn with trees behind them. Marge was wearing a dark velvet suit and matching hat. They were both smiling. Lynde's letter said "Marge and I are making each other very happy." They were in the midst of their preparations for going to Norfolk.

I'd never been to a wedding, and knew nothing about the customs involved, or that the families of both bride and groom would normally attend. If Ma and Pa sent a wedding gift I never saw it, and one was never mentioned in my presence. With the expenses of Grace's illness I doubt if we could have afforded to buy one—or afforded to go by train to Massachusetts to attend the ceremony. Even if poverty had not been a factor, I'm sure Ma and Pa were far too exhausted and demoralized to make such a trip. They'd have had to arrange to take me out of school for a couple of days, as well.

I learned no details of the wedding later, either. Lynde never mentioned it, and I never saw Marge again. No one knew of course, when they married, what would soon befall her.

The third grade at Nash School was supposedly a repeat of what I'd already had at the Leighton School but, as Ma had predicted, it was quite different. The school had several class rooms, so each grade had its own separate one. The building had a basement, too, where the toilets were, and where the janitor tended a furnace. Instead of being one of two or three children in a grade, getting less than half an hour a day of the teacher's time, I was now in a class of twenty-five third graders. For reading, arithmetic and work-book assignments we were divided into ability groups, though I didn't realize then that the division was by ability. This group work was in the morning. The afternoons were devoted to teaching the whole class the same things, such as geography, history, art and singing.

At Leighton I had sailed through the reading and workbook assignments, had no problem with the arithmetic, and had spent a great deal of my time listening to what went on in the higher grades. This had its advantages, as I heard information which I would not otherwise have been exposed to for years, and I was ready to absorb it. Now a great deal which I had not been taught at Leighton was presented to me at Nash.

One activity which stands out was working on a large group painting which was later mounted on one whole wall in the classroom. Music and Art were twice a week, not just once a week with an itinerant teacher as at Leighton. I could feel my mind expanding, and began to realize how little I had known before, and what a surprising place the world was.

My venture into the city school produced not only new friends but a new pet.

Autumn had arrived, and the yellow leaves were swirling along the street when I first saw Fluff. She was wandering along the sidewalk looking dazed and lost. Her coat was striped fawn and black, and her fur was long and fluffy. She was tiny, eyes still blue. She saw me and mewed. I picked her up. At once she snuggled into my arms and began to purr.

"Poor little thing, where do you belong?" I asked her.

Rosalie, who was in my grade at school and was walking back to Edith's with me, said, "She's a stray. Somebody didn't want her and put her out."

I looked at Rosalie in amazement. Did people really put kittens out on the street because they didn't want them? Rosalie assured me that they did. I walked up to the door of the nearest house and knocked. The woman who answered said she knew nothing about the kitten. "Probably a stray. Why don't you take it home?" she said.

Why not, indeed? I carried it back to Edith's and told her I was taking it home with me. Edith smiled wryly. "I wonder what your Ma will say to that!" she said.

The first thing Ma did was draw in breath. Then she turned the kitten upside down. "Female, of course," she said resignedly. "Probably born in August."

Puzzled, I looked up at her.

"Well, we can't just put her out into the woods," she said. Then she went all over Fluff, parting the fur with her fingers and looking carefully at the skin beneath.

"What are you doing?" I asked.

"Checking her for fleas," she replied. "See, look here. Those little black specks are flea droppings. And look! There goes a flea!"

I saw a tiny brown shiny body shoot across the area of skin Ma's fingers were exposing.

"We must get rid of them at once, or the poor little thing will get mange from their bites."

"What's mange, Ma?"

"Sore, itchy skin caused by flea bites and the cat's scratching."

"How do we get rid of the fleas?"

"Come, I'll show you. Bring Fluff."

Ma went to the kitchen sink and drew two pails of warm water. She took them and a cake of homemade yellow soap outside on the grass.

"We're going to lower Fluff slowly into this pail of water, tail first," she said. "As she goes in, the fleas will run upward to get away from the water and we can pick them off her head. I'll show you how to hold her. Look. I'm picking her up by the scruff of the neck like this. That's the way mother cats carry their kittens. See? Fluff just goes limp and doesn't resist. But wet soapy cats are slippery, and I might lose my grip. So I'll hold her hind paws too, keeping one finger between them so they don't rub together and hurt her, and then she's less likely to struggle free."

Ma lowered away slowly, and Fluff never even twitched. If anything, she seemed to enjoy feeling the warm water rising on her body. As Ma had predicted, as the kitten went down fleas began crawling up onto her nose and I could pick them off.

When no more fleas appeared, Ma said, "Now I'll raise her out of the water and you soap her all over with the yellow soap while I hold her. Be careful not to get soap in her eyes. Then we'll rinse her off in the other pail."

Fluff liked being massaged by my soapy hands, and just lay back and purred.

Next time Fluff needed a bath, I did the holding and Ma applied the soap. We repeated this as needed and never had the least trouble.

And so Fluff came to stay. She was to be an important part of my education.

Later in the autumn, some time after finding Fluff, I heard someone crying during a school recess period. Investigating, I found a girl in my class, Joan, being beset by two other girls. I rushed at them and they fell back, amazed at my sudden show of ferocity. I comforted Joan, who told me that Rose and Thelma often followed her home, calling her names and spitting at her. From that time on I accompanied Joan home after school to make sure there was no nonsense, often staying on to play at her home. We became close friends. I was heartbroken to learn at the end of the school year that her family was moving from the town.

Rose and Thelma showed me no enmity because I defended Joan. If they harbored any resentment for my interference, they never showed it.

In fact, I never felt any enmity from anyone at Nash school, although sometimes I was the cause of good-humored mirth. Coming from a farm, I wore the sort of clothing suited to hard-to-heat farmhouses and deep snow. As winter came on and we had to dress for it, my four-buckle overshoes were cause for comment. They were not the type of slender feminine snap-on overshoes girls in the city were used to wearing. Once I'd taken my four-bucklers off, it also became apparent that I was wearing long-johns under my heavy woolen stockings. The line where they ended just at the ankle was a dead give away, and for a while this caused no end of excitement.

Most of the city girls didn't even wear stockings in the winter. Navy, dark green, black or burgundy knee socks with colorful decorated bands on the top were in vogue. A few whose mothers refused to let their daughters freeze their bare knees were allowed to wear what everyone called "those fake knee socks" which had brown woolen extensions like regular stockings which covered their knees and thighs and were held up by a garter belt. I thought the whole commotion over leg wear was silly and stupid and persisted with my long johns. The others soon ceased to comment.

It was just as well that the problem of school had been solved. If it had not been, I think the events at the farm during that winter would have been past bearing.

Aunt Grace had grown steadily worse. Often I was not allowed to see her for days, and when I did, the change in her once round and pretty face—its gauntness and pallor—was terrible. I could never stay long, and sometimes she would burst out crying and say "Go away, oh go away."

I hung around the farmhouse and the outer rooms of Grace's bungalow like a gray ghost. My blinding headaches did not recur, but instead were replaced by a rash at the inner bends of my elbows. It itched like fire and oozed a thin colorless liquid. Also, boils appeared on my arms and legs and across my backside. At one time I had 21 boils at the same time on my bottom. I could sit down without too much pain if I did so slowly, because my weight pushed the blood out of the boils. When I got up, however, the blood rushed back in and it was agony. The doctor just said "She's got bad blood. She'll get over it when she matures." It didn't seem to occur to anyone that the boils and the rash might be a reaction to Grace's illness.

Boils are dangerous. The rich went to the doctor and had them lanced under aseptic conditions to avoid blood poisoning. Blood poisoning took a lot of people off in those days. Antibiotics weren't even imagined.

The poor treated boils as we did, and Ma trained me well in the art of bringing a boil to a head.

"If you try to squeeze a boil too soon, it can force the infection back into the blood," she told me when the first boil appeared on the inside of my forearm. "You must wait until it's ready to burst."

So I waited as the redness and swelling got worse, as the throbbing increased, during days when the pain let me think of little else. The damn thing wasn't called a boil for nothing. The heat it produced felt as though it would ignite my skin.

"A poultice will relieve some of the pain and help draw the boil to a head," Ma said. She soaked some bread in warm milk, rung it out and bound it onto the boil with a gauze bandage.

As the poultice "drew" on the boil over the next two days, a transparent membrane became evident on the surface of the boil, in a central position. Beneath this membrane pale yellow pus began to accumulate.

"When the pus goes from pale lemon to rich yellow, the boil will be ripe and ready to burst," Ma said. "It will probably do so spontaneously and drain into the poultice, but if it doesn't, we can burst it."

I didn't like the sound of this. I couldn't bear the thought of anything touching the throbbing boil, let alone bursting it. "How?" I asked apprehensively.

"With a sterile needle. I'll show you when the time comes. Don't worry, the needle won't hurt, and once the boil has burst the pain will go away."

I didn't believe the needle wouldn't hurt, but the pain of the boil was so bad I was ready to do almost anything to try and stop it.

Next day when Ma removed the poultice to check the boil, the area of pus under the membrane had enlarged and its color had deepened. "It's ready," said Ma. "Go and fetch me a box of matches from the cupboard and a needle from my sewing box. I'll get the rubbing alcohol and the sterile cloths."

When everything was assembled I asked what the alcohol and the cloths were for. "The cloths have been washed and then ironed with a hot iron to sterilize them. The surfaces that are folded inside are sterile and can be used to wipe the pus away. The alcohol will clean the boil and the skin of your arm afterwards."

Ma lit one of the matches. She took the needle and held the tip in the flame until the match was spent. The tip of the needle was now coated black with soot. "It's sterile now. The black doesn't matter, that's just carbon from the smoke. It's sterile too. Sit down at the table, Peggy, and rest your arm on it."

I did as I was told. I looked up at Ma as she approached with the needle. "It'll hurt," I said.

"No. You just watch what I do carefully so you can do it yourself if you ever need to."

She held the needle between thumb and forefinger and delicately pricked away the transparent membrane. I felt nothing, and the pus began to roll out. Ma kept wiping it away and dropping the used cloths into a paper bag. "We'll burn them in the stove when we're done," she said.

When the flow of pus stopped, I looked at Ma questioningly. "Don't move your arm yet, Peggy. We have to get the core of the boil out to get rid of the infection. The infection is walled off from the blood stream in a little sack. That sack full of germs and pus must be removed, or the infection will spread into the blood."

"How do we do that?"

"We must squeeze the boil."

I winced.

"Yes, it will hurt, but it is absolutely necessary—so you will have to grit your teeth and bear it. It must be done right, and it must be done now. I will show you how. Watch carefully. I'll be as quick as I can."

She placed the thumb and forefinger of each hand on either side of the boil, about an inch away from the drainage hole, and exerted slowly increasing pressure in an outward direction.

"You mustn't squeeze close to the hole. That would just drive the infection back in. You must press at the edges of the boil, pushing out away from it, to make the core pop out."

As she pressed, the pain was searing, but I clamped my jaws tight together and watched, as she had told me to do. Slowly more pus was expelled, then in a final rush of matter the sack popped out, followed by fresh blood.

"That's it," said Ma. "That's the core out. Now you'll be all right. I'll clean your arm up with alcohol and put on a sterile bandage. It won't hurt anymore. The red will subside and it will itch a bit while it heals, but that's all."

It was a good thing that I took in the techniques which Ma showed me. Not only did watching take my mind off the pain, but I had plenty of occasion to use them that winter. Ma squeezed the boils on my butt and other places which I couldn't reach, but I poulticed and squeezed the rest, under close supervision at first, then when Ma was sure I knew what I was doing, on my own.

Mostly we used bread and milk poultices, but sometimes tried mashed potato or cooked onion. Then a product called Antiphlogiston came on the market—a malleable clay-like substance. All these poultices seemed about equally effective in drawing the infection to the surface.

As bad as the boils, in its own way, was the rash at the bends of my elbows. "Weeping eczema," said the Doctor. This, too, he proclaimed was due to "bad blood." It itched incessantly and made sleeping almost impossible. Salves and creams were useless and only increased the itching. Only one astringent lotion, the name of which I forget, gave some temporary relief. It stung when applied, which was better than the the itching. Repeated applications dried the skin until it formed thick, ugly scales. For about a week the itching was kept at bay, but then the scales would slough off and one had to start all over again.

For both the boils and the eczema various pills and potions were available at the drug store. I guess I was exposed to most of them, but none of them helped.

Meanwhile, Grace continued to fail. In the depths of the winter a nurse, Mrs. Knowles, came to live at the bungalow. She was big and brusque and good-natured, but she raised no one's spirits. I heard Ma ask her one day "Is there any hope?"

"While there's life there's hope," was all she said.

The combined resources of Uncle Fred and my father were not enough to pay the nurse. Pa plumbed an old sink into one of the upstairs rooms of the farmhouse, put in a stove salvaged from a junkyard, and rented it along with our guest room as a two-room apartment to get the money.

A couple named Towle moved in. They were in their sixties and had lived in Massachusetts, as had Fred and Grace at one time. I think Fred and Herb Towle had worked together at a shoe shop in Haverhill.

Herb Towle was grim and silent. Like most other men I had known, except Pa and Merrill Lee, he was cross and cold and didn't like children. But Mae Towle was warm and wonderful. She was grey and wrinkled and the skin on her heck hung loose like a hen's wattles, but with her heart-shaped face and green eyes she must have been beautiful when young.

Herb was away during the day and Mae, at a loose end, was glad enough to become my companion and confidante. She didn't treat me like a child. She was a woman full of wisdom and willing to discuss life and the things that mattered and how the world worked beyond the confines of our farm. She told me strange things like the story of Pompeii and the discovery of Tutankhamen's tomb. She was from Boston, that big city to the south that she said was larger than any city in Maine, and where everything was different.

Mae was the source of several enlightenments that winter which would never have come from Ma and Pa or Aunt Grace. Mae thought in different terms, from a different perspective. For one thing, she pointed out that no cow could have a calf unless she had been taken to see the bull. She did not

97

elaborate, and I could think of no sensible question to ask about this interesting observation.

Although I was now eight years old, I had no inkling yet that young grew inside their mothers. My people took great care to keep this from me. No animal at the farm would dare copulate or give birth in my presence. It seems incredible now that my elders could have managed to sustain my ignorance so completely, but they did. Our yellow tomcat Sandy had been neutered and was no source of information, and Fluff was not yet old enough for the inevitable kittens to have been produced. When I encountered two cats copulating at the Lees, Dick simply said, "They're fighting." He was usually reliable, and I believed him.

I had tried to get information about the source of babies by my usual method of asking the same questions to everyone. When I posed the question "Where do babies come from?" to Ma, she sighed and turned away without answering. Then I asked Aunt Grace. She didn't know. Mrs. Lee just laughed and said, "Little girls would like to know that, wouldn't they?"

Pa had said, "You came because we wanted you." That was nice, but I couldn't see how wishing could bring this about.

Obviously this was another dark secret my elders wished to keep from me. Their resistance was total. I would have to figure things out for myself. Mae was the only one so far who had been any help at all. I suspected she would be even more helpful if everyone else were not so intent on keeping me in the dark. But her comment about the bull had at least given me something to ponder about. If it took a bull to create a calf, then who knows, maybe it took Pa to create me. Why wouldn't he tell me how he did it?

Mae Towle also told me a great deal about painting with oils. She showed me books full of photographs of paintings done by the old masters. She knew all their names and when they lived and how they had learned their trade. She showed me her set of oil paints which she kept in a large metal box with many drawers. All the tubes had been partly used. Most of them were small, but the tube of white was enormous. "You use lots of white to get lighter colors," she explained.

I loved art at school and was good at it, but I had never seen anything but watercolors before. I was so fascinated with the oil paints that Mae began to show me how to use them. She explained how to mix primary colors together to get secondary colors and how to lighten colors with white; also what complementary colors were and how to use them with each other for different effects. She showed me how to get flesh tints by mixing Indian red and white together. I loved the feeling of the oils under the brush and the way errors could be corrected, which could not be done with watercolors. I learned how to bring the paint to the right consistency with linseed oil and turpentine, and to enjoy the strange sharp smells of these solvents.

The names of the pigments delighted me—rose madder, prussian blue, burnt sienna, raw umber, crimson lake, cadmium yellow, viridian green.

Mae had been a talented artist, though now she painted only for pleasure. She and Herb had had one son, Vaughn, very talented, who had been training to be an artist when he fell from a ladder and broke his spine. The doctors available to him could do nothing, and after a few bedridden months he died. He kept on painting till the end. Mrs. Towle showed me his last work—a china plate with the bleeding heart of Christ on it, surrounded by a crown of thorns.

Mae liked to talk about Vaughn and about the girl, Irene, who was in love with him, but whom he hadn't loved. Irene never realized that Vaughn didn't love her and he hadn't the heart to tell her. After he died she never married.

My absorption in painting took my mind for brief periods off what was happening to Grace. Mae's friendship and instruction helped me greatly that winter, which I'm sure she knew, but even she could not work miracles. Death hung in the air over the two houses. Everyone waited.

Then one afternoon when I got home from school I knew the waiting was over, though nobody said anything.

Later that evening Ma said to me, "Come here, Peggy, I have something to tell you."

"I know what it is already."

"You know that Auntie's gone?"

"Yes."

"Aren't you going to cry?"

"No."

Ma turned her head away and wept. I could only stand there dumb with misery. It is not until now, years later, as I write about it that I can cry for Grace.

26. Learning the Game

It was early spring when Grace died. Ma spent the last night at her bedside, but at dawn she went back to the farmhouse and fell into a troubled, aching sleep on the downstairs couch. The weak March sun rose silently over the remains of snow in the dun-colored fields to hang brittle in the sky. About ten, Barton came to Ma in a dream and said: "Mother, I've come for Grace." She awoke to see Mrs. Knowles coming along the path through the raspberry canes to tell her that her daughter was dead.

The doctor was summoned to sign the death certificate, the undertaker to collect the body. The room was cleaned and fumigated, and Mrs. Knowles left. It was over.

No one had told me that Grace was dying, but the truth had come to me slowly over the last weeks. Without framing the thought in words, I realized that someone who had changed as much as she could not recover: The face and hands emerging from her nightgown were skeletal, and seemed no longer to be hers. Bones glowed through transparent skin. What I came to know as the smell of death was everywhere.

I was considered too young to go to the funeral, but I was too numb with grief to care. I had been the childless Grace's special love, and my life would have been far lonelier without her affection.

Uncle Fred wandered back and forth along the short path between the two houses like a grey ghost, longing for the comfort that no one could give. I had hated Uncle Fred because I thought he hated me—as he seemed to hate all children—but even I felt sorry for him now.

Mae and Herb Towle left to take an apartment in Hallowell near the shoe shop, so the family was alone with its grief.

For a time we shared our table with Fred, who seemed unable to cope with more than getting to work and back again. But he was not left alone for long. Hardly was the spring grass green above Aunt Grace when his sister Carrie appeared, uninvited.

She was a thin, grizzled, sharp-faced woman with a lower jaw that jutted ahead of the upper one. Her eyes saw everything and her lips sneered. She was older than Fred and must have been in her seventies. She had been divorced years earlier, after producing several children, and now lived with her two spinster sisters in Biddeford, a town fifty miles away on the Maine coast. She had visited Fred on several occasions when Grace was alive, always with her sisters. The three of them would arrive in a flurry of curly grey hair and pale lavender-and-white chiffon. I never recalled seeing any of them in anything but lavender-and-white chiffon, and Carrie arrived in it this time as well, but soon changed into a faded print house dress and got going on the cleaning.

Carrie did not arrive alone. With her came Rodney, her thirteen-year-old grandson. Carrie's daughter had recently divorced and, for reasons no one explained to me, Rod had been sent to Carrie. Rod, of course, had not been invited either. A big-boned clumsy lad with a sullen face and gruff manner, he glared crossly at me from under heavy brows when we were introduced. I could tell by Fred's face that he detested Rod on sight.

Everyone assumed at first that the visit of Carrie and Rod was to be a short one, but the two settled in and Rod was enrolled at a school in town. Fred said nothing in my presence, but grew even more sour and cross than usual and took no pains to hide his displeasure from Rod.

"Wonder what Fred makes of Carrie's cooking?" mused Ma. "No meat and potatoes for Carrie. She serves these little fancy dabby things with sauces and herbs—wouldn't be surprised if that's why her husband left her."

I was astounded at this quite out-of-character comment. Ma never spoke ill of anyone. And did men really leave their wives because they didn't like sauces?

Because of our first encounter, I decided Rod was ill-mannered and unpleasant, and fastened my attention on Carrie, who seemed to promise more in the way of entertainment. Though wrinkled and bowed, with a dowager's hump, she was alert and quick and never stopped talking. This was something new to me. My people, like most New England farming folk, said little and worked hard.

Carrie's chat was largely about people and things of whom I knew nothing, and mostly uncomplimentary. Clearly Carrie was hard to please, and never forgot a slight, real or imagined. Because of my silent family, I had spent my childhood listening at keyholes hoping to learn family secrets. Now here was someone who laid things bare for all who cared to listen. But the "secrets" Carrie was willing to share, it soon became apparent, were dull and petty—no great events or tragedies or love stories emerged, just day-to-day squabbles never forgotten. If anything more profound had ever happened to Carrie, she wasn't telling. Her spiteful diatribes soon became repetitious and boring, but were hard to interrupt. I kept finding myself caught in the doorway of Fred's bungalow shifting from one foot to the other in my eagerness to get away.

Ma smiled when I mentioned this. "That woman is a small-minded gossip," she said. "I wouldn't waste my time on her if I were you, Peggy."

Rodney and I sized each other up for a few days with the reserve characteristic of lonely children. There was a four-year gap in our ages, but there was no one else near the farm to play with. After a week of boredom pervaded with the pregnant atmosphere of Fred's disapproval, Rod made the first move. Seeing me in the swing Pa had hung in the elm tree for me, he crossed the raspberry patch, eyed me awkwardly, and asked, "Can I have a swing?"

I had pumped till I was flying high. I let the swing reach its apogee and jumped. I flew about fifteen feet before landing on my feet with no loss of balance.

"Sure," I said.

"Did you do that on purpose?" Rod asked.

"Yep. I've practiced it so I can scare people who come to visit."

"Well you didn't scare me! And you shouldn't be doing things like that. You're a girl!"

"Who says so? Girls can do anything boys can."

Rod dissolved in contemptuous laughter.

"Name something you can do that I can't," I snapped.

"Bet you can't shinny up the swing rope to the branch."

"Let's see you do it!"

Rod spat on his hands, leaped at the rope and began pulling himself up. It was a long rope, and was obviously a harder job to reach the branch than he had imagined. He made it, however, waved triumphantly and slithered down again.

I also spat on my hands, a ritual I had not seen before, and went for the rope. I was up to the branch considerably faster than Rod had done it, and my descent was more controlled. "Beat you!" I announced.

"It's not fair, you're lighter and it's easier for you. I'll tell you what. I'll race you from here to the barn."

"*That's* not fair. You're four years older and have longer legs!"

"Make your legs go faster, then."

I observed him narrowly. Clearly playing with Rod was going to be one long battle of wits. "I know how to make it fair," I said. "I'll run you an endurance race. Up the path through the woods, down the old trolley line to the main road, then back along that to the farm. We can do laps till one of us collapses."

"Right. That'll be easy enough."

It was a circuit of nearly a mile, and I had correctly guessed that Rod had never run any more than around the gym at school. I, who had more energy than I knew what to do with, had formed the habit of running some of it off by doing a circuit or two when there was nothing better to do. My wind was good and I ran easily, but Rod soon began to labor, and collapsed puffing and scarlet-faced, chest heaving, after about a lap and a quarter.

"Little . . . bitch," he gasped between intakes of breath. He lay on his side, unable to move. I was surprised and contrite. I had never seen anyone in such a state of exhaustion before. But Rod, after gasping for a couple of minutes, sat up. "You did that on purpose! You knew you could run longer because you're lighter. . . and I just had a big lunch."

"I didn't know anything about your lunch, but I'm sorry if you're feeling sick. Come on. Let's go back and you can have that swing you wanted."

Ma and Pa laughed when I told them of Rod's collapse, but Pa cautioned me never to run, or let anyone else run, on a full stomach. "That can strain the heart," Pa said.

"But the idea, him saying girls can't do what boys can!" I said.

Ma smiled. "Boys and men are stronger and heavier built, and there are some things they can do that girls and women can't. But girls and women are better at some things than men are, so it evens out."

"I bet he won't suggest any more competitions for a while," said Pa.

"Rod was trying it on," said Ma. "Just trying it on. You didn't let him get away with it, and now I expect you'll have a much easier time with him. He's not a bad lad. He was just trying to make an impression."

Although Rod was nearly full-grown and would be going into eighth grade in the autumn, cops and robbers was still his favorite game. Or perhaps it was simply the best compromise he could think of, considering my age. I had not played cops and robbers before, but learned fast. Rod had the advantage of size and experience and gave no quarter, but I soon learned to get by on my wits, once I had discovered that playing fair was no part of the game.

Rod also introduced me to softball, and we played two-man scrub for hours at a time. Rod could cover the ground faster, but I had strong arms and a good eye and soon learned to send a fly ball a long way.

Rod's conversation soon proved much more interesting and pertinent to my life than Carrie's had. It began with his observations about the cat. Fluff was now nearly a year old. Ma had muttered darkly about the disadvantages of female cats, but hadn't the heart to send her away. Rod now pointed out Fluff's enlarging belly and commented, "She's pregnant."

"What does that mean?" I asked in alarm. "Is she sick?"

Rod snorted. "No, for God's sake, she's going to have kittens."

All I had known for certain until then was that boys and girls were different. I was aware that cats had kittens and dogs had puppies and people had babies, but no one would admit to knowing how it happened. When I asked them, my elders told conflicting stories or just said "I don't know." There seemed to be an awful lot of things that adults didn't know. But Rod knew. His face was full of the superiority of knowledge and he was obviously itching to tell.

"How do you know she's going to have kittens?"

"You get four or five kittens in a cat's belly and she swells up as they grow, right? She's big enough now so she must be gonna have 'em pretty soon."

"Do they grow in the cat's belly?"

"Yeah."

"But how do they get out?"

"Through that slit below the ass-hole, dope."

I had paid no attention to the anatomy beneath Fluff's tail before. I did now. Sure enough, there were two round openings, one below the other, with a slit lying vertically between them. No kitten could get out of that!

"It's not big enough!"

"It gets big enough. It stretches."

"Poor cat, it'll kill her!"

"Nah, it won't kill her. Every cat in the world was born in the same way, and every human too."

I considered the implications of this statement. I did not like them. But the full import did not strike me until later.

"Does the vet come to help get them out?"

"For a cat? Of course not. Cats just shell 'em out like peas. For a calf the vet sometimes has to come if it's having trouble coming out. You heard Dick Lee's cow bellowing the other night. He had to get the vet for that one."

"How did you know that?"

"Uncle Fred saw the vet's car arrive, and you couldn't miss the noise."

"Ma said the cow was just exercising her lungs."

"Your Ma would never tell you anything!"

"But why? Why shouldn't I know if everyone else knows?"

"Because you're a girl and they don't want to let you know what you're in for and how dirty it is!"

"It's not fair! Why do they lie and say they don't know? Lying's wrong, and it's worse not knowing."

"I suppose it's because what girl would want to grow up if she knew what was going to happen."

"Rod, how do the kittens get inside?"

"The tomcat puts them in. He puts his thing into the cat's slit and squirts in some juice. The cat has eggs inside her, and the juice makes them grow into kittens. That's what those two cats were doing in Dick's barn the other day, when he told you they were fighting. Actually, it's called fucking. The male's thing is called a prick and the female's slit is called a cunt."

Many of the previously obscure conversations I had overheard in the school playground now fell into place. Of course. It was all beginning to make sense. And so did some of those words that Ma had told me not to say because they were vulgar. I knew that some of them had to do with going to the toilet, but now I realized that the others were about having babies. And everyone . . .everyone. . . had known but me. The kids at the country school had known of course, and wouldn't tell me because they wanted to prove they knew something I didn't. I was furious.

Later when I was alone I took a mirror and conducted my first self-examination. Sure enough. I was no different from a female cat—and presumably no different from a female dog or a female cow or a female elephant. We were all doomed to the same unpleasant process of producing the world's young.

I felt as if a cold, hard light had been directed where previously there had been only darkness. The world would never seem the same again. Everything . . . everything would be different and terrible because I was a girl. And all the men had to do was squirt in the juice—which Rod said was fun. Why should they have all the fun?

I questioned Rod about this the next time the subject came up.

"Women don't like it much," he said. "Except for whores."

"What are whores?"

"Women who like doing it. They'll do it with any man who pays them to. They put on floor shows where they strip to get the men excited and then they take the men into the back bedrooms afterwards."

"How do you know?"

"My father told me. Boys' fathers tell them things, it's just girls that don't know anything."

"It's not fair!"

"My Dad took me to a floor show last winter and all the whores were stripping and wagging their bottoms in the men's faces. One of them rubbed a towel between her legs and then stuck it on an old man's face. 'How does that smell?' she asked. 'Sweet,' he said, and everybody laughed."

"Did your father do it with one of the whores afterwards?"

"Yeah, but he wouldn't let me come along because I was too young."

"If the whores like it so much, why don't other women like it?"

"Because it's dirty. It has to be dirty, doesn't it, being so close to where the crap comes out. Nice women don't like that."

"Do nice men like it?"

Rod stopped short and looked at me, obviously at a loss how to answer. If he says no, I thought, what does that make his father? Still, I pressed the point.

"Do they, Rod?"

"Um . . . I'll ask my father when I see him again."

Rod's father had taught him how to play poker and had mentioned that it was most fun when played with a whore, using clothes instead of money or chips. Naturally, Rod wanted to play with a whore, but he didn't know where to find one. He decided to teach me how to play poker, using chips of course, since we had no money.

Pa had a supply of poker chips, so I borrowed them. After a few sessions Rod and I became reasonably proficient. Rod's father had taught him the fine art of bluff, but I soon learned to call it and to rely only on my cards. Like Ma said, Rod was always trying it on. We usually played in our sitting room, but one afternoon Rod said "Let's play in the loft."

We often used the loft in our games of cops and robbers. It fitted into many of our scenarios and could be reached either via a ladder and trap door from the stable, or by stairs leading up from one of the sheds. We also liked it because the grownups seemed to forget about us when we were up there.

We brought an old dairy table and two discarded chairs up from the shed. Rod pushed the bolt on the door, which surprised me. He'd never done that before. We set up the table and began playing. After a couple of hands Rod told me about strip poker and suggested we give it a try.

"Why not?" I said, shuffling the cards. Rod lost the first hand and doffed his shirt. He lost the second too, and kicked off a sneaker. I lost the third and took the ribbon off one pigtail.

"That's not clothes," snapped Rod.

"It is too. Ma says I'm not dressed properly unless I've got ribbons over the elastic bands."

Rod conceded, and in the next round lost the other shoe. Then I lost, consecutively, the other hair ribbon and my blouse, which, it being a warm day, was all I had on the top.

"Pity you haven't got tits," said Rod. "If I was playing with Madeline now I'd really have a hard-on!"

"Is that the girl at school you're sweet on?"

"Yeah. She's got lovely big tits."

"Have you played strip poker with her?"

"No, for God sakes, I haven't even asked her for a date yet."

Several hands later Rod finally lost the critical hand and was reduced to skin alone. It was the first time I had seen a male organ in full erection. It was nothing like the tiny pink spigot with which Kenneth had peed on Janet the pig. I noted with surprise the corona of black curly hair at the base and the two drooping plums behind. "Those are balls," Rod explained. "That's where the juice comes from that makes babies."

"Can I look underneath?" I asked.

Rod accommodatingly put one foot up on the table and I knelt on the floor to get a full view.

"Funny-looking equipment," I said. "Like a baloney sausage and two prunes in a sack."

"Not half as funny as yours. My father says women look like black cats that have been hit in the back with an axe!"

"Your father says? Haven't you seen one yourself?"

"Not close to, and the light was pretty dim at the floor show. But I'll see yours."

"Not unless you play better poker than you've played this afternoon!"

Sudden heavy footsteps sounded on the stairs leading to the loft and we looked at one another in horror.

"What are you kids up to in there?" shouted Pa, finding the door bolted.

"Wait a minute Pa, we've got to hide the loot," I shouted back, pulling my blouse on over my head and kicking the hair ribbons under a pile of sawdust. Then I leaned against the door in case the bolt gave, while Rod got his trousers on. "Hurry up and get the loot out of sight," I yelled for Pa's benefit. Then I pushed back the bolt and let him in.

"What are you kids doing?"

"We were playing cards but got tired of it and were just getting the loot ready to play cops and robbers."

Pa looked around suspiciously, but saw nothing he could object to. I could tell he didn't like Rod, though he had no concrete reason not to.

"Ma's almost ready to put the supper on the table. You should be helping her, Peggy. You run along Rod, your supper'll be ready too, I reckon."

Rod left, and I followed Pa down the loft stairs and through the connecting sheds to the kitchen. I was worried about my missing hair ribbons, but luckily neither Ma nor Pa noticed their absence.

In subsequent games Rod had a run of bad luck and ended up the loser several times running. I became thoroughly familiar with the topology of human male anatomy. Finally, however, my luck ran out and I lost my last stitch.

Rod's face dropped in disappointment. "Christ," he said, "There's nothing to see. You haven't got anything. No tits, no hair, just a little slit going out of sight between your legs."

"What did you expect?" I asked.

Rod didn't answer for a moment, just looked puzzled. Then: "Come on, put your foot up on the table like I did so I can see."

"Fair enough," I said, and did so.

Rod got down on his hands and knees and looked up. He studied the view intently. "God, it's ugly," he said finally.

"Nobody asked you to look at it. Yours isn't very pretty either!"

"Maybe it'll look better when it's got hair around it," mused Rod. "Of course you're only nine. It would look better on a real woman with tits and a little waist and big hips and hair in the right place. Like those whores in the floor show."

I clearly had not lived up to expectations, and Rod rather lost interest in cards after that.

As the weeks passed and school let out for the summer, I could see Uncle Fred's patience with Rod evaporating. He had actually said to Ma in my presence that he'd never seen a thicker piece of wood than Rod in his life, and he just wished it was still in the forest. Once school was out Rod decamped to our house during those hours when Fred was home. Ma and Pa weren't eager to have Rod underfoot either, but they felt sorry for the miserable hulking man-child and let him stay most evenings.

The situation came to a head in July. Rod appeared late one afternoon, a grimy paper parcel under his arm.

"I've got something to show you, Peggy."

"What is it?"

"Some magazines I got at the filling station. Come on up in the loft."

I followed him and he bolted the door behind us. He had half a dozen magazines with him, with plain outer covers. Inside the first one were cartoon strips incorporating a number of popular characters from the Sunday funnies.

But what Maggie and Jiggs were up to here was something quite different from what they did on Sundays.

"Wow!" I said. "I didn't know they sold things like this at the gas station."

"They wouldn't show it to girls, stupid. It's kept under the counter for men when they ask for it."

"You're not a man."

"If your voice has changed they'll sell them to you."

"Let's see the others."

There were photographs in some, mostly black and white but a few in color. The pictures were more interesting than the cartoons. Through Rod I now knew what men were like naked, but I'd never seen a mature nude woman except for the quick glimpse of Aunt Grace I'd caught through the hole in the bathroom door. Grace had been fat then, and rather shapeless. These women were different, all sensuously pretty with lovely curves. I thought they should have left off the garter belts, though. Why wear stockings if everything else was off?

It was nearly time for the evening meal, so Rod left the magazines with me to look over after supper. I hid them in my bureau drawer and then spirited them into the sitting room after the dishes had been washed. With the plain covers no one would know what I was reading. I hadn't reckoned on Pa's sixth sense, however. His antennae had been trained on Rod for some time, though he hadn't been able to catch him at anything.

"Peggy, what are you reading?"

"A magazine, Pa."

"What kind of magazine?"

"An adventure story magazine Rod lent me."

"Are those others on the floor adventure stories too?"

"Yes."

"What's the name of the magazine?"

"*La Paree*," I said, plummeting into the snare.

Pa leaped up roaring. "I know what those are. I'll kill that over-grown lummox. I knew something was going on. I'm going to tell Uncle Fred!"

I was quicker than Pa: I scooped the magazines from the floor and fled. I took the straightest line to Uncle Fred's bungalow, flung open the back door, raced into the front room where Fred, Carrie and Rod were sitting, and threw the lot on Rod's lap.

"Here. You explain them. Pa's after you," I said. In horror Rod fumbled with the magazines, which spilled off his lap onto the floor. I ran out the front door as Pa entered the back, and returned to the farmhouse. Ma was in the kitchen, and I told her I was off to bed. She gave me an odd, sharp look, but did not ask me what was going on.

Next morning at breakfast Pa said grimly, "Fred and I took the magazines back where Rod got them and gave the owner's head a twist. He had no business giving them to anyone under age. I should have called the police but I didn't want to distress Fred any further. That lad is not to come here again, do you understand? He's a blight on a decent neighborhood. Has he been interfering with you in any way, Peggy?"

I wasn't sure what "interfering" implied, but I decided to define it as "hands on," and Rod had never touched me, nor I him. Our investigations had been limited to looking.

"No, Pa, he's never laid a finger on me. If he had, I'd have screamed blue murder. He told me about some things people do, but he said I was too young to be any fun."

"Thank God for that," said Pa. I saw with surprised relief that he had decided to believe me. I realized he didn't really want to go into it with me any further. He seemed embarrassed and only too glad to let the matter drop.

"Poor lad," said Ma. "Everybody blames Rod for everything. Nobody likes him. Nobody wants him except Carrie. His mother and father don't, and his brothers and sisters are grown up and involved in their own lives."

"He's as unattractive a lummox as I've ever seen," said Pa. "Not a spark of anything interesting about him. He's a hard lad to feel sorry for."

"Divorce is cruel for kids," said Ma. "And the trouble in that family didn't start yesterday, either. Carrie says those two have been tearing at each other for years. Only God knows what it has meant for that boy."

"Yeah," said Pa.

Two days later I overheard Pa talking with Ma in the kitchen. "Fred's told Rod he's got to go, and that his mother can damn well take him back," he said. "Rod's been driving Fred crazy for weeks, and now he's shown what sort of upbringing he's had. 'Men will be men,' Fred says, but Rod is too young to be into that yet. He'll come to no good, that boy."

Carrie blamed me for Rod's impending dispatch. "If you'd behaved yourself and not acted like a little hussy it never would have happened," she told me.

The last time I saw Rod was the morning of his departure. I'd found some things he had left at the farmhouse: a belt, some marbles, and a pack of cards. When I saw him outside I slipped over unnoticed to return them.

"I'm sorry you're going," I said.

"Well, it's your fault, you little bitch. What the hell did you have to read those magazines in the living room in front of everybody for? You could have taken them up to your bedroom and read them when they thought you were asleep. That's what I thought you were going to do, for Chrissakes, or I wouldn't have given them to you."

"But Rod, I sleep with Ma. I couldn't read them up there. Besides, I never thought Pa could possibly know what those magazines were. He never reads things like that!"

"The hell he doesn't. All men do. All the time. What the hell else is there in life that's any fun but looking and fucking? That's all my father does!"

The shock and disbelief I felt must have shown on my face, for Rod gave me a smile full of hate and triumph. For once he'd rendered me totally at a loss for a reply.

"And I'm not sorry to be going, either," he continued. "Nobody should have to live with Uncle Fred. He's a mean bastard and he hates me."

I somehow managed to find my tongue. "He hates all children, Rod, if that makes you feel any better. He's always hated me. Ever since I can remember."

Rod was incredulous. "But he keeps telling my Gran what a 'paragon of virtue' you are and how awful I am."

It was my turn for disbelief. "I've never heard him say one good thing about me. When I was little he used to tie me to a chair or tie my hands behind my back for being naughty. Only Aunt Grace threatening him kept him from beating the pants off me."

"Well you'd think he idolized you to hear him talk to my Gran. It made me want to kill you. In fact, I could kill you, couldn't I? Or fuck you. Show you what it's like, what you've got coming to you. I could do it right now and no one would know. We're out of sight of everyone and they wouldn't even hear you scream."

The tone in Rod's voice was one that I had not heard before, and something in his eyes sent a series of shocks down my spine. Was Rod just trying it on as usual? Or was the threat real this time? He was a card player. He'd learned how to bluff. But so had I. I knew instinctively that I mustn't show fear.

"How would you get rid of the body?" I asked coolly.

"Hide it in the woodshed."

"They'd find it. And they'd know darn well you'd done it and be after you. Uncle Fred'd see to that."

The rage drained from Rod's face, and defeated resignation took its place. "Yeah. He would, the asshole," he sighed. "It wouldn't be worth it."

I knew the crisis was past. I could breathe again. "Well, I'd better get back before Pa finds out where I am," I said. "Good luck , Rod."

"Thanks."

Rod had changed my whole life, I thought as I walked back to the farmhouse. All the things he had told me had changed it. And I was sure there was more he hadn't told me, things he didn't even know himself. People were not what they seemed. I couldn't ask Ma and Pa about it. They wouldn't tell me. And because they wouldn't tell me they couldn't protect me from what was to come. I'd have to find the truth on my own and learn to cope without them.

Rod hadn't harmed me. Instead, he had given me a gift of knowledge that no one else had been willing to give—and that ominous knowledge might some day lead me to the truth.

As I returned to the farm kitchen, I heard the sound of a car coming up Uncle Fred's drive. That would be the car to take poor Rod away—to wherever it was he was going next.

27. Myths, Ghosts and the Search for Truth

Grace's death was a turning point in my relationship with Ma. She had lost two children—Barton and Grace—in as many years. All she had left was my father and me. Age and grief had gentled her. My temper tantrums were long a thing of the past. The trial by fire of the country school and Grace's death had muted my early feelings of aggression toward Ma. She had betrayed me, but she also tried to protect me. She betrayed me out of love. She'd tried to protect Grace, too, but failed. Perhaps she couldn't protect me either, but she was still trying.

I loved Ma, yet sometimes I hated her though I no longer showed it and no longer wanted to feel it. She had always been kind and patient with me, in spite of my terrible behavior. Any punishments administered had been richly deserved. All my people had been kind really, except Barton. Even Fred was kind some of the time, after I stopped being an impossible brat. Lynde had certainly been good to me. He told me of the endless nights he walked the floor with me when I was a baby, trying to get me to stop crying so Pa and our exhausted mother could get some sleep. I knew these things, so when I hated Ma and was angry at the others, I hated myself too. I was ashamed of my anger. My heart was black. I was rotten at the core, while outside I smiled and pretended to be good.

After Grace's death, Ma and I began to talk together, especially in bed before we fell asleep at night. Ma and I still shared a bed, as we had done since I was old enough to be taken away from my crib. It was the only sensible way to keep warm in winter, and it didn't occur to me to want a room of my own.

Perhaps Ma had talked to me in bed much earlier, but I don't remember it before Grace's death. The talks were very gentle and were about helping others, being a good person, loving one's neighbor—in short, a Christian message but with no reference to God or Christ.

Ma believed deeply in tolerance. "Don't condemn people, Peggy. If they act badly or do evil, remember that you don't know what they've had to live through. Try to put yourself in their shoes. If you'd been raised as they had, and endured the same things, you might have acted the same way."

Other than observing my people's silent example of strict honesty in their dealings with others and of helping people in need, these talks with Ma were the only "moral training" I remember.

Formerly, if I tried to question Ma about my mother she would turn away without answering. But now, in the quiet dark of our upstairs bedroom, without being able to see each others' faces or expressions, she seemed a bit more willing to speak. One night on impulse I asked her, "Ma, why don't you ever talk to me about my mother?"

She didn't answer for a minute or so, just lay there on her back staring into the dark. I thought she was going to ignore my question. But then she expelled a quick breath, half impatient, half resigned, and said, "What do you want to know about her?"

"Who was she? What was her name besides Bess?"

"Her name was Bess Lynde."

"Lynde? Like my brother?"

"Yes. Her maiden name was Lynde, and she named Lynde for that."

"Why is Lynde's last name Russell?"

"Because your mother's first husband's name was Russell. Lynde is his son."

"Oh. Pa isn't Lynde's father, then?"

"No. You are your father's only child. Lynde is your half-brother, because only your mothers are the same person. He's not related to your father at all."

"Oh. Did Lynde live with his father in Melrose?"

"No. His father is dead."

"Why did Lynde live in Melrose instead of living with us, then?"

"The Lynde family lived in Melrose and Lynde went to school there until your mother married your father. After your mother died, he went back there to finish high school."

"Why did my mother die? When did she die?"

"She had a weak heart. She died when you were a baby. And now, Peggy, we'd better get to sleep. The morning comes early."

Such halting questions. Such spare answers, pulled out against some unseen barrier. What else should I have asked? Would she have answered?

Another night I questioned her about Mrs. Cony: "Why does she come to see us so often and bring us things?"

112

Again Ma hesitated, arranged an answer, and drew it out as if it lived somewhere in her belly and was stuck there. "She's your legal guardian," she finally said.

I'd never heard that term before. "What's that?" I asked.

"A legal guardian is a person who is appointed by the Court to look after the interests of a child."

"But why do I have to have one? I've got you and Pa to look out for me."

"Your Grandfather Lynde left you some money in trust when he died. Since he lived in Melrose, the trust comes under Massachusetts law, which is different from Maine law. The Court in Melrose ruled that you had to have a legal guardian to make sure that the income from your money is wisely used for your benefit. They contacted Judge Cony, because he practices law in Augusta and has an excellent reputation. He suggested that his wife be appointed your guardian."

"Have I got a lot of money, Ma?" I asked, surprised.

Ma laughed. "No, don't get big ideas. There is a small amount of money in trust for when you're grown up, and it earns a small amount of interest from which Mrs. Cony can buy you things you need that we can't afford. Like the clothes and books from the rummage sales. And your piano."

With Ma's words a whole area of my life began to come clear. Why hadn't she or Pa told me before, for heaven sakes? Why those lean answers, so hard to wring out? What else should I be asking? There was so much I didn't know, more than I could even guess, I was sure. But after a few more attempts at getting more of the mystery out of Ma, I learned not to expect too much. I didn't keep pressing her for more because I felt the wall of her resistance was not worth the struggle to overcome. But someday, somehow, I was determined to learn the truth.

Luckily, Ma talked more willingly and spontaneously about other things, and she focussed our night talks on trying to guide me toward living a good and productive life. Religion, however, was never talked about at the farm, and no one went to church, although the Universalist minister used to visit Ma when she was ill and bring her fruit and flowers. After Barton and Grace died, the Minister of the Spiritualist Church came too, with messages from "The Beyond," but I never knew what Ma thought about this or what the messages were.

One autumn (was it before I began school or after?) I went to Sunday school for a few weeks. It was certainly before I went to the Nash School, for by then I had long since decided to disbelieve anything I was told.

It was Rachel Locke's mother who arranged for me to go to Sunday School. The Lockes lived about a mile down the Leighton Road beyond the country school. Their children, however, were driven daily into town to attend the Lincoln School, so I knew them only by sight.

I don't know how Mrs. Locke came to approach Ma about taking me to Sunday School. Since religion had never been discussed in front of me, I didn't really know what a church was, except a building with a steeple. Later when I asked Richard Lee what church he went to he laughed and said, "We're Home Baptists—because we stay home on Sunday." Ma, when pressed, had said she was a member of the Universalist Church, but I never knew her to attend.

Mrs. Locke, as a good Universalist, probably knew of Ma's tenuous connection with that church. Apparently she got the idea that my religious education was being neglected, and that she should attempt to remedy the situation. Ma and Pa did not object, so on Sunday mornings Mrs. Locke, with her two children on board, would pick me up and head for the church. Rachel and her brother Richard were in more advanced Sunday School classes. I was placed in the youngest group.

We cut out paper dolls, colored in pictures and listened to stories about God, Joseph, Jesus and Mary.

Being told stories was nothing new to me. As far back as I could remember people were telling me stories, and I was telling them stories back. Fairies, witches, goblins and other fantastic beings were Aunt Grace's specialty; anthropomorphic stories about my pet chickens were mine. One of the stories I was told—not by Aunt Grace—had been particularly unpleasant and shocking and had upset me. I can't remember what it was about, or who told it. Only the sense of shock and fear comes back to me now.

Though Grace had not told me the story, it was to her that I took my worries about it. She explained to me that stories about fairies, witches, goblins and strange happenings were make-believe. They didn't really happen. They were stories that had been passed down for generations and generations because most children liked them. I didn't need to be upset about that story, or any of the others, because they weren't really true.

From that day on I was able to put most of the stories I was told into the "Not True Category." This made me feel quite grown up, because now I could think about what I was told and decide myself whether it was true. For instance, it was into the "Not True Category" that I placed the Santa Claus myth. When Christmas approached and I declared to my father that I did not believe in Santa Claus, he said, "I'll take you to town and you can meet Santa Claus yourself. He's going to be in Chernowsky's store tomorrow."

Chernowsky's—that big new store where everything glittered, and they put people's money into little metal cylinders and sent them up in a tube that went across the ceiling and down to an office, where they took out the money and put in a receipt and some change and sent it back.

Next day we took the ten o'clock bus into town and paid the promised visit. We went up to the second floor of Chernowsky's and saw a line of children waiting to go into a booth with a curtain in front. We stood in the line

114

and watched children go behind the curtain at one side of the booth and come out a few minutes later from behind the curtain on the other side. When it was my turn, I went behind the curtain and found, perched on a stool, a fat old man in a red fur-trimmed suit with a mask and a fake beard on his face. He was saying "Ho, ho, ho." I could see his eyes through the eyeholes in the mask. I glared at him and said "You're not Santa Claus. You've got a mask on." I don't remember his reply.

So by the time I met Jehovah, Mary, Joseph and the Babe, I knew what category to put them in. Sunday School soon bored me, and after a few weeks I refused to go. Ma and Pa did not try to force me.

It never occurred to me that grown-up people actually believed in the Sunday School stories. This fact did not intrude on my consciousness until I went to the Nash School. During recess one morning, my classmate Tessie said something about God and I said to her, "You don't still believe in that do you?"

I couldn't understand why Tessie was so upset. She went home for lunch that noontime, and when she got back she came straight up to me and declared, "There is so a God, and my mother says your mother should give you a good talking to and wash your mouth out with soap!"

When I got home I asked Ma, "Do you believe in God?"

She gave me a sharp look and said, in her down-east Maine accent: "Of co's I do!"

I couldn't believe my ears. I went straight outside to find Pa. He was in the woodshed, sitting on the chopping block smoking and looking down at his feet.

"Pa, do you believe in God?" I demanded without preliminary.

He look up at me and thought for a minute. I think he was remembering about Santa Claus. He said slowly, "No, I guess I don't."

"Good," I said. I knew he'd given me a straight answer, one I could believe. I trusted Pa in most things after that. He might omit to tell me things that he thought might hurt me, but I never caught him out in a lie.

I had received what I considered to be a satisfactory answer from Pa, but I decided to enquire further in view of Ma's divergent opinion. Uncle Fred, Aunt Edith, Mrs. Lee and Gracie all declared that they believed. Even Mae Towle averred that there was a God. I couldn't imagine how all these people could have made such a mistake. Clearly Pa and I were right. Obviously not everyone believed the same things about the world.

My practice of asking the same question to a number of different people had long ago convinced me that "truth" was a matter of opinion, often stubbornly but sincerely held in the face of obvious facts to the contrary. I now decided that unanimity of opinion did not guarantee truth either. If I hadn't asked Pa, the verdict for God would have been unanimous. I could not see any reason why God should exist, or why He should be wasting his time poking into little girls' private lives even if he did.

I did what probably most young skeptics do: Went out into the field and yelled at the top of my lungs, "All right, if you're up there do something to prove it, or don't expect me to believe in you!"

I felt that the Deity's silence spoke for itself.

Much later someone, probably one of my high school teachers, told me that I could look things up in books if I wanted to find the truth. But when I had learned enough to know where to look for the right books, I found that they, too, did not agree with one another. They certainly contained more shades of opinion—many of them more interesting and stimulating than the ones I'd heard on the farm—and they were better argued, and had proper grammar and syntax. They had to seem compelling on the surface, of course, and not be sloppily written, or who would publish them? But hidden under the clever arguments were just as many flaws. Again, it was necessary to consider all these opinions carefully and then make up my own mind. I was beginning to understand about "the spurious authority of print," a phrase I heard many years later and recognized at once as valid.

Not believing in the heaven-and-hell stories, I had no thought of ever seeing Grace or Barton again in another world. If Ma and Pa died, that would be the end of them too. I knew Pa had heart trouble and could no longer do the heavy lifting required for the plumbing he did during the winters. His helper now had to do that. I knew people died of heart trouble, and Ma had said that was what had killed my mother. Ma was now eighty-one. How much longer could she go on? Death seemed to lurk in the farmhouse walls, waiting. It could swallow my family any time.

This apprehension condensed into fear one morning when I woke at dawn and started to get out of bed. I noticed no sound or movement from Ma. She was a light sleeper and usually woke as soon as I started moving. Now she was lying on her back beside me and did not stir as I sat up.

I felt my skin creep before I even looked at her. Then I saw that her eyes were open. They were staring past me. "Ma ?" I asked. No reply. No movement. I put my hand on her arm. It felt stiff to the touch. I tried to shake her. She was rigid. The impact hit me full in the gut. Dead, I thought.

"Pa," I shouted as I threw myself from the bed and headed for the stairs. I heard him thump out of bed below at the urgency of my voice, and begin running. We collided on the stairs. He pulled me back up with him, and we headed for the bedroom. Ma had not moved. Pa put his hand on her shoulder. "Mother?" he said. She blinked, and her eyes turned toward him. I saw her body go limp. "Mother, are you all right? What happened?"

She couldn't tell us. Said she hadn't felt sick or felt herself go rigid. Just thought she'd been asleep and woke when Pa spoke to her.

"Didn't you hear me yell for Pa?" I asked. She shook her head.

She managed to get out of bed without our assistance and said she felt fine. I stayed with her as she got dressed, while Pa went downstairs to get the stove going and the tea on.

This kind of attack happened to Ma several times after that, either in bed or without warning during the day. It would last only a few minutes, and coming out of it she would sometimes vomit. Always she would seem to recover completely and show no after effects. She refused to let Pa send for a doctor. "It's nothing—nothing—and we can't afford the doctor," she insisted.

From then on I kept waking at night to listen for her breathing. I feared finding her in the morning lying beside me stiff from the final attack from which she would never rise.

In spite of my disavowal of religion and an afterlife I had, incongruously, a fear of ghosts. Perhaps my early reading matter was the root of this. Or perhaps it is simply a basic human response to the unknown. Ma was certain that when Grace died Barton had come to her in a dream and told her.

She had also told me that her dead mother, Eliza, came to her sometimes at night to give advice. Once, long ago, when Ma had moved to another house she could not decide where to put the furniture. The house remained in chaos till Eliza appeared in a dream and together they went from room to room deciding where things should be put. Next day Ma, in accordance with these decisions, got everything in order.

Another time Ma had a badly infected hand and was worried that it would result in blood poisoning. Again Eliza appeared to her and told her to go into the woodshed. There she would find a wooden cabinet in which there was a bunch of dried herbs. She was to make a strong tea with the herbs and soak her hand in it. When she awoke, Ma did as she had been told and went to the woodshed. There she found the wooden cabinet, which she claimed never to have noticed before. Inside were the herbs, and after she soaked her hand as instructed, the infection came under control.

Ma also told the story of the friend who, before she had died, told her family that she didn't want anyone else to have her clothes. They were to be burnt. The family, being of the waste-not-want-not persuasion, felt it would be sinful to burn perfectly good clothes. They were washed and hung in the kitchen to dry while the family went out to the fields. When they returned, the clothes were charred fragments hanging from the rack. Whatever the source of the fire, it had burned nothing else.

Certainly our farmhouse was a marvelous setting for a ghost. Like most New England houses it was built of wood, and anyone who has lived in a wooden house knows how the timbers give and shift with changes in temperature and humidity. At night as I lay in bed, I could hear the wooden floors and stairs creak, and it was easy to follow the footsteps of the ghost across the attic floor and down the stairs.

My father's first wife, Florence, had died in our farmhouse. So had my mother. Edna Townsend had also died there.

The Morangs had sold the farm to the Townsends, and the Townsends sold it to us. Their daughter Edna was a college girl who had contracted tuberculosis and come home to die. In the attic I found a chest full of her books. One of them was Bright's *Anglo-Saxon Reader*, and I marveled over this strange tongue that had preceded English. Ma was upset when she found me reading it, but the doctor assured her that I could not catch Edna's tuberculosis from it.

Was it Edna Townsend's ghost I felt in the house whenever I was alone? Or Florence? Or was it my mother?

I was never sure whether to be afraid of the house or not. It had a presence of its own, a will, a thousand eyes. It knew my thoughts, saw my every deed, and smiled or leered as the mood took it. Was it sinister? Was it evil? Playfully mocking? I used to wander alone through the quiet rooms, savoring its presence. The doorknobs I had feared as an infant were still there, watching me. We had long ago taken the white cloth covers off, but I was still uncomfortable with them.

The dark closet in my father's bedroom, which sloped back into the blackness under the stairs, still frightened me when its door was open. Sometimes when I glanced quickly at it, I thought I could see a white, skeletal hand there in the darkness.

The attic fascinated me most. It was more alive than the rest of the house, more sensitive to one's presence. It ran the length of the house and had never been finished except for one small room over in the north end. Between the stairs and this room the flooring was incomplete. Only a long, narrow catwalk of boards stretched across the beams. When it rained, the water would begin creeping in slowly, murmuring through the cracks in the old roof which Pa could not afford to mend. It was my job to climb the long flight of wooden stairs to the attic burdened with pails to set beneath the leaks. I would step gingerly over the dead flies lying on the steps. The air seemed full of their humming, just on the edge of audibility. I would climb up and up through the dust and cobwebs till I could step out onto the narrow planking, then walk out along it to the place where the water was seeping in. Every board was vital beneath my feet and whispered back at each footfall. Then I would edge out along the beams toward the gloom of the gables, where little eyes of light would shiver at me, and faint, wraith-like figures would flicker across from beam to beam. I would set the pails down beneath the drips, then edge my way back onto the catwalk and start the long way back to the stairs. The air would be thick, electric, full of presence, but I would not run. The dark gables would laugh if I ran—laugh, or be angry and clutch out at me with their long fingers.

28. The Violin

In the fall after Grace's death I went to Lincoln School, which taught grades four through eight and took pupils who had finished the third grade at the Nash School. Luckily it was also within walking distance of Edith's apartment, so that routine carried on for a while.

The first week I was at Lincoln our fourth grade teacher, Miss Libby, announced that group violin lessons would be available once a week for fifty cents a lesson. We were given a note to take home to our parents. Anyone wishing to sign up should do so by Friday.

Dick Lee had taken violin lessons for a while and then stopped, but he still liked to play. He and Gracie played together sometimes. Uncle Fred had a violin too, but I'd never heard him play it. He kept it at the back of a closet and said he'd forgotten how to play.

I took the note home and asked if I could take the group lessons. Since I liked playing the piano and had learned quickly, Ma and Pa said they'd think about it, but violins were expensive.

"I could use Fred's," I said. Ma and Pa exchanged glances. "I'll talk to him after supper," said Pa.

After we'd eaten, Pa disappeared in the direction of the bungalow and returned a few minutes later with Fred, who was carrying the violin in its case.

"So you want to learn the fiddle do you, Peggy?" asked Fred, his jaw flapping. "Do you know which end is which?"

"No," I said truthfully, "but I know which end goes under my chin."

The violin case was long and black and plain of line. Narrow at one end, it tapered smoothly up to the wide end, like a coffin. Its handle and hinges and their fittings were of brass, badly in need of a polish.

Fred took a tiny brass key from his pocket, unlocked the case and removed the violin. It had four strings, but they were loose and hadn't been tuned in years. Fred started to tighten them up, and the first one broke. So did the second one.

"Hasn't been played for twenty years," he said. "You'll need new strings. But the bow works." He took it out and showed me how to tighten the horse hair. "You always leave the hair loose when you're not playing, 'cause if you don't, the tension of the hair will warp the wood." Then he produced a cracked and flaking piece of rosin and rubbed it over the horse hair. "That's so it will make the right sound on the strings and won't skid across them," he explained.

He handed me the violin. I put it under my chin and held it the way I'd seen Dick hold it. It felt funny.

"We'll take the violin to town tomorrow and get it fitted with some new strings," Pa said.

"It'll do the fiddle good to be played," said Fred. "Glad you're gonna use it."

"Thanks. Uncle Fred," I said. "Ill take good care of it. I promise."

I was surprised and touched by Fred's kindness in letting me borrow his violin. He could so easily have said no. He seemed to have mellowed toward me somewhat after the business with Rod.

Next day the man in the music shop restrung the violin for us and sold us a pitch pipe with four pipes marked E, A, D and G. He showed me how to tune the violin to the pipes and said I'd have to do it often for a few days because new strings stretched. They were already out of tune when I got home, so I tuned the violin as I'd been shown and took it over to show Dick.

It was out of tune again before I got over there. I hadn't brought my pitch pipe, but Dick said,"You don't need a pitch pipe, Peggy, you can tune it to the piano," and he showed me how. Then he played "Pop Goes the Weasel" for me. It started on the D string and when it got to the "Pop," which was the highest note of the song, he plucked the E string with his fourth finger to make the "Pop" sound. I was delighted and tried to play it myself.

"You sound like a skinned cat," said Dick, laughing. I laughed too.

Dick showed me how to hold the violin and how to go up and down the scale using open strings and the four fingers of my left hand.

Ma and Pa could hardly get the violin out of my hands after that. It wasn't easy to play like the piano, and it was terribly hard to get a note that sounded nice, but by the time the class met the next week I was beginning to get my fingers coordinated, and "Pop goes the Weasel" and several other tunes weren't sounding too bad.

At the first class about ten of us from different grades sat around in a semicircle. The violin teacher, a short, greying man with a heavy foreign accent, stood in front of the class and showed us what to do. His name was Joseph Korda. He passed out an exercise book—which cost 25 cents—to each of us, and then told us the names of the notes. He never called any of us by name, just pointed and said "Girl," or "Boy."

Playing tunes at home had seemed fairly easy after a bit of struggle, but learning notes was something else. Everyone thought I'd learned them on the piano, but of course I hadn't. With the violin, you saw a note on a line or a space, and you had to know which finger to move to play that note, and where it had to move to on the string. You were supposed to learn the name of the note too, but I decided that was one thing too many, so I just fixed in my mind which finger moved for notes on each line and each space, and never mind the names.

It was also necessary to coordinate the bow with the fingers and be able to run the whole length of it across the strings. Uncle Fred's violin was a full-sized one. I had no idea, nor did anyone else in our non-musical family, that children usually started on half- or three-quarter-size instruments. However, by stretching from the shoulder joint I learned to dislocate my arms far enough to accomplish the necessary, and no one told me the violin was too big for me.

By the end of that school year I had learned the first position and the notes attached to it and could play both the assigned lessons and most of the songs in *The Community Song Book*. Three of us in the fourth grade who had taken the lessons serenaded our class and also participated in Korda's end-of-the-year concert. It was great fun, in spite of the fact that about half way through the concert my A string broke with a ping. I didn't have a replacement string and wouldn't have had time to put it on if I had. Instead, I tuned down my E string to the pitch of an A and managed to play most of the notes. Next day our picture was in the paper, all looking smug and happy.

Unfortunately Korda only gave group lessons to beginners. Next year anyone who wished to continue would have to take private lessons from him in his studio, at a dollar a lesson, either after school or on Saturday mornings. Transportation in and out of Augusta on a Saturday morning would be difficult, and after school in the depths of winter when it was dark, even worse. Besides, a dollar a week was a lot of money, and farm finances were at rock bottom.

I didn't really mind not continuing. I'd learned to play the violin as well as I could play the piano, and I'd even learned the notes, so I could teach myself now. Besides, I had discovered the joys of making up my own tunes. If I started on any of the open strings there were natural jumps that could be made with almost no effort, and notes could be filled in easily between the jumps. It was more fun doing this than playing by note.

Half a century later I still play the violin, and still don't know the names of the notes.

29. Death Wish

The first winter after Grace's death—the winter I was in fourth grade—Ma collapsed entirely. She had held firm and kept the rest of us from falling apart all through Grace's illness and the summer and autumn that followed, but with the first snows of November she took to her bed. Heart trouble, Pa said, but surely it was more than that.

It seems odd that I can't remember more details of her illness, but my memory insists on giving way to holes when I think of the misery of that winter.

I do recall the pills the doctor left for Ma when she first collapsed. The bottle was sitting on the stand beside her bed, and I picked it up and read the label: Strychnine. Strychnine was used in rat poison. Had the doctor left the wrong bottle by mistake? Upset, I ran to Pa with it. He laughed. "Sometimes in medicine a little poison does you good," he said. "Strychnine used in tiny doses helps keep the heart going."

Ma's illness seemed to have no end. We moved her downstairs onto a bed in the sitting room to avoid endlessly going up and down to care for her. Pa looked after her during the day while I was at school. Whatever part-time plumbing jobs he did that winter were done on weekends.

I took care of Ma at night, sleeping on a mattress in the dining room so I could tend her. With the sliding doors open between the dining and sitting rooms, I was awake at Ma's slightest sound and could get the bedpan or a glass of water or whatever she needed. Or summon Pa if she seemed worse.

I liked sleeping in the dining room. The embers in the fireplace kept it warm through most of the night, and the many plants on stands and window ledges in the bay window freshened the air.

Sometimes the cats chased mice over me in the night. I liked mice and thought it was funny. A bat once buzzed me in the dark. I thought that was funny too, and got up, gently caught the bat with a butterfly net, and put it out.

I didn't mind giving Ma the bedpan. I'd warm it by the fire and she'd manage to raise up enough so I could slip it under her. I'd cleaned up after pets, mucked out our cow barn, helped Richard clean out the Lee's stable, and dug rotted manure into the garden. From the stench of the two-holers at the country school and the odors of Grace's sick room, I was familiar with the smells of human effluent. But vomit was something else. To me, nausea is the most unpleasant feeling in the world. The pain of injury is far easier to bear.

When anyone vomited, I always retched along with them. Pa knew this. Kind Pa. If he was in earshot and heard Ma start to retch he'd come and tend her.

Ma couldn't force herself to eat. When we asked what she'd like she'd usually say "Just tea and toast," but she frequently vomited up even that. Sometimes she'd ask for a raw egg beaten up with milk and flavored with cinnamon, and that seemed easier for her to keep down. She never complained, but several times I heard her say to herself, "And even this shall pass away."

As the days shortened and darkened and the snow piled deep outside, Ma was sinking rapidly. I thought death was inevitable. The whole family had tried to save Barton and failed. The whole family had tried to save Grace, too, and failed again. Now only Pa and I were left to save Ma.

Ma, once so vigorous and strong, lay white and strange in the bed, her face the color of parchment. She didn't talk, just stared at the corners of the room. She'd only speak if she needed the bed pan or wanted a glass of water, or in response to repetition of a direct question. I kept a pitcher of fresh water at her bedside, but she was too weak to sit up and reach for it.

"Wouldn't you like to try sitting up in a chair, Mother?" Pa asked her. "I can help you up, and Peggy and I will stay right by you in case you feel faint."

"I can't, Shirley," she said. "Just let me lie."

"Why does she just lie there?" I asked Pa when we were out of her hearing. "Why won't she talk to us? Why doesn't she try to get up?"

He looked at me sadly for a minute. "She's given up, Peggy," he said. "She's given up."

"She wants to die, doesn't she?" I asked. Pa's eyes filled with tears and he turned away.

Mrs. Knowles, who had tended Grace, was re-hired to stay at night. She slept on a couch near Ma's bed, and I went back to the cold bedroom upstairs.

One morning when I came down at six to get ready for school Knowles was already up, sitting by the stove in the kitchen clutching a cup of hot tea. "Your Ma almost went in the night," she said. "I heard her cry out, and by the time I was off my couch she was lying there with no pulse. I gave her a shot of adrenalin, and that started her heart up again. I didn't wake your father. He's exhausted and couldn't have done anything. He needs his sleep more than any of us."

So death had come knocking for Ma, and Knowles had sent him away.

That was the nadir, and then Ma began slowly to rise above it. Knowles, who again was costing us the earth, no longer came. With relief, I moved back downstairs.

Late in January Pa sickened too, with a fever and a wracking cough, and was temporarily unable to keep an eye on Ma while I was at school. A woman named Sturrock began coming in during the day.

I wasn't told that Mrs. Sturrock was coming, because arrangements had been made in a hurry the night before after I'd gone to bed. I was asleep on my mattress and woke up as she was sitting at Ma's bedside introducing herself. I heard her say ". . . and we're having to break up our home," and then she burst into tears.

I pieced together, from what I heard of her conversation with Ma, that her husband was a drunk, unfaithful, and had left her. The nearly grown children had decided to go off on their own, and she was staying with a friend till she decided what to do. Meanwhile, the temporary job of helping with Ma was just what she needed.

I think Ma recovered because she felt so sorry for the wretched Sturrock. Ill as she was, she reached out to this woman with warmth and sympathy. Sturrock blossomed under it, and so did Ma. After the first few dark days Ma was able to be out of bed, the two of them were laughing together, and the early spring sunshine had started to warm the earth again. The worst was over. For a little while, perhaps, we could breathe easy.

Slowly, gradually, Ma got on her feet again, and by April she had pretty much recovered.

30. Of Medical Charts and Dictionaries

Once Mrs. Sturrock had gone, Ma resumed her usual cooking and keeping things in order, but she complained of stiffness and soreness of her muscles.

"It's the weeks of inactivity," she said. "Nothing works right after you've lain in bed like that."

Trying to relieve pain and stiffness, Ma, on Mrs. Cony's recommendation, went several times to a chiropractor.

"He'll adjust your neck and spine and massage your muscles," Mrs. Cony told her. "It can make an amazing difference in your mobility, and it's well worth the money."

Ma went on several Saturday mornings and let me come with her, presumably to keep me out of mischief. Fred drove us in, did his own errands, and then picked us up at the chiropractor's office.

The chiropractor was Dr. Burns, a plump, fiftyish man with red hair gone mostly grey. He had two rooms—a waiting room and a treatment room. The first time we went, I was told to stay in the waiting room, but when it became obvious that I was quiet and "didn't get into things" I was allowed to come in and watch the treatment. Dr. Burns would have Ma lie on her stomach and would go up and down her spine with his hands, making cracking sounds. He said he was "adjusting" the spine.

Then he'd have her put her head on one side and say to her, "Just leave go," and he'd crack her neck. Then he'd have her put her head on the other side and he'd crack that too. I winced and gasped when I first saw him do it, but Ma assured me it didn't hurt, and she felt better afterwards.

Dr. Burns also had a glass tube that flared out at the end into a bulb. It was a sort of electric light that turned pink and blue and crackled when he turned it on. It was warm and prickly when I was allowed to touch it, and it gave out a strange smell which he said was the smell of ozone created by the electric sparks. He would run this magical bulb up and down Ma's spine, massaging her with it. He said it was to make her relax.

In the corner of the treatment room stood what Dr. Burns called a "diagnostic machine." Ma would sit on a seat in front of it, and Dr. Burns would "wire her up." He put things called electrodes on her arms, legs and head and then switched on the machine. Dials on the front lit up, and he claimed he could tell what was wrong with Ma by which dials became illuminated. Ma told me later the treatments helped her, but she didn't believe in that machine.

After my first captivation with the treatment room, I elected to remain in the waiting room. A large set of medical charts hung on the wall, one behind the other, and I could roll them up one by one to see what was at the back. The charts showed all the parts of the body and how they fit together.

Each structure had a black line running from it with its strange sounding name on a label at the end. Some of the names had wonderful sounds when I whispered them to myself. *Fibula* sounded like a brook tumbling over stones. *Trapezius* reminded me of a circus, and I liked the way the "z" and the "s" hissed in my mouth. Some strucures had double names: *foramen magnum, latissimus dorsi.* When I said two double names together it sometimes sounded like poetry: *Foramen-magnum-latissimus-dorsi.* Tetrameters, like they told us at school!

It didn't take long till I stumbled on the reproductive system, which was a special delight, since I could now enlarge my collection of forbidden information. That chart supplemented nicely what I'd learned from Rod. *Vagina, penis, testis, scrotum.* And that really strange word *embryo*, the baby that lay in the mother's *uterus.*

During these investigations, I always kept one ear trained on the treatment room so I'd know when Ma was about to come out. Then I would sit down quickly and busy myself with a magazine. I knew she'd have twenty fits if she caught me looking at those charts!

I didn't dare ask Ma or Pa why the parts of the body had such strange names, but I asked Mrs. Lee. She looked at me sharply, an amused smile playing at the corners of her mouth as if she knew what I'd been up to—but she was willing to answer my question.

"Those are ancient names from Latin and Greek," she said. "The ancient Greeks were the first ones to make a proper study of the human body."

I'd heard of Greeks but I hadn't heard of Latins. "Who are the Latins?" I asked.

"The ancient Romans spoke Latin," she explained, "but no one speaks it today. It's what is known as a 'dead language.'"

When I left Mrs. Lee, I went home and headed straight for the dictionary.

I already felt at home with dictionaries. After Grace had taught me to read, she'd shown me how to use one. "When I'm not around to tell you what a word means, you can look it up," she'd said. "And if there are words in the definition you don't understand you can look them up, too."

I loved using the dictionary. I'd soon found I could chase information through definition after definition. Sometimes the chase went in a circle and ended by returning to the first word I'd looked up. More often, it lead me far away from my original quest, into another subject entirely, and every bit of information was rewarding.

I'd soon found out there were other parts of the dictionary besides the ordinary definitions. When I ran across the section on common personal names, I looked up Brenda and found it was the feminine of the Norse name *Brand*, which meant a sword. Peggy was a diminutive of Margaret, which was from the Greek word for a pearl. Emma, Ma's first name which she didn't use, was from German and meant universal or whole. Her middle name, Mentora, which she did use, wasn't there at all. Shirley—Pa's name—and Barton weren't there either. Grace was from French and meant grace.

Of course I'd tried to look up the "vulgar words" I'd heard at school, but they weren't in the dictionary. That path was a dead end. But now, Mrs. Lee's information was just enough to make everything start falling into place. Now that I had the proper words from the charts, perhaps the door to the forbidden information might open.

Sure enough, the words were all there, each with its derivation from Greek or Latin. *Foramen magnum*, which was the hole at the bottom of the skull, was from Latin: *Foramen* meant hole, *magnum* meant big.

Embryo was from Greek and meant an animal before birth.

I was thrilled. I could feel my skull expanding with new knowledge, new potential.

Another source of information I discovered about this time was a book called *The Miracle of Life*, which I saw advertised in a magazine. The ad listed the chapters, and one was entitled "Reproduction." The book could be obtained for a ten-day trial, and could be returned without charge if the reader didn't want to buy. I sent for it, of course, and managed to intercept it at the mailbox before Ma and Pa saw it. I hid it in the woodshed until I had time to read the chapter on reproduction, which was clearly written and informative. It supplemented the information on the medical charts, and provided me with even more words to look up.

Once I'd pored over that vital chapter, I turned back to the beginning of the book and got my first taste of evolution: how life was thought to have arisen in the sea and then came onto the land as amphibians, which gave rise to reptiles and then mammals, the apes, and finally Man.

To me, this idea had the ring of truth. I was tremendously excited by it. No nonsense here about clay and Adam's rib.

It was cold and uncomfortable reading in the woodshed, and I knew my continued absence from the warmth of the kitchen would eventually cause suspicion. So I threw caution to the winds, brought the book into the house, and read with my feet keeping warm in the oven.

It was some time before the busy Ma spotted that I was reading something she hadn't seen before. Pa was sitting in his rocking chair in the kitchen, cat draped around his shoulders, reading *Western Story Magazine*, and hadn't noticed either.

"What are you reading, Peggy?" Ma asked.

"A wonderful book I got free on a ten-day trial," I said. "It tells all about different kinds of animals and about the different tribes of people in the world and is a sort of history." Keep off of sensitive topics, and perhaps she wouldn't look too hard.

She took the book and thumbed through it, luckily missing the chapter on reproduction and the drawings of man rising from the apes. "Looks interesting," she said, and handed it back, so I got on with it.

Pa noticed when I'd finished the book, and asked me what it would cost to buy it. I showed him the ad, and to my surprise he sent off a check. Then he took the book off to read himself. "Interesting book," was his only comment. I have no idea whether Ma read the book. If she did, she didn't tell me.

31. The Widow Beale

During the winter of Ma's illness, another drama was unfolding for Fred, but this did not become apparent until spring. Relations between Fred and his sister Carrie had become strained by the time Rod left the farm the year before. They became more so when Fred's affair with Charlotte Beale, who lived in town, came to light.

Charlotte was a friend of Edith's, and I had encountered her a number of times having afternoon tea with Edith when I was still at the Nash School. Charlotte was a big, blowsy woman, fat and sixtyish, with a round feline face and straight dyed black hair, cut Dutch fashion. She was good humored and expansive, and always had something funny or kind to say to me.

Fred met the Widow Beale at Edith's. It must have been shortly before Grace's death. They were introduced one afternoon when he came by to pick me up. I usually watched for Fred out the window about ten minutes past five so he wouldn't have to come in or blow his horn for me. But that time he came in to deliver some jelly from Ma that he'd forgotten to leave for Edith that morning. I noted nothing unusual at that meeting. The polite minor social interactions of my elders did not interest me.

I knew nothing of the developing romance between Fred and the Widow Beale until months later, after I had started at Lincoln School. I overheard part of a conversation between Edith and Angie Guild, another of her cronies who also came by sometimes in the afternoon. I was reading a magazine in the next room, and the two of them seemed unconscious of, or at least unconcerned by, my presence there.

"Grace was hardly cold in her grave when it started," I heard Angie say. My attention snapped at once from my reading to their conversation.

"It *was* a bit abrupt and a bit obvious," said Edith. "Not long after the funeral he began coming to the door instead of waiting for Peggy to come out. He wanted to see who was here. If Charlotte was here he'd come in."

"When I first saw them together here, he had a great line going with her," said Angie. "All jokes and sly glances and her giving him the come-on with her cat's eyes. He put his hat on her head and didn't take it off till he left. And you know what that means," said Angie.

I didn't know what that meant, or what that conversation implied at the time. I knew Fred was sometimes excessively charming with women. He had been embarrassingly so to Mrs. Crockett, the widowed librarian in the Children's Department at the Library. Fred sometimes took me there on the way home to return books and get out others. Mrs. Crockett would get red and flustered by his attentions and looked relieved when we left.

I'm not sure how long it was before Ma and Pa got wind of what was happening, but it must have been after Ma had recovered, or she might not have recovered at all. My first intimation of what was afoot was in the early spring when I walked in on a shouting match between Fred and Carrie.

Fred was in the doorway of the bungalow's kitchen, and Carrie was at the sink. She had suspended her dishwashing operation and was bracing herself on the sink, hurling venom at Fred. They didn't see me come in the outside door and stand behind Fred in the shadows of the entry way.

It soon became clear that the topic of conversation was Charlotte Beale, and that Carrie wanted Fred to quit this "immoral carry-on."

"You mean you want to move that woman into this decent farm neighborhood? Into this house? Into the very bedroom where Grace died?"

"Carrie, life goes on," said Fred.

"Goes on? Goes on? You, brought up to be a good Christian man, are going to 'go on' like this?"

"Charlotte reminds me of Grace."

"Don't insult Grace!"

Fred shook his head as if he'd been slapped, but said nothing.

"And what about me?" Carrie hissed. "I won't live in the same house with her!"

"No, you won't," said Fred. "You'll go back to our sisters, where you belong."

"Never," cried Carrie, stamping her foot. "I'll never go back there. This dalliance of yours is the work of the devil and I won't stand for it. You can't just put me out!"

The impasse between them was resolved shortly afterwards when Carrie came down with a temperature and had to take to her bed. I don't know what it was, probably flu. This was in April, just over a year since Grace's death. Fred had been through enough with Grace's long illness, and no doubt foresaw Carrie providing him with one medical problem after another to avoid leaving. He hired an ambulance and two men to remove her from her sick bed and transport her back to her sisters.

The first Ma and I knew of this was when the ambulance arrived and the driver and his assistant went into Fred's bungalow with a stretcher. Ma, who was now on her feet again and able to go outside, thought that Carrie's illness must have turned into pneumonia and they were taking her to the hospital.

"Come on, Peggy," she said. "Let's go and see if we can do anything to help."

Ma and I were just crossing the raspberry patch when Fred and the two men emerged with Carrie on the stretcher. She was weeping and protesting loudly: "You can't do this to me—that long ride in the cold in my condition will kill me. What kind of brother are you? You kicked Rod out because of that seductive little witch next door, and now you're taking me out feet first because of that fat floozy. God will judge you for this!"

Fred said nothing, and Carrie's voice broke into a wail as the ambulance doors closed between them. Fred turned abruptly and walked into the bungalow without looking back. The ambulance driver, who had left his motor running when he entered the bungalow, shifted gears and glided off down the driveway.

Ma and I had stopped in mid-raspberry patch when the stretcher came out with Carrie. I don't know if Fred even saw us. "Come on, we'll go back, Peggy," she said. "There's nothing we can do." Her face was white and she was clearly shaken, but she would not discuss what had happened. I was glad that Carrie was gone, but I said nothing.

In fact, Carrie survived the trip very well, but she and her sisters never forgave Fred. We never saw her again, nor, I think, did Fred. Certainly he never mentioned her thereafter in my presence.

The Widow Beale moved into the bungalow with Fred at once, without benefit of the clergy, and the neighborhood was predictably shocked. Ma was particularly upset because Fred had replaced Grace so soon, and with someone she considered an immoral woman. If Pa had an opinion he kept it to himself. He had, of course, replaced Florence with my mother even faster than Fred had replaced Grace, as I learned later.

The liaison continued in the bungalow for a few months under the cloud of Ma's anger and resentment. The whole ethos of the farm had changed. To Ma, Fred had betrayed us all—betrayed Grace, betrayed her, betrayed Pa. He had even betrayed his own sister. Much as Ma had come to dislike Carrie for her ignorance, her lack of tolerance and her incessant virulent chatter, she thought that Fred had treated her inhumanely.

I couldn't miss the change in the atmosphere, and for once Ma did not hide her feelings about the situation from me. I had never seen her so angry. She seemed obsessed by it. I could hear the unusual murmur of her voice talking at length to Pa in low tones after I had gone to bed, and his occasional brief, muffled rejoinders. I could not make out what they were saying, but I knew it was about Fred and the Widow.

One fragment, out of context, which I did hear meant little to me then, but it was a sufficiently striking image that I remember it:

"Do you really think, Shirley, that there has been an illicit affair going on all this time?" Ma asked.

"You gotta pay the Piper, Ma," Pa said. "You gotta pay the Piper."

To this day I don't understand Pa's reference, but I take it he believed that an affair had indeed gone on "all this time."

Ma tried to discourage me from going over to the bungalow, but when I got a chance I went anyway. I rather liked the Widow Beale, who was kind to me, and funny, and I think when Fred was away at work she was glad of the company. I couldn't see what all the fuss was about. Fred was lonesome and they liked each other. Why shouldn't they live together if they wanted to? It must have been hell for him living with Carrie.

I had even begun to think better of Fred. After Rod's departure he had been almost kind to me—as if he had decided that, compared to Rod, I wasn't so bad after all. And he'd been willing to let me use his violin, for which I would be forever grateful.

Whatever was done and said between the parties concerned I don't know, but after a few months, Fred and Charlotte packed their bags and moved to her apartment in town. Fred never asked for his violin back, so I kept it.

I don't know what Pa thought about all this, Pa who never spoke, who never bad-mouthed anyone, who kept his own counsel. But he would never go against Ma. Ma and I were his only loyalties now. We seldom saw Fred after he left the farm, and when we did, the atmosphere was acrid.

The bungalow sat empty for a while, then Fred rented it to two women. One, named Chloe, was blonde, thirtyish and quite pretty. She had a baby. Said her husband was dead. The other, called Terry, was short and muscular with shingled hair like a man's, and she swaggered around in real know-it-all fashion. I felt funny in her presence. Her eyes always took me in like she was making notes of everything.

The neighbors snickered about the women, saying things I only half heard or didn't understand.

"Queer as a three dollar bill," Pa commented, safe in the knowledge that I didn't know any other meaning for "queer" than strange.

32. Harriet's Wedding

In June of that year—1938, when I was ten—Harriet Lee got married. It came about because of her brother Bob, who was now in the Army Air Corps and stationed in the west. The year before, Bob's wife, Judy, had fallen victim to scarlet fever. We all knew about scarlet fever. Like tuberculosis it killed people, or it weakened them so they got tuberculosis later and died, like Beth in *Little Women*. Two children had died from scarlet fever in Manchester recently.

Harriet had been teaching in East Orange, New Jersey when she heard of Judy's death. She left her job and went west to become Bob's temporary moral support and housekeeper. Young, vibrant, dark-haired and beautiful, Harriet was immediately popular with Bob's unmarried friends and dated several of them. The last one was Bill Fraser, a young officer in the 13th Cavalry. The romance developed fast, and a small June wedding at the Lee farm was arranged.

The first I heard of the wedding was when Harriet brought Bill back to meet her family in mid-June. "It's going to be a very small wedding in the living room," she told me. "Father's too ill for us to have a big one, it's too far for Bill's parents to come, and Bob can't get away. It will be just a few of our relatives. But we'd like you and my cousin Ruth to come. You'll be the only young ones there."

Ruth was the daughter of Mrs. Lee's sister. She was two years older than I and lived in town.

I'd never been to a wedding, and Lynde's, two years before, was the only one I'd heard about involving people I knew. I was thrilled to be asked to go to Harriet's. She said it would be at ten in the morning on the following Saturday, and I ran home to tell Ma.

Harriet asked me to pick wildflowers for the wedding, so I got up at dawn on Saturday and went out into the fields. They were full of brilliant white daisies, their petals almost luminescent in the light of the rising sun. When I'd picked a barrow load I took them over to the Lees' kitchen and piled them on the table. Mrs. Lee, who was busy mixing batter, thanked me.

"Ruth and Harriet will arrange them in the living room," she said. "You and Ruth can stand in the living room doorway and watch the wedding. There's only room inside for a few people, and the old must have seats. Don't be late—come back at nine forty-five."

I went home and pressed my dress, which Mrs. Cony had brought me that spring from yet another rummage sale. It was pink silk with tiny embroidered flowers on it and had a wide sash. Its delicate folds pressed out beautifully under the cool iron. I'd never had such a beautiful dress before, and fell in love with its softness and the way it rested on my body. Two years previously, Ma had made me a blue frock which she told me looked like silk. The material felt heavy and clumsy, and Ma cut it large so I wouldn't outgrow it for a long time. I felt as if my skinny body were in a hot, heavy tent, and I hated it. When Mrs. Cony brought the pink silk one—real silk—I was amazed at its lightness and delicacy. I vowed I'd never wear the ugly blue thing again.

When I got back to the Lees at quarter of ten, Ruth, dressed in crisp lime-green muslin, was hopping back and forth across the hallway between dining room and living room like a nervous bird. Several elderly relatives including Nan Townsend were being seated in the living room by Dick. The seats faced the fireplace, which was festooned with ferns and flowers. The daisies I had picked were in two large matching vases sitting on the floor on either side of the fireplace.

Mr. Lee had already gone in and was sitting in the front row, slumped in his chair, grey and bent. His hand rested on his lap, shaking badly. Bill, dressed in his cavalry summer whites, stood by the fireplace talking with the minister. Gracie, in a simple floor-length gown of the palest yellow with puffed sleeves, was coming slowly down from upstairs. She clutched a bouquet of yellow roses in one hand and leaned on the stair rail with the other to help her negotiate the steps. She smiled at Ruth and me and went into the dining room, where she was joined by Dick and the bridegroom.

Dick looked very tall and elegant in his dark suit. At eighteen he was just over six feet, lean, strong and clean cut. Bill was not a tall man—just Harriet's height, as I had noted when I met him—but he looked very dramatic in his summer whites. His clean, fresh face was closely shaven and his quick smile showed a mouthful of large gleaming teeth. In spite of the smile, I could tell he was nervous by his extra quick movements.

"Come on," Mrs. Lee said to them. "It's time to go into the living room. It's almost ten o'clock. Mustn't keep the bride waiting!" Ruth and I watched as Bill, Dick and Gracie arranged themselves by the fireplace, facing the minister, their backs to us. When everyone was in position, Nan Townsend got up from her seat in the front row and sat down at the piano, which had been moved into the corner near the fireplace. The old grandfather clock in the hall began to strike ten. Nan waited until it had finished and then struck up the Wedding March.

There was a rustling at the top of the stairs and Harriet appeared, wearing her mother's wedding dress of white India linen and lace and holding a bouquet of white roses. On her feet were delicate white satin slippers. I had never seen a face so transfigured with joy. Light seemed to be coming from it. She began her descent, stepping lightly in a dance of her own: step-hesitate-step; step-hesitate-step on each stair, in time to the Wedding March.

Only Ruth and I from our stand in the doorway saw Harriet on the stairs. She was all for us. "Lord, she's beautiful!" I whispered to Ruth, who was rendered speechless. Harriet didn't look at us as she came to the living room door. She looked straight at Bill, who had turned toward her. When he saw her face his eyes grew wide with pleasure and surprise. I felt something almost tangible pass between them, and realized for the first time there was more between a husband and a wife than I'd imagined.

The wedding ceremony, which I had never witnessed before, obviously moved the watchers. I was surprised to see that Nan Townsend and Mrs. Lee were crying. More surprised to see that Mr. Lee was crying too. I never thought that a wedding would be sad.

When it was over, everyone went out into the garden where a table was spread with a cloth and adorned with bouquets of flowers. Mrs. Lee and her sister brought out trays of sandwiches and the wedding cake, made by Nan Townsend. Dick followed, carrying a large bowl of fruit punch.

After the wedding breakfast the bride and groom changed their clothes and left in Bill's car, which I'd heard Bill tell Dick was a 1935 supercharged Auburn four-door convertible touring car. The minister, who was a mountain-climbing friend of Harriet's, followed in his own car. The three of them were off to climb Mount Katahdin.

"Strange way to spend a honeymoon," an elderly relative commmented as she crossed the lawn, supported by two sticks.

I didn't understand this comment. What was wrong with newlyweds spending a honeymoon with a friend climbing a mountain? That's something I'd like to do!

33. The Next Enlightenment

The same summer Fred and his Widow Beale lived in the bungalow, another product of divorce passed briefly through the neighborhood. Her name was Elaine, and she was the granddaughter of the family who had bought Maude's house. She was to stay with them until her warring parents could decide what else to do with her.

Elaine was a loose-boned thirteen—three years older than I was— with a large nose and mouth, small eyes and straggly dark hair. She was all right on her own, friendly enough and willing to play with me, but she had a best friend, "Tossie," who used to come out to see her most days.

"Tossie" was so-called because of her habit of tossing her shoulder-length honey-blonde hair out of her eyes with a shake of her head. She was aware that she was pretty, and had perfected the hair toss because her family and friends thought it was "cute." She was also convinced that she was funny, and enjoyed using her humor to put me down when she could.

Both girls were going into the eighth grade in the fall. Since fifth grade they had been required to take gymnastics and had learned to do splits, handstands and cartwheels, and stand on their heads. They were good at it, and had just participated in the end-of-year gymnastic demonstration the school put on at City Hall.

All during summer vacation they wore either slacks or their lime-green gym suits, and spent a lot of time honing their gymnastic skills. They decided that I should learn.

I had no talent whatever for gymnastics. Try as I might, I couldn't do a proper cartwheel—I couldn't get my legs up high enough. Standing on my head produced a headache, and I couldn't balance well enough to stand on my hands.

"God, you're clumsy," said Tossie in exasperation.

"Gym sure ain't one of your talents," Elaine agreed.

They snickered at my inept attempts and shook their heads.

In spite of my inability and chagrin, I fell in love with the green gym suits. I hadn't seen one before. They were sleeveless and square cut at the top. The legs, which had elastic at the bottoms, stopped at the top of the thighs like bloomers. The suits were cool and neat and I wanted one. I wanted a pair of slacks too. I'd never seen a girl or a woman in slacks before meeting Elaine and Tossie, but I'd always envied boys the freedom that pants gave them, and the girls said they were much more comfortable than skirts. "And you don't have to worry all the time about your panties showing," added Elaine.

"You'll be going into fifth grade in the fall, so you'll have to buy one then anyway," Tossie pointed out. "Why don't you ask your grandmother if you can get one now?"

I approached Ma.

"I don't like nudity," she said. "Those gym suits are indecently short. Elaine and Tossie shouldn't be wearing them anywhere but in the school gymnasium."

"But Ma, Harriet wears shorts when she comes home in the summers. They're just as short as a gym suit, and don't even have elastic in the legs."

"It's even worse when Harriet does it!" Ma snapped. "She's in her twenties and shouldn't be showing her legs like that!"

"I'll have to buy a gym suit in the fall anyway Ma, why can't I buy one now?"

"Because we can't afford it. We'll wait till the time comes and see if Mrs. Cony can find one that someone's outgrown."

This put a new light on the subject. Next time Ma was out of earshot and not likely to come back for a few minutes, I phoned Mrs. Cony.

"Glad you mentioned that," she said when I told her about the gym suit. "I hadn't realized you'd be starting gym so soon. I suspect there's a number of outgrown ones in the stuff that's accumulating for the next sale. I'll check on it."

"And do you think there might be a pair of slacks?" I asked. "They'd be great for gardening in—much better than a skirt."

"That's a good idea," she said. "I'll see what I can find."

Three days later she appeared at the farm with a gym suit which looked hardly worn, a pair of navy blue slacks with a narrow red stripe and white stripe up the side of the legs to the waistband, and a pair of sturdy dungarees for farm work. I was delighted.

Ma gave me a sharp look, but I kept quiet about my phone call, and to my relief Mrs. Cony didn't mention it.

Ma didn't object to the gym suit, no doubt because I'd need one anyway, but her eyebrows shot up over the slacks.

"I don't like girls dressing like men!" she exclaimed.

Mrs. Cony just laughed. "Well, a lot of the young ones are doing it," she said. "Sporty clothes like that are quite sensible, really, and much more practical than a skirt if you have an active life. Slacks cover your legs after all, and woolen ones are wonderfully warm in winter. I wear them myself sometimes. One doesn't want to be too old fashioned."

Ma said no more, and Mrs. Cony's remarks proved to be the thin end of the wedge that resulted in my clothing liberation. Although Ma muttered crossly about my new apparel from time to time, she didn't forbid my wearing it.

This was one of many things Louise Cony did for me that changed my life, and this one, at least, was for the better.

Gymnastics aside, it was soon obvious that when Tossie was with Elaine the order of play was to make me do their bidding, be the loser in their games

135

and the butt of their jokes. I was just lonely enough to let them get away with it for a while. There was a payoff for this: They were the first adolescent girls who had deigned to play with me, and being city bred and socialized, they were aware of aspects of life as yet unrevealed to me. As had happened with Rod, I got information from them that Ma had gone to great pains to keep from me.

The three of us often went over to the Lees when we saw Dick working around outside. Elaine and Tossie were just entering the boy-crazy stage and thought he was "divine" and "cute." He welcomed our company, but never let it interfere with his work. In fact he usually enlisted our assistance. "Never let a spare pair of hands remain idle" and "Never stop long enough to sit down" were unspoken basic principles on Maine farms. No one ever wasted Dick's time.

Between chats with Dick we often climbed up into the hayloft of the barn from which we could jump down 15 feet or so into soft hay. From this repeated activity we got the thrill of flying without the pain of landing. One day when I suggested hay jumping, Elaine demurred. "I can't today," she said.

"Why?" I demanded.

"It's the time of the month."

"The what?"

Elaine and Tossie exchanged glances.

"What do you mean, 'time of the month'?" I persisted.

"She doesn't know," smirked Tossie contemptuously.

Richard was out of earshot. "Let's tell her," said Elaine.

Tossie shrugged. "You tell her."

Elaine turned to me, her face ominously serious. Whatever it was, I wasn't going to like it.

"You bleed," she said.

"What do you mean, 'bleed'?" I asked. "Bleed where?"

"From the place the babies come out, of course."

"When? What for?"

"For a week every month. Girls have bad blood and it has to come out or you get sick."

I looked at her in shocked disbelief. "Do boys have bad blood too?"

"No. Men and boys don't. Just women and girls."

"That's crazy. Why should we have bad blood if men don't? Why should anyone have it? It doesn't make sense!"

"We have to have it so we can have babies," said Tossie.

I turned on her furiously. "I don't believe you."

"You'll believe it all right when you start to bleed," she said smugly. "It'll happen when you're twelve or thirteen. It's called getting the curse." I could tell she was enjoying this.

Elaine came in again: "And you'll have to go buy Kotex or Modess at the drugstore and everyone will know why you're buying it, and you'll be all wet and sticky and worried that the blood'll come through the pad and show on your skirt."

Tossie added, "And you'll have cramps and have to take Midol for them and you can't run or exert yourself or go to the gym for a week every month—until you're forty-five."

"What happens then?"

"You can't have babies any more so you don't have to get rid of the bad blood any more."

"What you say can't be right. If you bleed, there must be a better reason than that. What you say is crazy! Why should things work like that?"

"Because God made us that way and you have to accept it," said Tossie.

I went steaming off home to absorb this shock, but knew better than to ask Ma about it. She'd never tell me. Elaine and Tossie's story sounded highly unlikely, and yet it pulled some of the pieces of the puzzle into a position where they might eventually fit. There was the bit about bad blood. The doctor had said my boils and eczema were caused by it, and I'd get over them when I "matured." By "matured" he probably meant when I started having times of the month—when I got the curse. But he was wrong: I'd gotten over the boils and eczema not long after Grace died, when I was nine, and wouldn't be getting the curse for three or four years. If I'd got boils and eczema because I had bad blood, why didn't all girls get them?

I'd gleaned other information which might fit from the ads in the women's magazines Mrs. Cony brought. Now I understood what the Kotex and Modess ads were about. And the Midol. Maybe the curse was why the ads advised women to get Lydia E. Pinkham's Vegetable compound, and to take iron pills. The information Elaine and Tossie had given me may have been mostly wrong and told to upset me, but it did begin to sound like the life of females over the age of twelve was painful, messy, inconvenient and bad for your health.

I did a quick calculation of how many years between the ages of twelve and forty-five I'd have to spend bleeding, and came up with seven. Clearly it would be better to have been born a boy.

I continued to play with Elaine and Tossie for the rest of the summer and tried to get more information about the facts of life, but they appeared to have told me all they knew, or thought they knew. I checked out with them the information Rod had given me about where babies came from, and it became clear that I knew as much about it as they did. More, I reckoned. I didn't tell them about the whores, the strip poker and the vulgar language. They didn't use those words, nor did anyone else I'd met at the city schools.

I was not sorry when, as summer ended, Elaine left her grandparents and went to live with her aunt in town.

137

I'd been getting increasingly uneasy about them and Dick. Being older and more in touch with popular culture, the girls had picked up jokes and ways of speaking that were currently in vogue, and this seemed to amuse Dick. I was being outclassed with my favorite boy.

The girls went into routines used on the Jack Benny and the Fibber McGee shows. Ma and Pa didn't listen to these weekly shows, but I'd heard them several times at Fred's the year before and couldn't understand why everyone thought they were so funny. I'd told Carrie I thought they were silly and I couldn't see what the audience was laughing about. Carrie had told me in disgust, "You have no sense of humor! That is a great fault, my girl. Everyone should be able to laugh. You'd better correct that."

I don't remember whether it was Jack Benny or the Fibber who used the routine "I mean, I mean, I mean. . . What *do* I mean?" but everyone thought it was hilarious, and Elaine and Tossie began using it at every opportunity. It always got a laugh out of Dick. Next time I saw him alone without the two girls I made some remark and then added "I mean, I mean, I mean. . . what *do* I mean?" with the same twitching, wide eyes and stupid expression that Tossie used.

Dick glanced up from the cow he was milking. He looked pained and upset. "Don't do that," he said.

"Why? Tossie and Elaine do it and you think it's funny."

"Don't copy those silly girls. Just be yourself," he said, "They're not funny."

He returned to his milking. I felt relief pour over me. It was the nicest thing he could have said to me.

34. Marge

For a few months after they married and moved to Norfolk in December of 1936, either Lynde or Marge would write us occasionally. They said they had found a nice small house to rent convenient to Lynde's work and were very happy. At Christmas they sent me a box of things Lynde had brought back from Honduras: A dress made of woven green, tan and brown material with a brown bolero jacket to go with it, a cloth doll with dark skin, long black hair and a flaming red and orange dress, and a string of carved wooden beads. My dress and bolero were made for the tropics, of course, so I put them carefully away to wait for summer.

Though our family was not great about writing letters, I wrote Lynde and Marge every few weeks. By spring, however, their letters to me had tapered off. "Just busy being newlyweds with a life of their own to live," said Ma. It was not until fall of 1937, after Grace's death, that we received a letter from Lynde saying Marge was ill—she'd had a "nervous breakdown." I'd never heard of that before.

"What does 'nervous breakdown' mean, Ma?" I asked.

"It's something that happens to some people if they're doing too much and get over-tired," she said. She had looked worried when she read the letter, but now her manner did not imply that such a breakdown was serious. I assumed Marge just needed to rest.

It was nearly a year later when Lynde came to see us. When he got out of the car in the farmyard I couldn't believe what I was seeing. My handsome young brother had grown old. His face was lined and his eyes sunken. His hair had receded back over the dome of his skull and gone grey. He was nearly bald.

He was kind to me as ever, asked about all my interests, and brought me books and writing paper, but his sadness was palpable. He told us that Marge was no better and he'd had to return to Boston to put her in a hospital there so she could be near her family. He said he was going to Rhode Island to work for a couple of years on a bridge to connect Kingston to the Island of Jamestown in Naragansett Bay.

Distress was obvious on Ma's face. "I'm sorry for your trouble, Lynde," she said quietly. He thanked her, but said no more about it. He stayed the night and left next morning. He wrote occasionally from Jamestown, where he had rented a room, but we didn't see him again as long as he was working there.

My heart was sore for him and for Marge. They had been so happy when they came to see us before they married, and their letters for a while afterwards sounded the same. What could have happened to point the lives of two happy people whom I loved toward this disaster?

35. With Gracie in the Model A Ford

By the time Fred moved to town with the Widow Beale, Gracie Lee had graduated from high school and had found a job in town working for Judge Cony. He travelled around the circuit courts to judge cases in other towns, but he also practiced law in Augusta.

Judge Cony was fat and bald and much older than Mrs. Cony. He'd been out to our house with her several times. He dressed like doctors I had seen: he wore a waistcoat that matched his suit, had a gold watch on a chain, and smoked fat Havana cigars. Gracie told me he drove her hard, but he was a good man to work for.

Since Fred was no longer around to deliver me to school, I started riding to town with Gracie. She'd bought a second-hand Model A Ford that had to be cranked to start on cold winter mornings. She went conveniently close to Lincoln School on her way to work and could drop me off. I was now in the fifth grade and old enough to walk the two and a half miles home after school. I liked this better than going to Aunt Edith's. I was a fast walker, and as school let out at 3:30 I could be home by a little after four. Quicker if I got a ride. It was common practice for local people to pick up farm children who lived far from the school. It wasn't considered dangerous then.

Mostly it was just Gracie and me in the car in the morning, but occasionally she would pick up someone else on the way. A lot of people she knew didn't have cars and walked to town if they had to go when there was no convenient bus.

The first baby lamb I ever saw was in the lap of a farm woman who had been given a lift by Gracie. There was not much sheep-farming in our part of Maine. The lamb was the color of fresh cream and had a clean, sweet smell. Only years later did I come to know that odor as the fragrance of lanolin.

Another rider of Gracie's, whom she picked up regularly for several months, was a young woman who worked in an office in town. She was always smartly dressed, with a different brightly colored scarf floating each day from the throat of her slim-fitting grey coat. The coat was trimmed with tightly curled fur on collar and cuffs. She wore high heels covered with rubber overshoes. The overshoes had hollow high heels for the shoe heels to fit into. She always ran, delicately and gracefully, down her often icy path toward the car. "How fleetly you run," said Gracie to her one morning, laughing. I'd never heard that word used for anything but deer or horses before.

Once Gracie gave a lift to a thin, weedy, grey-haired woman I'd never seen before, but Gracie knew her. She had a tight, white little face, and hands that seemed to be all bone. Her fingers gripped a cigarette on which she pulled hungrily. She told Gracie she'd left her husband, gone back to him, and then left him again. "Couldn't live with him and couldn't live without him," she said. It was the first time I'd heard that phrase—but not the last. It was a recurring theme throughout my life—friends, acquaintances, workmates, chance encounters—so many women trapped by that lethal kind of attraction and the cruelty that goes with it. It was a new phrase to me then, however, and it opened one of the many windows onto human relationships: People who are married leave each other, like Mrs. Sturrock's husband, and now this woman. And parents sometimes leave their children, like the mother of the Hunter boys.

Did my mother really die, I wondered? Or did she just leave? Why do people leave each other? When do they know if it's going to happen?

36. The Lees' New Bathroom

As the year rolled around toward spring, the Lees made a landmark decision. They, like almost everyone else in rural Maine, began life on their farm with no modern conveniences. At first, they hand-pumped water into their kitchen and had a two-holer outhouse in their back shed. Then, to facilitate the washing of milk bottles and processing of equipment for their milk business, they'd asked Pa to plumb hot and cold running water into their milk room and kitchen. Their bathroom had to wait.

Aware, I suspect, of the state of our own bathroom, they got a plumbing firm in town to do the job. For about a week we saw men carrying pipes and parts into the house and the plumber's truck coming and going. When the job was finished and the bathroom in operation, Ma and I went over to admire this modern marvel. The tub was a hollow rectangular ceramic block set flat on the floor. I'd never seen one like it—no dragon's-claw feet! Shiny, chunky chromium faucets graced one end, and the rim of the tub was flat so soap and other things could be set on it without falling into the tub. This bathroom enchanted me with its white half-paneling and freshly applied wallpaper with fishes swimming in swirls of bubbles betweeen strands of golden kelp.

As we were leaving, I asked Mrs. Lee shyly if I could please have a bath in the new tub. She looked amused and agreed. I shot off to get soap and towel.

For an hour I soaked in the incredible luxury of that gleaming white porcelain tub with its inexhaustible supply of hot running water. When I had finished, I thanked our neighbors and returned home. I had not been there five minutes when the phone rang. It was Gracie.

"You'll have to come back," she said. "You left a ring on the tub."

"But," I protested, "I wasn't wearing a ring!"

37. Compartments

My time in the city schools was mostly a happy one. The year I spent at Nash had prepared me to go on to Lincoln, and paid off in many ways. My classmates at Nash were more civilized and kindly disposed than those at the country school. No tradition of bullying had been allowed to establish itself there, and I made many friends with whom I could play after school until Fred came to collect me. It was my first experience with friendly children, but I soon learned to relax and enjoy them. These friendships became well established, and they carried over when our whole class transferred to Lincoln School for the upper grades.

My acceptance by others at school and my interest in what I was learning there helped me get through the troubles at home. I developed the ability to shut off all upsetting thoughts and throw myself totally into school life while I was there. This capacity to put my life into compartments allowed me, and allows me now, to keep one area of my life from poisoning another. It was not denial or repression: I could move from one compartment to another and compare them whenever necessary.

The only dark ripple on the otherwise fairly idyllic pond at school was Delia, the dimpled blonde Shirley Temple look-alike who had reminded me so strongly of my fantasy friend "Sylvia" when I first went to Nash. Delia decided to dislike me. She was the prettiest child at the school, and until my arrival had been the smartest. Now I, the skinny, unpromising farm kid, was giving her stiff competition. Luckily for me, the other children resisted her attempts to get them "on her side." I sensed little sympathy among them for the spoiled and imperious Delia.

Without support from the others, Delia had to rely on words alone to express her hatred. "You're ugly," she'd snarl. "With your skinny arms and legs and those stupid pigtails you'll never get a boyfriend!"

She was neither strong enough nor quick enough to attack me physically on her own. This I proved to her the day she lost her cool and gave my hair an excruciating yank. She got the reflex reaction of the back of my hand full in the face. After that she kept her distance.

In the end, as we approached the watershed of adolescence, she had to content herself with basking in the warmth of her increasing swarm of male admirers. In this she had no fear of competition from me.

38. The Gallop

From the time I was nine, Dick Lee had occasionally allowed me to curry his horses on Saturday mornings. In return, he gave me riding lessons.

I loved working with the two horses, Mollie and Ricky. The stable was small and close and full of the comforting smells and sounds of warm, breathing horses. Gentle snorts and nickers, and the thumping and shifting of hooves in the stalls blended with the odor of their sweat and the sharp, steaming tang of fresh horse manure. The cowshed on the other side of the barn smelled quite different. Each type of animal has its own distinctive set of aromas.

I stroked the horses' velvety noses, talked to them, and felt their gratitude as I went over them with the curry comb. They leaned into my hands as I worked the week's scurf out of their shining coats.

After currying came a lesson, provided the busy Dick could spare the half hour.

Dick started me out on Mollie, a tame and gentle old mare in her late twenties. First, he taught me how to control and direct Mollie at a walk. When he was sure I knew what I was doing, he taught me to post.

In the trotting gait, as Dick explained to me, one forefoot and the opposite hind foot come down together, and this alternates from side to side. When the horse shifts weight and changes feet, I was to stand in the stirrups to prevent the impact of bottom with saddle when the horse's other two hooves hit the ground. "That's called posting," Dick said, and demonstrated as he rode beside me on Ricky.

It is not easy to learn to post on a trotting horse, and the chances of being thrown off are fairly high. However, the pain of not posting provides ample motivation to learn fast. I still remember the lame, bowed-outward feeling of my legs and the soreness of my rump after my first session trying to post.

I'd known nothing about the different gaits, and assumed at first that trotting was all there was to riding a horse. I was enlightened during my third or fourth lesson when I had conquered posting and was taking Mollie for a fast trot. Suddenly she stopped trotting and was flying through the air. I grabbed the saddle horn and hung on for dear life with my legs, expecting to be thrown. Instead, Mollie came down smoothly and lightly and then took off again. Then down again. Off again. Down again. There was no bottom banging, no need to post. We were streaming through the air together as if we were one body.

"You're galloping, Gal! How do you like it?" yelled Dick. I was too amazed at what was happening to answer.

Mollie suddenly dropped back into a trot and my butt hit the saddle with a clunk. I resumed posting, then slowed Mollie to a walk beside Dick.

"What was she doing?" I asked.

"Galloping. Great fun, isn't it?" he said. "What happens is, she breaks out of the trot and leaps forward by pushing herself off with her back feet. She stretches herself out flat in the air and then brings her back feet forward to meet her forefeet as they strike the ground. Then she pushes off again. She just goes flying smoothly and gracefully through the air and takes you with her."

After trotting, the gallop was pure delight. At a later lesson I found that the canter is also a smooth gait. Both right legs hit the ground together, then both left legs, resulting in an even, swaying, side-to-side sensation. Again, no posting required.

Saturday mornings with the horses was always the high point in my week. Dick also taught me how to saddle and bridle a horse, and how to harness one

143

to the old-fashioned buggy, which he then showed me how to drive. I felt at one with Mollie and Ricky and was pleased and proud of my increasing ability to manage them. Later, when I was twelve and working at the Lees for money, I was able to turn my experience with horses to good use by driving the hayrick during haying season, and sometimes also the hay rake. The safety-conscious Lees never allowed me near the mowing machine.

39. Of Birthday Parties and Bluffs

Both at Nash and Lincoln Schools I always got stuck with sitting in front of Patricia, or behind her, or beside her. Every year.

I liked Pat, but sometimes I wished she wasn't so close. Pat had to sit near someone, of course, but why me? I still wore my hair in long braids, and she kept reaching forward and playing with them. They seemed to fascinate her, and she wouldn't stop when asked.

Pat had a hard time at school. Never seemed to catch onto anything. If an assignment were given to write an original poem or story she could never think of a thing to write about. So I, to whom poems and stories came easily, would write one for her. I'd make sure, of course, that the ones I wrote for Pat weren't as good as the ones I handed in myself.

Pat used to tell some awful whoppers—things you just knew couldn't be true. Like the time she came to my tenth birthday party. Next day she told everybody at school that the food at the party made her sick and she'd thrown up all over seventeen of her mother's clean sheets.

I was boiling. It was good freshly made cake and ice cream, made by Ma herself, and nobody else got sick. Pat had just made a pig of herself. "Seventeen sheets indeed!" I said. "I bet your mother hasn't even got seventeen sheets, and if she did they wouldn't all be on your bed at once!"

Later, during one of the weekly art periods, the class was painting some tulips and daffodils which the teacher, Miss Clark, had brought in. Pat made a few pink and yellow brush marks on her paper but they didn't look like anything, so she gave up and started playing with my braids instead. I turned and snapped "Cut it out!" under my breath, but Pat wouldn't stop. All my whisper accomplished was a sharp "No talking, Peggy!" from the teacher.

A few minutes later Miss Clark left the room, and the sound level immediately rocketed. This was when Pat decided to use the ends of my braids for her art work. She dipped them into her inkwell and, using one in each hand, began to cover her paper with curliques.

Furious, I took a large gob of paint on my brush and daubed it on the hands that held my braids. Pat dropped them and began wailing "Look what you've done, you horrid thing," and wiped her hands all over her own clean dress.

"You keep your hands off my hair," I snarled. Pat opened the top of her desk and began fishing inside while I turned back to my painting.

"Hey, Peggy, look what I've got!" Pat said, so I turned around. She had her large, heavy blue music book in her hands and hit me full in the face with it. I felt the blood start from my nose and begin trickling down onto my dress. I got out of my seat, determined to take Pat apart.

At this moment Miss Clark walked in. "Peggy Shaw, what are you doing?" she shouted as I reached for Pat's throat.

"She hit me in the face with her music book," I said, dripping blood onto the floor.

Pat burst into tears. "She painted my hands and it's all over my dress. My mother'll kill me!"

The teacher went to Pat to cuddle and console her. To me she said icily "Go to the Girls' Room and wash off the blood." I went, fuming. I wet paper towels and held them to the back of my neck and pinched my nose where the book had hit to stop the bleeding. How come nobody ever cuddles me when I get hurt, I wondered.

When the bleeding had stopped I went back to class, which was unnaturally quiet. The painting things had been cleared away and Miss Clark was reading a story aloud. All eyes looked up when I came in. I couldn't even hear anyone breathe. Miss Clark ignored my arrival and kept reading.

When the bell rang the others shot out of the room. I went up to the teacher's desk. "Miss Clark, I want my seat changed."

"Why do you want your seat changed, Peggy?"

"Pat is driving me crazy. She takes things off my desk, keeps kicking my feet, won't stop whispering to me when we're supposed to be writing an assignment, and I get into trouble for telling her to shut up. She's always pulling my hair or playing with my braids. She was dipping my hair into her inkwell and using it for a brush. That's why I painted her hands. I want to get away from her."

Miss Clark looked at me hard for a minute. Then: "No, Peggy, I'm not going to change your seat. Patricia is a poor, disturbed child with very little to look forward to. You're clever and you're strong and you're quick-witted. You're the only one in the class who can handle her. So you'll just continue to sit where you are."

She turned back to her papers. Evidently I was dismissed. As I turned and walked out I knew that the world would never be the same again. Beneath my anger at the unfairness, a small bud of pride had begun to open. Miss Clark might not like me, but the gift she had given me was priceless. She had recognized my strength and my ability to cope with trouble, thereby confirming them.

My tenth birthday party had other spin-offs besides Pat's seventeen sheets. I had invited Rosalie to that party, and now she asked me to hers.

I was surprised. She hadn't enjoyed my party. Someone early in the event, very likely Pat, had said something she didn't like, and she'd sulked for the rest of the afternoon. Ma took her aside and talked with her, trying to find out what was wrong, but to no avail.

But now Rosalie was having a party, and I was asked.

Before the cake and ice cream were served, we played games. One of them required that anyone who got caught doing a forbidden act must run quickly to the goal without being tagged by the one who had spotted her.

I got caught in a forbidden act at a strategically bad place. The girl who saw me was squarely between me and the goal. There was no hope. For me, the game was over. I shrugged and said, "Well, you've got me—there's nothing I can do."

Everyone relaxed and grinned. It registered like a flash that with everyone off guard I could probably get to the goal without being tagged. I shot off toward the goal so fast that my opponent was caught unprepared. She gasped in surprise and made no move to tag me.

The lesson was obvious, and I learned it well.

40. Of Rats and Dorothy

The year I turned eleven, Sam Simpson, Dorothy's father, decided to start up a business. I don't know what he did before that, but now he was going into rabbits. Breeding them. Selling them. That, it seemed, was something even Sam could do.

I heard about the rabbits from the Lees, and thought I'd go and see them. I'd had two when I was younger, but they'd died of old age and had not been replaced. I thought I'd rather like some more. I'd saved up some of the money I'd been paid for picking raspberries, so on Saturday I walked the half mile down the road to the Simpsons' and tapped on the front screen door. Dorothy appeared behind it.

"Haven't seen you for a while," she said, looking surprised.

It was three years since I'd left the country school, and I'd made sure our paths never crossed.

"Heard about your rabbits," I said. "Wondered if I could have a look at them. Is your father home?"

"No, but I'll show you around. Come on, they're out in the shed."

She'd been friendly at first on my home ground. Now apparently she was willing to be friendly on hers. But I'd have to watch her. Did her face really look wicked and sly, or was I just remembering that she was wicked and sly?

In the shed were rows of cages, one on top of the other, each with a rabbit inside. The shed smelled of warm fur and animal feed. At least Mr. Simpson was keeping them cleaned out and there was food in their feeding dishes. They looked healthy.

But more interesting than the rabbits were the creatures in the topmost row of cages. I'd never seen anything like them before. Slender, sinuous white animals, longer and thinner than the grey rats that populated the outbuildings on the farm. Their eyes were red and their noses quivered with curiosity as I approached the cages.

"What are those?" I exclaimed.

"Albino rats. Want to see one? They're tame." She opened a cage and brought one out. It ran up her arm and around the back of her neck, sniffing inquisitively but making no attempt to escape. Dorothy giggled as the rat shot down her other arm and tried to go up inside her sleeve. She plucked it off her wrist and handed it to me. It was warm and soft and quivered with life. It exuded friendliness and good humor.

"It's wonderful!" I gasped. It was my rubber rat come alive.

I left rabbitless, but in my arms was a box containing two albino rats. Both males, Dorothy assured me. I'd checked them over carefully, and they seemed perfect.

As we left the shed, Dorothy paused.

"I hear you got some strange people renting your Uncle Fred's house," she ventured. I looked at her sharply. What did she know about them?

"Two women and a baby," I said.

Dorothy smirked. Her face was full of superior knowledge. "Do you know what they are?" she asked.

"What do you mean?"

"They're morphydites."

"What are morphydites?"

Dorothy looked at me in contempt. "Oh, you wouldn't know, would you? Everybody else knows."

"Well, what is a morphydite then, if you're so smart?"

"Someone who's both man and woman. Got breasts and a cunt and a prick and balls too," and she went off into her obscene laugh.

I was shocked, and uncomfortably aware that I probably showed it. Chloe and Terry were certainly unlike anyone I'd ever met before—but surely not like that? Dorothy looked at me with scorn and triumph. She obviously thought she knew all about it. She spoke with the conviction of the expert.

I'd heard of two-headed calves and seen a six-legged stillborn lamb displayed in a bottle at the carnival last year, so this suggestion wasn't impossible. But it didn't seem very likely, either. I'd wait and see. I'd learned the hard way, many times over, that I couldn't trust a word that Dorothy said.

41. Of Rats and the Pedlar

He was deaf and dumb, and maybe twenty. His skin was smooth and pink, and he looked quite boyish.

I was eleven, and had heard about people who couldn't hear or speak but I'd never seen one before.

He came to the side door of the farmhouse and handed me a card explaining that he was a deaf-mute making his living as a door-to-door salesman. I gave the card to Ma, who was working in the kitchen, and she came and motioned him in.

People often came to the door, as our farm was near the main road. Most were disabled veterans who had fought in the World War, or older men who couldn't find work. They came on foot in summer sun and winter cold trying to eke out enough to eat by peddling what the farm wives might buy: thread, darning cotton, needles, buttons, bias tape, ribbon, shoe and boot laces, shoe polish, gauze bandages, iodine, Mercurochrome, sturdy cotton handkerchiefs.

Ma always asked them in and fed them and bought something from them, though we could ill afford it. The neighbors warned her she was "risking life and limb taking those men in." "Nonsense," was her only reply. None of them ever showed her anything but gratitude.

The deaf-mute's name was Jim. It said so on his card. He was too young to have been in the war. Ma pointed to her mouth and made motions of her jaw like eating, then pointed to him, to the stove, and to a chair, making it clear in those few gestures that she would provide food if he would wait a few minutes. I was fascinated.

As Jim turned toward the chair his eye caught the cage on the kitchen windowsill which contained my two white rats. "Eh .. eh .. eh.. ," he cried, and pointed to them. I ran over and together we looked at the creatures in the cage. Jim made excited motions and obviously wanted to know all about them. I opened the cage and took them out. I played with them every day and they were tame, gentle and without fear. They climbed up my arms, sat on the back of my neck. They tickled and I giggled. Jim giggled too. His face was alight with joy. He held out his hands. I handed him one of the rats. He cupped it gently in both hands for a moment, then began to stroke it. Then he let it run up his arms, nuzzle around his collar, investigate his pocket. He "spoke" to it with unintelligible sounds, then did the same to me.

I ran and got pencil and paper. "They are my pets," I wrote. "They are five months old," and handed him the pencil and paper.

With the rats running over both of us we wrote notes back and forth.

"I never see white ones."

"They're albinos — white fur red eyes."

"Long tails — snaky."

"But clean and beautiful — need tails to balance."

"Yes. I like red eyes."

The notes passed between us for the next hour while we enjoyed the rats and also my tame hen Cara Lou, who had the run of the house. Jim ate a hearty meal, and we used many pages of paper. Then it was time for him to leave, as he had many miles of road to follow, many farms to stop at.

"Would you like to take my rats with you, to keep you company?" I wrote in a sudden burst of generosity.

Another flash of joy lit his countenance for a second, then his face clouded. He shook his head. "Rats would jump out of pocket on way," he wrote sadly.

"Come back and see us and the rats again," I wrote.

"I will," he replied.

He never did.

Part Four: The Watershed

42. Boston and Melrose: Disillusion and Revelation

My father's cousin Hazel lived in Caribou, Maine, with the rest of her family until she was in her thirties, then in Orono for a bit, then took a job in Boston. She was still single, and I suspect she felt her life in Maine was going nowhere and decided to change it.

In Boston she had better luck, and within a year met and married Joe Aveni, a short, wiry, dark-haired man with a neatly clipped mustache. How she met Joe I never heard, nor did I learn why, in his early forties, this Italian Catholic was single and looking for a wife.

I was about seven or eight when they married. Over the next few years, before they separated, Hazel and Joe called at the farm fairly often on their way between Boston and Orono. Joe made a great fuss over me, throwing me up in the air and catching me, and tumbling about with me on the lawn. I thought he was wonderful.

Their car was the first Chevrolet I had ever seen, and it was in a new shape that Joe called "streamlined." Its back and front were sloped and molded to reduce air resistance so it could go faster and use less gasoline, Joe told me.

The summer I was eleven, Hazel wrote that she was going to visit people in Orono for a week. Joe couldn't come because of his work. On her way back she'd like to take me home with her to Islington, the suburb of Boston where she and Joe lived, for a few days. She knew I'd never been out of Maine and thought it was time I saw something different. She and Joe would bring me back at the weekend and continue on to a wedding in northern Maine.

I was ecstatic. I'd never been further from home than forty miles to the Maine Coast. Now, finally, I was going to see Boston, that mysterious city to the south Mae Towle had talked about. I couldn't wait to get away from the watchful eye of Ma and find exciting adventures in a new, strange place.

When Pa told me about the trip, he said he'd also arranged for me to spend a day with Aunt Rita in Melrose while Hazel attended to business in Boston. Lynde wasn't living in Melrose any more so I couldn't see him, but Rita could show me where he had lived.

As I thought about the approaching visit to Aunt Rita, I realized that I knew almost nothing about her, or how she came to be "a friend of the family." My curiosity now aroused, I asked Pa about this.

"She was a friend of your mother's," he said.

I was staggered. My mother's friend? If I'd only known before! Perhaps, now that I was older, and was going to see her alone, she would be willing to tell me something about Mother. I did not, of course, mention this possibility either to Ma or Pa, but I couldn't wait to get to Melrose.

On the day of departure I sat in the front seat of the Chevrolet beside Hazel and marvelled at everything I saw. The road to Boston was wider and smoother than the road to the coast, and had traffic lights as well as stop signs. I'd seen traffic lights in Augusta, but never on roads outside the town. The closer we got to Boston, the wider the road grew. First it became three lanes, which I had never seen in one road before, then it became four lanes, and finally there were separate roads going parallel to one another: one for cars going south and one for cars going north. It was a "turnpike," Hazel said. I remembered Uncle Fred saying that someday there would be roads going in two directions with a strip of grass in between. He was right, except on the roads we travelled that day there was no grass between.

I thought Hazel must be very clever to remember the way to Boston. It was nearly two hundred miles and there were roads turning off all the time. How did she know which ones to take? No one had ever explained route numbers to me or shown me a road map, as everyone knew the way to anywhere I had ever been.

I didn't say much on the journey, just kept looking. Everything I saw was so different I didn't even know what questions to ask. Hazel and I kept glancing at each other and smiling. I thought she was the pleasantest woman I'd ever known, so different from the sad and quiet Ma, who seldom spoke and was becoming increasingly forgetful.

As we neared Boston, we went through miles and miles of city streets, enough for a hundred Augustas, but we never saw Boston itself.

"We're just driving through the outskirts on the way to our house in Islington," Hazel explained. "Around Boston one town runs into another and becomes just one big super-city."

Finally Hazel drew up in front of a small, square pink house with a tiny patch of lawn back and front, and no fence. "Here we are," she said.

151

I didn't know what to make of the house. It wasn't wooden, nor was it brick or stone.

"It's stucco, coated over a wooden frame," Hazel informed me in answer to my question.

We went inside and found Joe waiting for us with Timmus, their half-grown yellow cat. Their small living room had ivory-colored walls decorated with pale green splotches instead of wallpaper. "That's the latest style down here," Joe pointed out. "The painter put the green on with a sponge. A lot easier than hanging paper!"

The rooms in the house had the lowest ceilings I'd ever seen—quite a contrast to the high ones in our farmhouse. Lucky Joe and Hazel are short, or they'd hit their heads, I thought.

A corridor ran off one side of the living room to the bedrooms and bathroom. It had a shiny polished hardwood floor that would be fun to slide on in stockinged feet. Hazel took me along it to leave my bag in the guest room and show me where my towel was.

I couldn't believe the bathroom when I saw it. The tub, toilet and wash-basin were reddish purple, like blood. The towels and bath mat were reddish purple to match.

Joe and Hazel then took me through an archway that led from the living room into the smallest kitchen I'd ever seen. Adjoining it was what they called a "dinette" to eat in. Hazel fixed sandwiches and soup for supper while I stroked Timmus, who had an enormous purr.

Joe seemed glad to see us and was pleasant enough during supper. It was 8:30 by the time we finished. "It's been a long day for you, Peggy. Are you tired?" Hazel asked. I admitted that I was, and by nine o'clock I was in bed. Before I fell asleep I could hear the mumble of their voices. Joe's had changed tone. He seemed to be cross about something, but I didn't stay awake worrying about it.

Next day was Saturday and Joe and Hazel drove me around while they did errands in Islington. It was just like coming into the Boston area the day before: one continuous city wherever we went—wide concrete roads with several lanes in each direction and forests of stoplights for miles ahead. These big roads went between regions with lots of shops and regions of streets full of little box-like houses with tiny lawns in front. I wouldn't want to live here, I thought. No green fields or brooks. There'd be no place to play.

Joe was jumpy and bad tempered all day, and I could tell this made Hazel uncomfortable. She seemed to be trying extra hard to be nice to me.

That evening Joe and Hazel took me to see a movie called "The Three Feathers." I offered to pay my way in with the spending money Pa had given me. Joe gave me a funny look and said, "I'll take care of it."

"Oh, let me pay it," I said. "Pa gave me some money." I thought it was the polite thing to do.

"I said I'll take care of it," he snarled. There was an edge in his voice I hadn't heard before. I could think of nothing else to say, so I shut up.

The movie was set in the desert and had a lot of action involving camels. The main character had his tongue cut out in the end.

Later, back at their house while Joe was in the bathroom, Hazel apologized for his snapping at me. She explained that he was nervous and not quite himself. By now I had the clear impression that it was I who was making him nervous. He was showing the signs, familiar enough to me, of a man who disliked children, particularly in large doses. I was disappointed. He hadn't acted like that when they visited the farm.

Joe was still in a foul mood next day, which was Sunday. His sister, who lived nearby, had offered to take me and her own children to Franklin Park Zoo for the day, but at the last minute she backed out of the arrangement. Joe made no attempt to hide his anger at this betrayal, and left the house, not to return until evening.

He took the car, so I helped Hazel do some cleaning in the house. She asked me to sweep the corridor while she made the beds. I took the opportunity to try out what I'd thought about doing when I first arrived. I slipped off my shoes, took a run at the corridor, and slithered the whole length of it. It was great. I did it again. When I turned around Hazel had come out of the bedroom and was standing at the other end, hands on her hips. "You mustn't do that, you'll scar the floor," she said sharply. I couldn't see how stockinged feet could scar a floor, but I didn't say so.

I finished the jobs Hazel asked me to do, then went out into the tiny back yard. Timmus was there prowling about, and as I watched him he pounced on a bird. I shrieked at him and managed to grab him. He hadn't killed the bird and I was able to get it away from him. The sparrow was shocked but apparently not badly injured. Its heart was thumping, and it was gasping with fear. I soothed it in my hands. When it calmed down I would let it go and see if it could fly.

"What have you got there?" demanded Hazel, coming out of the house.

"Timmus caught a bird, but I got it away from him. It's not badly hurt. I'll let it go in a minute when it gets over the shock."

"Give it back to the cat at once," said Hazel. "If he eats that one he'll be satisfied. Otherwise he'll just go catch another one."

I couldn't believe my ears. Ma would never do a thing like that. She had shown me how to get a bird away from a cat without further injuring it. Often it would recover and fly away. If it were too badly injured, we would put it to sleep with a little chloroform. Injured birds and animals seemed to like the smell of chloroform, and would nuzzle their noses into the cloth as if they knew it would help them. Ma would never, never, give a bird back to a cat to torture before he killed it!

"No, Hazel," I protested, "That's cruel!"

She snatched the bird out of my hand and passed it to the cat, who was mewing in frustration at her knee. He sank his teeth in and headed for the bushes. I burst into tears.

"Don't be a cry-baby," Hazel snapped. "You're a farm girl— you should know better than that!"

That pleasant, smiling woman who had driven me to Boston had turned into a monster. And she was married to another one. It was Ma who was wonderful. Ma who was kind. Ma who loved animals. Why had I wanted to get away from her? People are not what they seem, and I should have known it.

I spent the rest of the day and evening furious at both Hazel and Joe. I missed Ma and Pa. If only I could just shut my eyes and wish myself back at the farm.

Luckily, next day was Monday and Joe had to work. I was to visit Aunt Rita that day, so Hazel drove me to Melrose and dropped me off.

Aunt Rita's house was more like the houses I was used to. It had large rooms with high ceilings and tall windows. She greeted me kindly and called me Brenda—then said, "Forgive me, I just can't call you Peggy. I know you prefer it, but Brenda was the name your mother chose for you. I hope you go back to it one day."

"Brenda" sounded strange to my ears. No one called me that now except Lynde—and Rita when she came to visit. I didn't associate myself with that name any more.

Rita—tall, spare and graceful in her movements—conducted me into the living room. With her unlined face and pink-and-white complexion she looked much younger than her mid-fifties. Even her white wig did not age her. She still had the tic in her forehead which made the wig move about.

Something Ma had said popped into my mind: "Rita has an aristocratic face." I hadn't known then what she meant, but now I decided that "aristocratic" meant having a long, slender face and a delicately molded narrow nose like Rita.

Rita gave me milk and cookies and then drove me to a store where racks and racks of children's clothing occupied a large part of the lower floor. I'd never seen so many clothes before. As far as I can remember, this was the first time I'd had a new dress from a store. Before that, Ma made my dresses or Mrs. Cony brought them from rummage sales. Recently it had all been from rummage sales. Ma didn't sew much any more. I hadn't seen her use a needle for some time, and then only to do mending. The will and the spirit seemed to be going out of her.

I can't remember what clothes I was wearing that day, or what state they were in, but I must have looked so shabby that Rita decided to act. I'd never thought much about clothes. Ma had taught me that they must be washed when dirty and worn till they wore out. It was a matter of pride to make something last as long as possible. Many of the children at school had been taught the same, and were as threadbare as I. The rich kids who lived on inner Western Avenue and Winthrop Street always had new clothes, and as soon as they didn't look new they were sent to the rummage sale. I didn't know the rich kids well. They only spoke to each other.

Aunt Rita and the salesgirl discussed sizes and prices and had me try on a lot of short-sleeved cotton dresses. The ones that didn't fit were taken away and six were left.

"Which four of these do you like best?" Aunt Rita asked.

Four? I must have heard her wrong. Surely she wasn't going to buy me four dresses? She read my face and smiled at my surprise.

"You'll need four dresses for the rest of the summer and for school when it first begins. The ones you have are too small for you and very worn. I want to buy these for you. Your mother would like that."

I can still remember the ones I chose, and I wore them till I could no longer force myself into them. One was a blue flowered print, with little pink buds and blue piping around a V-shaped panel in front. It had a full skirt and a fitted top. Another was pale corn yellow with burgundy and green designs on it. The third was straight and slender, wine red with small white polka dots. It tied at the back. The fourth was a "dressy" dress: Navy blue, fitted, and without a belt. A single white flower on a long white stem went up the front from hips to collarbone on each side. I thanked Rita as best I could. They were so beautiful, how would I ever dare to wear them?

On our way back to Rita's, she brought up the subject of my brother.

"Brenda, do you often hear from Lynde?"

"No, not often. Not since Marge has been sick. But he did come to see us just before he went to work in Rhode Island. He looked terrible, Aunt Rita. He's gone bald and he seemed so unhappy."

Aunt Rita sighed. "Poor lad," she said. "It's such a tragedy about Marge. She won't even talk to Lynde. Doesn't seem to know who he is. When he goes to see her in the hospital she just turns her face to the wall and won't look at him."

"But why, Aunt Rita? What's wrong with her? What is a nervous breakdown?"

"Marge has a mental illness which is very difficult to treat. What will happen to her is quite unpredictable. It's not just Lynde she won't talk to. She can't, or won't, recognize her parents either, or other relatives or friends.

Everyone feels so helpless. We're just waiting and hoping she'll snap out of it. People do, sometimes."

"You mean she might be in that hospital forever?"

"We just don't know what will happen. Do write to Lynde often, Brenda. Even if he doesn't answer you, it will help him to know that you care about him."

"I will, Aunt Rita," I promised.

When we got back to Rita's house she gave me a delicious lunch of fricasseed chicken and showed me some photographs of her grown children and grandchildren. Then she put the album down beside her on the living room couch where we were sitting and took up an envelope. It had pictures in it of a woman holding a baby.

The baby looked about four months old and was wrapped in a wooly shawl. It just looked like any baby. The woman had a mass of grey curly hair, full on top but shingled severely at back and sides. She looked mid-forties and seemed to have no shape beneath her loose white dress. The skin on her arms and neck was flabby and her face, though smiling, looked tired. The pictures had been taken on the porch of our farmhouse. In one picture the woman was standing, in the others she was sitting or kneeling. In all of them she was looking at the baby and smiling.

"Do you know who that is?" Rita asked.

"No," I said.

"That's you—with your mother."

Astonished, I looked up at her. "Is that Bess?" I asked when I could find my tongue.

"Yes," said Rita.

I took up each picture in turn, studying it minutely, trying to take everything in.

"The pictures are for you to keep, Brenda," she said when I looked up. "I had duplicates made for you."

"I can take them home with me?" I asked, incredulous.

"Yes, Dear," she said.

"Aunt Rita, you knew my mother, didn't you?"

"Yes, of course I knew her. I was her best friend. Did no one tell you?"

"They only said you were a friend of the family. It wasn't till just before I came down here that Pa told me you were my mother's friend."

Rita shook her head and sighed. "Brenda, what do you know about your mother?"

"Just that her name is Bess, and she died when I was a baby."

"Nothing else?"

"That Lynde is her son but not my father's, which makes him my half brother."

156

"And is that all?"

"Yes."

Rita's grey eyes widened, then clouded slightly. Her forehead twitched and her wig rode back and forth. "Dear God!" she said. "You'd have thought in all these years that someone would have told you something! You never heard how your mother and father met? Didn't Grace tell you?"

I shook my head.

"Incredible! I cannot understand why they won't talk with you about her. She was such a wonderful woman, and she loved you so much. Your life would have been very different if she had lived to bring you up. She nursed you at the breast till the day she died. She used to call you 'Brenda Betsy Blueberry Shaw,' because you had eyes like two blueberries."

I didn't know whether to laugh or cry. "Why did she die?" I asked.

Aunt Rita hesitated, as if uncertain how to begin. "Have they mentioned your Grandfather Lynde to you?" she asked.

"Yes. Ma said he had left me some money, and because he lived in Massachusetts I had to have a guardian to look after it."

"They did tell you that your Grandfather Lynde was your mother's father, I presume?"

They hadn't, actually, but I'd seemed to realize it without particularly thinking about it. I nodded.

"Well, that's something. Let's begin with how your mother and father met. About four years before your birth your father had a serious accident. He was walking along a sidewalk in Augusta when a car went out of control, left the road and hit him. He was quite badly injured. When he was convalescing, your Aunt Grace and Uncle Fred, who were living here in Melrose at the time, invited him to come and stay with them."

This surprised me. Several disparate bits of information were coming together in an unexpected way.

"I knew Grace and Fred lived in Massachusetts before they came to live at the farm," I said, "but I didn't know it was Melrose. I thought it was Haverhill where Fred worked in a shoeshop."

"They may have lived in Haverhill at one time, but they were certainly living in Melrose when your father met your mother."

"So Grace and Fred lived in the same town as Lynde. Did they know him?"

"Not till after your parents met. Grace and Fred had recently bought a duplex house across the street from your Grandfather Lynde's farm. They lived in the bottom unit and rented the top one. Your mother and Lynde were living at the farm, helping to take care of your grandmother, Sarah Lynde, who had not been well. Grace knew that one of your grandfather's cows had just freshened, and thought giving your father a quart of warm new milk every day might help his recovery. He began going over each day to get the milk, which your mother would have ready for him. That's when the romance between them started."

"Over a cow?" I asked, delighted. Aunt Rita smiled at my reaction.

"How long before they got married?" I asked.

Rita hesitated, as if she were deciding what to say. "About a year," she said. "And three years after that, you were born."

"But why did my mother die?"

"She had been very ill with pneumonia about a year before she met your father. Although she recovered, the pneumonia had damaged her heart, and she was told she could not return to work. When she became pregnant, we all feared that she would not survive your birth. Not only because of her heart, but because she was forty-four, which is considered quite old to have a baby. But, thank God, she came through it with no trouble and brought you safely into the world. She died the following summer, when you were seven months old."

"But why?" I insisted.

"Your Grandfather Lynde had just arrived from Melrose that day. It was easy then to come from Melrose to your father's farm. The Melrose Wyoming Station was just behind the Lynde farm. All he had to do was step onto the train there and get off at Augusta four hours later. Then he took the trolley car out to Morang's Crossing, just at the edge of your land, and walked up to your farmhouse.

"It was August—haying season—and your father and Lynde were working out in the back field. It was near noon by then, and the temperature had risen into the nineties. Your grandfather was hot and flushed when he arrived, and your mother took him out on the front porch where it was cooler. He was sitting on the hammock and she on the porch steps, holding you in her arms. They chatted for a few minutes, but then your mother asked him something and he didn't answer. She looked up. He'd had a stroke and was sitting there on the hammock, with his eyes bulging out and his false teeth hanging from his mouth. Then he pitched forward and fell to the floor beside her. She screamed for your father and Lynde."

I saw in a flash of vision the eyes bulging out of my grandfather's head, the teeth, him falling, hitting the floor hard—the eyes dilating, going black and still. This blended into another flash of vision—the black doorknobs that had so terrified me when I was younger—and then Bart's eyes, black, wild, staring at me.

Aunt Rita couldn't know what I'd just seen, and went on:

"Your father and Lynde heard your mother scream and came running in from the field. They found your grandfather lying dead on the porch floor, eyes still open and staring, and your mother kneeling beside him, hysterical. She started to tell them what had happened, but collapsed at their feet from a heart attack and was dead twenty minutes later."

I could *see* the scene: The woman in the picture with the baby—she was screaming and screaming and then falling over—Pa was taking her in his arms—what did she do with the baby?

"And they told you none of this?" asked Rita.

The vision flashed away and I was back in Melrose, sitting on the couch.

"No," I said.

As Rita spoke, I could only feel the physical shock of revelation. That I had been there. That I had witnessed those deaths, which in some form I knew now that I remembered.

I didn't think to ask Rita why my people hadn't told me what had happened. I took it for granted that I knew why: They thought it would upset me, just as they thought it would frighten me if I knew in advance about my tonsils coming out, and about where babies came from. As if being deceived about everything that happened in life and then finding out the truth later weren't infinitely worse!

Instead, it was Rita who asked the question: "Why do you think they didn't tell you, Brenda?"

I wasn't sure how to say it. "I guess they thought it was for my own good not to," I ventured.

Rita shook her head. "No, Brenda, it wasn't for your own good. It wasn't for your own good at all!"

When Hazel came at four o'clock to pick me up, my world view had totally changed. I knew much more than before, but realized there was infinitely more to learn. It would still be a struggle to find the truth in this bizarre, expanding story.

Luckily, the next day was Tuesday, and in the early morning Hazel and Joe drove me back to Augusta before going on to the wedding. We left before dawn. The streets were deserted, the houses dark. I sat in the back seat, watching the light slowly spread up the eastern sky.

If I ever actually crossed the line into the city of Boston on that trip, I didn't know it. From one place to the next everything looked alike. The joys of Boston Common, Beacon Hill, the gold dome of the Statehouse and the Charles River Basin were far in my future.

I was glad to get back to Ma and Pa, because no matter what our problems and troubles were at home, no matter what might happen to us, I was sure they loved me. Even though they kept vital information from me, I knew they were kind and well meaning all through—not like Hazel and Joe, likely to lash out with something cruel and vicious when I least expected it.

Aunt Rita had been wonderful. She was like Ma and Pa and Lynde. I could trust her to do me no evil, even if she stopped short of telling me all of the truth. I sensed she would tell me more later, when she thought I was old enough to hear it.

But I was furious with Ma for not telling me about my mother—what she was like, how she and my grandfather had died. Why did I have to wait until I was eleven, when Rita showed me those pictures, to even know what my mother looked like? Why did the information have to come from Rita?

I don't know why I blamed Ma more than Pa for not telling me. Perhaps because he was always more silent than she, so I really didn't expect him to say anything. We usually communicated on a non-verbal level, but somehow, for us both, that was enough. I was used to it; we were good at it. But Ma did talk with me about some things. She had a tongue in her head and could use it when it pleased her. She only shut me out, it seemed, about the things that really mattered. I'd thought for a while that she'd gotten better after Grace's death, but she hadn't, really. She'd just parried my questions with tiny bits of information until I realized that asking her anything about Mother wasn't worth the effort.

I decided to tell Ma nothing about what Rita had said. Two could play the secrets game.

43. The Allens

By the time I visited Aunt Rita, the Shaw farming operations had almost completely run down and Pa was working in town. He had faced the fact the autumn before that he could no longer cope. Fred's departure had been the beginning of the end. When both men were able-bodied and committed to the farm, Pa and Fred together could just about carry it. Although Fred had only evenings and weekends for farm work, his contribution had been vital.

Aunt Grace's illness and death had bankrupted our family financially, physically and emotionally. Pa had turned sixty and was in poor health. Something was wrong with his heart, but the doctor hadn't put a name to it. Pa's legs also bothered him. He couldn't walk any distance without pain in them.

"Poor circulation," said the doctor. "You'll just have to put up with it."

Fred was older than Pa by ten years, and, like almost everyone else I knew, also had heart trouble.

Pa, exhausted, sold the last cow—Vivian—and told Ma and me that he was going to let the west back field revert from vegetables to grass. We would keep the west front field planted just for our own use, and wouldn't try to supply the shops in town any more. We'd keep the raspberry field between the houses so we could sell the fruit and Ma could continue to make jelly. For the rest of our income, we'd have to depend on Pa's plumbing jobs.

Pa began catching the 7:50 a.m. bus to town every day and returned on the 5:10 bus. His jobs in autumn and winter entailed heavy work in miserably cold conditions, and he always came back drained and chilled through. He caught one cold after another that winter and often had to stay off work, growing more and more gaunt and haggard. Ma worried that he'd go into pneumonia, or have a heart attack, and then where would we be? In spite of her fears, he managed to get through till spring without collapsing.

I was concerned about Ma, too. She'd never completely got back to normal after her illness, and ever since the time I woke to find her stiff beside me in bed, she'd go through periods of not seeming to remember things she couldn't possibly have forgotten. But then she'd snap out of it and be all right again.

The farmhouse was showing signs of neglect, too. It had been becoming shabbier ever since Grace's illness began. Its light colored wallpapers had darkened into an ugly, greyish tan, the designs seeming to disappear as if into fog. Even the dark, elegant wallpaper in the stairwell of the front hall had lost its luster.

The large oriental rug in the sitting room, which filled it to within a foot of its walls, was getting threadbare. More and more of the backing showed through under its colorful repeating patterns. In the kitchen, the surface of the linoleum had worn off everywhere except under the stove, the table and Pa's rocker. That's the only way we could remember what the pattern was like.

"Why don't we just take it up, Pa?" I asked. "There's a hardwood floor underneath, isn't there? That would look better than this."

"Then this room would be even colder and harder to heat than it is now, Peggy. What's left of the lino serves as a layer of insulation. We'll have to keep it down. There isn't enough room in that oven for everyone's feet at the same time, you know."

Outside, the house and outbuildings all needed paint, but paint would cost money we didn't have.

Ma no longer had the strength to keep up her flower borders to her usual high standards, and they were becoming choked with weeds. I did what I could to keep them up, but between school and my other chores I couldn't do enough, and most of the beds were slowly reverting to grass.

The general dilapidation of our home had happened so slowly that I didn't realize it at first. Rather, I felt a general sense of unease, a sense that things were no longer right without being able to pinpoint it.

I knew nothing about the details of family finances, and though I realized things were bad, I had no idea how desperate they really were until early May when Aunt Edith came out to spend Sunday with us.

Edith arrived just before eleven, left her new navy blue straw hat on the hall table and went to join Ma and Pa in the kitchen. I was upstairs, and as I came down I spotted her hat on the table and went over to examine it. Pale blue plush forget-me-nots with yellow centers clustered along its band. I touched them lightly. Their petals were soft and velvety like the backs of bumble bees.

As I admired the forget-me-nots, I overheard Pa say to Aunt Edith, "We've got to sell the farm. The money's gone. I can't pay the mortgage. There isn't even enough to eat on."

I felt my stomach plummet through my feet. The farm was the only home I had ever known. Where else could we go?

I knew better than to go into the kitchen and tell them what I'd overheard. They wouldn't discuss it with me. I'd always been excluded from the family griefs and strategies. Why should I expect them to include me now?

I tried to push what Pa had said out of my mind while I helped Ma get Sunday dinner and talked with Edith. But every time I went across the hall I'd see the blue forget-me-nots on the hat and feel my stomach hit bottom again.

Next day Pa put the "FOR SALE" sign up on the front lawn. I saw him through the living room window, and went out to join him.

"Have we got to sell the farm?" I asked.

"Yeah. I gotta give up plumbing, Peggy. Even with a helper I can't keep it up. My strength is gone and there's a mortgage payment coming up mid summer I won't be able to meet. We've got no choice."

"But what'll we do when you sell it?"

"Put some of the money into a small place in town and live on the rest till I get my strength back enough to find a lighter job."

I couldn't imagine living in town, with no fields and woods around me, no animals, no Lees across the street. I turned away and went back into the house so Pa wouldn't see my tears.

Weeks passed but nobody even came in to inquire about the farm. In those hards times, who had the money or the recklessness to buy one? Like us, many other farmers in Maine were trying to meet their mortgage payments by taking second jobs. Who'd go into farming if they could do anything else?

By the first of June, I could see that Pa was desperate. Maybe someone could afford to buy an acre, he said. That would allow him to meet the mortgage payment and settle the long outstanding bill at the grocers so he wouldn't have to worry for a few months. He changed the sign to "HOUSE LOT FOR SALE." The field down across the road from McAuley's wasn't much good for anything but pasture—too wet. But someone could put a house on the higher part near the stone wall. It was only June, and a house could easily be got up before winter.

I felt a surge of hope. Maybe we could get by without selling the farm after all.

Several couples came by to look at the land and shook their heads. Too much money. By the time I left for my visits with Hazel and Rita, Pa had lowered the asking price to just the amount that would meet the mortgage payment and pay the grocer.

I was relieved to be going away for a few days and not have to think about what might happen to us. As I did at school, I could put my troubles into a compartment in my brain, close it, and forget about them until it was necessary to remember.

The week after my return, a man from town came with his family to look at our acre. His name was Ron Allen. He was small, lean, of dark complexion and, he told Pa, part French-Canadian, though he spoke no French. His puffy eyes gave his long face a sleepy look, but this was belied by his quick movements.

Anna, his wife, was sharp-faced and skinny, hair frizzled from a cheap perm. With a little thrill of recognition, I realized that their three children all went to my school, and one of them, Rena, was in my class. We smiled shyly at each other, but didn't speak.

The three of them had the look of children in families that had always been poor: gaunt, pale and underfed. Bony arms and legs emerged from their clothing. The two girls had thick manes of straight dark hair falling loose down their backs, and Rena had the long face and sleepy eyes of her father. Beryl and Charlie resembled their mother.

The Allens viewed the house lot, liked it, and the price was right. Allen was a jack-of-all trades with no particular talents, but like many men in those days he could turn his hand to anything. He'd managed to make a living and somehow save enough to get a loan to buy land and erect a house. Said he'd helped put up enough houses for other people so he reckoned he could build his own with his son Charlie's help. He'd like to get onto the lot right away.

I breathed easy for the first time in weeks. Our farm was one hundred acres, eighty of it woods. The houses and outbuildings took up about two acres. The rest we had used for planting and pasture in rotation. Pa said we could sell off an acre at a time till things improved. The Depression couldn't last forever. It was 1939 and already the papers were claiming things were better now that there was a war in Europe and America was mobilizing in case we were drawn in.

I was delighted that the three Allen children would be our neighbors. No children my age lived nearby. Dick Lee was nineteen now and out of high school. Life on our farm was lonely and silent. The Allens had hardly driven out of sight when I began dancing in a spasm of excitement. "Oh, Ma, this is great! Rena's in my class at school, Beryl's a year behind, and Charlie's going to high school in the fall."

"They seem like nice children—very quiet—rather shy," Ma commented.

"Rena never says much, and always looks sad. She's hardly ever spoken to me, actually. She just looks unhappy and kind of discouraged. She should be a year ahead of me, but she had to stay back 'cause she couldn't do the work."

"Beryl has a lovely smile," said Ma. "With that round face and enormous black eyes she'll be a beauty one day."

"I don't know much about Beryl except she's supposed to be smart," I said. "But everybody knows Charlie. He's good at art and his teacher brings his drawings around to show the other classes. He can draw anything!"

"It'll be good for you to have someone to play with, Peggy," said Pa. "You're alone too much with us old folks. But take it slow till we get to know them better."

Pa and Ron Allen wasted no time getting the land transfer arranged. The day after signing the papers the Allen family appeared on their plot, put up a large round tent supported from a central pole, and erected a two-holer outhouse. We went down to welcome them as soon as they arrived. Pa helped Allen and Charlie erect the tent. I was impressed by Charlie. He was tense, wiry, sharp-witted, and incredibly strong for his thin build and fourteen years.

"Being town dwellers, do you know poison ivy when you see it?" Ma asked Mrs. Allen. Anna Allen looked quite taken aback and shook her head, as did the girls.

"Come on then," said Ma. "While the men are getting the tent up we'd better inspect the lot and I'll show you what it looks like. You won't want three itching children on your hands."

We went over the ground foot by foot looking for the dark green, glossy, three-leaved vine which sneaked through stone walls, under fences and invaded surrounding grass. Luckily, we found that the poison ivy was largely confined to the stone wall on the west boundary and easily avoided.

I'd never seen such a big tent before, outside a circus. When it was up, Mr. Allen and Charlie made several trips to and from their former home with a pick-up truck to collect their belongings. Ma and Pa returned to our farmhouse, leaving me behind to help carry things in from the pick-up. These included a large table, chairs, a kerosene stove and lamps, four mattresses, bedding, an assortment of cooking gear and dishes, and several boxes of clothing.

On the last trip they also brought the rest of the menage: an infant of nine months which they were fostering for the State; Fay, Mrs. Allen's younger sister who had agreed to help with the baby during the summer; and two old ladies that the State was also paying them to house and feed. One of them, Mrs. Minot, must at one time have been fat, for her loose skin hung about her like a drapery. When she arose from a sitting position, I noticed that the back of her dress was always wet, though it wasn't hot enough yet to sweat that much. She had a coarse laugh and a fund of dirty stories. She spotted me as a potential recipient of this largesse and immediately told me about the billy goat who "jumped from precipice to precipice and stopped to piss again." Anna Allen caught my look of embarrassed surprise and smiled. "Don't mind her," she said. "She goes on like that all the time. Something missing upstairs."

Old Mrs. Drury was scrawny and bent and kept her thin hair slicked down with Vaseline. She spoke only when shouted at.

"Where's everybody going to sleep?" I asked Rena, noting the eight people and four mattresses. Their tent was huge, but I still couldn't imagine how everyone and everything could possibly fit in.

"Mummy and Daddy share one mattress, Beryl and I one, the old ladies one, and Charlie has one to himself."

"What about Fay?"

"She goes home at night. She lives with Granny in town and just comes out during the day to take care of the baby."

"What's the baby's name?"

"The Blat. 'Cause it blats all the time."

Next day Allen and Charlie began digging post holes for the new house, and a load of lumber arrived. It was already the last week in June and the house had to be habitable before the frosts came in September. The post holes rapidly filled with water.

"They'll have a hell of a time building the house on that corner of the lot," said Pa. "Should have put it on the high end near the wall, where it's dryer. But Allen's got his own ideas."

The Allens had no water, but the well would have to wait till later. They had no time to dig it themselves, and no money to pay anyone else to do it, so twice a day two of the children appeared at our farmhouse with two large water containers pulled on a home-made hand cart. This pleased me, as it meant that there were no formalities to go through in order to see my new friends. We began spending a great deal of time together, mostly at the Allen's when I was not busy with chores at home. At least when I helped the Allen children with their house-building it was a change of pace, a welcome novelty. And I liked Fay, who arrived daily on the eight o'clock bus out from town.

Fay was only twenty-one—"An afterthought to five other children," said Anna Allen when I commented what a young aunt the girls had. Fay was rectangular in both face and body, with no visible waistline. Like Mrs. Allen she had ruined her hair with a cheap perm, and a mouthful of decayed teeth spoiled an otherwise comely face. "She's too scared to go to the dentist," Beryl confided.

I was horrified at the teeth. I'd never seen a mouth like that on anyone so young. Pa had let his teeth go because he couldn't afford a dentist, but he'd always made sure I went to one regularly. But I forgot Fay's teeth after a while and just took her as she was. She was a kind person, quiet and gentle and always ready to help. She was certainly kind to The Blat. A good thing, too, I thought, since no one else paid the baby the least attention, except to stick the bottle in her mouth when she cried after Fay left in the evening.

"I love babies," said Fay. "I'd like to have one of my own." I made no comment. I thought babies were over-rated.

Mr. Allen was a quick and efficient workman, as were most men in the area. They had to be to survive. He and Charlie had the framework of the house up in a week, though Allen admitted to Pa that he had no more formal training in carpentry than that provided in the manual training course he'd taken in high school years before.

Ma took a quiet interest in the events on our former property, although she was too busy with her own work to do more than look in occasionally with a bag of vegetables or fruit for Anna Allen. Ma was a woman of quick sympathy and could see well enough what her new neighbor was facing that summer.

Though the Allens said little, Ma's concern was noted and appreciated. This became clear in early July when Ma had her "operation." She'd had a lump on her back for several years but had done nothing about it. Couldn't afford unnecessary doctor's bills. But now the lump, which she referred to as a "wen" had become inflamed and nasty looking. Something had to be done. It was foolhardy to risk blood poisoning. So Dr. Murdoch was consulted and he said the wen must go.

He wouldn't put Ma in the hospital, which we couldn't afford anyway; he'd do it at the farm. He arrived as scheduled at ten a.m. "I'll just freeze it with novocaine, slit the top and slip it out," he said as Ma took him through to the bedroom.

He was back out in less than ten minutes with something in his hand. It was white and shiny and looked like a flattened disc of cartilage. "It's just a lipoma—a fatty tumor," he said. "Nothing to worry about. If you throw it on the fire it'll just sizzle and melt."

Pa lifted one of the lids on the top of the stove, and Murdock tossed the glistening lump in. We heard it crackle and spit in the flames.

"I've stitched and dressed the wound, and I'll come back in a week to take out the stitches. Let her rest for today, she'll be right as rain by morning."

So Ma was treated to an unheard-of afternoon in bed, and commented that she should have wens removed more often. Fay, who liked Ma and felt grateful for her interest in The Blat, came up with Beryl in the late afternoon and handed in a pint of ice cream for Ma to have all to herself. An undreamed-of luxury!

44. The Blat

As June turned into July the heat increased, and life in the Allen's tent became nearly unbearable. The heat and the incessant crying of The Blat kept the family from sleeping.

"That kid had better watch it. I eat babies!" Rena commented after a particularly restless night. She said it under her breath so her mother wouldn't hear, but I caught it and laughed. Rena was turning out to be quite a character. Nothing like the shy child she seemed at school.

Swarms of flies invaded the tent, and The Blat and the old ladies stank. "They sit a lot and don't like to wash," Rena explained to me, apparently discounting the fact that there was neither the water nor the privacy in which to bathe.

The Blat was put outside as much as possible to keep the smell down. This helped reduce the problem in the tent, but proved disastrous for The Blat. One day when Fay was away and Rena was left in charge she didn't cover the baby's bare legs, which were soon severely sunburned.

I had no idea how dangerous sunburn could be. I was outdoors constantly from spring onward each year, and my own skin tanned gradually. I'd only experienced the mildest of sunburns. However, I didn't like the look of The Blat's red legs and mentioned it to Ma. She made no comment, but within the hour she suggested casually that we stroll down the road to the Allens with some raspberries for their supper.

Ma sized up the situation in a glance, but said nothing till we got home.

"That baby will die if she's left with those people. Flies over everything, lighting on the nipple of her bottle which is stuck in and out of her mouth continually to try and shut her up, her legs are burned raw and she's feverish. I wouldn't give her a week if she stays there!"

I knew nothing about babies and their proper care. We had screens on our windows and doors at the farm, but no one had explained to me the connection between flies and disease. I just thought flies were a nuisance. I was shocked, but I believed Ma. She seldom spoke, but when she did she never exaggerated.

I had to thin turnips next morning, but in the afternoon I went down the road to the Allen's tent. Allen and Charlie, having finished framing the house, were now boarding in the walls. Beryl was handing up nails and running to and from the piles of building materials on command.

Mrs. Minot was just limping back to the tent from a trip to the two-holer outhouse. She hailed me.

"Peggy, I gotta joke for ya. Did ya hear about the butcher who backed into the meat grinder?"

"No," I said.

"Got a little behind in his work!" She began to cackle like a tickled hen.

I giggled and accompanied her back to the tent, where she joined Mrs. Drury who was sitting outside on a rickety chair.

Inside, I found Mrs. Allen and Rena talking with Fay, who was in tears. Talk stopped when I appeared.

Fay got up, wiping her eyes. "I'll be going," she said. "There's a bus due in five minutes, I'll catch it at McAuley's."

"Are you coming out tomorrow?" asked Rena.

"What for?" said Fay, and left.

"What's the matter with Fay?" I asked. "How come she's leaving so early?"

"She's upset about The Blat," said Rena.

"Why, what's wrong?"

"They took it away."

"Took her away! Who took her away?"

"The State. The inspectors came out and said the tent was no place for a baby."

I was struck dumb, and Rena continued: "They said it was no place for the old ladies either, and they'll be going as soon as the State can find another place for them."

"I don't know how the hell the State thinks we're going to live if they take away our boarders," said Mrs. Allen. "We got $10 a week for each one, so that's $30 a week down the drain. Your Dad isn't bringing in any money while he's putting up the house. What the Christ are we supposed to live on?"

Ma never said that she had called the State Childcare Office, nor did I ask her. You didn't ask Ma questions about important things and expect an answer. But logic dictated the answer. With Ma, to think was to act.

I didn't see Fay again for over a year. Now that The Blat was gone, she no longer visited the tent. Within the week, the old ladies had followed The Blat to other quarters, and Rena told me that Fay had taken a job as a waitress in Wiscasset, a small town near the coast.

As the summer wore on, I spent more and more time with the Allens. They provided me with something which I had lacked before: the opportunity to watch members of a different sort of family interacting with one another.

Unlike our family, the Allens were talkers as well as doers. The talk was often aggressive and the language strong. They constantly picked at one another. No one was free from receiving barbs except Rena, who got at everyone else but who was never picked at in return. Within the family she was the undisputed Princess. Even Charlie deferred to her. She was clearly her father's favorite, and he gave her anything she asked for that he could afford. Which at the moment was nothing, but promises cost no money. Sure, she could have a horse of her own, as soon as they had enough cash.

Charlie was Mrs. Allen's favorite, but of the two girls she always paid more attention to Rena—possibly because Beryl made fewer demands.

I was at a loss to explain Rena's dominance. Of the entire family she seemed the least intelligent, yet she had everyone's number. Even Charlie catered to her moods. If Rena went into a sulk, anything initially refused was always given later.

To my surprise, I found myself deferring too, like everyone else. Rena's will was too strong for me. Even though I liked Beryl better, I kept finding myself aligned with Rena against her in our games of cops and robbers or cowgirls and Indians. I was ashamed of this, and apologized to Beryl later, when we were alone.

"Don't worry," she said, "I know what Rena's like."

Rena fascinated me. I'd had no practice dealing with other children except in the formal setting of school. In Rena I encountered for the first time the strength of will as distinct from the strength of intellect. I knew instinctively that I should resist Rena, but I couldn't seem to make myself do it.

45. The Gathering Storm

Until that autumn, 1939, I was hardly aware of the worsening situation in Europe, except being shown in school a map with the mouth of Germany enclosing the drumstick of Czechoslovakia. Before that, from time to time, I'd heard the ranting voice of Hitler gnashing out his German on the radio, and the elegant, suave voice of Roosevelt with its clear, clean syllables stressed in ways I hadn't heard before.

I had only the vaguest idea of Europe. From geography classes I knew what it looked like on the map, and we'd been taught that all Americans had originally come from there, mostly from the British Isles. We'd had no European history, and I knew nothing of Europe's rivalries and hatreds and wars, except for the Revolution we had fought to get the British off our backs.

Every year we had American History. It was always about the same things. Over and over. Names, battles, dates. Us against the British, us against the French and the Indians. Us against each other, over slavery. I didn't really know what war was, except that we always won.

We also got a few names and dates about who invented what machines for the Industrial Revolution: James Watt and his steam engine. Somebody-or-other and his spinning Jenny. I remembered the names and dates long enough to get an A in the tests and then forgot them.

Then on September 1, 1939, Hitler marched into Poland, and the papers and the radio were full of it. Still, it didn't seem anything to do with me. Or with Rena, Beryl and Charlie. There was talk of it at school, but at home no one spoke of it. Whatever Ma and Pa and the grown-up Allens thought about it, they didn't tell us. It may have been talked about in other children's homes, but not in ours. We all had more immediately pressing concerns.

At the beginning of school, the Allens were still in their tent. Work had gone slower than expected, some of the framing had to be undone and re-done, and now Charlie was at high school from 8 a.m. till half past one.

The high school was in session during those hours to allow children to take afternoon jobs so their families could make ends meet. There was no bus to the country till 2:10, so whether Charlie walked or took the bus it was nearly 2:30 before he could get his hands dirty.

Still, Allen kept insisting that things would be ship-shape enough to move in by October. But Mrs. Allen was getting increasingly tense about the situation. The temperature had plummeted during the last half of August, and in September the frosts set in. The nights under canvas were becoming increasingly uncomfortable.

Rena, Beryl and Charlie didn't seem to mind. To them it was still an adventure, and the girls were out of it until late afternoon anyway. Lincoln school let out at 3:30. There was no bus till 5:10, so they walked back with me. We could do the two and a half miles in forty minutes if we hurried; an hour if we lagged.

Charlie soon reported a growing tension among his high school classmates about the war in Europe.

"Jim Franks' and Adrian Phillips' big brothers have quit school to sign up," he told us when we got back from school about a week after the invasion of Poland had begun. "They're sure America's going to be drawn in and they don't want to miss the fun."

"Fools!" said Anna Allen, who was cutting up vegetables at the sink.

Charlie laughed. "Why stay in school if you can get trained, have a uniform and impress the girls, Ma? There are posters all over town saying 'Join the Navy and see the World' and 'Uncle Sam Wants YOU!'"

Anna snorted but did not comment further.

We girls were too young to to feel the cold breath of war on our necks and paid little attention to what was going on. The war in Europe was as yet having little effect on the farming community.

"It's a tragic and stupid European squabble," said Pa. "Let's hope we keep out of it."

In October, I got my first away-from-home job. Apple picking at the Lees on Saturdays and Sundays. They were short-handed, and I already knew how to handle apples from picking our own trees. Dick came over and checked with Ma and Pa to see if they would be willing to let me, and they were glad to do so.

I loved apple-picking, now even more so since it meant being with the Lees. The weather during the day was warm and golden, and the air was full of the fragrance of McIntosh reds. We each had our own tree to strip, but since the pickers moved through the orchard together we were in easy talking distance. Gracie couldn't climb ladders, nor could Mr. Lee now, so it was usually Dick and me, a couple of young boys from down the hill, and Mr. and Mrs. Harrald. The Harralds lived in a shack on the flat land near Leighton School.

Harrald was French-Canadian—small, lean, with a thin, sharp face and cold, shifty blue eyes. His wife was Indian from some tribe in the north. Her dark face was round and handsome, her eyes large and black. She seldom spoke but observed everything as if life was important to her. Her long black hair was piled onto her head and held in place with a red bandana. Her skinny body and work-hardened hands made her appear older than she probably was.

The Harralds spoke English with us, but French with each other. Harrald was a jack-of-all-trades and had come to the area some time after I left Leighton School. Their four older children, James, Martin, Peter and Mark, had gone through seventh and eighth grades at Leighton and all but James, who was Dick's age, were now in high school. The two little ones, Ted and Tony, were four and three. They came with the Harralds and played quietly beneath the trees. Though Mrs. Harrald was quiet, she radiated warmth and strength, and I liked her. Harrald was more forthcoming, but nothing he had to say seemed to be of much interest.

I had first met the Harralds just after Ted was born. The family had moved into their shack only weeks before, in the depths of winter. After the home birth, which I learned later had not been attended by a doctor, Ma went down to find out if Mrs. Harrald needed help. She took me with her.

The Harrald's shack had only two rooms with an outhouse in the back. Mrs. Harrald was in bed nursing the baby in the main room, which functioned as both a living and a sleeping area. The room was warm and smelled of human milk, human flesh and dirty diapers. A large cast-iron wood-burning stove stood near a chipped enamelled sink at one end of the room. A table, four rickety-looking straight chairs and a piano were the only other furnishings.

I was surprised to see a piano there. It looked out of place with the table and chairs and bed. Having no interest in babies and talk of babies, I asked Mrs. Harrald if I could please try the piano. She smiled at me and said "Oh, *oui, oui,* yes, yes!" so I occupied myself at its keys until Ma was ready to leave. It was badly out of tune and smelled moldy.

Ma kept her eye on Mrs. Harrald and the baby till she was sure she was coping with the bitter weather and the needs of the infant. She did the same thing a year and a half later when Tony was born. She made no comment about either grown-up Harrald in my presence, but I overheard her say to Pa, "That man is a strange one. He makes me nervous. Poor woman."

I knew what she meant. Harrald had seemed odd and furtive to me then, and now at the apple picking he still did, but he was a good fast picker, wasted no time, and the Lees seemed to like him.

By the end of October the apple picking was finished, and I ended my job satisfied that I had done it well, earned my ten cents an hour, and the Lees were pleased with me.

Because of the war in Europe the munitions factories were girding themselves for action that fall, and the shipyards were coming to life. The last week of October, Allen applied for work in the shipyard at Bath, and was taken on at a wage he would never have dreamed possible. The house, now boarded in and water-tight, was left hanging and the well remained undug as he began leaving at six a.m. in the pick-up and returning twelve hours later.

After his first week, he came to see Pa, with his wage voucher in his hand. "Come with me, Shirley," he urged. "I've made a down-payment on a new car with a back seat and a proper heater so we won't freeze to death when winter sets in. It'll be available next week. They're desperate for trained men, and with your journeyman plumber's license they'll welcome you with open arms."

"Don't know as I could stand it," said Pa. "I quit plumbing because of my heart and the trouble with my legs. We've had to get rid of the farm animals, and my mother and Peggy have been carrying most of the load of what's left. But Jesus, how we need the money!"

"Give it a try," said Allen. "Come with me on Monday and talk to them."

Pa went, and came home grinning like a gargoyle. "I think I can do it," he said. "I had a talk with Allen's boss. They can put me on a fairly light job with a helper to do the heavy lifting. I can start as soon as I can produce a birth certificate to prove I ain't a German spy. Christ, I don't know how I'm going to do that, they didn't issue birth certificates when I was born. Allen's boss suggested that I write the Town Clerk in Woodland and see what he can do."

The Town Clerk was most helpful and found several solid citizens of Pa's generation to attest that Pa had been born in Woodland on June 17, 1879. This satisfied the shipyard, and Pa began the long daily trek with Allen and two other local men in Allen's new car. He found the work utterly exhausting, but gritted his teeth and said nothing. Now we could eat without guilt. Nevertheless, Ma and I noted that he took to his bed earlier and earlier each night until he was going off soon after supper.

Since no major work could be expected on the house until spring, the Allens moved into their shell of a dwelling and commenced the job of making the three downstairs rooms habitable and cold-proof. One room held an old wood-burning stove and provided the day quarters. The second room, divided by a curtain, slept Rena and Beryl on one side and Charlie on the other. The third room slept Mr. and Mrs. Allen. The stove was supposed to provide enough heat for the main room and sufficient overflow to take the chill off the bedrooms. Although the cellar was unfinished and flooded, Allen had built the floor of the house clear of the ground because of the wet, and the air space would provide some insulation—he claimed.

Mrs. Allen didn't believe it. She'd known Allen too long. "It'll be cold as the hocks of hell," she predicted. "And no water. Do you realize those kids'll have to make two trips a day up to the Shaw's through ice and snow all winter to keep us in water?"

"Never mind, Anna," said Allen. "I'm making enough to give you and the kids a whole new wardrobe and new warm blankets for the beds. You can throw out all that old stuff. We're rich! Rena can have her horse in the spring!"

"Rich my ass," said Mrs. Allen as she wrestled with the ash blocking the grate of the stove. "I'm sick of this whole shittin' match!"

The new clothes and blankets were bought, along with a new set of dishes and pots and pans, and the old quilts were hung on the walls to keep out the drafts. During the day, at least, with the stove going, things might be just bearable.

46. Winter 1939-1940

Winter came with uncommon severity in November that year. The ponds froze solid to the bottom, and by Thanksgiving three feet of snow lay on the ground. Rena, Beryl and I threw ourselves into the delights of the Maine winter. Charlie, though he pretended to consider girls beneath his notice, was more than willing to join us in this.

First, I introduced them to skating. Allen had treated his three to their first pairs of skates, and we headed for the nearest sheet of ice, each of us bearing a snow shovel. At the boundary where the Lees' land adjoined the Connors farm, a dirt track ran up to an abandonned granite quarry in the forest. We called it "Lees' Quarry" because it was surrounded by Lees' woods, but the Lees didn't own it—it belonged to the granite company.

I hadn't taken the Allen children to the quarry before, and on the way up the track in hip-deep snow I told them what I knew of its history.

When I was five, the quarry was still in operation. One of the quarry workers, a young, sun-tanned Italian named Fantini, was living for the summer with his wife and baby in a log cabin beside the quarry. He had married Sarah, a Protestant girl, against her family's wishes and they had disowned her.

Ma was worried about Sarah and her new baby in such primitive conditions. The cabin had no well, and drinking water had to be brought up from the Connors, as quarry water was only fit for bathing. Ma and I used to go up often to see Sarah and the baby, and Sarah sometimes wheeled the baby down to the farm to see us. It was uncertain what they would do or where they would live when winter came.

In the end, that problem never arose. One of Fantini's teeth, which he had neglected for too long, ulcerated. By the time the pain drove him to a dentist he was already running a fever, and within a week he was dead of blood poisoning. Sarah's family took her and the baby in, and the quarry hadn't been worked since.

"That's so sad," said Beryl. "That poor girl." The story had stopped us in our tracks and we were leaning on our shovels.

"Helen Connors says that Fantini still works the quarry," I said. "Sometimes, early on still, sunny mornings she hears the clang of his mallet on the stone."

Beryl shivered. Charlie laughed nervously. Rena's sleepy eyes went wide, but she said nothing.

I had never heard Fantini's mallet clang since he died—but I liked to tell Helen's story.

We continued on up the track and finally came to the deserted cabin. It was almost completely buried in snow, and heavily laden branches from the giant cedar behind it leaned on the roof. The door, when we dug in and tried to open it, was frozen shut.

"We won't get in there till spring," I said. "Come on, the quarry's just ahead."

The quarry was a sheer cliff of stone with ledges where blocks of granite had been blasted off. At the bottom, where rain-water had collected, lay a pond, frozen solid and covered with a deep blanket of snow. At one end, a large hump rose above water level.

"What's that?" asked Charlie.

"The wreck of a Model T Ford, half under water. It's been there for several years and no one knows where it came from. Pa says someone must have driven it up here and deliberately run it into the pond, but nobody ever reported it missing."

"Did they find a body in it?" asked Charlie.

I'd never thought of that possibility. A shiver ran up my spine.

"I never heard that they did," I said.

Ma and Pa wouldn't have told me of course. But surely the Lees—or someone—would have mentioned it.

174

We got our shovels working and uncovered the Model T first. Its back end protruded forlornly above the ice, but not much was visible except the spare tire fastened to the back and the framework of the black canvas roof. We turned our attention to clearing the ice. Fortunately it had frozen hard before it had begun to snow, so its surface was smooth and inviting.

Our fingers were numb with cold, but we managed to struggle into our skates. "Be sure to get them laced tight at the ankles," I advised. "Otherwise you won't have enough support to skate properly."

The Allens had never skated before and pushed off onto the ice cautiously. The woods soon rang with the hilarity of learning, as their feet went unbidden in opposite directions and they landed in undignified positions. Our ankles were weak and wobbly, and our toes congealed in the sub-zero temperatures, though our bodies were warm enough with our efforts to keep ourselves upright. When we had finished, exhausted, we transferred our feet to the sheepskin slippers which we all wore inside our four-buckle rubber overshoes. This contact with sheep's wool soon thawed our feet and prevented frostbite.

Next day I took the Allens for another "first"—skiing. I had demonstrated what could be done on the little hill behind the Lees' barn, and the ever-willing Allen then provided them with the necessary equipment.

My first pair of skis had been barrel staves fitted by Pa with thongs when I was five. On my sixth birthday he had given me a pair of second-hand real skis, which were traded for larger ones as I grew.

After an initial practice on the little hill, I took Rena, Beryl and Charlie, fumbling and slipping, through the deep snow to the big hill on the other side of the quarry. Here they gradually lost their fear of height and gained balance. We could exert little control on direction. We simply started at the top and went straight down, wind howling in our ears. Skiing had not yet become a leisure industry for the rich, and our skis were held onto our four-buckle overshoes by a leather thong over the instep. The thong was anchored in place by a jar rubber placed around the toe and anchored behind the heel.

The first time down the hill was slow in the deep snow, but once the trail had been broken and packed hard with use, we went like lightning. The only way to get up the hill again was to "herringbone" up, ski tails together, points spread at a wide angle, weight on the inner edges to get purchase on the snow. It was hard work, and as the weeks passed our leg and abdominal muscles hardened like steel.

We kept at it on weekends and in the twilight hours after school, even going back for more after supper on moonlit nights. Afterwards, we would go up to the Lees' barn where Dick was doing evening chores and warm our tingling hands on the belly of a cow.

If there had been a fresh fall of snow, we would go back to my house and make snow ice cream by mixing fresh heavy cream, Hershey's chocolate syrup, vanilla extract and sugar into a bucket of snow. I've never tasted ice cream since that could match it.

As our skill on skis increased, we built ski jumps by packing snow over existing rocks, and soon got used to the feeling of being airborne.

Finally I decided the Allens were ready for the short-cut trail through the woods. It was steep and bumpy with trees in inconvenient places. Luckily our bones were young, and bent rather than broke.

Dick Lee watched us go shooting past his logging team one day on our way to the big hill and yelled at us, "Come on over Sunday afternoon and I'll take you ski-joring." When questioned, he would not elaborate. "You'll see," he said.

When Sunday came he saddled Ricky and attached a heavy rope to the back of his saddle. "You four grab holt of the rope, one in back of the other, and hang on," he directed, then galloped the horse flat out. Of course we all fell off, but kept re-attaching ourselves until a workable order of precedence was discovered: The one with the least balance, which was Rena, went on the end of the rope; the others ahead of her in increasing order of skill so that the first to fall would not knock off the rest.

By the Christmas vacation we were all proficient skiers, and were doing backward figure eights on skates.

In spite of the joys of snow and ice, it was a bleak Christmas for both the Shaws and the Allens.

Pa was finally forced to give up work at the shipyard. He'd been going on his nerve since the beginning, and one night in mid-November he came home and collapsed and could not rise from the bed. I could see his heart pounding through his shirt. Ma phoned Dr. Murdoch. He listened to Pa's chest, took his blood pressure, poked and probed.

"You'll have to cut out the shipyard. No question. Otherwise you'll kill yourself," he said. "I'll give you a prescription which you're to take regularly without fail, and you're to stay in bed until I tell you to get up. It's all I can do for you, the rest is up to you. Do you understand?"

"Yeah," said Pa.

After the first few days when his exhaustion had lifted a little Pa was bored and restless, so I spent the evenings playing Parcheesi, poker, shipwreck or gin rummy with him. Then on Christmas day the whole Allen family appeared at our farmhouse to give him the newest game out: Chinese checkers. We played several games on the spot to learn how to play. For the rest of the winter I played Chinese checkers with Pa till I dreamed of triangles full of marbles in my sleep.

Luckily, Ma's health had improved slightly over the preceding summer and she did not fall ill that winter. If she had, I can't imagine what we would have done.

Life was hard for the Allens, too, that winter. Only the area directly around the wood stove in the kitchen was warm, and at night the temperature in the bedrooms was cruel. I told them about heating short lengths of wood in the oven to use as bed-warmers. This helped, but only part of the night. The wood held the heat until past midnight, but the early mornings were grim. Charlie suffered the most, as he was the only one without a sleeping companion. A dog was provided to take care of this, and carefully de-fleaed before being allowed between the sheets. She was a half-grown mongrel named Susy that one of the neighboring farmers wanted rid of. She had a sweet disposition and at once attached herself to Charlie, who claimed the privilege of feeding her.

The Allens still continued to fetch water from us, though during the time Rena had whooping cough the children were not allowed to see me. After the first few days Rena was not kept in bed, but she whooped for weeks—longer than necessary, Charlie implied. Whooping cough wasn't normally considered dangerous—not like scarlet fever, diphtheria, rheumatic fever or T.B.—but a child in Manchester had died of it, and Ma and Pa didn't want me exposed.

No immunizing jabs except smallpox vaccinations were given in school. About all the school nurse did when she came around was weigh and measure us and send notes home to the parents of those who were underweight. Those children were to receive free milk at school every morning.

I was lean but strong and never ill, now that the terrors of the country school were behind me, but since I was found to be twenty pounds under weight I qualified for the milk—and chocolate milk on Fridays! The Allens, even thinner than I, qualified as well.

In spite of a hearty breakfast, by mid-morning when the free milk was brought out I was ravenous. I drank it eagerly, even though it was pasteurized and didn't measure up to milk fresh from the cow. The children who didn't qualify for milk looked on enviously, especially on Fridays when we got chocolate milk. I felt we were the lucky ones.

Once the nurse gave us all tuberculin patch tests to see if we had been exposed to tuberculosis. Several times I'd heard T.B. referred to as "the white death." Bed rest and fresh air were the only prescriptions, and the sanatoria were full of the dying. It was the most dreaded of all diseases, hanging in the background like a pale cloud, ready to engulf the unlucky.

47. Maisie

By the end of February, Dr. Murdoch allowed Pa to get up from his bed, but with a warning to restrict his activities very carefully until summer.

As if to make up for the wicked winter, spring came early that year. By mid-March the snow, which usually lay until mid-April, began to break up, and our skiing and skating activities tapered off. It was time to turn our minds toward warmer pursuits.

My venture into apple picking for the Lees the autumn before paid off in the spring. I suspect the Lees were aware of our financial plight and were glad to make an arrangement that would be helpful to both our families. Mrs. Lee approached Ma about my giving her a hand in the milk room for a couple of hours on Saturday and Sunday mornings.

"Caring for Mr. Lee is taking up more and more of Mrs. Lee's time and energy," Ma explained to me. "With your help she could cut the time of her milk room duties in half. She'll pay you twenty-five cents an hour, which is about the same as you make berry picking. Would you like to do that?"

"Oh yes, Ma, I'd love that," I said. Any excuse to see more of the Lees was welcome.

"In the summer, after school is out, they'll have other jobs besides the milk-room work you can do for them if you'd like—weeding, thinning vegetables, picking fruit, perhaps helping with the horses. Since our own farm work has been cut to the bone, there won't be as much for you to do here any more. Working for the Lees will give you the spending money that we can't afford."

This was sounding better and better.

Maisie Lee had always been one of my favorite people: cheerful, sharp, interested in everything and everyone, and always on the move. I don't recall her sitting down in all the years of my childhood, except at Harriet's wedding. Even when the family was seated for a meal, she always seemed to be on her feet serving food.

Maisie appreciated the droll or funny side of everything, her laugh always at the ready. It was never snide or cruel or needling, but the laugh of one who loved living and loved the world and took people as they came. She passed this on to her children—her vibrancy, her interest, her humor, her genuine good will. But I had never really got to know Maisie. In her busy life there had never been chunks of idle time in which to talk with a neighbor's child.

The following Saturday I began work. The hours were to be eight to ten in the morning. When I arrived, Dick had already been out on the milk route for some time. I found Maisie in the milk room, her masses of curly grey hair swept up into a "pug" on top of her head.

I'd been in the milk room many times before when I came for milk during periods when we had no cow. Maisie would raise the heavy lid of the milk cooler, a long white wooden chest that ran the length of one wall, and get out the milk I had asked for.

Inside, the cooler was lined with galvanized metal. It held ice water deep enough to come up around the necks of the milk bottles. Several blocks of ice lay half submerged in the water to keep the temperature at the freezing point. Milk was brought fresh from the cow, bottled, and placed there to be kept cool until Dick took it off on his milk route.

Along two other walls were racks with drip pans beneath for drying pails and bottles, and along the fourth wall was a long, deep sink with three compartments.

That first morning Maisie had already filled the three tubs with chemical solutions. She greeted me, then began explaining what we were about to do and why.

"Luckily, the law doesn't require heat sterilization, so we haven't had to invest in expensive equipment. We couldn't have afforded that," she told me. "But we're very carefully and frequently inspected. Our milk business is one of the few still allowed to sell unpasteurized milk, and there's a strict routine we must go through to make sure it's safe. The herd has to be regularly tuberculin tested, the cowbarn kept clean, and the cows' udders swabbed down with disinfectant before milking."

"Why do you have to do all that, Mrs. Lee. What would happen if you didn't?"

"Several diseases can be caught by drinking contaminated milk, Peggy. Cows' milk itself is sterile, but it's very easily contaminated by germs from cow manure on the cow's udder, which can get on the hands of whoever does the milking. Pasteurization kills any germs that get into the milk, so most milk on the market is pasteurized. Our milk isn't pasteurized, so we have to be extra careful and clean in our milking habits. Everything that comes in contact with the milk, such as pails and bottles, must be sterilized."

"What kind of things can you catch from milk, Mrs. Lee?"

"Anything from mild stomach upsets to undulant fever and tuberculosis."

"T.B.?" I asked, aghast. "Do cows have T. B.?"

"Cows carry bovine tuberculosis, a kind that can affect not only the lungs but any part of the body—bones, kidneys, anything. Have you noticed the little metal clips in our cows' ears, Peggy?"

"Yes, what are they for?"

179

"So many people, especially children, were dying of bovine tuberculosis that a law was passed that all cows must be tested and certified free of it. The cows wear metal clips on their ears to prove to the inspectors that this has been done. T. B. isn't as prevalent now as it was because of this. There's no cure for T. B. except rest, fresh air and luck, so milk businesses like ours which sell raw milk are carefully watched."

I was fascinated by this. I'd gathered little separate bits of information about germs causing disease. I knew germs from boils could spread to different parts of one's body, and germs could get into cuts or into bad teeth and cause blood poisoning, and that you could catch some diseases if infected people breathed on you, but this was all very disconnected. I hadn't realized that milk could be dangerous. Could Edna Townsend, who died in our house, have caught her tuberculosis from cow's milk?

"No," said Maisie when I asked her. "She got T. B. of the lungs from someone she roomed with at college. But here, Peggy, the three tubs of solutions are waiting for us to get going. I'll show you how. Another time I'll show you how to mix the solutions, but today you'll just help me at the sink. I'll give you a pair of rubber gloves to put on. You'll need them to keep the chemicals off your skin."

I'd never seen rubber gloves. Before she handed them to me, Maisie sprinkled some white powder into them and shook them around. "That's cornstarch," she explained. "It will keep your hands from sticking to the inside of the gloves and make them easier to get on and off."

The gloves fit tightly. The cornstarch felt smooth and cool, but even with that I had to work my hands into them carefully.

"What do I do now?" I asked.

"We'll wash the milk pails first, so they'll be finished by the time Dick brings the empty bottles back from the milk route. I'll scrub out the pails in this first solution, then hand them to you. Rinse them thoroughly in each tub and set them upside down on the rack."

She demonstrated the whole procedure with one pail, then scrubbed another and handed it to me. I plunged the pail into the second tub and got busy. The chemicals had an odd, sharp, metallic smell, but it was not unpleasant, and I soon got used to it.

We hadn't quite finished the pails when Dick appeared, bearing wire baskets full of empty bottles. He grinned when he saw me. "Welcome aboard," he said. "Guess you're going to be mighty helpful to us from now on."

Through my work in the milk room, I began to learn more about the world I lived in and to understand some of the things everyone else seemed to know except me.

The situation in Europe had been becoming steadily more dangerous, Maisie said. The feeling was growing that a catastrophe was about to happen there. She explained to me that, although America was still a neutral nation, Congress had repealed the arms embargo in November. This allowed the sale of American munitions to the Allied Powers on a cash and carry basis.

The German push into Scandinavia began early in April, and Denmark fell the week after I started work. The Lees, unlike our other neighbors, had a strong, direct interest in what was happening in Europe because of their son Bob. He had graduated from West Point in 1931 and had been rising rapidly in the Army Air Corps, which would separate from the Army to become the U. S. Air Force. No one realized then that soon Brigadier General Bob Lee would be Deputy to the General directing the European Operations of the 9th Air Force.

The Lees had a copy of *Mein Kampf* and had long suspected what was coming. I could just remember, as a smaller child, hearing Hitler on the radio, giving a speech in German. I had never heard of him before and had no idea what he was doing, but the sound of his voice barking out in that strange gutteral tongue had made the hair rise on my neck.

Now, from Maisie, who was willing to talk with me about it, I learned something of the background of Hitler's rise to power. She told me many things as the German armies occupied Norway, swarmed across the Netherlands and Belgium, pressed on to the Channel ports to rout the British Expeditionary Force at Dunkirk, then turned south to cut the French army to pieces. On the 10th of June, Mussolini entered the war and Paris fell five days later.

It was an enlightening and stimulating time for one who had been kept as sheltered and as ignorant as I. The information now coming to me from Maisie was not confined to the European war. Though that was often the topic of our conversations, she told me much else of interest as well.

The Lees subscribed to *Readers Digest* and *Life* magazine, and Maisie was always telling me of some marvelous or incredible or just plain interesting article she had been reading. She sometimes let me borrow a magazine to read and return.

My family subscribed to no magazines, and never spoke of world or national events. Ma read women's magazines brought by Mrs. Cony. Pa's reading was mostly the daily *Kennebec Journal*, about which he made no comment, and *Western Story Magazine*, which he or Fred would pick up at the Shell Station down the road.

Maisie, in contrast, was interested in everything from the smallest insect or tiniest flower on up to the stars, and delighted in expressing this interest.

As the weeks passed, she also told me, a bit at a time, the story of the Lees' life on their farm. Mel brought her there in 1909, just after they married. He'd bought the farm with what he'd earned in the previous five years of dawn-to-dusk hard labor on someone else's farm. Now it would be more years of dawn-to-dusk hard labor on his own land, with no let-up.

His 200 acres were mostly woods, and Mel had to claim his fields from stony New England by sweat of brow. He and a hired man cut down trees, hauled out stumps and roots and dug rocks out of the thin soil with pick and crowbar. They hooked two horses to a wheelless drag, piled on the rocks and took them to where they would build dry stone walls between the fields.

It was at that time that Mel first met Charlie Fifield, the meat man. Charlie was toothless, and leather-lunged from self-rolled Prince Albert Tobacco fags. He came on Wednesdays with his horse-drawn meat cart to the farms along the dirt road from Augusta to Manchester where Lee had settled. He passed the Lees' rocky meadow, saw the drag and the flying pickaxes, and decided to stop and watch operations. Grinning like a toothless skull, he dragged on his brown-paper fag and called out:

"Got pwenty o' wocks and woots, en't ye, Mr. Wee?"

Mel had to admit that Charlie was quite right.

The Lees' first two children appeared in quick succession, Bob in 1910 and Harriet in 1911—the same year as my brother Lynde. Gracie was born in 1914, and Dick in 1919. The milk room was very much part of these events:

"Dick was born in the milk room," Maisie told me one day. "In fact, all my children were. It used to be our bedroom—the warmest one in the house, just off the kitchen. When Dick went to school and the teacher asked the children where they were born, meaning what town or village or state, Dick piped up and said, "I was born in the milk room.""

As I was now twelve and had reached what Maisie considered a suitable age for the enlightenment of a girl, she enlarged on the milk room story by telling me of the introduction of anesthetics for use in childbirth, and what a blessing it had been. Bob, Harriet and Gracie had been difficult, painful births. With Dick, the doctor had let her sniff ether. She told me that after Dick's painless emergence she had wept with gratitude as she thanked the doctor.

The Lees had not been spared tragedy. The first one occurred in 1924, before my birth, and it happened to Gracie. The whole family had felt off-color, and had cold-like symptoms, but only Gracie developed full-blown polio. The family and the farm community waited anxiously as she battled for her life.

The Lees' milk business, which could not be run from their quarantined house, was quietly taken over by my family, then composed of Ma, Pa and his first wife Florence. They took the necessary equipment to our farm and carried on until the crisis was past and the quarantine lifted.

Thankfully, Gracie's handicap, though a life-long impediment for her, had not involved her breathing. There were no iron lungs in the 1920's. She was left with deformed hands (with which she nevertheless became an excellent piano player) and a stiff right leg. The nerves to the tendon in her knee had been destroyed, so she had to walk stiff-legged and use a cane to avoid falling.

Never did I hear Gracie issue one word of complaint. Maisie told me Gracie was the same with her family. She had inherited, by gene and by example, Maisie's amazing cheerfulness and resilience.

The second tragedy was Mel Lee's illness. By the time I began working in the milk room, he was already suffering from the disease that eventually killed him. But because of the courage and cheerfulness of the whole family, it did not poison their family life any more than Gracie's illness and its aftermath had. Yet as Mel grew worse, the load fell heaviest on Maisie and Dick. Harriet and Bob were already away from home, and Gracie's range of activity, though she did everything she could, was limited.

Mel's illness began when I was seven or eight, and progressed slowly. Although I knew he was ill, I'd heard no details until Maisie told me.

He'd begun having trouble milking his cows. He couldn't close his fingers around the teats properly, and he was losing strength. He thought it might be the early onset of arthritis. Then he began having trouble keeping his footing. It was difficult to pick up his feet, and he kept stumbling. Neurological examinations resulted in a diagnosis of Parkinson's disease, something no one in the neighborhood had ever heard of.

Several theories were current in medical circles at the time: It might be chemical poisoning from the spray farmers used for their apple trees. Since many people who developed Parkinson's had a history of influenza in the 1918 epidemic, perhaps there was a link there. Did apparent recovery take place when the virus went dormant, only to cause trouble later on? No one knew.

Not only did I learn about the Lee family during my milk room sessions, I also learned about my own—an unexpected bonus. Since Mrs. Lee's revelation, when I was five, that Ma was not my mother, she had never mentioned the matter. Why had I never asked her about it? This puzzles me. Perhaps I thought it would be rude, or that she, like Ma, would refuse to talk about it. I lacked the imagination to realize that if she knew Ma was not my mother she must have known who was, and what had happened to her.

When I found out from Rita that Mother had died on our farm along with Grandfather, my first thought should have been to check out what she had told me with Maisie, but this possibility never occurred to me. I was desperate for information, but I had been kept in the dark so totally all my life that I was convinced certain information was off bounds and not to be inquired about.

Now that contact with Maisie was a weekly occurrence, the subject came up naturally. Something Maisie told about one of their farm cats amused me. She noted this, and said, "You know Peggy, when you look up at me and smile like that, you're very like your mother."

"Did you know my mother?" I asked, surprised.

"Of course I knew your mother. She lived across the road from us!"

"Oh," I said.

"Haven't your father and grandmother told you anything about her?"

"Not much, except that she died when I was a baby. I didn't know that she and my grandfather died on the same day at the farm until Aunt Rita told me last summer."

Mrs. Lee shook her head. She looked stunned. "Well, I'll tell you a bit more," she said. "Your mother was a kind and wonderful woman, and I was pleased to have her for a neighbor."

Just then Gracie came into the milk room to get milk from the cooler for a customer who would be coming by for it. She entered just in time to hear what her mother was saying.

"Oh Peggy, I just loved your mother!" she said. "She was so kind and beautiful and full of fun. She always made me feel like a princess! I remember one time she came over for something and I was wearing a yellow dress Mother had made me. She stopped and gave me such a pleased look. 'Gracie,' she said 'yellow is your color. It's lovely with your dark hair and eyes. You must wear it often!'"

Mrs. Lee laughed. "I remember that," she said. "Gracie wore that dress until it was in tatters."

An image of Gracie in the long yellow dress she wore at Harriet's wedding flashed across my mind. "She was right," I said. "You looked lovely when Harriet got married."

Gracie flushed with pleasure. At that moment a knock sounded at the kitchen door. "That'll be Mr. Cross after his milk," she said, and went off with the bottles.

Why hadn't I realized it before? Of course the Lees all knew my mother. But for how long? I had no idea.

"Mrs. Lee—how long did my mother live across the street?" I asked.

Maisie straightened up from the tub and thought for a minute. "Just under three years. She came here to live in September, 1925, and she died in August, 1928."

"So you must have known her quite well?"

Maisie hesitated. "I knew her as a good neighbor and as a kind and lovely person. I didn't know her as long or as well as I knew your father's family, of course. They had been here much longer."

Gracie, who had finished dealing with the customer, returned and joined the conversation again.

"Your mother was so bright and sparkly. She used to look up at your father, who was taller than she, and smile at him. He'd just glow when she did that. You could tell he adored her. Your father was such a handsome man, Peggy, with those warm blue eyes."

This surprised me. I'd never thought of Pa, old as he was now, as handsome, he was just Pa—thin, gaunt and lined, looking rather ill, and his nose was crooked.

"Was he?" I asked. Maisie and Gracie exchanged glances. "Yes, he was, very," said Maisie. "But he aged ten years when your mother died. He's had a lot of ill health since. And he fell and broke his nose. He never bothered to have it reset."

"And he kept trying to straighten his curly hair and finally succeeded," said Gracie. "What a shame, it was so nice!"

"Wish I'd inherited his hair," I said. "I hate mine, it's straight and awful. Did my mother have curly hair?"

"Yes, but I'm not sure if it was naturally curly or if she used a curling iron," said Maisie.

Dick arrived just then with the bottles, so the conversation turned to other things.

Again my world had changed. Now I had a clearer picture of my mother than even Rita's pictures had given me. The woman in those pictures had looked old and tired at forty-four. Her flesh had gone slack, and her arms, coming out of her sleeves, were flabby. The picture the Lees painted was quite different, was of someone bright and joyful whom I'd have liked to know.

That was on a Sunday, so a week intervened before I had a chance to ask Maisie more about my mother. She must have been thinking about our conversation too, for she brought it up herself.

"Did you know, Peggy, that I took care of you for a few days after your mother died?"

"No," I said, surprised.

"When your mother and grandfather died on that terrible afternoon twelve years ago it shook everyone to the bone. Your father had to make arrangements for your mother and grandfather to be taken to Melrose for the funeral and burial. Your whole family went down there, but they didn't want to risk taking you, a tiny baby, on such a trip, so I offered to bring you over here and take care of you while they were away.

"Your mother had breast fed you—you'd never been near a bottle. I had to wean you—and believe me, you didn't like it. You were one upset baby. But we managed. And when the family came back, your grandmother took over from me."

I'd always loved the Lees, but it was now that I began to wish I had been born into their family, that Maisie Lee was my mother, and that Dick, Gracie, Harriet and Bob were my brothers and sisters.

48. Bicycles

As spring progressed, Pa was feeling better, and of course was trying to take on more than he should. He seemed to be at least as well as he had been before going to work at the shipyard and mumbled something about going back. Ma and I told him he would return there over our dead bodies. He'd managed to save enough to keep us going through the summer and the following winter if we were careful, and then perhaps we could sell another house lot. People were beginning to have money again, now that the long Depression was lifting, and new houses were starting to spring up in the area.

As soon as the snow was off the ground, Allen and Charlie resumed work on their house at weekends, and arrangements were made with a town firm to drill a well as soon as the earth was frost-free.

It was lucky that Ron Allen had built his house clear of the ground. As the snow melted, true to Pa's prediction water collected around it, temporarily forming a muddy pond. No one without knee boots could get near the place, and the pick-up, Allen's new car and Charlie's bicycle had to be kept on higher ground near the road. The mud, of course, got tracked into the house, and Mrs. Allen's already flavorful vocabulary ripened in variety and vigor.

Maisie Lee laughed when she heard about the Allen's pond, and showed me a picture in *Life* magazine of houses in Central America that had been built on stilts at the edge of lakes. "The Allens are becoming Lake Dwellers," she said.

By the end of April the water drained away and the mud receded. Rena, Beryl and Charlie appeared at my door early one Saturday afternoon, each in control of a gleaming new bicycle, just bought at Augusta Hardware. Charlie had been the only one of the three to have a bike before—a cheap skeletal thing with no frills and chipped paint. His new one was sleek and fast, bright red with white stream-lines painted on, and a flat metal shelf at the back for carrying his gear.

Ron Allen had bought girls' bikes for Rena and Beryl. The frame above the pedals sloped down to accommodate skirts, and was sturdier than Charlie's to compensate for the lack of a cross bar. Their bikes were royal blue and had no stream-line stripes.

Rena and Beryl had learned to ride on Charlie's old bike, so the three had pedaled up to show me their new acquisitions. I marvelled at the elegance of design and the gleaming paint work.

"We'll be able to go all over on these," said Rena. "No more walking or waiting for Dad to drive us somewhere."

"Mummy says we can take them to school in spring and fall when there's no ice and snow," said Beryl.

"Peggy, how'd you like to buy my old bicycle?" asked Charlie. "You can have it for five dollars, and then you can come with us up to the reservoir to swim, or out to Lake Cobbossee, or in town to the movies."

In a flash I saw freedom spreading out before me. Now that Fred had gone, our family was totally dependent on the bus and on our feet. But with a bike . . .

I'd had a tricycle, but had never been on a bike in my life. Still, it should be easy enough to learn to ride one. I'd already saved $3 out of my milk room money.

"Can I give you $3 down and the rest in two weeks, Charlie?" I asked.

"Sure," he said. "Come on down with us now and you can take it home."

"I don't know how to ride yet."

"We'll show you. Come on. Sit on the carrier at the back of my new bike and hang onto me and I'll give you a ride down."

Not only didn't I know how to control a bike, but I'd never ridden as a passenger either. I did as Charlie suggested and hung on tight. I was amazed at how fast we covered the ground between our houses.

Now it was the Allens' turn to teach me something, and Charlie proved to be a natural teacher. First, he adjusted the seat to my height and demonstrated how to mount the bike and then balance it by putting my toes down on each side.

"Now you've got the feel of that, put your right foot on the pedal and push off with your left," he said, and demonstrated.

I tried it and fell flat, of course. We all laughed, and I kept at it until I got the feel.

"Okay, I see what I'm supposed to do," I said. "I'll push it home and practice on the driveway."

Pa was just emerging from the stable as I came wheeling the bike into the yard. He stopped short and stared.

"Where'd you get that?" he asked.

I told him about my financial deal with Charlie. The deal didn't bother him, but the bike did.

"Bicycles are dangerous, Peggy. I don't want you out on the road with that thing."

"But Pa, I'll be careful. I won't go on the road till I know how to control it. And just think, now that it's good weather I can take it to school. I won't have to walk home any more."

"You will not take it to school. You are not to take that thing in town at all! Town traffic is dangerous. It's bad enough out here, especially on weekends when every fool on the road is doing sixty miles an hour between here and Manchester. The cops have been setting up speed traps to try and control it, but they can't be everywhere."

"All right, Pa, I'll just go on the back roads. We can explore a lot of places on back roads."

"Let me look at that thing," he said. He examined it minutely. "Well, in spite of its looks it's not in bad shape," he admitted. "The frame isn't bent, the wheels aren't warped, and everything's put together right. But don't take it off this property until you can control it perfectly, you understand?"

"Yes, Pa, I promise. I'll go practice."

"Show me what you've learned."

I mounted and wobbled off, only managing to go about six feet without losing balance.

Pa laughed. "It'll be a while before you're on the road," he said, and left me to it.

I practiced going up the drive past the house, around the curve at the top of the raspberry patch, and down the other side past Fred's bungalow to the road, then back up around the drive to where I started. Within a couple of days Pa agreed that I could go back and forth on the road between us and the Allens. But no further.

I didn't tell Pa about my one near catastrophe while I'd been practicing. I'd gone up the grass track through the fields as far as the wood road, then back down to the farm. The last part of the track was fairly steep and I'd become over-confident. When I was half way down I realized I was headed straight for a log sticking out into the track on one side. I was going too fast to swerve before I hit it. The bike and I struck the log and flew over it. I got bruised and lost some skin, but miraculously the bike was stronger than it looked and showed no signs of damage.

Pa kept a sharp eye on me and soon began to relax a bit. On Saturday and Sunday afternoons the Allens and I began exploring back roads and soon became familiar with local fields, copses, brooks and potential swimming holes. One day we went down the dirt road past Leighton School further than we'd ever been before. We came upon a steep hill, at the bottom of which was an old grain mill with a water wheel perched on the side of a stream. We'd never seen anything like it, and were delighted.

"Oh, you got as far as the Bond Brook Mill, did you," said Pa when we got back. "it's still a working mill, the oldest one around."

At the end of May, a different kind of mount became available to the Allens—the horse that Allen had promised Rena. He was specifically Rena's, and she absolutely had first call, but she was to give the others time on him. His name was Petey, and the weather was now warm enough for him to stay outside. Allen and Charlie would build a snug stable for him during the summer.

Petey was a tall, well-built creature with a shiny brown coat and a white forelock. Pa had gone with Allen and Rena to look at suitable specimens, and had helped them select a gentle, well-trained older animal with a smooth, even gait.

I undertook to teach the Allens how to ride. I was eager to pass on what Dick Lee had taught me.

"It's easy enough once you learn to post," I explained. "When you've mastered that, you won't feel like you're going to be thrown off every time he breaks into a trot. And he's got a lovely canter and gallop. You won't have any trouble with those."

Pa and I kept a careful watch on the situation to make sure that the Allens, inexperienced in animal care, did the right things for Petey.

49. Haying

When school recessed for the summer, my commitment at the Lees expanded. At first, my outdoor duties were confined to garden work: weeding, thinning, hand cultivating, harvesting. Helping with the haying was a delight which I had not expected. Dick and his father had originally done the haying, together with whatever odd assortment of local boys were available, but now Mel Lee was housebound and other help was sometimes hard to find. A minimum of three men was needed to get in a load of hay. I'd watched the haying operations from a distance and thought what fun it must be for the men out in the fields with their pitchforks and horse-drawn mowing machine, rake and hayrick.

I'd done plenty of running and jumping in hay during the time we had our cow, so hay was no novelty to me. I knew its tickle and prickle and how it felt when someone put a handful of chaff and dust down my neck. The hay's sweet aroma and its bounce when I jumped in it made up for this. I'd watch the motes of hay dust dancing in the sunlight streaming through our high barn window. It was like watching a fine shower of gold.

Ma couldn't go near the barn when there was hay in it. Her eyes and nose streamed and she couldn't stop sneezing. "Hay fever," she called it. Luckily, I was spared this. If I'd inherited it, an important part of my life would never have happened.

One day in early July when Dick got back from the milk route, his mother told him that fifteen-year-old Jerry had called in to say he'd got a better job in town and wouldn't be available any more. Dick groaned, then turned to me:

"Peggy, if you can drive a buggy, you can drive a hayrick. How would you like to join the hay crew?"

"I'd love it!" I cried. To get away from the weeding, to be out in the fields, driving horses!

Maisie Lee looked taken aback. "Wait a minute, Dick, that's no kind of work for a girl—out in the fields with the men! It's hot, heavy work and I'm sure her grandmother would not approve."

"Oh, please, Mrs. Lee—I'd love to do it. I love horses and I'm strong for my age—you know I am! And it's not hard work driving a horse."

"I'm sure she could manage it, Mother," said Dick.

Mrs. Lee got on the phone to Ma.

"Of course she can, if she wants to," said Ma. "I'm delighted she can help you out."

As soon as the milkroom routine was finished I shot back home, drank a pint of milk for sustenance, and got into dungarees and a halter. By the time I returned Dick had Mollie harnessed to the hayrick and he and his other helper, Freddy, were ready to go out to the hayfield.

Freddy was about my age, sturdy and freckle-faced. Like the rest of us he wore a wide-brimmed straw hat to keep the sun off his head. He and Dick were stripped to the waist and deeply tanned.

The hayrick was a large home-built wooden wagon, about six feet by twelve. Its tall, skinny-spoked wooden wheels had metal bands around the rims, and were set in underneath the wagon. The hayrick floor was high at the sides to accommodate the wheels beneath it, but in the middle it was about a foot and a half lower, creating a three-foot-wide depression the length of the wagon.

At front and rear, four wooden posts about five feet tall established the four corners. The front and back sides of the hayrick consisted of an open framework made of two crossed boards running diagonally from the top of one post to the base of the other. The long sides consisted of single boards running from the post top in question to a point on the wagon's side just clear of the wheel.

"Up you get, Peggy," said Dick. "You're the driver."

I vaulted up onto the side of the hayrick, stood behind Mollie and took up the reins. There was no driver's seat, so I had to stand to drive, but my balance was good from skiing and skating, so I wasn't worried about it. The crossed boards at the front of the rick would keep me from falling out of the wagon should I lose my footing.

Mollie snorted, twitched her skin to dislodge flies, and shifted her weight from one foot to another as if impatient to be off. "Now listen," said Dick. "There's nothing difficult about driving a hayrick except for one thing. You can't turn it too sharp. If you do, those big wheels are gonna start to scrape the underside of that low strip of floor. If you keep turning when it does that, you'll upside the wagon and it'll go over. Get it?"

"Yeah," I said.

"Well, we'll see if you do. Get Mollie into a slow amble and then pull that left rein real easy. Keep easing her round till you hear the wheel start to scrape, then straighten it fast."

"What if I tip it over?"

"You won't, as long as you listen for that first scrape and correct for it. Go on, try it."

I clicked Mollie into a walk and guided her gently to the left. No sound. A little further. No sound. A bit more, and I was rewarded by a grinding screech. I relaxed the left rein and tightened the right one slightly. The screeching stopped.

"You got it," said Dick. "Now you know what the tolerance of this wagon is. You'll be all right if you don't get over-enthusiastic. Just keep your mind on what you're doing till you get used to it."

Dick and Freddy threw their three-tined pitchforks, and another one for me, into the hayrick and climbed aboard. They sat with their legs dangling over the edge as I headed Molly off toward the hayfield.

"Driving this thing isn't hard," said Dick. "What's hard is building the load. That's tricky, and if you don't do it right the whole thing'll fall off."

Freddy laughed. "Jerry lost a load like that last week, an' he come off with it. I think that's why he quit."

"He lost that load because you two were horsing around and he forgot to watch what he was doing. And he quit to get more money."

"How do you keep the hay from falling off, Dick?" I asked.

"Tell you when we get there. I'll demonstrate."

The wagon had no springs, and the wheels creaked and wobbled over the rough field. Dust rose from the stubble, and field mice scuttled out of our way.

Dick had cut the hay two days before with the horse-drawn mowing machine. Its long arm-like blade was lowered close to ground level and it cut the grass into flat, thin windrows which were left to dry in the sun. He let it lie all that day and the next, then went out with the rake in the cool of the evening.

The rake was also horse-drawn and, as on the mowing machine, Dick perched on a metal saddle above the frame. At the back was a set of long curved metal teeth that could be lowered with a lever in order to rake the hay into bunches. When the teeth were full, Dick would raise the rake with the lever to release the hay. Each bunch was the size that one person could easily lift with a pitchfork and throw onto the hayrick. The hayfield, when we arrived, was covered with bunches of hay in neat rows, far enough apart for easy access of the hayrick.

"Start down the outside row and stop between the first two bunches," Dick directed.

"Freddy, take your pitchfork and get off," Dick said when we stopped. "You pitch those bunches up and I'll show her how to build a load."

"How come you never showed me how to build a load?" asked Freddy. He sounded a bit resentful.

"Cause it takes brains instead of muscle," said Dick, laughing.

Freddy stabbed the first bunch, lifted it over his head, and made a run at the hayrick with it. He flung it off his fork into the middle of the wagon.

"You gotta fill up the middle first," Dick explained to me as he spread the bunch along the floor. "We tramp each bunch down well so it's less likely to shift. Once this low part is full, you start filling up the four corners. When you've got a bunch in each corner, put a couple of bunches along each side. Then bind those side bunches on by first putting more in the middle and spreading some of it over the side bunches, and then putting more in the corners and spreading some of that out so it covers the edges of the side bunches."

I must have looked a bit doubtful, for he grinned at me.

"In other words, Peggy," he continued, "every bunch in every layer you put on has to be positioned so it binds on the hay below it. You'll have to take special care with the side bunches. That stretch of side between the corner frames has no support and is hard to keep hay on. We've got the middle strip filled up level with the rest of the floor, so we can start on the corners now. We just have to tell Freddy exactly where we want him to place each bunch."

"That ain't fair," complained Freddy. "How'm I supposed to keep up with the two of you?"

"I'm just going to show her through the first two layers, then I'll be back down with you," said Dick.

I could see the binding-on pattern emerging as we worked. I was surprised at how effectively it kept the slippery hay from sliding off at the sides.

After Dick hopped down to help Freddy, things went faster, and I could feel the load rising beneath me, pushing me up higher and higher, making it more difficult for Dick and Freddy to get the bunches up. It was hot work placing and tramping down each bunch, and I had to be fast to keep up with the boys. I could feel my sneakers filling with chaff, the sweat running down my neck, and my face glowing with heat. The hayrick filled to the level of the corner tops, then the boys threw a few more bunches into the middle to provide further weight for the side bunches.

"Those are the last ones," said Dick. "Tramp 'em down real good." He stepped up onto the singletree and then pulled himself up the cross pieces of the wagon front to the top of the load. He inspected my work carefully.

"Fine," he said. "Good work. That won't shift—unless you tip us over."

192

I was already hot from the work, now I was even hotter from his praise. I felt that I'd accomplished what he'd wanted me to do, and he was pleased about it.

"Now we've got a full load, you can sit down to drive," said Dick. "Sit back a bit from the front and brace your feet against the wagon frame."

I did as I was told. The ground looked very far away, and I felt a little twist of apprehension in my stomach.

"Get used to the feel of the reins now that you have to pull them from this height," Dick instructed.

I took up the reins and looked down their length. I realized I'd be okay as long as I kept my feet carefully braced.

"It feels different, but I think I can manage it," I said.

"Good. I'll sit just behind you and make sure you're okay."
Then he shouted down to Freddy: "Are you comin' up?"

"I'll walk," said Freddy with emphasis, and Dick laughed. From Freddy's tone I concluded he thought walking was safer.

"Okay, get her going," said Dick, and I clicked to Mollie. She leaned into her harness, and slowly the hayrick shuddered into motion and the load was under way. The empty wagon had rattled and jerked. The full one lumbered and lurched, but with a reassuring sense of underlying stability. It was odd at first, sitting down and controlling the reins from above, but I soon got used to it. It was certainly easier than trying to balance standing up. I wasn't seriously afraid that I'd upset the load. I'd done several sharp turns of the rick at the ends of the rows and negotiated them without a single scrape. After the first few minutes driving the full load I felt reasonably confident, and the track back to the barn presented no problem.

"Stop her right in front of the barn door," said Dick when we arrived. "I'll drive the load in. Then you can help me unhitch the horse and hook her up to the hayfork."

The barn door was wide, but still looked too narrow to get the load through. The hayrick creaked and shuddered up the gentle ramp to the door, and Dick maneuvered it through, just barely touching the sides.

We climbed down and were joined by Freddy. The three of us gulped down cupfuls of cool water from the barn faucet. "Take a piece of rock salt out of that bucket and lick it, Peggy," said Dick, helping himself to a bit. "Drinking water and licking rock salt will replace the salt and fluid you've lost in sweat so you won't get heat stroke."

Then Dick and I unhitched Mollie and led her out the back door and around to the front again. Meanwhile, Freddy had gone up into the haymow to lower the big hay fork down onto the load. Dick went up onto the load again to check the fork. The prongs had to be pushed down deep into the hay and then cross prongs released to anchor the fork in the bunch to be lifted. Then Dick jumped back down, the end of the fork rope in his hand. The rope went from the fork up through a pulley attached to the roof of the barn, and then back down to ground level. Dick showed me how to secure the rope to Mollie's harness.

"Okay. Now you lead out the horse in a straight line from the barn. That pulls the forkful of hay up into the mow. Then Freddy'll yell 'Whoa' and release the bunch from the fork. When he's done that he'll yell 'Lead back!' and you'll bring her back to the barn and the process repeats till the hayrick is empty. Okay?"

"Okay."

"Good. Do it through one cycle while I watch. Then I'll go back up and change places with Freddy. He'll stow the hay away in the mow, and I'll set the fork in the load."

Mollie had done this routine so many times she knew exactly what to do and when. While waiting at the barn end for the "Lead out!" command she stood patiently, her only movement an occasional twitch or stamp to scatter flies. I talked to her and stroked her nose, and she nickered to me softly with evident pleasure. Sun glinted from her coat.

I loved the smell of her aging leather harness and the pong of sweaty horse. They blended into the sweet country air, both seeming to enhance the other.

When hay was out ready for the barn, we could bring in one load in the morning and two in the afternoon, Dick said. In order to get hay ready, however, he had to cut or rake it most evenings till dark. He had a long day from 5 a.m. when he started the milking until dark when he fell into bed, but he insisted he liked doing it. Farming was in his blood. By the end of my first day of haying, I realized it was in mine, too.

I could think of no way of thanking Dick without sounding silly, but I felt the Lees had enlarged my life out of all bounds. They had trusted my ability to learn a demanding job and do it well.

Later that week Rena and Beryl, who had never watched a haying operation, came up to see what was going on. Dick was happy to let them look on. He allowed them to ride on the empty hayrick up to the field we were stripping, and after we'd got the load on he boosted them up on top of it for the ride back. "Aren't you lucky," Beryl said as we jounced along toward the barn. "Learning how to do all this and getting paid for it too!"

"Humph," said Rena. "A lot of hot work and sweat. I'd rather be riding my own horse."

I couldn't tell whether that was just sour grapes or whether she meant it.

50. Harrald and the Axe

One night in mid-July, about nine when we were just ready for bed, Mrs. Harrald and the two little boys appeared at our door. I hadn't seen them since the autumn before when they were picking apples at the Lees.

Pa went out onto the porch with her and closed the door. She spoke so softly that I, who was in the kitchen with my ears strained to their utmost, couldn't hear what she was saying. I couldn't catch Pa's replies either, and they held a muffled conversation for a few minutes. Then Pa opened the door before coming back in, and I heard him say, in a strained, upset sort of voice I hadn't heard before:

"No, I'm sorry. I can't do it. I can't take that risk. I'm sorry."

Mrs. Harrald and the two boys walked off into the night. Pa came in, his face held in tight as if he might cry. He shook his head at Ma without speaking and went into his bedroom.

"You go upstairs to bed, Peggy," Ma said. "I've got some things to do down here."

After I went up I heard the hum of voices in the kitchen. Something very strange was going on and—as usual—I wasn't being told. "For my own good," I muttered angrily.

I found out what had happened next day at lunch time when Rena and Beryl came up to see me before I went back to haying. I could tell by their faces that they had something big to tell.

"Mrs. Harrald and Ted and Tony are staying with us!" Rena said proudly.

"Why?" I asked.

"Mr. Harrald got drunk and was chasing her around the table with an axe."

"He cut the cat's tail off," Beryl broke in. "Mrs. Harrald and the boys ran away."

"So that's why they came here last night!"

"Yeah," said Rena. "She said your father wouldn't let them stay with you."

This shook me. It was the first time I'd known my family to refuse someone in need. And Mrs. Harrald was so kind, and in such desperate trouble. Why had he done that? If the Allens took her in, why couldn't we? I was angry at Pa, both for refusing the Harralds and for not telling me what was wrong. He was as bad as Ma.

After Beryl and Rena left, I went out back and found Pa turning over the compost heap.

"The Allens are letting Mrs. Harrald and the boys stay with them. Why couldn't they stay with us, Pa?"

I could tell by the strain on Pa's face that he hated what he'd done, wanted to explain it to me, but didn't know how. Finally he said, slowly, "When Harrald is drunk he's dangerous. A man like that will hunt his wife down if she runs away. He could do damage not only to her and his children, but to anyone who tried to shelter them. I admire Allen for taking them in. I'm glad someone was willing to help. But I'm not willing to risk my family. That man is bad medicine."

Over the next week I got daily reports from Rena and Beryl. Mrs. Harrald, once away from her husband, opened up and in spite of her troubles showed them for a few days the spirited young woman she must have been before she met Harrald. She told them of her youth with her tribe in the north, the way they lived, the food they gathered in the wild and ate. She told how late the girls matured. She was sixteen before she had a period, seventeen when she met Harrald and he took her away and got her pregnant. She'd had four children, many miscarriages, and then Ted and Tony. She was only thirty-three, and we'd all thought she was in her forties.

The Allens were clearly enjoying the Harrald Experience, and I was jealous. All the action was taking place down the road and I was missing the drama. Worse, Rena was rubbing it in and putting on airs about the Allens' virtue in being willing to help when no one else would.

When I went down to the Allens, which I did as frequently as I could get away, Mrs. Harrald would greet me kindly, and the change in her appearance was remarkable. She could have passed for twenty-five now that she was out from under Harrald's thumb. Mrs. Allen had lent her clothes and shoes and she looked like another person. Her long hair was loose and hung down her back nearly to her knees.

The Harrald drama, however, only lasted eight days. When Beryl came up the day after the denouement she reported that Harrald had appeared at their back door the afternoon before.

"With an axe?" I asked apprehensively.

"No," said Beryl. "He was sober, polite and just said 'I need to speak to my wife. It's about Peter. There's something she should know.' Mummy told Mrs. Harrald what he'd said, and she went outside to talk with him. After about ten minutes she came back smiling and said, 'It's all right. I can go home now.' She changed back into her own clothes, took the little boys by the hand and went off with him."

"Wow," I said. "Wonder what he'll do to her?"

"She seemed happy when she went. Mummy says if they've been together sixteen years without him killing her, and she can still go back with a smile, she'll probably be all right."

I could not understand this. Why would *anyone* stay with a man who had chased her with an axe? Why didn't she just take her two little ones and go back to her own people? The older boys could look after themselves, they were all bigger and stronger than Harrald.

When I got home, I asked Ma those questions.

"Where do you think she'd get the money to go home to her people?" she asked. "It's a couple of hundred miles. And what's to keep Harrald from going up there after her with his axe if she did? He'd never let her keep his children. She had no choice but to go back to him."

I couldn't believe this. There must be some other way out. I was absolutely sure that no man would ever force me to stay with him out of fear.

I asked Dick if he'd heard what had happened. He hadn't, but he didn't seem to think it was as serious as I did.

"It's happened before," he said. "I heard that when they lived in North Augusta the neighbors had to call the police one time. The cops came out and told Harrald to behave himself. Next time he got drunk he called the police himself, pretended to be someone else and said, 'Harrald's beating his wife again. Come out here quick and make him stop.' Then he hid in the branches of a tree and watched the police while they hunted for him."

I couldn't help laughing, but it didn't make me feel any better about Mrs. Harrald.

I was beginning to wonder about marriage. It didn't sound like a very good gamble. Was anyone, except Mr. and Mrs. Lee, happily married? It was beginning to seem unlikely. I'd been told that Eva Fuller's husband sometimes got drunk and beat her. It was well known that Sandstrom did the same to his wife. The man who lived with poor Maude used to beat her. And that woman Gracie gave a lift to several years ago—she'd left her husband, gone back, then left him again: "I can't live with him and can't live without him," she'd said.

51. The Laundry

About a week after the Harrald episode, Rena and Beryl came up to the Lees on their bikes looking for me. It had rained the day before so the hay was too wet to bring in, and they found me thinning turnips in the side field that ran from the Lees' barn down to Maude's brook. I was glad enough to get up off my hunkers and stretch for a minute. I'd been at it since I'd finished in the milkroom at ten, and it was nearly noon.

Rena's face was white, her eyes angry. I could tell she was in a fury about something, but it was Beryl who spoke:

"Our granny—Dad's mother—got rushed to the hospital with pain in her side last night and they had to do an emergency operation to get her appendix out."

"Gosh, I'm sorry," I said. "Is she all right?"

"I guess so. They got it before it burst, but she'll have to stay in the hospital for a couple of weeks and then take it easy for a while."

"We've got to do her goddam laundry," Rena burst out. "Just when I want to ride my horse!"

I didn't understand this outburst and looked questioningly at Beryl.

"Granny runs a laundry business," she explained. "She and our grandfather used to run it together, but he died a couple of years ago so she's been doing it on her own. Now while she's sick Mummy and Rena and I have got to keep it going."

"It isn't fair," snarled Rena through clenched teeth. "I won't do it!"

"We don't want to interrupt your work, Peggy," said Beryl. "When you're through here come on down and we'll tell you about it. Starting tomorrow, we'll be gone during the day."

"I should be done by mid-afternoon. I'll come down then," I said, and they wheeled off.

I was finished thinning by three, went home and downed a pint of milk, and biked off to the Allens. I found Charlie nailing siding onto the stable he and Allen were building for Petey. They'd got the frame up over the last two weekends.

"How's it going?" I asked.

"Kinda slow on my own," he said. "But another couple of weekends with Dad and the outside will be close to finished and we can start on the inside. And the guys are coming next week to begin digging the well."

"I hear your granny's in the hospital."

"Yeah. Glad I've got this to do, otherwise I'd be spending the summer tending laundry machines."

"Rena and Beryl came and told me this morning. I'm just going in to hear about it."

"Have fun. The air's so thick in there you could cut it with a knife," and he snickered as I headed for the house.

The tangy smell of fresh yeast greeted me. Mrs. Allen was making bread, and Beryl was kneading it for her.

"Have a hunk of fresh dough," she said and tore off a bit for me.

I loved the taste of fresh dough. It was tart enough to make the saliva flow. Almost as good as fresh bread. The smell of yeast, however, was not the atmosphere Charlie was talking about. Rena was standing in the middle of the kitchen floor in a state of cold fury. She didn't even look at me as I came in. Her eyes were fixed on her mother, who was trying to get the oven going.

"It isn't fair! Now that I've got a horse I don't want to be stuck in town all summer in a hot laundry doing the shit work!"

"We've got to," said Beryl calmly. "It's the only living Granny's got. She'd have to come and live with us or starve if she lost the laundry business."

"Oh, you sound just like Mummy and Daddy. Why is it always us who get stuck with taking on squalling brats and stupid smelly old ladies and more work than we've got to do already?"

Anna Allen turned on her. "You think you're the only one who's put out? You think I'm happy about dragging in there and back in the pickup every day and working like stink in between and then coming back here and getting supper for the lot of you? Just in the hottest part of the summer? Don't you think I'd like a little let-up after coping with last winter? Why should you be the only one not working in this family? We're all in this together, and we've all got to pitch in or we'll sink. Do you understand? You can ride your horse on Sundays!"

Rena looked at her mother with what I can only describe as pure hate. "Only Sundays?" Rena stormed. "Dad told Charlie to feed and exercise Petey, so he gets to ride him Monday, Tuesday, Wednesday, Thursday, Friday and Saturday! Why can't I pound the nails in the goddam stable and exercise Petey, and Charlie tend laundry machines? Why do the men always get the best of everything and the women have to do the shit?"

Mrs. Allen didn't say a word. Her face was white and she started forward. I thought she was going to strike Rena, but Rena turned, marched into her bedroom and slammed the door so the house shook.

Mrs. Allen exhaled sharply, collapsed into a chair at the kitchen table, and wiped sweat off her brow with the back of her hand.

"Can I do anything to help?" I asked her.

She smiled at me. "You've got enough on your own plate working at the Lees, Peggy. But thanks for offering. If there's an emergency with Petey and Charlie can't cope, we'll let you and your Pa know."

As I wheeled home, I felt torn in two directions. I was appalled at Rena's total disregard for everyone in her family except herself. Yet I could see why she was upset and frustrated by not being able to spend more time with her horse, especially since Charlie was getting the privilege of exercising him in her absence. It didn't seem fair. I'd have been mad too in the circumstances. But couldn't Rena see that it was a family crisis? They all had to do what they could.

52. Swimming

In late July a boy named Leon Bunker joined the hay crew temporarily. He was about fourteen, blond and strongly built. With three pairs of hands to pitch hay, the work went faster. Three pitchers and one driver was about optimum.

A few days later the heat soared. The temperature hung in the nineties for three days, while we labored to get the hay in. Between loads we drank gallons of water and licked pieces of rock salt to protect against heat stroke. On the fourth day it was 109 degrees in the shade—quite unheard of for Maine—by the time Dick returned from the milk route.

Dick, for possibly the first time in Lee history, declared it was too hot to go out in the fields. "Let's go to Cobbosseecontee and cool off," he suggested. "I'll drive us out there in the milk van." Leon and Freddy cheered, and I dashed home to get into my bathing suit and make a sandwich to take with me.

I found Pa waiting for me so he could demonstrate the frying of an egg on the cement slab path to our back door. He cracked the egg carefully, then bent low over the path so the yolk wouldn't break when it dropped. The egg sizzled as it hit the cement, and its translucent 'white' went opaque within seconds. Pa laughed at my amazement, and called the cat to eat up the egg.

Cobbosseecontee was a lake about three miles west of the farm, just past the Manchester Forks. "Contee" was the local Indian word for lake. Cobbossee was the finest lake in the area, and the Augusta wealthy had built elegant houses all around one end of it. At the other end the Augusta Country Club had snapped up Sandy Beach, one of the best sites on the lake, and put a golf course and an expensive club house on the land behind it.

For years Manchester residents had used Sandy Beach. It was their local swimming place. When they heard they were about to lose it to the country club, they put up such a ruckus that an agreement was hammered out between village and club stipulating that Manchester residents could continue to use the beach, but no one else. Pa said the club probably agreed to this to avoid sabotage of their beach by the locals.

Technically, the Lee and Shaw farms were in Augusta, about a quarter mile from the Manchester Line, which was at the top of Pelton's Hill, but no one ever questioned us when we went.

Fred had taken us to Cobbossee occasionally when I was little, and it was there that I'd learned to swim. I hadn't been out there since Fred left, as Pa still had the back-roads-only rule in force for my bike.

I'd never seen the lake more beautiful than it was that day, with sun dappling the calm water and willows drooping over its edge. The heat was too fierce to lie on the sand, so we spent the next several hours in the water, which was warm and soft but seemed cool and delicious in contrast to the air. I loved swimming under water, my face close to the bottom, watching the sand ripples slipping by beneath me.

"Can you do an egg float, Peggy?" asked Leon. I'd never heard of one, and shook my head.

"You just hold your breath and make yourself into the shape of an egg. You bring your knees up under your chin and hold them there with your arms. Then put your forehead on your knees. You'll go under water, but your back will rise to the top and you can just hang there till your breath gives out."

He demonstrated. I watched him disappear beneath the water, then his curved brown back appeared and broke the surface. Leon floated with just his back showing till he needed air.

I tried it. I quickly sank almost to the bottom, but then I felt my body rotate in the water automatically till my back was pointing skyward, and I rose like magic to the surface. I hung there enjoying the sense of weightlessness until I could hold my breath no longer.

Freddy had never seen this done either, and tried it as well.

The temperature dropped to the nineties next day so we were back in the fields again, but the trip to Cobbossee was the beginning of a tradition. Leon suggested we go again after the last load of hay was in.

"No can do," said Dick. "Got chores before supper, and milking after. But I can be done by seven, and it won't be dark till nearly nine. Why don't we go this evening?"

It was agreed, and we began going every night that Dick didn't have either mowing or raking to do after the milking.

When I got back from our third evening swim, Ma was awaiting my return and questioned me about who had gone with us and what we did. I thought this was a bit odd and couldn't understand why she was asking, but I didn't worry about it. "How old is this Leon?" she wanted to know. "Where does he live?"

"He's about fourteen," I said. "I don't know where he lives, he comes back with Dick from the milk route and takes the bus home after work."

Next morning when I reported for work in the milk room, Maisie said, "Your grandmother and I have decided that it's not proper for a young girl to go off swimming in the evening with the boys. I'm afraid you won't be able to join them any more. I'm sorry."

This came as a complete shock. I could see no reason whatever why it was 'not proper.'

"Why' for heaven sakes?" I asked.

"You'll have to ask your grandmother about that. It's for her to explain. All I'll say is that I'm very sorry."

I managed to keep my anger and hurt under control while we washed the bottles, but when I went home to change for the hayfield I went straight to Ma and demanded an explanation.

201

"It's not decent," she said. "You shouldn't be off in the evening with the boys without supervision. Nice girls don't do that sort of thing."

"Why isn't it decent? We wear our bathing suits out there and back, we don't undress in front of each other. What's wrong with that? You've known Dick all his life, Ma. You know he wouldn't do anything improper!"

"You'll understand when you're older," she said.

"I want to understand now," I shouted.

"Don't talk back to me! You're being rude and impertinent. If you don't stop, I'll forbid you to go haying over there."

She turned abruptly and left the room. There was nothing I could do. If I said any more, I'd lose my job, and the summer would be completely ruined.

I'd never been so angry with Ma before. I'd been resentful, yes, felt betrayed and bitter, yes, but now I felt sheer fury. How could she be so totally unfair, pig-headed and stupid? Why couldn't I go and have fun like the boys could? I'd worked as hard as they had.

It flashed across my mind that Rena had a point in saying men always get the best of it. But it wasn't the men's fault in my case, it was Ma's, and there was no reason for it!

I went looking for Pa, but he'd disappeared. He didn't want to get into it, I thought. He'd never be willing to argue with Ma.

Dick was upset and apologetic when I told him about it. He'd already been told by his mother, of course.

"It's not fair," he agreed. "You work as hard as any of us and you deserve to cool off as much as we do. But Mother won't go against your grandmother's wishes."

I sizzled with anger the rest of that hot summer as I saw Dick drive off about seven in the evening to pick up the boys for swimming. I never forgave Ma for that. I still haven't.

53. Marge's Death

Because of my work at the Lees and the Allens' involvement in the laundry business, I saw little of Rena and Beryl for the rest of the summer. By late August, however, Mr. Allen's mother had recovered sufficiently to take over the business again. Rena, according to Beryl, had vented her spleen on both parents and siblings for the entire time they were away. Now she was able to ride her horse again and was in better temper.

We returned to school the Monday after Labor Day, and the Allens continued their efforts to make their premises more habitable for the winter. The well had been dug and was now providing a good supply of water. The burden of the quarter-mile trek with a cart in sub-zero weather would not have to be repeated in the coming winter.

The combined efforts of Allen and Charlie quickly finished Petey's stable. Then they turned their attention to the house, hoping to install insulation and plaster board before the cold set in.

We'd only been back at school a few days when I got a letter from Lynde. He hadn't been in touch for some time. The letter stunned us all:

September 16, 1940

Dear Brenda,

> Marge died on September 11 and was buried in Wyoming Cemetery, Melrose, on the 13th.
> It is very sad. There was nothing they could do for her. I'm sorry to have to tell you this.

Love to all,
Lynde

That beautiful girl dead? How could that be? Barton and Grace were old, and the old got sick and died. But Marge? She was the same age as Lynde, and she'd been happy and full of life. Then she'd had a nervous breakdown, but how could that kill her? She'd had plenty of time to rest, and doctors and nurses in the hospital to help her.

When I asked Ma why Marge had died she shook her head sadly and said "I don't know." I didn't believe her. Surely she must know.

"I'll write Lynde and find out," I said.

"No, don't, Peggy. You mustn't ask people about tragedies like that. If he wants us to know, he'll tell us. Just write and say how sorry you are and how fond you were of her. Pa and I will write him also."

I couldn't understand Ma's answer. Why would Lynde not want us to know? We were his family. Why should he and Ma and Pa always keep things from me? Did other families do that, too?

Why do people keep secrets from one another? What are they doing to each other when they do that? How can you ever tell for sure if someone is lying? And why they're lying?

There seem to be two kinds of lies, I thought. Ones told to hurt you, and ones told to protect you. But the protecting lies don't work. They make things worse in the end. Surely the people being protected don't want *not* to know. To deal with life you've got to know what's true so you can decide what to do about it and perhaps find out how to make things better.

I felt sick with grief for Lynde, and for Marge. But there was nothing, nothing I could do.

54. After the Trip to Town

"Come into the sitting room, Peggy. I have something to tell you."

Ma is dressed in her 'town dress.' It is navy and white organdie with a lace collar and cuffs. Her white hair is swirled into its usual "pug" on top of her head, but it's loose at the sides—not skin tight like some farm women wear theirs. I am struck by how handsome she is, how tall and strong. She does not look eighty-five, in spite of her many illnesses.

Ma wears her town dress only when she goes to town, which is seldom. If a neighbor is going, she asks for a ride. She does not try to take the a bus any more, as her knees have become "tricky" and she fears falling when getting on and off.

It's Saturday afternoon, and Ma has just returned from such a trip. She got a ride in and back with Gracie, who was doing errands for her mother. They were gone about two hours. Ma came back with several packages half concealed under her cloak and took them straight to her room. I knew better than to ask what they are. If she wants me to know, she will tell me.

Now, a few minutes later, she confronts me in the kitchen where I am playing with Fluff and her kittens. She motions me toward the sitting room. She is carrying a small paper bag and a box about nine inches square and four inches thick, wrapped in brown paper.

I know instantly what it is.

I've seen boxes of Kotex and Modess in the drugstore and in Woolworths, and have noticed how the women and girls approach the counter grimly, eyes darting around to see if anyone is watching. They whisper something to the clerk and are handed a box of the identical dimensions wrapped in brown paper. Money is paid. They slink off, the guilt of the world upon them.

Now Ma has such a box in her hand. I'm in for it.

She seats herself on the couch, motions me to a chair opposite.

"Peggy," she begins, her face tight with embarrassment, "Have the little Allen girls told you that some day something will come from you and you'll have to . . .wear something?"

I feel my own taut face reflect the embarrassment in hers.

"Yes, Ma. I know all about it."

Surprise and relief battle for control of her face. She extends the parcel in my direction, saying "This is . . . "

"I know what it is, Ma," I say, and take it from her.

"There's another bag—it has a belt in it," she says, passing it to me. I take it, say nothing.

"Do you have any questions?"

"No, Ma. I'll just put these in my room."

I exit at speed.

It is over. The subject is never—but never—referred to again.

55. The Initiation

My October weekends were again taken up with apple picking at the Lees, but by November Rena, Beryl and I found ourselves with the unusual luxury of extra time after school and weekends—a vacuum which cried out to be filled. I'd heard a program on the radio about witches, which set my thinking off in an unusual direction.

"I've got an idea," I said to Rena. "We could start a Witches Club."

It was a Saturday, and I was helping Rena cut up apples for a pie while Beryl took her bike the mile and a half to Robbins' store on an errand for her mother.

Rena looked up. "What do you mean?"

"You and me and Beryl. We could use that room up in my attic as a Coven Room. One of us could be President—the 'Grand Witch.' The other two would take witch-like names and act as Secretary and Treasurer. If Charlie wanted to be a warlock, he could join too."

"What's a warlock?" asked Rena.

"A male witch. And we'd need a couple of familiars. My two cats would do for that. Or we could use that stuffed weasel your father found and gave to Charlie—if Charlie doesn't mind."

Rena had never heard of familiars either, but the idea of the Witches Club appealed to her. "I shall be Grand Witch," she declared.

Just like Rena, I thought. "All right, I don't care. I'll be Secretary. Unless Beryl wants to be."

"Maybe we won't let Beryl in. Maybe she won't pass the initiation."

"What initiation?"

"You can't take people into a club without an initiation, idiot."

"Well, it won't be much of a club with only two of us! I meant Beryl to be in it. I would have told her at the same time as you, only she isn't here."

"We will have an initiation and that's that. I'm the Grand Witch, and you have to do as I say!"

"Maybe Beryl won't want to join anyway."

"She'll want to join, all right. You'll see."

We told Beryl about the club on her return and, as Rena had predicted, she was eager to join even though Rena made the initiation sound frightening. "You may not be able to pass it, Beryl," she warned. "Such things have turned white the heads of better people than you!"

When Rena and I approached Charlie about warlockship, he snorted with disgust. "I'm not interested in baby stuff like that. Witches Club for Chrissakes—are you nuts? I'm in high school now!"

Rena sulked, but for once Charlie held his ground. We were beneath his contempt.

The initiation was set for a week later to give us time to prepare and for Beryl's anxiety to deepen. Rena and I spent considerable time fixing up the attic room.

The attic was creepy at the best of times. The farmhouse had more than its share of creaks and groans. I'd told the girls about the footsteps I'd heard in the attic at night, the something that walked across the guest room floor when no one was there, and the strange rustlings like silk skirts of a lady passing from room to room. Pa said it was just mice and the wooden house expanding and contracting, but I only believed him when it was daylight. Even then, I never voluntarily went to the attic alone.

If someone was with me, however, everything was different. Then the attic no longer terrified, and I could laugh at my fears. The house was no longer an all-seeing presence, it was just a house, and the attic was just an attic.

Rena and I hung some old black curtain liners across the entire front wall of the attic room so the light from the single window could be completely obliterated. I crocheted an enormous white spider web, pinned it onto the curtain liners and made a frightful looking spider of black yarn to place in the center. We suspended another spider by a string from the ceiling.

We cut bats from black paper and hung them from strings or stuck them onto the walls. I made a skull from an old sheet cut to the proper shape, stuffed it with wadding, and painted hollow eye sockets and teeth on it. We set it on an old plant stand donated by Ma, who was told she was not to come up to the attic while work was in progress. We stood a broomstick in a corner of the room, ready for rapid transport in case of need. Charlie had lent us his stuffed weasel, and it shared the table top with the skull.

We painted plant pots black, and stuck candles in the bottoms. When lit they gave an eerie glow. "We can only have them lit when we're actually in the room," I warned, with the wisdom of those who live in wooden houses.

When all was ready, we allowed Charlie up to inspect. In spite of his early derision, he was curious about what was going on. He was impressed in spite of himself.

"Look, I'll help with the initiation," he offered. "Four heads are better than three. I won't join the club, but I'll be glad to advise."

As our plans developed, Charlie agreed to laugh like a fiend at appropriate times during the ceremony and to help carry Beryl. He cut a skeleton from cardboard and stood it in the corner opposite the broom, and donated the skin and bones of a long-dead cat he had come across beside the road.

The initiation was scheduled for the following Saturday afternoon and was to begin at the Allens'. I went down just before two and joined Rena and Beryl in their bedroom. Charlie would join us later. Beryl had not been told of his participation.

Rena and I blindfolded Beryl with a Kotex lifted from Mrs. Allen's supply, fixing it in place with a black scarf. After the blindfold had been checked for adequacy, Beryl was led out through the kitchen and down the steps to the outhouse. Here we were joined by Charlie, who kept silent so Beryl would not know he was there. We placed an old horse collar (borrowed from Pa) around Beryl's neck for extra weight, and attached to it a pair of reins. We explained to her that we were going to guide her like a horse with the reins. Then we spun her quickly around several times and told her to set off.

Rena held the reins and drove Beryl through the marshiest bit of field and into the woods. There was no path, but Charlie had blazed trees with red paint to lead us to a shallow pond that had formed during recent heavy rain. It was only knee deep, but Beryl had no way of knowing that when she started to wade in.

As she did so, Rena intoned:

> Drowning by water
> Drowning by water
> Lizards and snakes
> Frogs and eels
> Entrails of foxes
> Talons of owls
> Drowning by water
> Hear how she squeals!

"Aieeee!" shrieked Beryl as the icy water squished over her low shoes and up her legs. "How deep is it?"

"What does that matter? You can swim," said Rena.

"Not with this weight around my neck."

She's got more guts than I'd have, I thought as Beryl plunged ahead and made it to the other side without further protest. Beyond the pond there were no blazes on the trees, but as long as we kept a roughly straight path we couldn't avoid hitting the disused trolley line. This was set on a steep embankment up which Rena urged Beryl. Then we proceeded along the line a few hundred yards to where our logging trail crossed it. At this point Charlie gave forth with a chilling cackle and tickled Beryl's neck with a long feather. She screamed most rewardingly. Rena then ordered her to turn right onto the logging trail, which led us through woods and fields to our farm buildings. Charlie and I removed the horse collar from Beryl's neck and carried her into the back shed. A stretcher was leaning against the wall. We had constructed it from two cross-braced lengths of board attached to two long poles. Charlie laid it flat on the floor.

"Lie down on this, flat on your back," Rena directed. We guided Beryl down onto the boards and strapped her on. Then with Charlie at one end and me at the other, we raised the contraption off the floor and supported it on our shoulders with the poles. I was surprised by Beryl's weight. She didn't look that heavy, but the poles cut into my shoulders.

We carried Beryl through a complex of sheds and through the stable to the barn. Here we managed to manhandle the stretcher up through the trap door into the loft, although we very nearly dropped Beryl when Charlie's foot slipped as he was trying to pull her up. Then Charlie and I rolled the stretcher and its occupant in the hay, while Rena scattered chaff in Beryl's hair and down her neck. Then back down through the trap door to visit the hen house, where I captured a hen and induced it to flap its wings by holding its head down over Beryl's chest. It cooperated magnificently.

"Don't let that thing shit on me," pleaded Beryl. Charlie let forth another volley of wild shrieks.

We were just passing through the final shed on our way to the attic stairs when we encountered Ma on her way to the orchard to look for windfalls. She stared at Beryl with horror.

"What are you doing to that girl?" she demanded.

Desperately I signalled her to be quiet. "It's the initiation. Don't say anything. It's all going according to plan!"

"Beryl, are you all right?" Ma was not going to be put off.

"Yes, Ma'am," said Beryl with a reassuring giggle.

"Where are you taking her?"

I pointed up toward the attic, frantically signalling silence.

"Well, you be careful. We don't want any broken bones. Are you sure you can manage that?"

We nodded vigorously and silently.

Ma watched as we maneuvered the stretcher up the stairs to the second floor. Reassured, she let us proceed, and went off toward the orchard.

We crossed the bathroom and went on up the attic stairs. The stretcher cleared the top of the stairwell with some difficulty, nearly breaking the attic window, but Charlie and I managed to get it turned, and then started down the narrow planking toward the attic room.

"Let me go first," demanded Rena. "I've got to get my robe and mask on!" She tried to push by Charlie, who lost his balance and fell sidewise off the planking. The stretcher fell from his shoulders and clattered onto the boards. I was thrown down heavily but, luckily, did not go off the planking.

"Fucking son-of-a-bitch!" said Charlie, whose leg had gone through the lath and plaster into the room below. He was supporting himself with his arms and upper body on a crossbeam to keep from going further through. I leaped up and grabbed him around the middle.

"Rena, for God's sake help me pull him up!" I shouted. Rena was standing rooted to the planking, but unfroze when I shouted at her. With the two of us pulling, Charlie managed to free his leg and scrambled back onto the planking.

"Are you hurt?" I asked.

"No. I'm okay." He turned on Rena: "You little bitch, you pushed me!"

"I did not," she shrieked. "You lost your balance. I never touched you. You're just clumsy."

"You give me that crap and I'll take you apart! Look what's happened to the Shaws' ceiling!"

"Lucky Ma went out," I said. "She'd have heard the crash and been up here like a shot!"

"What's happened?" demanded Beryl. She was still blindfolded and lying on the stretcher, which had luckily landed right way up and straight along the planking.

"Oh, just your dear sister who lets everyone else do the heavy work. She pushed by me to get her goddam costume on and I fell through the plaster," said Charlie.

"I didn't even know you were here," said Beryl.

"You weren't supposed to."

"Oh, come on," said Rena. "Let's get her into the room and finish the initiation. That's the best part of all."

"Jesus Christ," bellowed Charlie. "Can't you think about anything else? Don't you realize what you made me do to the Shaws' ceiling?"

"Ma probably won't be back for at least half an hour," I said. "We can't do much about the ceiling anyhow till Pa looks at it. We might as well carry on with the initiation. Then we can go clean up the mess."

"All right. Gosh, I'm sorry about the ceiling, Peggy," said Charlie. "But Dad'll know how to fix it, and I'll come and help him with it."

"We've got to get our robes on," hissed Rena. "Come on."

We left Beryl on the planking while we costumed ourselves with more black curtain liners decorated with snakes and toads, and peaked hats cut from cardboard and painted black.

"Light the tapers," ordered Rena. "And don't forget to light the wick in the sulfur jar. Peggy, have you got the incantations and the Order of Service?"

I had written them for the occasion. "They're here on the table," I said. "Your names are on your copies."

"Are we ready?"

"Yes. Let's get Beryl."

Rena remained in the room while Charlie and I carefully maneuvered Beryl along the planking. Once inside the room, we undid the straps and allowed her to stand up, though still blindfolded. Rena mounted a stool so she, as Grand Witch, could stand higher than the others. Charlie gave another fiendish cackle and we all banged on baking tins with metal spoons.

"Do you swear, Beryl Allen, never to divulge that which you are about to see and hear?" Rena demanded.

"Yes, I swear."

Charlie undid the blindfold, which fell away from Beryl's eyes. She told us later that at first she was aware only of darkness lit by the eerie glow from the plant pots. Then she saw three forms all in black, with stark white faces and eyes like black holes. She knew, of course, who it was behind the sheet masks, but still, she said, the effect was startling.

In the corner opposite we had placed the table bearing the weasel and skull. Charlie's skeleton hung behind it, with the dead cat at its feet. An ungodly stench was rising from the sulfur pot, which was well alight and burning with a blue flame.

Grand Witch raised her arms toward the dark ceiling and began to speak:

> Spirits of earth
> Spirits of air
> Come and join us
> In our lair.

Then I, who had taken the name Huldah the Weasel, continued:

> Spirits of living
> Spirits of dead
> Let our 'cantations
> Ring in your head!

Then Rena and I continued, alternating verses:

> Grand Witch:
> Lizards and toads,
> Snakes and flies,
> Scarabs and termites,
> Eaters of eyes,
> Come join our meeting

As soon as you please.
Hell is made up
of friends such as these.

Hulda the Weasel:
Familiars join us:
Come with the breeze.
We hear you padding
Soft through the trees.
Come and find Beryl,
Judge on your own.
If she is worthy,
To us make it known.

Grand Witch had learned her lines well and declaimed her parts of the incantation in an impressive voice, hardly recognizable as Rena's. Huldah the Weazel was amazed. She'd no idea that Rena had any declamatory ability. Rena was good!

But then a completely unrehearsed and unexpected thing happened. The speed of the alternating verses increased. Grand Witch was declaiming faster and faster, carrying Huldah the Weasel along with the increasing tempo until the words became nearly unintelligible. I reached the end of my allotted dozen verses and expected Rena to stop, but instead she continued faster and faster, her voice rising in pitch. Now the words passing her lips were nothing that I had composed. It was a fiendish gibberish about demons, body organs and functions, blood, cannibal acts and horrible happenings with animals. The recognizable words rapidly became fewer and fewer until what we were hearing appeared to be a completely foreign tongue. Then Rena stopped and said slowly and clearly in a ringing voice:

"Satan, I call thee!"

There was a moment of dead silence, then a bone-shivering howl began, rising in intensity to a shriek. It put the bones of my jaws vibrating, and the shock waves ran the length of my vertebrae. I'd never heard Charlie produce such a sound before. Obviously Rena had prepared him for her little act and he'd been saving the best for last.

As if in answer to the shriek the light from the potted candles brightened, then sputtered and went out with a series of little "phuts," leaving us in total darkness.

"Christ, Charlie, what have you done to the candles?" I asked.

"Nothing," said Charlie, surprised. "I didn't touch them! Where's the flashlight? We'll have to get them lit again."

The candles responded quickly to the touch of a match, and again the room was suffused with an eerie glow.

"Satan has spoken," said Rena dramatically. "We can now go on. Beryl Allen, do you, under pain of fire and agonizing death, promise to renounce all your human ways and take on those of this Coven, to forsake all loyalties to family and friends and to honor only ours?"

"I do."

"Then sign your name here, in your own blood!"

"How do I get my own blood?"

> Water to water,
> Blood to blood.
> Prick your jugular
> And there'll be a flood!

replied Grand Witch.

I was shocked. I hadn't written that into the service either. I said hastily to Beryl: "Just prick your finger. Here's a needle. It's all right, I've sterilized it, and here's disinfectant to put on your finger first and a plaster to use afterwards."

"I can't do it," said Beryl.

"Yes, you can," I said. "I tried it out on myself earlier. It doesn't hurt if you just jab it quickly."

"I can't!"

"You WILL!" said Grand Witch.

Beryl took the needle and jabbed. Three bright drops of blood fell into the empty inkwell Huldah the Weazel held beneath the finger. "That's fine," I said. "That'll be just enough. Well done, Beryl!"

"Here's the pen," said Charlie.

Beryl signed.

"We now christen you Sybil the Snake and welcome you to our Coven," declared Grand Witch.

"Here are the robes of your office as Treasurer of this Coven, to which you are now duly appointed," said Huldah the Weasel, arranging a curtain liner around Beryl's shoulders and setting a peaked hat on her head. "Do you swear to honor the responsibilities of your office, and be answerable only to the members of this Coven for your actions?"

"I do," said Beryl, starting to giggle with near-hysterical relief. I began to giggle too.

"How dare you!" shrieked Grand Witch. "This is a solemn and awe-inspiring occasion!"

Beryl controlled herself with difficulty, then: "Gosh, Charlie, I've never heard anything like that yell you gave. It nearly split my eardrums!"

"I didn't give that yell," said Charlie. "I thought it was Peggy."

"Not me," I said. "I thought it was Charlie, too."

"Rena, was it you? It didn't sound like your voice at all," said Beryl.

"It was the Shriek of Satan," said Rena. "I summoned him and he answered."

I felt a chill begin at the top of my head and run to my heels. I didn't believe Rena, of course. She must have made the noise herself, although it seemed incredible that a human throat could have produced it.

"Girls! Charlie! What has happened to the bedroom ceiling?" cried Ma, who was thumping up the attic stairs. "Come down here at once. I want an explanation!"

56. Voodoo

Once the initiation was over and regular coven meetings commenced, Charlie opted out except for special occasions. Obviously something had to be done to keep interest going.

"Let's start a newspaper," I suggested. "We can write it in special ink and run it off on the school Hektograph. Then we can sell it and make some money."

I regularly did duplicating at lunch time for Miss Pierce, the first grade teacher at the school. The town kids went home for lunch, but those of us who came in from the farms brought ours and sat in one of the classrooms under supervision while we ate. Then we were allowed out into the playground until classes resumed.

Miss Pierce wrote a lot of her own work sheets for her pupils and asked me if I would like to make the copies for her. I considered it an honor to be allowed to help.

She'd taken me to the little closet-like room where the Hektograph was kept and showed me how to use it. The working part of the Hektograph was a heavy cloth covered with a layer of white gelatin-like material which gave off a heavy, sour odor.

Miss Pierce drew or wrote on special heavy paper with purple Hektograph ink. She shook a drop of it from her pen onto a piece of scrap paper to show me how the surface of the drop sparkled with little gold flecks.

Miss Pierce pressed the paper with the ink on it down onto the gelatin with a roller, and this transferred the ink onto the gelatin. Then she pressed ordinary paper onto the inked area a sheet at a time and rolled hard. Up to fifty copies could be produced before the ink faded. The remains of the ink could then be removed from the gelatin with special fluid.

"If Miss Pierce doesn't mind, after I do her Hektographing we could run off copies of the newspaper. You and Beryl can help. I'll show you how to do it."

"Who's the head of a newspaper—what's the boss called?" Rena wanted to know.

I was ready for her this time. I'd thought it all out. "Editor-in-Chief," I said. That should sound impressive enough to satisfy Rena, who of course immediately claimed the title as her own.

Page one of the first issue turned out even better than we'd hoped. Beryl did all the art work and designed the page carefully to include symbols of witchery and of the arts of writing and drawing. At the top she inscribed the name of the paper, *Neighborhood News*, on a scroll from which bats and demons peered. In the right-hand column an insert between two news items contained a crossed pen and pencil and an inkwell.

Beneath the scroll, the masthead read:

> A monthly paper by the Witches Society
> Editor-in-Chief: Grand Witch (Rena Allen)
> Written by: Huldah the Weazel (Peggy Shaw)
> Art work by: Sybil the Snake (Beryl Allen)
> Reporting and Production: Sybil the Snake and
> Huldah the Weazel
> Price: Five cents

That'll settle Rena's hash, I thought. Let her be Editor-in-Chief. It'll be clear enough that Beryl and I have done all the work and should get the credit. Everyone knows Rena can't string two words together and get them right.

Beryl and I planned the paper in three parts. The first section had items of interest about local farm people to ensure a market near home. The second section was "What's Going on at School" to interest the school kids and teachers. The last, and longest, section included short stories and poetry. I'd always had a head full of stories, and the paper was a good excuse to write some of them down. I'd made a bit of money the year before by charging a nickel a poem to friends who couldn't think up their own for class assignments—taking care to fit the quality of the poem to the brain of the buyer, so the teacher wouldn't get wise.

Getting news around home was not as easy as expected. Farming people were a quiet and reserved bunch and tended to be suspicious of anything new, so I'd relied largely on what I'd heard about outside the interviews. At school it was different. All the kids wanted something about themselves in the paper, and the teachers saw it as a chance for some positive propaganda.

Beryl and I did all the interviewing. Rena informed us grandly that since she was Editor-in-Chief she didn't have to interview anyone. It was up to us. This suited us fine. We were sure Rena wouldn't have known what to ask.

This spontaneous production by three girls in Grades Six and Seven was a phenomenon unknown at the school before. Our newspaper became the talk of the Teachers' Room, and the first issue was snapped up as soon as it came out. On our way home that day we also saturated the neighborhood with copies.

The first trouble came after Ma and Pa saw one. Ma read it first, but said nothing until Pa, who had gone to town, got home. By then, several people had phoned asking for Ma. They didn't want to speak to me. I began to feel uneasy. Something appeared to have backfired, but what was it? Whatever it was, it was serious enough to put off supper. Ma and Pa had shut themselves into the kitchen with the *Neighborhood News.* It was bad enough having to wait supper till Pa got home, and now I was feeling quite weak with hunger.

Finally Pa called me into the kitchen. "Did you girls write all this stuff?" he demanded.

"Yes."

"Where did you get this information?"

"From talking to people, mostly."

"I'll bet your Uncle Fred didnt talk to you about what you put in about him!"

"No, but everybody around here knows about it."

"Around here, mebbe, but not in town, and now every teacher in the school will be sniggering over it. Thank heavens Fred doesn't know anyone there, or anyone with kids there, except you. If he finds out what you've said about him and the Widow Beale, he'll flay you alive! You'd no business mentioning that he and his 'girlfriend Charlotte' had bought a new house!"

"And," said Ma, "Mrs. Potter did *not* want everyone to know that she had gone into the hospital for an operation, and most particularly she didn't want it known what it was for!"

"Oh," I said lamely. "I thought people would want to send her get well cards."

"I expect Mrs. Potter will send you more than a get well card," said Pa. "More likely a rocket with your name on it."

"And that note about Jenny Sim getting a job at a certain farm because of a certain handsome farm-hand," said Pa. "That's none of your business, and both Jenny and the young man will be terribly embarrassed. If there was a chance of a romance going on, that'll be enough to kill it."

"All the gossip about who's sweet on who at school seems fairly innocent to us older folks, and it's written with a lot of humor and a sense of fun," said Ma. "But I suspect a lot of children are going to be pretty embarrassed if their parents see the paper or hear about it. And I can't imagine what Miss Patterson

215

is going to say about your linking her name with that teacher at another school!"

"But Ma, most of it is just plain news items like about how Ralph Hutchins' barn roof collapsed and about the Smiths being burned out because of the fire that started in the chimney."

"Most of it is all right," said Pa, "but it only takes one item like that on Uncle Fred to put the fat in the fire, and you've got half a dozen uncalled-for things in here. You cannot write salacious stuff about people's personal lives. If you weren't under age, those people could sue you. As it is, I suppose they could sue me."

This had never occurred to me. We hadn't really meant to harm anyone, the excitement had run away with us. I didn't want Pa to get in trouble, but why did everything interesting have to be kept quiet and not talked about?

"I can see how it happened," said Ma. "You three girls get your heads together, one thing leads to another, and you carry things too far. And I bet Charlie had a hand in it too, didn't he?"

"Well, not really—he just suggested several interesting leads to follow up."

"I'll bet they were interesting," muttered Pa. "Now you listen to me, Peggy. I want you to go round and apologize to every one of the people who could have been hurt by anything in here. I'll give you a list of them, and I want it done this evening around here, and at school tomorrow morning. Do you hear?"

"Yes, Pa."

"As for your Uncle Fred, we'll just let it lie. Perhaps he won't find out. He doesn't come out here any more, and he doesn't know anybody at the school. If he does find out, I don't know what we'll do, but we'll worry about that if it happens. And don't you sell any more copies of this rag. Destroy what's left."

"They sold out," I said. "There's none left of the fifty we ran off."

"Oh, Jesus!" said Pa.

Not a word about the stories and poems and Beryl's art work, I thought. Everyone was too mad about the rest of it.

That evening and next day I did my best to make amends, and offered money back to the buyers. To my relief, no one took the money, and only Jenny Sim and two or three girls at school whose parents had got wind of it were really distraught. I'd been worried about Miss Patterson, the fourth grade teacher, but Miss Patterson said it was all right. She and Mr. Black were unofficially engaged, and it would be announced in the local paper soon anyway.

The school Principal, Mr. Stewart, who taught one of the two eighth grade classes, called Beryl and Rena and me into his office at the afternoon recess, and had a serious talk with us.

"I've had a couple of phone calls from parents," he said. "I think you girls should consider some of the possible consequences of your actions before you go into print again. There is a strict code of ethics associated with newspaper work, and if you are going on with this it's your first priority to find out what it is. If you like, I'll make an appointment for you to see the editor of the *Kennebec Journal*. Better still, perhaps he will come and talk to Grades Six through Eight about newspaper work, since everyone is now most interested indeed. Yes, I can see this serving a wider purpose."

We looked at each other in pleased surprise.

"I don't want you to feel I'm trying to discourage you," continued Mr. Stewart. "Far from it. I think it's marvelous that the three of you thought up this paper, and that you've done such an excellent job designing and producing it on your own. It's very well written. Your stories and poems are excellent, Peggy, and your drawings are superb, Beryl. You've got Charlie's gift, and you should develop it. I hope you three will put out many more issues. But you'll have to tone it down."

"Gosh, he was nice about it," said Beryl after we had left. "I'm glad someone had something good to say."

It was then that I noticed the expression on Rena's face. She looked like a thunderstorm about to erupt.

"What's the matter?" I asked.

"Mr. Stewart didn't say anything about me," she exploded. "Not one word! And I'm Editor-in-Chief. It was all about how clever you and Beryl are!"

Beryl and I said nothing. What could we say? Rena would sulk for a while, but she'd snap out of it.

For the rest of that year and the next, until I had gone up to high school, I recognized sly references by the teachers to Issue One of *Neighborhood News*. Principal Stewart was addicted to asking me how my Uncle Fred was. But as far as I knew, Fred never found out.

Next month we produced Issue Two. The draft was scrutinized thoroughly by Ma and Pa, the Allens and Principal Stewart, and certain changes were dictated before they agreed that it could be duplicated. The sanitized version was praised by all the grown-ups, but it was disappointing to everyone else.

"You know," I said, "I don't think we should do a third issue. It just isn't fun anymore with everyone looking over our shoulders telling us how to do it."

"You're right," said Beryl. "The grown-ups just want to take over. We'll have to think up something else."

The something else was not long coming. This time it was Rena who had the idea. Although she was Editor-in-Chief of *Neighborhood News*, as she had demanded, I could tell it had begun to dawn on her that the real heroines of the piece were Beryl and I.

Rena began asking me a lot of questions about what real witches did. I knew nothing about witches, except that they were said to be wicked old women who flew around on broomsticks, kept black cats as familiars, stewed up toads and snakes in cauldrons, and got together at coven meetings to plan trouble for people they didn't like. They were just make-believe, of course, like everything else children were told. No one talked about them, except at Halloween.

However, Rena's questions prompted me to go to the library to see if I could find out more. The books in the children's section told me nothing I hadn't already heard, and the librarian said children were not allowed in the adult section till they were in high school.

"There's no such thing as a witch," Pa confirmed when I consulted him. "That's just a lot of nonsense."

When I told Rena the results of my enquiries she was furious.

"Your father doesn't know what he's talking about," she snarled. "There are *so* witches, and they're in league with the devil. Everyone but a fool knows that!"

"Go look it up yourself, then, if you're so clever," I snapped back.

At the next coven meeting a few days later, Rena arrived with an uncommon look in her eye. "We've been wasting our time writing newspapers," she declared. "That's long-haired stuff. No proper Witches Club should be doing that sort of thing. Do you realize that this club hasn't done anything that a real coven would do?"

"What sort of thing would a real coven do?" asked Beryl.

"If you were a real witch you wouldn't have to ask that question," snapped Rena. "Well, I'm a real witch and I know what we're going to do. And we're going to do it now!" She spat the words out.

I reacted to her tone as much as her words. They gave me a tight feeling in the pit of my stomach. There was a coloring to Rena's voice that I hadn't heard before and didn't like.

"What do you mean?" asked Beryl.

"Voodoo," declared Rena. Then she paused for dramatic effect. Beryl and I stared at her, waiting for the next thrust.

"On the radio last night it told how you make a doll like your victim. Dress it in clothes like hers. Then put a pin through where you want her to hurt. Then she dies."

"Oh, that's nonsense," I snapped. "Just like ghost stories. They put them on the radio because people enjoy being scared silly. Voodoo doesn't really work!"

"Oh, you don't think so? You didn't hear that program. It really happens in Africa. The witch doctors can do it, and ordinary people can do it too. The victim just curls up and dies over about two or three days. In agony!"

"It's true," whispered Beryl, wide-eyed. "I heard it too. It scared me half to death."

"Twaddle," I said.

"Be careful," said Rena, "or I'll put a Voodoo curse on you. Then it won't be twaddle any more."

"I'm not scared of your curses. I'm as good a witch as you are."

"Who are you going to Voodoo?" asked Beryl.

"Miss Roberts."

Miss Roberts was the fifth grade teacher at the school—mid-fifties, tall, angular, horse-faced with big breasts sagging to her waist. I liked her. In fact everybody liked her. She was kind, and she told funny stories. "Why Miss Roberts?" I asked.

"Because that bitch made me stay back when I was in her year at school. She hates me and she used to mark my tests wrong so I'd fail. I had to sit and listen to that old fart for a whole extra year while everyone else went ahead. Now that I know how, I'm going to kill her for it."

"I seem to remember she gave you a lot of extra help at lunch time and after school," I said. "That doesn't sound like she hates you."

"She made me stay in while everyone else went out, and she made me do extra work, and kept writing home to my mother. Mummy got cross about it and told her to lay off me."

"She was nice to me," said Beryl, who had been in her class the previous year.

Rena turned on her like a snake: "Well, you're going to make the doll, Smarty. And you'll make it look just like her, do you hear?" Beryl went white.

Then Rena turned to me. "And you are going to write the incantation to pin on it."

"Write your own incantation. It's your idea."

"You'll write the incantation. As Grand Witch I command you to. You must obey."

I shrugged. This was all silly and stupid. It wouldn't work anyway. It didn't matter whether I wrote the incantation or not.

219

Beryl sorted through her mother's rag bag and found some peach-colored cloth for the doll's body. She also found some beige jersey almost the color of one of Miss Roberts' dresses, and a black scrap for the short jacket. She made a paper pattern and cut the doll out carefully. She sewed it together, leaving a gap big enough to stuff cotton into. The doll assumed three dimensions before our eyes. Then Beryl closed the gap and drew Miss Roberts' face on the front of the head. It really did look like Miss Roberts.

I wrote the incantation:

> Heckity peckity snakity Xoo
> Abarak Mabarak Zabarak Roo
> Entrails on fire
> Agony dire
> Ethne Roberts
> You're going to expire.

"It's just a silly poem," I said as I pinned it on the doll. "It won't do a thing to her."

"You'll see," said Rena. "It's my power that will make it work," and she took from her pocket a small coil of hair and sewed it on top of the hair Beryl had painted on. "What's that?" asked Beryl.

"Miss Roberts was combing her hair at the basin in the girls' room. Her hair's been falling out a lot lately, it's getting really thin. After she went out I scooped the hair out of the plug hole. You have to have something of the person's on the doll or the curse won't work."

The doll was now complete. Rena took a long darning needle from her mother's sewing box and pricked her own finger with it. Then she drove the needle diagonally through the doll's abdomen, saying "Blood to blood, hatred to hatred. Ethnie Roberts, I'll see you in hell!"

I winced as the needle went through; Beryl covered her eyes.

That was Saturday. On Monday I opened the morning paper and came face to face with Miss Roberts' picture. The headline read "Local teacher dead."

The story below told how Miss Roberts had been rushed to the hospital on Saturday and had died undergoing surgery for an intestinal blockage. The lines of print swam dizzily in front of my eyes. I couldn't believe what I was reading. I must be dreaming this. It couldn't be true.

Ma saw me go white and grip the edge of the table. "What is it?" she asked.

"Miss Roberts. She's dead."

"So soon?" said Ma.

I looked at Ma incredulously. Did she know. . . ?

Ma read the article. "Poor soul," she said.

I was in such a state of panic I could hardly get my words out: "Ma. . . someone. . . at school put a. . . curse on her. A Voodoo curse. Nobody thought it would work, Ma. How could it work? How does Voodoo work?"

"Peggy, what are you saying? Calm down and tell me slowly and distinctly what you are talking about."

"One of the girls at school hated Miss Roberts and she made a doll to look like her and ran a needle through it. I saw her do it."

Ma let this sink in for a minute, then said carefully: "Peggy, Miss Roberts has been a very sick woman for some time. Do you remember she was off for a few weeks about a year and a half ago?"

"Yes."

"There is a disease called cancer that older people sometimes get which causes tumors to grow inside them. When that happens the doctors have to take the tumor out or the disease will spread to other parts of the body. Miss Roberts had a tumor removed, but they didn't do it soon enough. The cancer had already spread. Perhaps you noticed that she hadn't been looking very well."

"She'd gotten awfuly thin and her hair's been falling out."

"The treatment they give sometimes makes the hair fall out. And I'm afraid in Miss Roberts' case the treatment just didn't help her at all. According to the paper, the cancer blocked her intestine. The doctors tried to remove the blockage but she died on the operating table."

I could feel the blood draining from my head. My lips and forehead felt all prickly and things started to go dark.

"Put your head between your knees, Peggy, and you won't faint. Better still, just lie down here on the floor for a few minutes. That will let the blood come back into your head." Ma wrung out a face cloth with cold water and bathed my face and neck.

"Now listen to me," she said. "Voodoo had nothing to do with Miss Roberts' death. Nothing at all. She was dying anyway, and that wicked girl no doubt had heard about it. Most of us grown-ups knew."

"Why didn't you tell me?"

"It's not the sort of thing that children ought to be worrying about."

"You never tell me anything important."

Ma sighed. "There's time enough to find out these things when you're grown up."

As if menstruation and childbearing were not enough to look forward to, I thought. And I'd heard about those from others, not from Ma. What else did being grown up have in store for me? What else wasn't Ma telling?

"Ma, how can you be sure Voodoo had nothing to do with it?"

"Because Voodoo only works in countries where everyone believes in it. If a person is sure that a Voodoo curse will kill him, and he knows that someone has made a doll to look like him and put a curse on it, he may die.

221

It's mind over matter. It sounds ridiculous to us, but it does happen in some places. Miss Roberts could have had no idea that girl was putting a curse on her. Thank heavens. It wouldn't have helped her to know that someone hated her so much. She was such a kind person and so good to the children."

"But how could it happen so quickly? The girl put the curse on her Saturday, and now she's dead!"

It didn't occur to me till much later that mentioning the deed had been done on Saturday would tell Ma at once that the doer could only have been one of the Allen children. I'd spent Saturday with them. But Ma never let on that she'd made the connection.

"Coincidence," said Ma. "Or, more likely, she'd heard that Miss Roberts had been rushed to the hospital. She could have died any time in the next few weeks and that girl could still have claimed it was the result of Voodoo."

Was Ma telling me the truth? Ma was an honest woman, everyone knew that. But I'd learned the hard way that Ma was quite capable of lying to protect me from unpleasant facts.

When school assembly began that morning, Rena and Beryl were conspicuously absent. I saw them come in about half way through. Beryl looked ill. Rena handed the Principal a note and took her seat, giving me a look of triumph as she did so.

At first recess I met the two girls in the playground. "You see?" said Rena. "I told you it would work!"

Beryl started to cry. "I shouldn't have made that doll. I didn't really think it would work. Miss Roberts was good to me. I didn't mean to hurt her."

"You didn't hurt her, and neither did I," I said. "She was dying of cancer. Ma told me so. And you must have known it, Rena. Miss Roberts didn't know anything about your old curse anyway, so it couldn't have done her any harm. The victim has to believe that Voodoo works and to know that she's being cursed."

Rena grabbed me by the shoulder. "Did you tell your Ma about this?"

"I just told her that someone at school had put a Voodoo curse on Miss Roberts. So Ma told me how Voodoo works, and that in our own culture it wouldn't have any effect." I shook myself free of Rena's grasp.

"Well, you believe that bullshit if you want," snapped Rena. "But I know better and so does Beryl. I can get rid of anyone I want with Voodoo. I've proved it. And why do you think Miss Roberts got cancer anyhow? I've been willing it on her ever since she kept me back."

"Well, I'm getting out of the club," I said. "You're evil, Rena. I don't want anything to do with your curses. They didn't harm Miss Roberts, but that's no thanks to you. I'll never write anything you ask me to again, *never.* And here's your four nickels back for those poems I wrote for you for English class last year. I don't want your money."

"I'm getting out of the club too," said Beryl.

Rena rounded on both of us. "You just watch it, Peggy Shaw, and you too, Beryl. I can put the curse on both of you. You just watch what you say and what you do!"

"The club's finished," I said. "It's childish and stupid and I won't have any more to do with it."

The bell sounded for the resumption of classes, and I turned and walked back into the building, leaving Rena and Beryl staring after me.

It was several days before I spoke to either Allen girl again. At school we avoided one another. Then on Saturday, a week after Miss Roberts' death, Beryl appeared at my door. Her eyes were dark and enormous in her drawn face.

"I had to come and see you. I've hardly slept since Miss Roberts died, and every time I do she's there whispering to me."

"You're just having nightmares, Beryl. Don't worry about them. I've been having them too. They'll go away. People always have nightmares after someone dies that they know," I said, remembering the dreams I'd had about Barton and Grace.

"It's not a nightmare. She's there, I tell you! Trying to say something but I can't make out the words."

"With me she's just standing there in a garden full of flowers looking very sad, as if someone had hurt her feelings."

"You'd better come with me, Peggy."

"Come where?"

"To the priest. My granny, Dad's mother, is Catholic. I went to see her yesterday and asked her if I could see a priest because I'd done something terrible that I couldn't tell anyone about and I wanted to confess. She's arranged for me to see him this afternoon. Why don't you come too?"

"I've got nothing to confess," I said.

"Wouldn't it help to cleanse your soul?"

"My soul isn't dirty. I meant no harm and I caused no harm. And anyhow I haven't got a soul. I don't believe in God."

Beryl was shocked. We'd never discussed religion before.

"Surely everyone believes in God!" she gasped.

After her session with the priest, Beryl came back to see me. "It's all right," she said. "I told him everything. He said I was free from mortal sin, and so are you. Since you and I meant Miss Roberts no harm our only fault was in not confronting evil and denouncing it. He said we can't be held accountable because we aren't Catholics. We live in ignorance of God's law, and he can't absolve us unless we join the church. Only then can we be released and allowed to take communion. I'm going to become a Catholic, Peggy. I'm taking instruction. Are you sure you don't want to come too? The priest said he would welcome you."

"No. I won't go with you. But I'm glad if he helped you. Very glad."

Beryl's conversion was never made final. She went for instruction and to mass for several weeks. It helped. She told me that Miss Roberts came to her in a dream—not a nightmare this time—and now she understood what she was trying to tell her:

"Peggy, she took both my hands in her own and said, 'Dear child, do not grieve for me, for I have become well. You did not harm me, for your heart bore me no evil.'"

Beryl's father, although a lapsed Catholic, did not want to brave his mother's wrath. He drove Beryl to and from her religious commitments without complaint, but, as he admitted to Pa, he hated having to rise early on Sunday, which was the only morning he could sleep late. Mrs. Allen, a Protestant, was furious and uncomprehending. What had gotten into the girl? Though Mrs. Allen had not been to church since she got married, Beryl told me, she still felt some commitment to Protestantism when she happened to think about it.

Rena and Charlie said nothing in front of their parents, but Beryl reported that they teased her unmercifully when they got her alone. Once her guilt and the fear of Miss Roberts' ghost had faded, she began to lose enthusiasm herself for getting up early to worship, and for learning yet more questions and answers. As her keenness ebbed, Mr. Allen—relieved—did nothing to renew it. Having served its purpose, the matter died a quiet and natural death.

Though I never admitted it to Beryl, I was profoundly shaken by the whole episode. I'd been shocked when Rena suggested Voodoo. Her desire to injure someone who had only tried to be kind to her was evil and wrong. But I was so sure what Rena was planning wouldn't work that I'd gone along with it for what I expected would be the pleasure of proving her wrong. Instead, Miss Roberts had died.

Fortunately, Ma had been able to convince me that her death had nothing to do with Rena's curse. But that didn't change the fact that Rena was willing to kill, and would have if it had been in her power.

I knew I should tell Rena I wanted no more to do with her. But if I did, I'd lose Beryl's and Charlie's friendship, and wouldn't be able to go down to the Allens' anymore. I was fond of all of them, in fact, except Rena. They'd been the source of much fun and pleasure for me.

There would still be the Lees, of course, but that wasn't the same as having friends my own age. My resolve to avoid evil doers was overcome by impending loneliness, and I took the easy way out.

Ma and Pa made no comment one way or another. I guessed that they had written off what we'd done as a foolish but harmless children's game.

57. Forbidden Fruit

LEARN THE TRUE FACTS ABOUT SEX!
Ignorance about the vital life force can damage your marriage and your health. Dr. Long's new book *Sane Sex Life and Sane Sex Living* can change your life for the better. If you are 21 years old or over you may order this comprehensive and clearly written account by a famous authority in the field. Place your order today and see how this classic text can improve your marital relations. Only $2.50 post paid.

I had received this advertisement with fill-in coupon attached in the morning mail. It was not unusual for me to receive solicitations to purchase by mail. Everyone in the town and countryside seemed to be on several mailing lists of one sort or another. But never had I received one of such immediate and pertinent interest. A book such as this might answer some of my questions, fill in the blanks in my knowledge, perhaps spell out some of the things which, for good or evil, lay in wait for me.   I filled in my age as 23, enclosed a money order purchased with some of the money I had saved from working at the Lees, and sent off the coupon.

A month passed before the package arrived, fortunately in a plain brown paper wrapper. Ma saw me returning from the mailbox. "What have you got there?" she asked.

"A letter for you, a circular for Pa and a seed catalogue that I sent for," I lied.

Ma went off to read her letter and I shot upstairs to the attic. I'd already prepared a hiding place for the book to avoid confiscation. Under the rug in the attic room I had found a short board in the flooring, about eighteen inches long, from which I had loosened the nails. The board could now be lifted up at one end to give access to the space between the flooring and the lath and plaster of the ceiling below. Now, with the rug pulled back and the board up in readiness for a quick transfer if necessary, I settled down for as long a read as I could get away with before Ma wanted me for something.

Luckily, my friendship with the Allens and the Witches Club had one positive result: I was no longer afraid to be alone in the attic. I had made it my territory.

The book was not a thick one, and I managed it, between interruptions, in two days. It was well written, clear, direct and fascinating. It changed sex from a smutty, guilt-ridden practice that people had to do to produce children into a joyful expression of love to be cherished and savored. A great cloud lifted from my mind. It wasn't awful and embarrassing after all. All the old ladies with their obsession with wickedness, and all the sniggering boys in the corner of the school playground were equally wrong. It made sense for a natural act of such importance to be wonderful.

There was only one problem: How could you do this marvelous thing and not have a baby? That the book didn't say.

As soon as I read the book and digested its contents, I told Rena and Beryl about my treasure. Over the next few days we read it aloud to each other and discussed it from cover to cover. Like me, the girls already knew the basic mechanics from one source or another, but had never before heard sex called an expression of love. They, too, did not know how to avoid having a baby.

"It isn't fair," said Beryl. "The one thing in the world which is the most fun can get you into the worst trouble. And the books never tell you how to stay out of trouble."

"Fay says it's against the law to give birth control information in books," said Rena. "You can only get it from doctors if you're married. Fay says the church is afraid that if people knew how to avoid having babies nobody would have any, and they'd just have sex for fun."

"That sounds like a good idea," I said. I didn't think much of the idea of childbirth. I didn't think much of the church, either, for that matter. God only seemed to be invoked when there was some danger of people enjoying themselves. I could never understand how Ma, usually so sensible, could claim not to be superstitious and still believe in God.

58. Winifred

Toward the end of March, six months after Marge's death, a letter arrived for me from Jamestown, Rhode Island. It was in a square, ivory-colored envelope and looked like it might be a birthday card. But my birthday was in January. Why would Lynde send me a birthday card in March?

I opened it carefully. Inside was a matching, engraved, announcement card. It read:

Mr. and Mrs. William Alonzo Clarke
of Jamestown, Rhode Island
announce the wedding of their daughter
Winifred French
to
Lester Lynde Russell
at a candlelight ceremony on
March 28, 1941
at Norfolk, Virginia

Lynde had betrayed Marge. She hardly dead, and he'd married someone else! Someone he must have met in Jamestown.

Speechless, I handed Ma the announcement. She read it, and I saw her mouth set into a hard line.

"How could he do that so soon?" I asked.

She looked at me sadly. "It's his business," she said, handing me back the card.

I found Pa in the shed, chopping kindling. I showed him the announcement and asked him the same question I'd asked Ma.

"He's been through hell and he's lonely. I hope they'll be happy. We'll all write and congratulate them."

All? I wondered if Ma would, after seeing her face when she read the announcement. Nevertheless, three letters of congratulation went off to Lynde and his new bride, and the story of Marge closed forever.

59. Pa and City Hall

The winter of 1940-1941 had not been a good one for Pa. He never seemed to completely recover from one cold before getting the next. He'd been spending his days smoking and coughing in his rocking chair by the kitchen window, with the cat making a permanent bed on his lap.

Pa was also worried about finances. The money we had received from the acre of land Allen bought was nearing exhaustion. In mid-March he put the "House Lot for Sale" sign back on our lawn, hoping to catch the eye of someone who dreamed of building a house once the snow was off.

With jobs becoming plentiful in response to the war, money was easier, and several people came by to look at the acre between 'Barton's' bunglow and the Allens' west boundary.

A house and garden would fit in there nicely, said Pa, and the single pine tree near a rock outcropping would lend character to the place. "It's where I'd build if I had the money," he said. "Nice snug little bungalow, no stairs to climb, low ceilings and proper insulation so it'd be warm."

The people who came, however, didn't want to buy land where a well would have to be dug. When they learned that the city water district stopped half a mile short of our farm, they lost interest. Pa was grim and preoccupied, and I could tell things were serious.

"The city damn well should have put in water right out to the Manchester line," he said. "I suppose they didn't because when they made the decision the only things out here were farms that had their own wells. Now all the city land suitable for housing has been built on, and people are wanting to move to the country. But having to pay for digging a well on top of buying the land and building a house is the last straw for most of them."

A couple of days later when I got home from school, Pa had something to show me. In the dining room, spread out on the table, was a large sheet of paper with a neatly drawn plan.

"It's our farm," Pa said. "I did a tracing of the original plan I got when I bought the place, and I've put in the details of how we could divide it up into house lots and make a packet of money if the city would supply the water."

The plan was meticulously drawn and the printing clear and professional looking. When had he ever learned to do that? I wondered.

"Part of my plumbing apprenticeship included drawing plans of where to lay pipes," he explained when I asked him.

"Look here," he said. "Here's our farmhouse. Here's Allens', and here's the old trolley line. If the city put a street with a water main up that trolley line, it would open up our eighty acres of woods for development. Another street could come down our logging road and exit onto the road between our farmhouse and the west field. That would open up land that wouldn't even need clearing. They're going to have to build streets out here eventually. The population of Augusta is going up, and pressure is growing to expand."

"Do you think the city would be willing to do that, Pa?"

"I'll find out tomorrow. I got an appointment to see the big cheese at City Hall Planning Department at 10:30 tomorrow morning."

When I got home next day, Pa was nowhere to be seen.

"Where's Pa?" I asked.

"In his bedroom," said Ma. "He's not feeling well. He had a cold coming on yesterday. He shouldn't have gone to that meeting this morning. He got chilled through waiting for the bus back."

"What happened at the meeting?" I asked.

"They weren't interested."

"But why not?"

"He didn't go into it. Not feeling up to it."

228

I didn't like the sound of this. Was Pa seriously ill? He'd always had a cough, like Fred, from smoking their home-rolled Prince Albert tobacco cigarettes, but did his repeated heavy colds mean he had something worse?

At half past five, I took a tray in for his supper and sat with him while he ate it.

"I'm sorry you've got another cold, Pa," I said.

"I think it's bronchitis," he said. "I'll lie low for a couple of days." His voice was husky and his eyes rheumy and red.

"You do that. There's nothing to be done that Ma and I can't handle."

"Good girl."

"Now what about City Hall?"

"They said there wasn't a hope of their putting city water or streets out here in the foreseeable future."

"But why not?"

"They weren't about to tell the likes of me why not, but I can guess."

"Why, then?"

"There's no pressure from the rich for them to do it. The rich have their mansions in town already and have filled up all the nice spots outside such as Cobbosseecontee. They've no interest in buying an acre of land on a former farm. They want to live next to their own kind. So there's no demand for putting water three miles out of town: the rich won't vote for it and neither will the poor, since it would raise everyone's taxes. There's more of them in the city to vote agin' it than there are of us in the country to vote for it."

"So what are we going to do, Pa?" I asked. I was afraid he'd say sell the farm.

"There's one thing left to try," he said. "I'll go see Judge Cony."

"What can he do?"

"You know about the money that's in trust for you, that Mrs. Cony handles. That's yours, and thank heavens no one can touch it till you need it yourself. But there's another trust fund as well. I guess we've never mentioned it to you."

"No, you never have."

"It was your mother who inherited from your grandfather, not you. When she died, her share of your grandfather's estate was divided between you, Lynde and me equally, as her heirs. Each of us has a trust fund, but the long hand of your grandfather has ensured that the three of us can only get money under the conditions laid down by him in his will. He tied up his estate in such legal knots that none of his heirs can get their hands on any of it when it's needed."

I opened my mouth to ask why, but Pa shook his head before I could speak.

"Don't ask me to explain. The legal language is so dense that only Judge Cony and your grandfather's lawyer in Massachusetts can understand what the old man did. And I suspect maybe they don't really understand it either. Anyway, Peggy, I'm going to phone Cony tomorrow—I'm too sick to go see him—and ask him if he can exert some pressure so we'll have enough to eat till I can sell another house lot."

"Pa," I said, "I've saved quite a bit of the money I've earned at the Lees. That'll buy food for a while."

"No, Peggy, that's yours, and you're to keep it. "We're not quite at the door to the poorhouse yet."

60. The Draft

In September, 1940, the first draft law was passed to register men between the ages of twenty-one and thirty-six. A lottery was drawn the first of October, and the first draft notices went out in November. These began their message with "Greetings."

The draft had opposite effects on two groups of men: The aspirations of many a farmer's son to leave cow and turnip patch in order to serve his country were thwarted. Farm workers were needed and draft-exempt. On the other hand, there was an exodus of vulnerable young men from the city to take jobs as hired farm hands. They were willing to work for peanuts to keep out of the Army, and this eased somewhat the killing hours of the farm owners.

This directly affected the Lees in the spring of 1941. They suddenly had more requests for employment than they knew what to do with. I regarded this development with trepidation. Now that grown men were available, would they still want me to drive the hayrick?

I need not have worried. Dick assured me that he was hiring only one man, Noah Robbins, who had recently bought the grocery store half way between Augusta and Lee's farm. Though recently married and running a business, he was in the vulnerable age group. His wife and her sister would run the store while he did farm work.

Noah was a quiet young man with a high tenor voice. According to Maisie, he had delicate skin that had never produced whiskers or seen a razor. Noah, Dick and Freddy would pitch the hay up onto the load, and I would keep my job as load builder. Noah would also work some evenings mowing and raking hay when needed, which would lessen Dick's work load.

I found this new arrangement very convenient. It meant that if some interesting adventure with the Allens came up I could take a day off without seriously inconveniencing the Lees.

For Maisie Lee, Noah's advent lightened a considerable burden of worry. She had been concerned about Dick's health for some time. The preceding summer's work had left him in a state of near exhaustion, and she insisted that he consult Dr. Murdoch. Murdoch had told him, "You've grown too fast and are too thin for your height. You need rest and more protein and carbohydrate in your diet for energy."

Murdoch prescribed several Hershey bars and three bananas per day, plus a mandatory half hour rest in a darkened room after each noonday meal. Now, with Noah's help, this prescription would be easier to carry out.

61. Willard

In mid-May Fay married Willard Peaks, a widowed farmer in his thirties. He lived on the coast near Wiscasset where Fay had been working as a waitress. Ma said it must have been a whirlwind romance when I told her no one in the family had heard of Willard until just before the wedding. I met him briefly when he came to pick up Fay after the "little miscellaneous shower" given by her mother.

I'd been invited to the shower, and went with Mrs. Allen, Rena and Beryl. I'd never attended one before so knew nothing about them, but Ma said it was unusual for a mother to give a shower for a daughter. It was supposed to be given by the girlfriends of the bride-to-be.

Willard had large, sensuous features, big bones and a mop of longish curly brown hair which fell down over his forehead. There was something coarse about him that I didn't like. He looked at me in a way that made me uncomfortable without knowing why, but Fay seemed utterly captivated by him, smiling up at him tenderly when he arrived.

They were married by a Justice of the Peace two days later, and left at once to go back to Willard's farm in Wiscasset. He couldn't leave the farm long enough for them to go away for a honeymoon.

In mid-July Rena was asked to go to Wiscasset for a month or so to help Fay, who was pregnant and suffering from morning sickness. Rena was furious. Working in her grandmother's laundry last year was bad enough, and now this. Waiting on a sick aunt and cooking for Willard Peaks was the last thing she wanted to do on her summer holiday. She wanted to relax, forget about school—at which she was doing badly—and ride her horse.

She protested long and loud and then went into a monumental sulk, but Anna Allen stood firm. "You'll go, Rena, and no nonsense!" she snapped. "Fay needs you, and Willard has two horses you can ride, for Chrissakes. I don't want to hear another word out of you!"

Thus for a month I had Beryl all to myself, and the two of us luxuriated in the relief of being out from under the dominant hen. We declared undying friendship for each other, and did all the things Rena disapproved.

In mid-August the Allens went to collect Rena and asked me to come along with them in the pick-up. It was a Sunday, and the Lees said they could get along without me.

Though less elegant than the new car, the pick-up was more fun. Beryl and Charlie and I bounced along the bumpy country roads for forty miles in the open back, laughing and singing in the hot sun. Outings were few, especially now that gas was rationed, and there was to be a cookout on the beach in the evening before we returned home.

When we reached the Peaks farm we found Fay cheerful and glad to see us. Her morning sickness had ceased, and she seemed rested and in good spirits.

Willard's welcome to Beryl seemed surprisingly warm to me, whose family was undemonstrative. He kissed and cuddled Beryl, and called her a beautiful sweet little thing; then he kissed and cuddled Rena, keeping both girls in his arms for a long time.

We ate lunch in the big farm kitchen which served as a living room as well. Fay had prepared a massive spread of New England boiled dinner with side dishes of fresh corn, peas, sliced tomatoes and cucumbers, followed by hot homemade apple pie and ice cream.

When we'd eaten all we could hold we sat around the table and talked for a while, except for Rena and Willard, who claimed they were too full to sit up and lolled on the couch in the corner of the room.

Then, while Mrs. Allen and Fay were cleaning up and Willard was showing Mr. Allen and Charlie his "new" second-hand milk-delivery van, Rena took Beryl and me to explore the farm buildings and to see the recently born litter of puppies. Rena had obviously been bursting with something she couldn't wait to tell. We were hardly out of sight of the adults when she announced dramatically:

"Willard and I are in love."

"What do you mean by that?" I asked.

"In love, idiot, like man and woman, not like some silly high school romance."

Beryl gave a nervous giggle. "You mean he touches you?"

"Touches!   Don't be a fool. We make love—all the way—it's marvelous!"

"Really, Rena?" I asked.

"Yes, really. Several times a day. Every time we can get out of Fay's sight."

"I don't believe you. That's wicked!" I exclaimed.

"It's true."

"Fay'd have found out."

"Fay's an idiot. She never suspects anything. And neither did you. There in the kitchen when we were all talking just after lunch and Willard and I were lying on the couch with that blanket over us. He had it in me then, from behind, and no one knew anything about it."

"I'm damned," I said.

Beryl began to giggle and couldn't stop. She seemed on the edge of hysteria. "That's adultery, Rena. Adultery's a sin!" she gasped when she got control of herself.

Remembering her Catholic instruction, I thought. "It's also against the law," I pointed out. "Remember you said your mother told you the age of consent was sixteen? Willard could go to jail for what you've been doing!"

"Oh, sin! Law! Age of consent! What are you talking about? I'm a witch, you fools. I don't have to listen to that crap. And don't you dare tell Charlie or anyone else. This is between us. Or I'll do to you what I did to Miss Roberts. Do you understand?"

Willard was a big man, and my imagination produced an organ to match. "Didn't it hurt the first time, Rena?"

"A little, but we'd played around so much before that I didn't want him to stop. Oh, at first I kept saying I didn't want to, but you just don't know how good it feels. God, it's wonderful. We just do it over and over now—all the time."

"Fay'll find out and kill you," said Beryl.

"No, she won't. She's too stupid. And when I'm grown up Willard's going to divorce Fay and marry me. He says I've bewitched him and he'll never love anyone else. He says Fay isn't sexy like I am, even though my breasts haven't developed yet. He plays with them all the time and says that'll bring them on."

Beryl and I were speechless. Rena looked at us with contempt.

"You're shocked, aren't you? You poor virgins, you don't know what you're missing!"

"You're almost thirteen, Rena, you'll get pregnant if you don't watch it," I said.

Rena preened herself and looked at us with sultry eyes. "Don't be silly," she sneered. "Real witches don't get pregnant! Only bitches do that. Come on. I'll show you the puppies."

She led us through a maze of farm buildings to the shed where the pups and their mother were. There were six of them. The mother was part collie, the father part Belgian police dog, Rena said. The results were pure mongrel, but the pups were sleek and beautiful. They were about a month old, not yet weaned, eyes still blue. One was particularly lovely—black with a tan and white face, white paws and white tip on her tail. I picked her up. She sucked on my fingers and seemed to smile.

"She's your dog," said Rena.

"What do you mean?"

"Willard's got to give them away because he's already got two dogs. He doesn't want to drown them. He told me to see which one you liked and you could have it. You can take it home with you tonight."

What would Ma say? We hadn't had a dog since Max got killed on the road. That happened when I was too young to remember, but I'd been told about him. Traffic past our farm was getting worse all the time, we were too near the road, and Ma had said she didn't want to put another dog at risk. But if no one took this pup, Willard would have to drown her. I couldn't let that happen.

"I'll take her," I said. I'd risk Ma's wrath. I figured if she saw the pup she wouldn't be able to refuse.

Willard was pleased when Rena told him. "She'll make you a nice pet, Peggy," he said. "After our cookout on the beach tonight we'll come back here so you can take her home with you."

Later that afternoon Willard suggested that Rena, Beryl and I be allowed to stay on for a week at the farm. The Allens could come back for us the following Saturday. I said I was sure my folks wouldn't let me. Anyway, I was working at the Lees and the haying wasn't finished yet. Beryl giggled uncomfortably. The Allens said they'd think about it.

"He just wants to do to us what he's doing to Rena—to get us in it too so we won't blab," said Beryl when she got me alone.

"Well, he won't get me," I said. "I wouldn't stay for a million dollars, even if my folks let me."

"I'm not staying either," said Beryl. "I'll tell Mummy I don't want to. But didn't it make you feel funny when Rena was telling us all those things that Willard does with her? Sort of like you want to do them too?"

I shuddered. "Yes. Yes, I'd like to. But not with anyone's husband. And not till I'm grown up, either."

The Allens thanked Willard and Fay for their invitation to the girls but said there was too much to do to get the house finished inside before school began.

I'd cooked hot dogs and toasted marshmallows over a fire in the Allens' yard a couple of times, but had never been to a beach cookout before. The beach was about a mile from Willard's farm, and we took both his car and the Allens' pickup to transport the food and people. Willard, Mr. Allen and Charlie got a fire going and put potatoes and corn in its husk beneath the hot coals to bake. We each cooked our own hot dogs on sharp sticks. It got dark soon after we got there, and the moon and stars came out in full brilliance. The heavens were awash in the light of the milky way. Our faces, lit by the flickering fire, seemed very different than when seen by day in sunlight.

After the cookout we returned to the farm and picked up my puppy, which I had decided to call Judy. Fay gave me a soft old towel to wrap her in. I sat with her in my lap in the back of the pickup, and she slept contentedly as we rode back home under the stars.

Ma muttered, "Female, of course," when she examined the pup. She'd said the same thing when I brought Fluff home. She folded her lips tightly, but as I had predicted she did not object to my keeping her.

"She'll be a lot of joy to you," said Pa. They agreed that Judy would be a good name for her.

Ma found an old medicine bottle with a dropper on its cap and filled it with warm milk. "You'll have to hand feed her for a while," she said to me. "She shouldn't have been taken away so young, but she'll be all right."

About a week later, I received a letter in a strange hand-writing. It was from Willard.

Dear Peggy,

I'm enclosing a letter for Rena and would be much obliged if you would give it to her without telling anyone. Fay and I are planning a surprise for Rena's mother and don't want anyone to know that we've written to her about it.

Thanking you for your kindness, Peggy.

Sincerely,
Willard

I examined the seal on the letter addressed to Rena. It was not firmly stuck and I had no trouble getting the flap up by gently rolling the end of a thin pen holder underneath.

Darling, Darling Rena,

I'm sending this to Peggy to give to you, as I promised. You can't guess how much I miss you, how much I miss your body every minute of the day. I can never get enough of you. Remember all the loving I've given you, how we can do it over and over without me going limp.

I've got a plan. At Thanksgiving vacation you could take a couple of extra days—get your Ma to write a note to school saying you're sick. You could come up here by train. I'd meet you in

Wiscasset. We'd say it was to help Fay, who will be 8 months on by then. Maybe you could come up for Christmas, too. Nearer the time I'll start working on Fay about it, and then get in touch with your folks. I'm sure it'll work.

Oh Darling Girl, I wish I had my arms around you and my prick up your lovely tight little cunt.

Your loving sexy Willard

So it was all true and then some! Rena was willing to break up Fay's marriage and not even think twice about it. Willard knew Rena was under the age of consent, and he was breaking the law. He didn't care a whit about Fay or about their baby. He and Rena were wicked and cruel.

I put both letters in my pocket and walked down the road to the Allens'. Beryl and Rena had gone over to McAuley's for hot dogs, and only Mrs. Allen was in.

"I thought you'd better see these," I said, handing her the letters. I hadn't bothered to re-seal Willard's to Rena.

Mrs. Allen read them and went white. "The bastard! Filthy bastard!"

"Rena'll kill me, but I thought you ought to know."

"You did right to give them to me, Peggy. Oh, that son-of-a-bitch!"

"I'd better be going," I said. "Got to help Ma with jelly-making this afternoon."

I knew it was the end of my friendship with Rena, but I didn't care. Rena was too proud of herself, too arrogant, too scathing to everybody, too nasty to Beryl. And incredibly wicked in what she had tried to do to Miss Roberts, and what she had actually done to Fay, who had always been so kind to her. Serve her right to be taken down a peg, stuck-up brat.

Anyhow, Beryl will still be my friend, I thought. And I'm not scared of Rena's threat about Voodoo, either. There's no God and the only devils are human ones.

I heard nothing from the Allens all that day and part of the next. By three in the afternoon I could stand it no longer and walked down the road to see what was happening. Not knowing what was going on was worse than braving Rena's wrath.

A car I hadn't seen before was parked in their driveway. As I climbed up the steps to their door, I saw Mr. and Mrs. Allen, Beryl and Charlie sitting in the kitchen looking at the closed door to the girls' bedroom.

"Dr. Browning is in there with Rena right now," said Beryl, her eyes enormous.

"Why, is she sick?"

"No, he's examining her!"

236

"Dr. Browning is the police doctor," Mrs. Allen explained. "He talked with Rena, and she told him how she tried to fight Willard off for four hours before giving in."

I glanced at Beryl, who flushed crimson and avoided my eyes.

"Can't you see poor little Rena lying there in the grass trying to hold off that big son-of-a-bitch?" continued Mrs. Allen. "And if you hadn't given me that letter, Peggy, we might never have found out!"

The door to the bedroom opened, and a big-bellied elderly man in a brown three-piece suit with a gold watch chain dangling from his vest pocket came out, wiping his hands on a towel.

"Well," he said without preamble, "your daughter is certainly no virgin. However she doesn't appear to have been harmed in any way. I see no evidence of violence, nor does she claim to have been injured. She is, of course, too young and under-developed to have become pregnant. I've taken blood and smears to make sure there is no venereal disease present, but everything else seems to be in order."

"In order?" snapped Mrs. Allen. "A twelve-year-old girl gets raped and you think everything is in order?"

"Whether the rape was any more than statutory I can't say from an examination such as this so long after the occurrence. But clearly the child is under age, and you have damning letters that will certainly get your man either behind bars or very heavily fined. But I wouldn't push the story of the four-hour fight, if I were you. No judge is going to fall for that one."

"The bugger should be put away for ten years," said Allen.

"That will be up to the judge. I must go now, I have other calls to make," and Browning left abruptly.

"Poor little Rena. . ." Mrs. Allen began again, when poor little Rena came out of the bedroom looking rather pleased with herself.

"Has he gone?" she asked.

"Yes."

"He told me all the right words to say in court. Like 'in course with a woman' instead of screwing."

Charlie roared with contemptuous glee. "Intercourse, you nitwit!"

"I bet you didn't know that, Peggy," Rena said, ignoring him. "And I'm to say, 'He penetrated my vagina with his penis,' instead of 'He put his prick in me.'"

I was thunderstruck. Rena wasn't angry with me at all. She was the center of attention and loving every minute of it! Instead of being taken down a peg, she'd taken command. Just like she'd taken over the incantations at Beryl's initiation. Her face and gestures were full of the drama of her situation. Beryl, too, seemed completely caught up in it.

"Oh, Rena," she burbled, "you look just like an actress!"

A couple of weeks later I was walking back up the road from the Allens' when I saw Pa coming to meet me. His leathery face was knotted up with worry.

"Peggy, I've just received a summons from the Wiscasset Circuit Court for you to appear on the tenth of November as a witness in the case of the State of Maine versus Willard Peaks. What in hell is it all about?"

"Fay's husband Willard has been fooling around with Rena and he sent me a letter to give to her. I gave it to her mother instead, and she called the police."

"Oh, Jesus Christ! I knew I shouldn't have let you get involved with that cheap bunch down there, Peggy. They've got the morals of a bunch of tomcats!"

"I'm not in any trouble, Pa! They're all glad I gave Mrs. Allen the letter. Even Rena."

"Peggy, do you know what 'fooling around' means?"

"Of course. But she's too young to get pregnant."

Pa looked at me, taken aback. I could tell he was wondering where I'd got that sort of information. "You don't seem to be very upset about this," he said. "Do you realize you're going to have to get up in court and tell the judge all you know about it?"

"Yes, but all I've got to do is tell the truth and answer the judge's questions."

Pa groaned. "At least Judge Cony is on circuit at Wiscasset in November. We know him and he knows us. He's a good man."

I felt no qualms about going to court. We'd been taught about trials by jury at school, and there'd been one in a play I'd heard on the radio. It would be exciting to see what a real trial was like. I'd learn a lot. I wasn't afraid of being cross- examined, either. After all, I'd just be telling the truth.

62. The Court Case

On the tenth of November the Allens and I travelled together to Wiscasset by car. Rena and Beryl looked very fine in new coats and matching knitted caps and mittens bought specially for the occasion. Charlie, too, had a new jacket. Rena was radiant with excitement. It was her day in court, as well as a day off school. She'd practiced all the proper terminology over and over. She'd shortened the four hours' resistance to "as long as I could hold him off."

I had very little idea of what a court session was, but, like Rena, I fully expected to have to tell my story to judge and jury and a packed courthouse of worthy citizens—and to be challenged on every point by the counsel for the defense. This still did not frighten me. I thought it would be exciting and rather fun. The long faces and obvious apprehensions of Ma and Pa as they saw me off did nothing to dampen my spirits.

We got to the courthouse with half an hour to spare before the morning session began, and were joined by Dr. Browning and the Allens' lawyer. We all took seats in the middle of the courtroom and, while the Allens conferred in low tones with Dr. Browning and the lawyer, Rena, Beryl, Charlie and I watched the people as they came in. Those whose cases were coming up that morning were fairly easy to spot: they were nervous and accompanied by family members and lawyers. As for the rest, they were a miscellaneous assortment of older men, mostly drifters off the street looking for a morning's entertainment in a warm room.

I kept my eye on the door, and saw Willard and Fay enter with their lawyer. Their eyes were downcast, and Willard was supporting the hugely pregnant Fay with his arm. As they passed the row where her family was sitting, Fay looked up suddenly. She caught my eye for a second, tried to smile, then her face crumpled and she turned away. They took seats near the front.

The Court Bailiff came out and scanned the assembled gathering. "Is the little Shaw girl present?" he asked loudly, and I jumped.

"Here," said Allen, pointing to me. The Bailiff came up to me. "Will you please come with me?" he said. "The Judge wants a word with you in his rooms."

Judge Cony was a globular man with short fat legs. This shape seemed to be an occupational necessity for professional men. I had noticed that all doctors, lawyers and successful business men looked like this. "Gluttony," Ma had said when I mentioned this to her. "They can afford to eat like pigs." Now, as Judge Cony sat behind his desk and leaned back in his swivel chair, legs off the ground, I mentally compared his girth to that of Dr. Murdoch and Dr. Browning. There wasn't much difference, but I reckoned that Cony had a slight edge on the others.

"Now, Peggy," the Judge began. "I didn't want to embarrass you in front of that crowd out there. So will you please just tell me here about this business between your friend Rena Allen and Willard Peaks? When did you first learn that something wrong was going on between them?"

"In August when I went with Rena's parents to collect her from Willard's farm."

"And what did you learn at that time?"

"She told me and her sister Beryl that Willard was making love to her 'like man and woman.'"

"And what did you understand 'like man and woman' to mean?"

"Not like just 'necking' in school. Going all the way."

239

"Peggy, I'm afraid I'm going to have to ask you to be more specific. What do you mean by 'going all the way'?"

"Having intercourse, like you would do if you wanted to have a baby."

"Did she tell you that he put his organ into her?"

"Yes, Sir."

"How did she express this to you?"

"She said it a number of different ways when she was explaining what he did to her. One was 'He put his prick in my cunt.'"

The Judge's eyebrows lifted slightly and his lips puckered. He looked rather shocked, I thought. "I see," he said. "And did she try to stop him?"

"She said she did at first because she was afraid, but then after he'd handled her she wanted him to do it."

"Did they do it more than once?"

"Oh, yes. All the time after that. Several times a day."

"And did she suggest to you that she was reluctant to do this?"

"Oh, no, she loved it."

"And did she ever say that she regretted what she had done?"

"No. She was proud of herself for it."

"And is she still proud of herself?"

"Yes."

"I see. Now did Willard Peaks make any promises to Rena about the future of their relationship?"

"He told her that when she was sixteen he was going to divorce his wife and marry her."

"Did she believe him?"

"Yes."

"Now I understand that you received a letter from Willard Peaks toward the end of August. Is that right?"

"Yes, Sir."

"Is this the letter?"

"Yes."

"And is this the letter which was enclosed in it to be given to Rena Allen?"

"Yes."

"What did you do with these letters?"

"I gave them both to Rena's mother."

"Why did you do that?"

"Because I knew what Willard was doing was wrong and against the law, and I thought her mother ought to know about it."

"All right Peggy, I think that is all I need to know. Thank you for being so helpful."

Judge Cony pushed a button on his desk and the Bailiff appeared to take me back to the courtroom. As I resumed my seat, the Bailiff called the court to order and the assemblage rose as Judge Cony entered.

"Where's the jury?" whispered Rena to the lawyer. "The jury box is empty."

"There isn't a jury in a case like this," he replied. Rena's face fell.

"First case on the docket is the State of Maine vs Willard Peaks," said the Bailiff. "Willard Peaks, will you stand."

Willard rose to his feet and faced the Judge. Cony glared at him, then:

"Willard Peaks, you are accused of having unlawful intercourse with a minor and of enticing her with promises of marriage. How do you plead?"

"Guilty, Your Honor."

I was flabbergasted. Willard wasn't even going to deny it!

"Since you have entered a plea of guilty, no witnesses will be called in this case. The testimony of the Shaw child has already been recorded in camera. Mr. Peaks, this is a most serious offense and if it were not for mitigating circumstances I would jail you forthwith for as long as the law permits. However, due to the fact that your wife is expecting a child, and since you have not been in trouble with the law before, I will instead fine you $100. As far as the girl is concerned, I wish to issue a warning to her and to her parents. Fornication under the age of sixteen is a crime, and should there be any further reports of misconduct on this girl's part I shall send her to the Girls' Reformatory at Hallowell!"

Mrs. Allen gasped. Rena stared at the Judge, her face full of fury. She wasn't going to be allowed to tell her story after all. Everything was out of her hands, had been decided without her.

"Next case," said Judge Cony.

"Come on," said the Allens' lawyer. "That's it."

"Wait," said Mrs. Allen. The family all looked in the direction of her glance. Fay and Willard had risen and were walking toward them up the courthouse aisle. But when they were opposite the Allens' row they did not pause or glance in their direction. Looking straight ahead they left the court, walking together hand in hand like lovers.

When Dr. Browning and the lawyer had left and we were back in the car, Mrs. Allen exploded: "Of all the nerve. Rena in Hallowell! Can you believe it? That son-of-a-bitch seduces her and the Judge makes it sound like it was her fault!"

"The Judge had his mind made up before he came to court this morning," said Allen. "He's not fond of the likes of us. By law he couldn't do anything but find Willard guilty, but he wasn't going to give us the satisfaction of seeing him jailed. Cony doesn't like the poor. Thinks we're all immoral or we wouldn't be poor."

I was shocked that he could say anything like that about Judge Cony. We were poor, and he and Mrs. Cony had shown us nothing but kindness. It didn't seem to occur to anyone that my testimony in camera had anything to do with Rena's telling off by the Judge. I had rather expected an ugly scene where I would be denounced as a traitor. The whole thing had been too easy. No jury, no witnesses, no cross-examination. I hadn't thought the law worked like that. In this case it had been all right, but what if I had been a liar, a twister, completely unreliable? How many people had been unfairly convicted on evidence given by a protected child in camera? Why, I hadn't even been under oath! What if Rena had been the one giving evidence against me?

63. The Split with the Allens

Although no recriminations were laid at my door, my friendship with the Allens seemed cooler after the trial. Rena had been denied her denouement and now was no longer the focus of interest and wonder that she had been during the preceding three months. We continued seeing each other, but I felt that Rena was filled with resentment against me, though no questions were ever asked about what I had said to the Judge.

The Allen children were now frequently not at home when I dropped by on the weekends, and their parents did not volunteer information on their whereabouts. Rena seemed suddenly to have lost interest in her horse and to have taken up some other activity elsewhere.

While I could to some extent understand Rena's resentment, there was a core in Rena that remained utterly unfathomable to me. I couldn't for the life of me understand her attitude toward Fay. Or that of the other Allens, for that matter. They seemed to have cast Fay off entirely. Fay had always been fond of her sister's children and had shown it in many ways. Now, as far as I was aware, there was no communication between her and any of the Allens. If Anna Allen had contacted her sister since the trial, she had not advertised the fact. And Fay's baby was due sometime in December.

Something else was also due in December that no one had expected. It changed in many ways the tenor of our lives.

"Keep 'Em Flying" with Abbott and Costello was playing at the Colonial Theater in Augusta on Sunday, December 7, and the Allens and I went to see it. No bus convenient for the 3 p.m. show went on Sundays, so we walked. It took longer than expected. Snow had fallen heavily the day before, and by the time we reached the theater only two seats were left in the house. We were wild to get in, and offered to pay four fares if the usher would let us double up on the seats. He must have been full of Christmas spirit, for he let us in free.

Beryl and I jammed into one seat and Rena and Charlie took the other, two rows behind. It wasn't comfortable, but the film was so funny we hardly noticed. Our stomachs were lame from laughing by the end of it.

As soon as we emerged from the theater and started up the street toward the station, we sensed something unusual going on. People were hurrying, or gathered in little knots in the street talking. We ran past them, as we had to catch the 5:10 bus or walk home in the cold. As we approached the station we saw that a crowd had assembled, including many soldiers and sailors kissing passionate goodbyes to their girlfriends. The 5:20 train for Boston was due in a few minutes, so they must be waiting for that, but it was an unusually large crowd.

Our bus was just about to pull out, so we flung ourselves on board and thought no more about it.

Pa enlightened me when I got home. "What movie did you see?" he asked.

"*'Keep 'Em Flying,'*" I said.

"We've got to keep 'em flying now, Peggy," he said. "The Japs have attacked Pearl Harbor."

I'd never heard of Pearl Harbor and must have looked totally blank, for Pa said, "We're at war, Peggy. Roosevelt has declared war on Japan and Germany, and now we're in it up to our necks."

"So that's why everyone was acting so strangely when we got out of the movies! A big crowd of servicemen and their girlfriends were waiting for the Boston train."

"All leaves have been cancelled. They've all got to go back and face God knows what."

Pa and Ma and I glued ourselves to the radio for the six o'clock news, and next morning the *Kennebec Journal* was full of it. Some incredible number of Navy personnel had been killed in a sneak attack on the Naval Base at Pearl Harbor. I got a fast orientation in the geography of the Pacific at school that morning. Girls with older brothers in the service were in tears, the boys were twitching with frustration that they weren't old enough to join up.

Three days later, Lynde phoned to say he had volunteered for the Navy Civil Engineering Corps and would be sent initially to the Naval Base in Argentia, Newfoundland. He and Winnie had been married only nine months. She'd be going back to Jamestown to stay with her parents while he was in the Navy. He would contact us again when he knew his departure date and mailing address.

In spite of the initial furor, the commencement of war had little effect on my own life, and within a week the immediate shock and excitement had died down. Ma and Pa assured me that Lynde would be in little danger, as he would be building bridges and roads instead of fighting. For once I didn't think to question what they told me.

The Allens, too, were little affected. I noted that Charlie did not appear to regret being too young to serve.

About a week after Pearl Harbor, as the Christmas vacation approached, I finally brought up the subject of Fay with Rena. It was a Saturday, and we were alone together in the girls' bedroom.

"Rena, what do you hear from Fay? Is she still with Willard? When is the baby due? Is she coming home to have it?"

Rena stared at me for a moment, then said slowly: "I don't know if Fay is still with Willard, and I don't care. I don't know what day the baby is supposed to arrive, and I don't care. I don't know whether Fay is going to Granny's to have it or not, and I don't care."

"You don't care at all about the trouble and grief you've caused Fay?"

"Why should I? Fay's no better than she ought to be. She's brought everything that happened to her on herself. At least I didn't get pregnant."

"I know Fay must have been pregnant when she married Willard. But so what? At least they got married."

"I'm not talking about that. I'm talking about the other one."

"What other one?"

"The Blat."

"What do you mean?"

"The Blat was Fay's baby."

I was struck dumb. The Blat that Ma had . . . Oh, God!

"Granny wouldn't have Fay in the house after she started to show. Said she wasn't going to be shamed in front of the neighbors, and wasn't going to have any bastard in her house. So she sent Fay away to a home till after she'd had it. Said Fay should have it adopted, but Fay wanted to keep it. So Mummy agreed to take it. Told everyone she was fostering it for the State, and they believed her 'cause they knew the State was paying her to keep the old ladies. Dad and Charlie and I didn't like it, I can tell you. There was a hell of a fight, but we still got stuck with taking care of The Blat."

"But Rena, the State social worker took The Blat away. She couldn't have done that if it wasn't under their program, could she?"

"The social worker and a doctor came out to check on the old ladies. They just do that from time to time without any warning to make sure they're being treated right. They just happened to see The Blat—remember how burned its legs were? The doctor took its temperature and said it had a high fever and something else wrong inside. So they took it to the hospital. Said the tent wasn't a clean enough place to keep a baby in."

"Where did she go to after that?"

"Nowhere. It died in the hospital."

I felt the blood leaving my head and had to sit down and put my head between my knees. Rena regarded me with contempt. "Oh, for God's sakes what's the matter with you, Peggy? You're such a stupid sissy!"

"Why didn't you tell me before, Rena?" I asked when the blood had come back into my head.

"We didn't want that story to get around, idiot. Mummy said she'd kill me if I told anybody."

"Is that why Fay went away?"

"Yeah. She was upset. Didn't want to go on living with Granny, so she took that job in Wiscasset where she met Willard."

"Poor Fay. Oh, poor Fay! She lost her baby, and now you've ruined her marriage."

"Me ruin her marriage? Fay did that, not me. She was lazy, she didn't keep the house half decent, and she kept pushing Willard away when he wanted her."

"She was pregnant and she was sick, and that man's a real tomcat, as you've made clear enough. Don't you understand anything, Rena?"

"I understand what a man wants, which is more than you do. You stupid virgin! You couldn't keep a man even if you were able to get one. But don't worry. Fay can keep Willard. I don't want him."

"I thought you were in love?"

"I am, but not with Willard."

"Who, then?"

"It's none of your business. But he's young and he's handsome and he's not married. Willard's an old man. God, he's thirty-six, a year older than my father. My new guy makes him look sick. Do you realize if I married Willard at sixteen, when I'm old enough to, he'd be forty?"

"Rena, you'll be under the legal age of consent for another three years yet. And before you know it you'll be pregnant. It could happen any time, now that you've turned thirteen!"

"You're a fool, Peggy. There are things you can do. Willard told me all about it."

"How come he got Fay pregnant, then?"

"Fay didn't do it right. It was all her own fault."

"All right, smarty-pants, tell me—what do you do?

"Oh, you'll never need to know. No man would want you with your silly pigtails and your old-maid ways. But I've told Beryl. My new boyfriend's got a friend for Beryl and she thinks he's super!"

"Who are they, Rena? Come on, tell me."

"What, tell you and have you tell Mummy like you did with Willard?"

"I gave that letter to your mother because Willard was Fay's husband and had no business doing what he was doing to you. I thought you'd realize that you'd done wrong after your mother found out. Since you don't, I don't care any more what you do, or who you do it with."

"Well, that's good. Glad you're not losing any more sleep worrying about what's none of your business."

"Tell me, then, Rena."

"All right, I will—since it wouldn't make any difference whether Mummy finds out or not. She can't stop me anyway. Larry Palmer's my boyfriend, and Tom Brenner is Beryl's."

Larry Palmer, who was at the country school when I was there! He was one of the unpleasant older boys who had made my life miserable. And by now I knew his family's reputation. They lived down the road about a mile beyond the Allens, across from Dorothy Simpson. Larry's mother had twelve children, each resembling a different local farmer. "Keep clear of that cheap bunch down there," Pa had warned. I'd needed no warning. I was afraid of the lot of them. They were coarse and they were cruel.

"How did you meet Larry?" I asked.

"Charlie met him at high school and brought him around. Charlie's sweet on his sister Sylvia."

That was it. I knew that my friendship with the Allens was over. It was as if a glass wall had been lowered that could never again be raised. It wasn't only this new association with the Palmers. It was The Blat, the Voodoo, the business with Willard, and what Rena had been willing to do, with no regrets, to Fay. Rena and I had nothing in common any more. Nothing to give each other. The fascination was over. Rena and Charlie had chosen their path, and they would take Beryl with them. I would be lonely now. I'd miss Beryl, but blood was a stronger tie than friendship.

I wouldn't tell Ma about The Blat. She had enough worries already. Come to think of it, Ma probably knew and just hadn't told me. Typical!

"I don't know Tom Brenner," I said. "But I remember Larry from school."

"Isn't he cute?" Rena smirked.

"Yeah, I suppose so. Well, I've got to go. Good luck. If you can't be good, be careful."

"Oh, don't you worry about Rena-gal. Rena-gal's going to be OKAY. But before you go, don't you want to know how The Blat really died?"

I stared at Rena's smirking face. Everything suddenly fell into place. "No, Rena," I said carefully, "I don't want to know. Don't tell me. I wouldn't believe you anyway."

"No?" said Rena. "I don't need to tell you, do I? And just wait until you see what I've got in store for Judge Cony!"

I didn't answer. Rena was still smirking as she watched me walk out the muddy driveway and out of her life.

Part Five: Beyond the Watershed

64. Beyond The Watershed

I had little time to miss the Allens until the Christmas vacation. My days at school were full. Then came the long walk home at 3:30, and dark fell before I got there. But during the holidays with outdoor farm work suspended for the winter, I had only my morning contact with Maisie Lee in the milkroom to look forward to.

I found myself feeling lonelier than I ever had before. I'd grown used to the companionship of others my own age. If the Allens did any skiing or skating that winter it was with others, and I never heard about it. Ron Allen still came by occasionally to see Pa but, other than that, contact between the families stopped altogether.

Rena and I ignored each other in class and did not seek each other out during recess periods. Beryl always smiled when she saw me if Rena was not in view, and I smiled back. I understood without being told that Rena had forbidden her to make contact with me.

No word had been uttered to acknowledge the end of my friendship with the Allen children, but both families knew. Certainly Ma and Pa approved and were relieved, although they never spoke of it. In silent families, communication takes place, but without words. The look of an eye, a gesture with a hand, the drawing in of breath, the turning away from a question, all had their meanings.

As soon as classes ceased, I began going out on my skis alone under the sapphire skies of a sunny December to break the trails through the woods and down the big hill. It was another world now, just sky and snow and silence, unbroken by the cries and laughter of the Allens. But this world had its own language, and with no one there to distract me the fields and the forest could speak. The cedars and hemlocks hung heavy with newfallen snow which sifted down upon me with a swishing sound as I passed beneath them. The footprints of mouse and bird left delicate tracery across the fields, and I could hear little scufflings and scuttlings whenever I stopped to listen. The brook running through the wood uttered softly under its coat of ice.

In the mornings it was chill, often well below zero, but if I went out immediately after the noon meal the sun had warmed the air and moistened the surface of the trails so I flew down them. By three, the sun was low and the snow pink and gold between the long shadows. By four, nothing was left but a rosy glow in the west and the chill had set in. Then my exhaled breath turned to frost, and I could feel the hairs freezing in my nose.

Sometimes on my way through the woods to or from the big hill I would come upon Dick and Noah out with the logging team, but I never met anyone else. I would stop and chat for a few minutes before shussing off again. They never mentioned the Allens, and neither did I. The knowledge had diffused silently around to those who should know.

It was a bleak Christmas that year. Not only for us, but for the many families with loved ones killed at Pearl Harbor, or drafted, or volunteering. Colin Kelly, the first American service man killed by the Japanese after the December 7 attack, became a national hero, and a young soldier from Manchester soon followed him to the grave.

In January, as the year turned on its hinge, I turned thirteen. I was thrilled to have reached my teens, but only Pa seemed to notice. To Ma, I was still twelve and always would be.

That year was a turning point for her, too. The brief resurgence of strength she'd had about a year and a half after Grace's death could no longer hold. Her muscles, always plagued by stiffness during the cold Maine winters, now weakened as well, and she lay her snowshoes aside forever. She'd been off to make sure her friend at Granite Hill was safe after every blizzard ever since I could remember, but now that had to stop, and she phoned her friend instead.

Ma had been slightly forgetful for some time, always wondering where she'd put things. "Just old age," Pa had said. "She's eighty-five. It happens to us all." I accepted this until Marguerite Hunter dropped by to see Ma. In the course of their conversation Marguerite asked her how old I was.

"Peggy is twelve years old," Ma told her.

We were in the kitchen, and I turned from the sink where I was scrubbing a pan with washing soda. "I'm thirteen, Miss Hunter," I said.

"No," said Ma. "You are twelve years old."

I shook my head at Marguerite and mouthed "No!" silently. She just smiled.

I was furious. Ma knew better than that. After Marguerite left I rounded on her. "You're mistaken about my age, Ma. I'm thirteen."

"Don't argue with me," she snapped. "I saw you trying to contradict me to Marguerite—and don't you dare talk back to me!"

I threw the scrubbing brush down into the sink and walked out. Ma was totally unreasonable and pig-headed. She just didn't want me to grow up. Didn't want me to start making eyes at the boys "like those other silly girls at school" she was always going on about. Just because Rena had made a fool of herself over Willard didn't mean I was about to do the same.

I didn't mention the incident to Pa. He'd just say it was old age, but I was sure it wasn't.

65. The Golden Rule

The concepts of altruism and selfishness had preoccupied me for some time. I was beginning to understand that in spite of all the idealistic and altruistic words I heard at home and at school, people were all basically selfish.

I remember the precise moment when this thought came to me. I was up in one of the Lees' apple trees, plucking the perfect fruit into my basket and enjoying the mild heat of the October sun cut by fresh wind.

Everyone worked for their own ends, I thought, whether they realized it or not. The virtuous were supposed to be rewarded in Heaven. If you were afraid of Hell, you behaved yourself. Ma was afraid for her own soul, and for mine as well. If she keeps me under control it'll up her chances in Heaven, I thought.

I wonder where she thought Bart went? I'd never asked her.

I tried to think of examples that would prove my thesis to be untrue, and could not. Except possibly Pa. Pa gave me pause for further thought. He didn't believe in God or in Heaven or Hell, and he was kind to everyone and loved me not because I was good but because I was me. What reward did he get? Whatever it was, he must be getting it in this lifetime.

One day I asked him: "Pa, you're good and kind and honest, but you don't believe in God any more than I do. Why do other people have to fear Hell in order to be good?"

"I dunno, Peggy," he said, "but that's what some of 'em need, I guess."

"But why are you good, Pa?"

He looked off into the distance for a while before he answered.

"I guess it's because I believe the Golden Rule makes sense," he finally said. "We're all in this boat together, and if we treat other people decent they usually treat us decent. You kick someone in the teeth and he'll do it to you if he gets the chance. Look what's going on in the world."

So it was self defense. Who was it that said more bees are attracted with honey than with vinegar? And the story of the man who clasped his cloak to him in desperation when the cold wind blew, but took it off when the warm sun came out? I began to see the side of the fence Pa was on and why. Why not? What better reason could there be? We're all in it together. Why not help one another? It had more chance of succeeding in the long run than trying to gouge and cheat everyone else. Again, self interest—selfishness. Of course selfishness included the desire for self-respect, as well as for the respect of others. At least this was a benevolent selfishness. A way of helping one's self and helping others at the same time. Or helping one's self without hurting others.

66. Rena's Parting Shot

The previous autumn, Ma had made some attempt to prepare her beloved flower borders for winter, but as spring came she sighed and shook her head.

"I just can't get down on my hands and knees to weed any more," she said. "I'm too stiff."

I'd been helping with the borders when I could for some time. I loved them too. The farm wouldn't be home without Ma's flowers. But what I could do wasn't enough, and other jobs were crowding in on me.

Pa, now struggling against what appeared to be an almost continuous cold, was in no condition to do more than keep wood split for the stove and furnace. The circulation in his legs seemed to be getting worse. He had difficulty walking any distance, and I could see he was struggling as he tried to keep the lawn mowed. He had to sit down and rest after every few swaths, so as the grass began to grow in May, I took over the care of the lawn. It was a big lawn, extending from porch to road and up along the driveway as far as the stable, but I was strong from the other farm work and could finish it in under an hour.

I could tell Pa hated my having to do it for him, but in the state he was in he could hardly object. After I'd finished a mowing he always gave me enough money to "go get us thirty cents' worth at McAuleys." That was the price of a pint of ice cream.

One day when I was mowing down near the road, Rena and Beryl came past on their bikes from the direction of Pelton's Hill. I hadn't seen them except at school, or from a distance, for months. They saw me and stopped. "How come you're doing the lawn?" asked Rena.

"Pa's legs are so bad now he can't do it any more," I said. "I'm really worried about him. He has one cold after another and coughs a lot, and spends most of his time in his rocking chair in the kitchen looking miserable."

Rena gave me a look of mingled disbelief and delight.

"Jesus, Peggy, you don't still believe that crap about him having a cold, do you?" she asked.

Beryl's face went white and she said "No, Rena, don't!"

"What do you mean?" I asked, feeling a cold knot roll up inside my stomach.

"He's drunk all the time, for Chrissakes. Sure he looks like he has a cold with his eyes all red and his nose running, but that's from booze, and his cough's from cigarettes. And the smell in your kitchen ain't cough syrup, girl, that's whiskey."

"You don't know what you're talking about," I snapped.

"Oh, yes I do. My father told us all about it. He said your Pa's been drunk ever since he got out of bed after that heart attack made him quit the shipyard. After that we could see it for ourselves."

"Rena," cried Beryl, almost in tears, "Dad told us never, never to say anything about it to Peggy!"

"She always wants to know the truth, doesn't she? Well, that's some of the truth she wants to know. Come on. We've got to get home."

They wheeled off.

I sat down on the grass beside the lawnmower and felt my world spinning out of control. Was what Rena said true? Or was it a vicious lie? If it was true, did Ma know? Did the Lees know? Was drink, like sex, something everyone knew about but me? How could I find out?

What was being drunk like? I'd seen drunks in town who staggered about, being noisy and nasty and falling over. Or being sick in the gutter. Pa wasn't like that at all. He was gentle, kind to everyone, never raised his voice, and loved us too much to be a drunkard. He'd never dare drink in Ma's presence. She'd never permit it.

But had he fooled Ma too? Did she, like me, just think he was ill? Even if she knew, she wouldn't tell me. And if she didn't know and I told her, she wouldn't believe me.

I got up and finished the lawn, then went off to McAuley's to get the thirty cents' worth. I said nothing to anyone about my encounter with the Allens.

Over the next few days I kept my eyes and ears open. Pa seemed worse in the mornings, but mornings are always bad when one has a cold. He'd perk up as the day went by and go out to the woodshed to putter around and chop wood.

251

About four he'd come back to his rocker while Ma and I got supper. He'd be foggy-headed, "coldy", and generally miserable. After supper, he'd sleep in his chair until he went to bed.

If I said anything to him, his reply was usually, "Oh, my gosh!" His tone varied according to the import of my words. If we were having something he partricularly liked for supper, he'd say "Oh, my gosh" with delight. If I told him the water pump had ceased to function, he'd say it with disgust. If I was planning some escapade that worried him, he showed his worry with those same three words. He could adapt them to anything, and he'd been doing it constantly for a couple of years.

I began taking careful note of the various smells in the air at different times, and soon distinguished two medicinal sorts of scent, one from his bottle of cough syrup, and a quite distinct one from something else, stronger the closer I got to Pa. Was that what whiskey smelled like? I could also detect that smell (but not the smell of cough syrup) in the woodshed. Is that where he kept the whiskey?

I searched everywhere I could think of, but couldn't find a bottle. Yet everything else seemed to point to the conclusion that Pa was drinking. I reckoned Rena, for once, was telling the truth. It was her way of getting even about Willard.

How could Pa possibly afford to spend money on whiskey?

Did Ma know? Should I ask her? If I did, she'd probably say "Don't be silly, of course he isn't drinking," whether he was or not. Worse, if she didn't know and I told her, and she did believe me, it might kill her.

For the first time, I realized that in some cases the truth could be deadly.

67. Silence

The pall of silence that settled around me after the break with the Allens deepened as the weeks passed, and I withdrew more and more into myself. The Allens had, for a time, broken the shell of my shyness and let me emerge to become one of them. I found we could share information and learn from one another ways to use it, both for good and for evil. The Witches Club had stimulated my creativity and freed me from the terror of my own attic.

The Allens showed me how another sort of family functioned, and allowed me to make comparisons with my own. The drama of their ups and downs and interactions had relieved the boredom and sadness of my own home life. They were so different from us in every way—open with each other, sharing their family tragedies—as they'd done with Fay and The Blat, and later with Rena and Willard.

They used rude language and obscenities as part of normal living, among themselves and with others they felt comfortable with. If we'd used those words in our family, they might have fragmented what bonds we had. Instead, the Allens' shared vernacular drew them closer together, was a badge of who they were, and identified them as part of larger groups who related with one another as they did.

My family hid their tragedies from one another and dealt with them alone in silence, each separate and distinct. They shut out the world, taking care to keep others from knowing about their private lives. In thinking about this, I began to be reasonably sure that neither Ma nor the Lees knew about Pa's drinking.

Although the Allens had brought me out of my shyness for a while, the old habits of solitude were now creeping back. Over the past year I had started to grow taller, and my skinny 120-pound frame had now reached what seemed the incredible height of five foot eight. I was taller than all the girls in my class, and most of the boys as well. I felt uncomfortably conspicuous and clumsy. Ma kept telling me, "Stand up straight, Peggy—why are you slouching?"

I now felt at ease only with my own family, the Lees and my classmates at school with whom I'd long since reached an equilibrium. Others seemed foreign and a source of fear.

The Hunter boys, whom I'd known by sight and by name all my life, were now old enough to act as delivery boys for their father's store. One or the other came to the farm about once a week with groceries we had ordered. They now filled me with apprehension. They were fourteen and fifteen, and I felt their eyes appraising me and finding me wanting. Smiles of contempt seemed to lie just behind their lips and were reflected in their eyes.

When the delivery van arrived, I began disappearing into the outbuildings or retiring to Pa's bedroom where I couldn't be seen. This apprehension soon spread to other people who came to the house on business. Pa noticed and was worried, but didn't know how to help. "Don't hide away, Peggy—don't hide away," was all he could find to say. Ma, wrapped in her own preoccupations and growing forgetfulness, seemed to have no idea anything was going on.

The Lees kept me sane that summer, by simply being there. They were a force of life acting against dissolution, and the regular routine of bottle washing and farm work with Dick and the hay crew kept me in regular contact with them. They had begun for me a pattern that continued to serve me well. If I were useful to someone, it was a way of becoming valuable to them. Hard work brought respect. Brought admiration. Brought something close to love. I worked hard. I worked hard.

Harriet added yet another dimension to the Lee experience that year. Bill was off to War, and in the spring she arrived with her two-year-old daughter Mimi to stay with her family until she could rejoin him.

I'd always admired the beautiful Harriet, but she'd been away most of the time since I could first remember her. Now I got to know her better. She was full of her mother's sense of humor and fun, but in a younger, lighter, more colorful mold, and full of new ways of doing things.

When she first brought Mimi to the farm a few months after her birth, she announced, "Diapers are hot, smelly and produce rashes. They shouldn't be worn in July in Maine."

To the consternation of neighbors and relatives, she kept Mimi naked in her carry cot, lying on a clean spread-out diaper, beneath which was a rubber sheet to protect the mattress. When the diaper was wet, it was immediately changed.

"No putting on or taking off of diapers," she pointed out. "Much easier."

As an added protection against rashes, Harriet gave Mimi a carefully supervised sun bath every day—ten minutes on each side. After the sun bath came Mimi's daily doses of cod liver oil and orange juice.

Older relatives clucked and fussed about Harriet's "silly new ideas":

"Everyone knows sunshine is bad for skin. . . ."

"That baby will have the hide of an elephant when she grows up. . ."

"Don't you know, Harriet, ladies who have beautiful skin won't go out without a parasol to protect them from the sun? . . ."

Harriet smiled sweetly and ignored them. Her own skin was beautifully tanned and flawless.

The baby had been named Mary Lee Stuart Fraser, the "Mary" after Maisie and Mary, Queen of Scots; the "Stuart" because some time in the misty and heathery past the family had an infusion of Royal Stuart blood. Hence Harriet calling the baby "Mimi" infuriated those relatives imbued with a sense of tradition:

"'Mimi' is such a silly, wispy French name, why do you call her that?" a cousin inquired, to which Harriet replied,

"Why, because I like it."

I was delighted by this reply. It was the first time I had ever heard anyone defend a frivolous decision by saying, without embarrassment, "Because I like it." I would never have dared give the reason of my own pleasure. It was one that Ma and Mrs. Cony would never accept. Now I realized why. It was the ultimate declaration of independence:

"I act because it pleases me, not because it pleases you."

Mimi was now two, a lively, happy, into-everything child with a joyful disposition. The relatives and neighbors had quieted, seeing that their objections were ineffective.

Sometimes Harriet, to give her mother a break and allow her to play with Mimi, would take over washing bottles with me for a morning. During those sessions she often spoke of the absent Bill. I'd seen Bill so seldom I had no idea what he was like until now.

"Bill wanted to go to M.I.T. to train as a physicist," she told me one day as we were mixing the washing and rinsing solutions. "But his father was a military man, and wanted him to go into the Cavalry. Bill insisted he was going to be a physicist. He had some brilliant, unconventional ideas, and the only way to find out whether they were valid was to study physics."

"What made him join the Cavalry, then?" I wanted to know. It sounded like surrender to me.

"His father suggested that Bill take the West Point examinations just to see what his scores were—whether he was, in fact, Cavalry material at all. Bill was interested in finding out what his I.Q. was, and this was a way to do it, so he agreed to take the exams."

"What's I.Q.?" I asked. I'd never heard that term before.

"It stands for Intelligence Quotient. At one end of the intelligence scale are the feeble-minded, and at the other end are the geniuses. Your I.Q. tells you how smart you are."

"What was Bill's?"

"He tested at the genius level."

"Wow!"

"West Point was very excited about Bill's scores, but he was adamant that he wanted to study physics."

"Who won?" I asked, putting the first batch of bottles into the tub.

"Everybody."

I stared at her. She laughed at my puzzled expression.

"The military took him into the Cavalry and sent him to M.I.T. to study physics. His father got what he wanted, the military got what they wanted, and Bill got to study physics—for free!"

"Are his ideas being used in the war effort?" I asked.

"That is TOP SECRET. We'll both have to wait till after the war to find out!"

Later, when pressed, Harriet gave me some examples of Bill's unconventional thinking. She was reluctant at first:

"They may shock you, Peggy. They're definitely not ideas that most people would accept."

This, of course, made me even more curious. Finding out forbidden information had been my driving force for years.

"Please tell me, Harriet. I don't think like most people either."

Harriet looked at me with a glance both of amusement and understanding. "No, you don't, do you," she acknowledged. "All right, you asked for it. For instance, Bill thinks it's a waste of good material to let dead bodies rot away in

255

overcrowded graveyards, or be cremated and allowed to go up in smoke. After the farewells and the religious ceremonies the bodies should be ground up for use as fertilizer, after being sterilized to kill any disease germs present."

"What a sensible idea," I said.

Encouraged by this response, she declared, "Bill doesn't believe in God—he's an agnostic." She looked at me with interest to see what my reaction would be.

"I don't believe in God either," I said. "What's an agnostic, Harriet?"

"*Gnostic* is the Greek word for knowing, and *a* is the prefix meaning 'not.' Bill thinks no one knows the meaning of the universe, or knows whether or not there's a God, and there's no way of finding out. We should base our morality on what is good for the human race—the humanistic approach. So we don't go to church."

I grinned at her and nodded my head in agreement. So there were other people in the world who thought as Pa and I did. Bill, I realized, was a man I could like and respect, and my already high regard for Harriet soared.

68. Mrs. Cony and the Commercial Course

In the second half of the eighth grade, when I was fourteen, our teacher told us that we must discuss with our parents what course we would be taking in high school. Those who were going on to college would take the academic course. Boys not going to college would do manual training or technical studies, and girls could choose between home economics and the commercial course.

I knew nothing about any of these courses, and when I broached the matter to Ma and Pa, neither did they. No one but Grace on my father's side of the family had finished high school. Pa, in an unusual burst of confidentiality, told me that he had dropped out at age fifteen to help support the family after his father deserted them. Ma had started doing tailoring from her home, but couldn't make enough money to support her three children without Pa going to work. Pa also confided that Barton had "a lot of trouble" of an unspecified nature at school and also dropped out at fifteen.

"So I guess we better talk your high school course over with Mrs. Cony," Pa said. "She'll know more about it than we do."

By then I realized that Louise Cony, as my legal guardian, had quite a lot to say about what I did and did not do. So far, she had done me only good. The clothes she provided from the rummage sales were better than anything we could have afforded to buy new, and as our finances worsened she'd started bringing things for Ma and Pa as well.

After Pa phoned her, Mrs. Cony came out to the farm to discuss my education. We sat in the kitchen over cups of steaming liquid: coffee for the elders, Ovaltine for me.

"What would you like to do, Peggy?" Pa asked.

I knew precisely what I wanted to do, and had for some time. I'd been telling stories before I could write, and I wanted to be a writer. As soon as I'd heard about famous artists and got my hands on Mae Towle's oil paints, I wanted to be an artist. And when I found I could play the piano by ear, I wanted to be a musician. It hadn't occurred to me to wonder how any of this would happen, but I was sure it would.

"I want to be a writer or an artist or a musician," I said.

Mrs. Cony looked at me in amazement and disbelief. "My dear girl," she said, "where did you ever come across such ideas? You cannot afford to go to college, or train as either an artist or a musician or a writer. You must learn how to make a living in case no one wants to marry you. I strongly suggest that you take the commercial course and learn to type."

Nobody I knew had been to college, and I didn't know what it was like or what it was for—just another four years like high school, as far as I knew. Lynde had gone to engineering school, but I knew nothing about engineering and had no interest in learning about it. Harriet Lee had gone to normal school to become a teacher, but the last thing in the world I wanted to do was teach. Such a dreary profession in which to grow old. All the young pretty ones left to marry after a couple of years. In Maine, married women were barred by law from teaching. They must stay home and care for their husbands and children. To me, that seemed an even more dreary fate than teaching.

I certainly didn't want to take home economics. We'd had it once a week in eighth grade and I hated it. They'd had us making pot holders and aprons and fixing fruit salad by opening a can and adding salad dressing.

Typing looked like it might be fun, fingers flying over the keys—like playing an instrument. Gracie was Judge Cony's secretary and enjoyed it. Mrs. Cony had been the Judge's secretary too, before she married him.

Ignorant of alternatives, I agreed. But I promised myself that someday I would do all three of those other things. I said to myself, "I shall be a writer, I shall be a musician, and I shall be an artist. No one is going to stop me."

How I was going to achieve these dreams I hadn't the faintest idea. I just knew it was going to happen.

69. The Picture

The Saturday after school let out for the summer, Aunt Rita arrived at the farm on her way to her Camden cottage. I never knew when she was coming, but she appeared almost every summer. If Ma and Pa knew, they never told me. I suspect Rita just dropped in, knowing we were always at home. We didn't dress up for company or do anything special for them except provide tea or coffee and whatever ordinary home baking Ma had done. When Rita came, we'd have our refreshments in the sitting room and talk for a while, then she'd be on her way.

Today, after tea and baking powder biscuits with raspberry jam from last year's crop, Rita asked me if I'd like to walk her around the farm. She didn't suggest that Ma and Pa come with us, and they made no move to do so. I think they realized that she wanted to see me alone.

I took her around the outbuildings. The only animals we had now were a few hens, Fluff and her latest litter, and Judy, but I showed her the remains of Fred's old Model T Ford, which was still on the floor of the barn. Then she asked if there were any wild flowers in the fields, and I led her up the track to the back meadow. It was alight with daisies, buttercups, blue vetch and gold and vermillion hawkweed. She gathered a little mixed bouquet, then we sat for a few minutes on a large rock enjoying the June sunshine.

"Brenda," she said, "Though you don't know it, this is a very special day."

I looked at her questioningly.

"It's your mother's birthday. She was born on the 8th of June, 1884. She'd be fifty-eight years old today if she'd lived."

"Oh," I said.

"People usually get birthday presents on their birthdays, but today your mother is giving you a present. It's something she'd want you to have."

What on earth could she mean? My mother was dead. How could she give me a present? I felt the hair rise on the back of my neck. I scanned Rita's face, but couldn't read what lay beneath her sad smile.

Rita opened her handbag, removed a white envelope and handed it to me. It was unsealed. I opened the flap and drew out a photograph, obviously an old one, measuring about four by six inches and mounted on thick dark cardboard which was worn at the edges. It was a studio portrait of a young girl in a wide-brimmed straw hat. She was standing, leaning against a Victorian bentwood chair.

I glanced at Rita. "My mother?" I asked.

"Yes. It was taken on her fourteenth birthday. Her parents had several copies made up, and she gave me one of them. I've had it all these years, but now I'd like you to have it. You're fourteen now, just the age she was when this picture was taken."

It was Rita giving me the picture of course, not my mother. Why had she said it the other way?

I looked at the girl in the picture. I could see no resemblance to what I'd observed in my own mirror, yet I felt a physical shock of recognition that I couldn't explain. It was as if she had touched me. I couldn't express this in words, so all I said to Rita was, "I don't look anything like her, do I?"

"Not much," said Rita, "except for your eyes. Hers were the same shape and the same dark blue as yours. And her brows, like yours, were heavy but neat. But when you look up at me sometimes it's as if your mother were looking at me again."

Almost the same words Maisie Lee had used! I was glad to have it confirmed, to know something of my mother had been passed on to me.

I examined the picture carefully. It was an old sepia portrait, and my mother was wearing a dress in a style I'd heard Ma refer to as late Victorian. If, as Rita had said, Bess was fourteen, it must have been taken in 1898.

The big straw hat with its wide brim was turned back from her face, and her hair fell onto her shoulders in loose dark curls. Her eyebrows were wide, dark and well shaped, but certainly not plucked. Her eyes were large, her nose neat and freckled. Her shy smile showed even white teeth. She wasn't beautiful in the usual sense, yet she gave off a sense of beauty. Her face looked friendly, open.

She wore a thin dimity dress with long sleeves and a V-shaped yoke made of lace which ruffled under her chin. Matching ruffles outlined the V of the yoke, circled her upper arms and formed cuffs at her wrists. A wide satin sash emphasized the slimness of her waist. One arm rested on the back of the bentwood chair; the other hung at her side, the hand holding three tulips.

So many questions I should have asked Rita about that picture, questions I didn't think of until years later when she was dead and gone and couldn't answer. Instead, I asked her about the wall of obscurity that separated me from Mother.

"Why didn't Ma and Pa tell me when my mother's birthday is, Aunt Rita? Why will they never tell me anything? Why is everything secret?"

Rita shook her head. "Your father isn't a talker, Brenda. Men don't talk easily, and he's the shyest man I've ever known. He's a good man. He loves people and he doesn't want any trouble. He loves you. He loved your mother, but he also loves his own mother, your grandmother. Your mother and grandmother didn't get along well, and your father walked a tightrope between them trying to keep the peace and not lose either. I hope one day he will find himself able to talk with you about all this. It was a tragedy for both you and him that you lost your mother."

This wasn't much information, but it confirmed what I had already suspected: That my mother and grandmother had hated each other, and my father had tried to please both. But why the hatred? What had happened between them? It was no use asking Pa, for he would fear that telling me would cause problems with Ma. For the time being I'd just have to wait. Perhaps when I was older if I went to Melrose to visit Rita again, she'd be willing to tell me.

Rita interrupted my thoughts. "These wildflowers are so beautiful, Brenda, why don't you put this little bouquet by your mother's picture? Then when they fade you can replace them with others. It will be a kind of memorial for her."

I nodded assent but didn't like the suggestion. I couldn't see any sense in it. Mother was dead and couldn't know about the flowers. I felt Rita expected some emotional reaction from me that I couldn't give. Did she want me to cry? I didn't feel like crying—I felt angry and confused.

Nevertheless, I took the flowers from Rita, and after she had gone I put them in a slim violet-colored glass vase and set them next to Mother's picture on the corner knick-knack stand in the living room. It was the only place I could think of. I knew Ma wouldn't want my mother's picture in our shared bedroom.

I was in the sitting room when Ma first noticed the picture. After arranging it with the flowers, I'd taken my violin from its case on the piano and began to play—not playing from notes, just things out of my head. Ma heard me and came in. She listened for a moment before her eyes caught the picture, and I saw her move to the knick-knack stand. I kept playing, but watched intently for her reaction. She stared at the picture and went rigid, then folded her lips tightly and left the room without a word.

In spite of Ma's reaction, I kept the picture on the knick-knack stand. I didn't replace the flowers when they faded. They were irrelevant. I was grateful and happy to have the picture, however. I wanted to keep it where I could see it. Each time I looked at it, something seemed to pass from it to me, wordlessly telling me what I could find out in no other way.

Ma never mentioned the picture, nor did she try to remove it, but I never again saw her as much as glance at it. If Pa noticed the picture, he never told me.

70. The Carnival

One Saturday in midsummer I got a surprise phone call from Dorothy Simpson.

"Carnival's in town," she said. "Thought you might like to go this afternoon."

Why was she asking me? We never went anywhere together. Ever since we had diverged into different schools I'd done my best to avoid her. Except for our encounter when I bought my white rats, we'd never seen each other except by chance on the bus or in town.

"Um—I hadn't thought about going," I said.

"There's something there I think you ought to see. Come with me and I'll show you."

Whatever it was, she wasn't doing this for my good, but for hers. It was no doubt something she could embarrass me about, or with which she could show up my ignorance. But I was curious. I was also bored, now that the Allens had gone elsewhere for company, even though I had no wish to join them. There was no hay to be got in that day, so I agreed to go.

We arranged that I would catch the 1:10 bus in front of the farm and she'd get on it down the hill at her place. I half expected her not to be there. It would be just like her to get me on a bus to the carnival and then stand me up. But she was waiting at the road.

"Okay, now tell me what this is all about," I said as she settled into the seat beside me.

"Wait'll we get there," she said. "All will be revealed."

We got off at the station and walked to the carnival ground. The rides were whirling away with their screaming cargo, and the air was full of the smell of popcorn, hot dogs and cotton candy. It was crowded. All the farm hands, in groups of their own or trailing their wives and children, had come in from the countryside to join the fun. We cruised around to see what was going on, bought hot dogs, went on a couple of rides. Darned if I was going to ask Dorothy again why she was so keen for me to come.

At the carnival a few tents were always set aside "For Adults Only." You had to be sixteen to get in. Mostly men and boys went inside, but they didn't turn girls away if they were old enough. As Dorothy and I passed the row of forbidden tents, she stopped in front of one of them.

"That's where they have the morphydites," she said, pointing to the banner emblazoned across the entrance. It said "Genuine Hermaphrodites" in large letters with spiky black and red outlines. She saw my puzzled glance.

"That's just the way it's spelled, but its pronounced 'morphydites.'"

How come she always knew everything? She must have been born knowing everything. Also it appeared that she never forgot anything. She had remembered our conversation of three years ago about Fred's odd women tenants, and she now wished to further my education, to make sure I understood our neighbors—who, by this time, had already moved on.

"Come on," she said, "let's go in."

"They'll never let us in. That sign says 'Sixteen or Over.'"

"They'll let you in. You've grown a foot since last year. You can pass for sixteen. Maybe they'll let me in if I'm with you."

It was true. I'd gone from being too short to being too tall almost overnight. At five foot eight, I was taller than the average man. Although we were the same age, Dorothy was barely five feet. And now she needed me as an entry ticket! I almost laughed out loud. There were some advantages to being tall, after all!

"Let's go," I said.

I went boldly up to the window and paid my money. They let me through without a word. Dorothy came up to the window behind me. I heard the ticket taker say, "Uh, uh, little girl. This is for the big folks. No children allowed."

"But I'm with her," she cried.

I didn't even look back, but I can imagine her fury.

Inside the tent was a small stage with standing room in front of it. The space was filled with about a dozen men and boys in overalls and cowboy hats. The reek of manure and sweat mingled with cigarette smoke and the pong of moldy canvas and aging wood. Three other girls huddled together near the stage, their apprehension scarcely masked by nervous giggles.

The curtains at the back of the stage parted and a middle-aged woman with dyed black hair emerged. She was overly plump, and a jeweled bra held in her voluminous breasts. A long skirt with a full-length slit down the side was draped around her hips. She regarded the audience of leering farm hands with a look of total contempt, then began her obviously memorized spiel.

"My brother and I were born with the organs of both sexes. We are gen-u-ine her-maph-ro-dites." She paused and looked around as if to see if this audience of idiots could cope with that long word. Some of the men smirked at each other and shuffled their feet. The three girls stood rigid.

The woman unhooked her bra and flung her breasts outward, glaring at the lecherous eyes in the front row. The tent went suddenly quiet. No one seemed to be breathing. Next, she undid the tie at her waist and slid her long slit skirt back around her hips. She'd shaved off her pubic hair. She reached two fingers in between her labia and pulled out a pink object about four inches long.

"This is my penis," she declared. I was fascinated. Was it real? It could have been plastic, for all I could tell. She exhibited it, supporting it with her hand, turning slowly so everyone could get their money's worth.

"My penis is incapable of erection and cannot perform sexual intercourse. My testicles are undescended and remain within my body. Although I have both ovaries and testicles within me, they are sterile. I cannot produce children," she stated slowly and clearly with no hint of emotion.

Then she replaced the penis within the labia and drew her skirt around her with dignity and decorum.

"My brother will now show you his organs," she intoned, gesturing toward the curtains at the back of the stage. An obese, balding middle-aged man issued forth. He wore only bejeweled undershorts. His hairy chest crowned an enormous beer belly.

"My brother will now show you his breasts," said the woman, and turned to put on her bra.

The man stepped forward, cupping his "breasts" with his hands, turning to give everyone a view. He looked to me no different from any of the fat men who walked the streets of the town shirtless on hot Saturday afternoons. They all had "tits" as big as that. Then he dropped his jewelled undershorts and displayed his penis, moving it aside to assure the spectators that he had testicles as well. He hadn't shaved his pubic hair. He looked bored and rather dazed.

Was he a fake? Were they both fakes? If they were really like that, why would they want to show everybody? Was it the only way they could make a living?

The woman came and stood beside him. She riveted the audience with a look that left no doubt that she wished us all in the fires of Hell.

"The Demonstration is over," she announced. "God Bless you."

The "God Bless You" was said with such utter contempt that I cringed. How she must hate us, I thought.

They turned and left the stage together. For a moment there was stunned silence. Then the tension broke and I heard a few perfunctory claps, sneers of derision and obscenities from the men. The girls couldn't even muster a nervous giggle, and left without a word.

So those were morphydites. Was that what our neighbors were? Surely not! Chloe wasn't sterile, she'd had a baby. She and Terry were unusual, yes. They were somehow different—but it wasn't this!

I went outside to enlighten Dorothy.

71. A Haircut and a Quilt

"Ma, am I pretty?"

Ma looked at me thoughtfully for a minute. "No," she said. "You're a good, plain little girl."

That stung. "You mean I'm ugly?" I asked.

"No, you're plain. Plain is not ugly. You're not one of these silly little girls with cupid bow mouths and dimples. They look like china dolls and are as vain as peacocks. They make eyes at everyone because they've been told they're beautiful. You're a good, plain little girl, and that's the best kind to be."

I knew she was wrong about plain not being ugly. I'd heard people say about other children, "Too bad she's so plain. She'll never get a boyfriend." I didn't want to be good and plain, I wanted to be bad and beautiful.

I went upstairs and adjusted the swinging mirror over the bureau carefully until I could see my full length in it, tilted but complete. Five feet 8 1/2 inches tall. Weight 120 lb. Long skinny neck. Bony. Clumsy. Thin, straight honey-colored hair too fine to do anything with but braid. No one wore braids any more. How could I go to high school looking like this?

Mrs. Cony had regarded my head with disgust when Ma talked me into wrapping the braids around it. "They're bad enough hanging down your back," she said. "Pinned up like that they make you look like an old maid schoolmarm."

I felt a shudder go through me at her words. That's the sort of thing that could happen to a plain girl—to remain a spinster in the prison of school forever and ever and never escape. Only the pretty teachers got carried off, swooning with love, toward the altar.

Plain. Good, plain little girl.

Plain I was. But not little, and I was damned if I was going to be good. I went downstairs, found the kitchen shears and returned to the bedroom. I adjusted the mirror so I could contemplate my head and shoulders. I unwound the braids from around my head. They hung down to my hips. I placed the scissors up under my ears. Stopped. Thought. I hadn't liked that short shingle I'd had before Ma told me to let my hair grow. I lowered the shears to mid-neck. Nobody wore hair that length, did they? I wasn't sure. I lowered the shears to shoulder length. I could always shorten it later.

I crunched the scissors together. The braid parted neatly, and four fifths of it fell to the floor. I eyeballed the length of the other braid against the cut one. Crunch. Four fifths of that braid fell to the floor. I pulled my fingers through the stumps to unbraid them, shook my head, and my hair fell about my shoulders, wavy from the ears down where the braids had shaped it.

I surveyed the result and felt a surge of delight go from head to toe. My neck didn't look long and skinny any more. My face didn't look bony either, and the sour look of anger and tension had evaporated. My eyes were large and wide open, and my nose was neat with a pert tilt upward at the end.

I shook my head about and felt the hair swirl around my shoulders, light, fine, free. My hair was free. I was free. And I'd done it myself!

The haircut wasn't the only declaration of independence I made that summer. Some time before that, it had occurred to me that I'd like to have a room of my own. One of Mrs. Cony's *Good Housekeeping* magazines ran a feature on bedrooms. It showed pictures of rooms for people of different ages, each arranged and decorated in its own particular style.

I began to look longingly at our second guest room. It shared the wide middle part of the upstairs floor with Lynde's bedroom. The front main guest room was to the north of it, and the bedroom I shared with Ma to the south. It was light and airy and would suit me perfectly.

I knew Ma would object to this. She didn't like change, and she was sure to feel abandoned. I didn't want to hurt her feelings, and I didn't want an argument. Already, Ma and I had too many things to get angry about.

I said nothing for a while, but ideas for decorating "my" room kept coming to me unbidden. I would put on new wallpaper. Paint the woodwork. Make some colorful cushions for the bed.

The opportunity to act came in mid-July. The temperature shot up into the nineties, and sleeping two bodies to a bed was insufferable. In past years I'd taken a mattress out into the field behind the sheds and slept under the stars during heatwaves. But this time I decided to stay inside on principle.

"Ma," I said after we'd sweltered all night even with no sheets over us, "It's too hot to go on like this. I'm going to move into the other room. That way we can each have a bed to ourselves."

She gave me a surprised look and started to speak, then checked herself. Ma disliked extremely hot weather, and the timing of my announcement surely helped my case. Still, the emotions crossing her face were almost audible.

"Well," she said finally, "perhaps for the hottest part of the summer it might be a good idea. When it cools off you can come back. You'd freeze there in winter."

We'll see about that when the time comes, I thought.

I made up the bed and asked Ma if I could borrow a couple of the brightly colored quilted cushions she'd made till I had time to cover some for myself. I think this pleased her. She apparently took it as a compliment, and agreed at once.

I also appropriated the guest room chamber pot for my own use. Ma and I had been using a plain white earthenware one if we woke in the night. The guest room pot was fine China, decorated with blue violets. Guests could have it back when needed.

I knew the family finances were at rock bottom, and I had other things I wanted to do with my pay from Lees, so instead of repapering, I contented myself with painting the wide board floor dark red and the bedstead sky blue with paint we had in the shed. The result pleased me.

Ma did not comment, but set her mouth in a thin hard line when she saw what I was doing. I think the colors shocked her. To paint a white Victorian iron bedstead (with brass fittings) blue was not something she would have suggested.

Pa chuckled. "We can certainly say this room is yours now," he said. I think he was pleased.

When the paint was dry, he brought up a quilt from the cedar chest in his bedroom. I'd seen it there, but hadn't thought anything about it one way or another. It was white with blue baskets quilted on it in a diagonal pattern.

"The blue in the baskets matches the bedstead," he said. "Thought you might like to use it as a spread."

It was perfect. I knew at once it was right for the room.

"Yeah," I said, and grinned at him.

"Your mother quilted it the year before you were born," he said, and left the room hurredly.

I was stunned. It was the first time he'd ever voluntarily mentioned my mother. And to have a quilt she had made! To be able to sleep under it—to have it as my own.

This was an outcome I could never have imagined.

72. High School and a Friendship

As autumn and the beginning of high school loomed, I became more and more apprehensive. We'd been told before leaving eighth grade that instead of remaining in one room all day we would shift to a different classroom for each subject. Ten minutes of every hour would be consumed just getting from one place to another. It sounded crazy to me. Four hundred students changing rooms every hour? Why didn't the teachers change rooms instead?

Even the process of getting to the high school and back was a cause for trepidation. The school day began at 8:00 and ended at 1:30 so pupils could get to afternoon jobs. Gracie left for work at 8:30, so I could no longer ride in with her. Our farm was three miles from the high school, so walking was out of the question, and there was no school bus. I'd have to take the regular intercity bus which passed our farm at ten to eight, and wasn't due at the high school till ten past.

I began having nightmares about being late, not knowing what room to go to, everyone else knowing what to do and laughing at me for being stupid.

"Walk to school the first day, Peggy, so you can get there early," Pa advised. "Plan to be there by quarter of eight and go to the high school office. They'll tell you what to do. I'll get you up at five so you'll have plenty of time."

I did as he suggested, and it was good advice. The large woman in blue behind the counter at the office smiled at me reassuringly when I told her my tale of woe.

"I'll give you a permanent tardy pass," she said. "Don't worry, you're not the only one affected. All the children from farms to the west of Augusta come in on that bus. It'll be a good chance to get to know them. All you'll usually miss is part of the half-hour home room period where attendance is taken and announcements read. If you do miss home room period, just report here at the office and then go to your first class."

The first few days were nerve-wracking, trying to interpret our schedule cards, find all the different rooms in the ten-minute breaks between classes, remember what we needed to take with us for each class, and learn the names and expectations of our teachers. After the first week, however, the shell of routine began to harden around us, and we had learned the names of our classmates.

I never got used to the embarrassment and pressure of coming in late. I always arrived out of breath from running the hundred yards from the bus stop. It was worst in winter. The bus was frequently so late that I missed home room period altogether and never knew about last minute schedule changes or unscheduled events. Everyone looked up and stared at me when I came in. Red faced and breathing hard, I had to struggle out of my coat and boots in front of everybody, having had no time to leave them in the coat room.

Typing was the first class of the day, and once winter set in my fingers were so cold that I could hardly move them for the first twenty minutes. My aching extremities went from white to purplish red and swollen as they warmed up.

All freshmen in the commercial course had to take typing, filing, basic accounting, English and civics. Typing was fun, and I found it easy. As I had suspected, it was like learning to play an instrument—but playing it blind on keys without letters on them so we couldn't cheat and look at our fingers.

"Can't get up any speed if you don't keep your eyes on the copy you're typing from," warned Mrs. Varney, our teacher.

Filing was a bore, and repeated the obvious over and over. Accounting was common sense. Civics was enlightening because it taught us how city government worked, about voting, and what our responsibilities were as citizens. I also liked English, for we were given *The Merchant of Venice* to read. I'd not been introduced to Shakespeare before and fell in love with Elizabethan English. Even the teacher, a drab and sour woman in her sixties who talked as if she had a mouth full of hot potato, couldn't spoil it for me.

As had happened when I first went to school in town, I felt my world expanding. It occurred to me that I'd been surrounded by a vast bank of fog all my life, not knowing what was outside it. At first, the only fog-free places were our farm and the Lees' farm. Then the way to the country school cleared ahead of me, as did the way to the city schools later. At each school, spots in my mind lit up as new information came in, and these spots magically corresponded to a region of clarity in the outer world. My visits to Hazel and Rita added to the process by de-fogging the route to Boston. Knowledge was a bringer of light and a disperser of fog.

High school caused a whole rash of lights to glow in my head: The eastern part of town where the high school was, as I became familiar with it; the network of government operation, as we learned about it and took class trips to some of the offices; the Venice of Portia and Antonio, and the part of Shakespeare's London that included a theatre called the Globe.

The girls in my commercial classes were pleasant, neat, clean and appeared willing to learn. None of them had gone to Lincoln School, so all were new to me. They were a remarkably friendly and open group, mostly from town, but a few were from outlying areas on the other side of Augusta. We went our separate ways after school, however. I could not linger to chat, as I had to get the 2:10 bus, so friendships with the town girls seemed no more likely than they had at Lincoln School.

In November, however, one of them—plump, quiet, dark-haired Kay, asked if I would like to come and watch her swim.

Her invitation took me by surprise. Watching her swim seemed an odd thing to invite someone to do.

"Where do you swim?" I asked.

"At the Y.W.C.A. pool on Tuesday afternoons. Only people who join the 'Y' can swim there. You wouldn't be able to swim with me, but you could sit in the gallery and watch. Then if you thought you'd like to, you could join and we could go together. It isn't expensive."

"I've never been to a swimming pool," I admitted, "but I'd like to see one. Yes, I'll come with you."

We went the following Tuesday. Kay showed me the entrance to the viewing gallery, then went off to the locker room to change into her bathing suit.

I opened the gallery door, and there below me lay the pool, a blue-green jewel set in white marble. The water was completely clear and I could see the mosaic floor with three black lane lines running the length of it. No one was in the pool yet, but the water's surface moved gently, making the black lane lines waver and fragment.

Then I became conscious of the warmth and damp of steam heat and the shock of chlorine to my nose. No chilly breezes in here!

A door at the side of the pool opened and a man in sporty dress came in, followed by half a dozen girls in bathing suits. I spotted Kay at once. She looked up and waved.

The girls sat down on the edge of the pool with their legs dangling in the water, and at a command from the man pushed themselves forward into the blue-green depths with a great splash. They surfaced spluttering, and he directed them from the side of the pool. I watched as he coached them through several different strokes. It looked like fun, and I was confident of my ability to learn. I longed to be in the water with them.

After the lesson, the girls were allowed to splash around in the pool till the hour was up. Then Kay went to get changed and met me a few minutes later at the gallery door.

"What did you think of it?" she asked. She looked a bit apprehensive.

"I'd love to swim in that pool," I said. "I've saved enough money from working on a neighbor's farm to pay the entry fee."

Kay's plump face lit up. "Wonderful. Come on, I'll take you to the office and you can sign up right now."

I had my first go the following Tuesday. Swimming in a pool with hard tile sides and floor and green water that stung the eyes and smelled of chlorine was a totally different experience from swimming in a warm, sun-dappled lake with a sandy bottom, fresh, sweet air above, and willow trees dipping their tresses into the water. I much preferred the lake, but the blue-green pool had its own delights, and Kay's companionship made it well worth continuing to go. She was a kind and friendly girl and I found myself liking her more and more. In summer I could introduce her to Cobbosseecontee—she said she had never swum in a lake!

Kay had started swimming lessons the year before, so during the informal times after the lessons she helped me with my efforts to do a proper crawl with my face under water. She also showed me how to do the frog-kick backstroke. In return I taught her the egg float, how to surface dive, and how to swim under water. After our Tuesday afternoon swims we had just time to indulge in ice cream sodas before I had to catch the 5:10 bus.

Kay was the first person my own age who had ever approached me specifically with the idea of becoming my friend. In grammar school I had played with whoever happened to be in my grade, in a rather random manner. With my background of earlier harrassment at the country school, I seldom made a first move toward anyone for fear of rejection or treachery. Kay was unique in my experience thus far, and her spontaneous invitation began a friendship I hoped would last all our lives.

In reciprocation for my first swim at the "Y" I invited Kay to the farm for the weekend. Snow already covered the ground, and the water in Lees' quarry was frozen hard. I told her to bring her skates. Her father drove her out on Saturday morning and would come for her late Sunday afternoon.

Kay had no pets at home, and she fell in love with my dog Judy, who came up to her wiggling and bouncing as soon as she arrived. They were captivated with each other. Fluff and her kittens were more reserved, but soon found their way onto her lap.

After the noon meal, I took her over to the Lees, and Dick showed her the cows and horses. Next, we headed for the quarry. We were about equal in ability on ice, and stayed till the light was gone at four. Kay told me she had never skied but was eager to try and would ask her father if she could get some second-hand skis.

And so began our friendship.

Ma hated Kay on sight. I had not noticed her displeasure, but she made it clear as soon as Kay had gone. "How did you ever get acquainted with that silly girl?" she demanded.

I looked at her incredulously. "What did she do that was silly?" I asked.

"Isn't it obvious? She hasn't got a brain in her head!"

"She's one of the smartest girls in my class, Ma."

"That doesn't say much for the class. And she has an irritating laugh. I wouldn't waste my time on her, if I were you."

I didn't know what to say, and sensed that it would do no good to say anything. Ma apparently wasn't looking for an answer, for she turned away and got on with her own concerns.

It didn't matter what Ma thought. I knew that Kay was anything but silly. She was quiet and serious and I could see nothing wrong with her laugh. It was not loud or harsh, but it did sound like she was enjoying herself.

Ah, that was it, I thought. She was enjoying herself. And I was enjoying myself. And Ma couldn't stand that. Why was it that Ma couldn't bear to see anyone happy?

Ma had always tried to ensure that I didn't spend too much time with anyone except her, but with the Allen girls she had not actively opposed the friendship. She'd felt sorry for the family and was generous with her own time and efforts on their behalf. But she'd always tried to make sure I didn't see more of them than she thought I should, and I had become expert at spending more time with them than she thought I did.

I think Ma so bitterly disliked Kay because she sensed our relationship would develop into a strong friendship over which she would have no control. She was still convinced that I was only twelve years old, and as she slipped further into old age she was becoming more demanding and possessive. I, on the other hand, was becoming more independent, even as she tried to stifle me.

Pa told me, without being asked, that he liked Kay and had no objection to her coming out on weekends, so I ignored Ma's objections. I'd learned that trying to argue with her only resulted in the order "Don't talk back to me!"

Luckily, Pa was in good shape that weekend, so I had no immediate concern on that score, but I did worry about Kay's reaction to her first encounter with Ma. Had she noticed her hostility? I didn't dare ask her. What if she never wanted to come to the farm again? I dreaded seeing her in class next day for fear our friendship had been spoiled.

I shouldn't have worried. Kay didn't mention Ma, but told me what a wonderful time she'd had. Though we didn't discuss it, I got the idea that Kay understood exactly what was going on but thought it was wiser to leave such things unspoken. As time passed, it became clear to me that Kay was very perceptive, and a determined enough friend to put up with Ma's rudeness.

Kay even persisted when she found out she was allergic to cats, dogs and house dust. I couldn't understand why she always "caught cold" when she came out to the farm. By Sunday her eyes and nose would be streaming. Her father insisted she see a doctor, who diagnosed it as an allergic reaction and tested her for various allergens. Supplied with antihistamines, she kept our friendship going.

Arthur Moore, Kay's father, doted on his three daughters, and Kay, the youngest, was especially dear to him. Although his job as furnaceman at the local hospital paid a low wage, he indulged his girls as much as he was able. He bought Kay skis and poles as soon as he learned I was a skier, and we spent almost every weekend during that winter cross-countrying through field and woods to the "big hill," shussing straight down it, then herring-boning back up. The first few times we went out, I spent much of my time pulling plump Kay out of snow drifts, but as her muscles toughened and her wind developed she improved rapidly.

I soon discovered that Kay and I shared a love of music. She had a beautiful singing voice and was taking lessons. Next time she came to the farm she asked if I would play the piano for her. I got out *The Community Song Book* and she picked out the songs she liked. I played them by ear and we both sang. Next time she came, she brought a book containing easy classical pieces and a few opera arias. Since I didn't know those pieces by ear, I switched to the violin and played them by note while Kay sang.

I had never been introduced to classical music or opera, but Kay had. Her older sister Eleanore had been well known for her beautiful singing voice when she was in high school, and had sung in public.

One day in early December, Kay came into typing class clutching a bit of paper she'd torn from the *Kennebec Journal*.

"Look, Peg," she said, handing it to me. "On Saturday, *A Song to Remember* is coming to the Colonial Theater. We've just got to see it. It's got Cornell Wilde and Merle Oberon, and it's about a famous pianist!"

I took the clipping.

"The story of Frederick Francis *Chop*-in," I read aloud.

Kay withered me with a look. "Fredereek Franswah Show-*pan*, you idiot!" she hissed.

That movie changed our lives. The beautiful, black-haired Oberon in her stunning white gown, the handsome Cornel Wilde leaning over the piano while floods of music poured forth, the shocking spatters of blood on the keys as he played on and on despite tuberculosis.

And the music. The music! We couldn't believe that sounds so wonderful could exist. We stayed on to see the movie through a second time. Next day, we went back and sat through it twice more. Then we bought all the records of Chopin's music that we could afford. I set out to try and play Chopin by ear and made some clumsy approximations, but began to realize my mistake in not learning to read piano music.

Ma couldn't have avoided hearing the music being played in our farmhouse living room, but she never said a word about it, nor showed the slightest interest. Her hostility toward Kay did not diminish, but she disclosed it only by facial expression and frigid silence.

I sensed that Pa was trying to make up for Ma's animosity. He never became talkative, but he tried his best to be friendly to Kay when she came. Although he was usually blotto during the week, he seemed to make a special effort to remain sober if Kay was coming.

Kay never commented on Ma's behavior and showed no sign that it affected her. We both wordlessly understood what was going on, and just as wordlessly ignored it. But I wondered, and I'm sure Kay did, in her own separate way, what action Ma would eventually take. Surely, it was just a matter of time.

Through Eleanore, Kay heard of the winter Community Concert Series, and Mrs. Cony allowed me enough money to buy a season ticket. Neither Kay nor I had seen an orchestra perform live before, and it was a powerful experience for both of us.

I couldn't believe how complicated it was, all the different instruments blending together to make one magnificent sound coming at us. All those blowing, scraping, striking, donging, whistling shapes producing one sound.

But it wasn't one sound. As we listened and watched, it became clear that it was a texture of many sounds. But which instrument was making which thread of the music? We couldn't tell, and even by the end of the year's orchestral series we were still trying to train our ears to single out the instruments.

I renewed my vow: Someday I would be a musician—moreover, I would play in an orchestra and by then would have developed the ear to understand it.

73. McGraths'

The summer before I started high school, a new phenomenon arrived in the neighborhood in the form of McGraths'. Before anyone realized what was happening, Mr. and Mrs. McGrath had set up business in the vacant building across the street from the Palmers and next door to Dorothy Simpson's house.

Like McAuley's, the McGraths sold sandwiches, hot dogs, hamburgers and ice cream, but there the resemblance ended. Harry McGrath made his ice cream on site, and it ran to seventeen flavors instead of McAuley's repertoire of vanilla, chocolate and strawberry.

McGrath made orange-pineapple, pistachio, maple walnut, butter pecan, banana, mocha and brandied peach, all (except for the brandied peach) with fresh fruit when available. The tastes of these exotic ice creams were enough to put me into a state of bliss.

When McGrath learned that we sold raspberries, he added fresh raspberry to their list. Pa admitted to him, when questioned, that we also had blackberry and black raspberry bushes out back of the house, and McGrath wanted those berries, too. Since Ma's jelly making had by now been reduced to what she produced for our own consumption, Pa told McGrath he could buy all we couldn't use ourselves.

In addition to several tables with chairs, McGraths' had a long counter with seats where one could sit and savor delightful treats composed of several flavors of ice cream, various exotic sauces and syrups, whipped cream, and nuts. Some masterpieces were decorated with cherries on top as well.

McGrath and his wife also made and sold their own candy. Along the wall to the left of the counter, a glass cabinet displayed chocolates with cream centers flavored with orange, lemon, strawberry, raspberry, vanilla, toffee, mint, and wintergreen. They also sold several kinds of fudge, with or without nuts; clusters of raisins or nuts dipped in chocolate; peanut brittle; and toffees without a chocolate covering. These toffees were neatly wrapped in wax paper and twisted closed. Walking into McGraths' was a sensory experience that set the saliva running and the stomach contracting with expectation. Now that I had a bike, it was to McGraths' I went for Pa's "thirty cents worth."

McGrath was an enormous man with a belly like a full shelf which went before him as he walked slowly and purposefully about his premises. He was bald except for a thin crescent of close-shaven white hair, and the red top of his head shone like a beacon. He had a face that never smiled, and he made it clear who was in charge. He must have been in his late sixties or early seventies.

His wife was much younger, but due to her size it was difficult to guess her age. Probably late thirties or early forties. She was shorter than McGrath, but just as broad. Her hair and eyes were jet black; the skin of her smooth round face olive, tinged with pink. Her features were rounded and smooth too, and her nose bulbous. She said she was from New York, and she spoke in an accent I'd not heard before.

In contrast to their own massive bulks, the McGraths had a dog named Tiny—a miniature fox terrier with bones as delicate as a mouse's and a murderous bark that made the doors rattle. "We keep him for a watchdog," McGrath said. "When he goes off at night he sounds like he weighs five hundred pounds."

That would be about the McGraths' combined weight, I thought.

McGraths' rapidly became the place to go in Augusta, and on weekends their gravelled front parking lot was jammed with cars. The average weight of members of the community must have risen as a result. The McGraths' first summer and autumn was a resounding success for two reasons: Their ice cream and candy were better than anything ever tasted in the region before, and the war had provided people with the money to buy it.

They kept their business open till the end of October, then closed for the winter and went to Florida with Tiny for a well-deserved rest. They would re-open in April.

When the McGraths first started up their business they had scanned the local talent for possible employees and soon took on a couple of the younger Palmer boys, ages eleven and thirteen, for general clean-up and errand-running services. Rena, who like her siblings, was now attached to the Palmer clan, was hired as a dishwasher for ten cents an hour, but lasted only a week. Dick Lee told me he'd heard that she claimed the work was beneath her. I heard later from the McGraths that she'd been hopelessly clumsy and what she didn't break was not properly washed.

I learned this information because, several months later, I came into their employ. When they returned from Florida in March, McGrath came up to see Pa. It was a Sunday afternoon. I thought it was a bit early to be discussing raspberries.

He drove up our driveway as far as the stable and stopped. Pa went out to see what he wanted. They spoke together for a few minutes and then he drove off. Pa came into the house. Ma and I were in the kitchen.

"Peggy," he said, "how would you like to work for McGrath?"

This possibility had never entered my head. I looked at Pa in astonishment.

"He says he's heard that you're a good worker, and reliable, and he'd like to talk with you about working for them."

"What would I be doing, Pa? When?"

"He wants you to come by after school tomorrow and talk with him and his wife. He'll tell you all about it. Says you could start working Mondays through Fridays from 2:30 to 5:30 till you learn what you need to know and get used to it. They won't be open to the public till Wednesday, which is April first, but they'd like you to start on Tuesday so you can begin learning what goes on behind the scenes, where everything is, and help them get the place ship-shape for opening day."

"Gosh," I said.

"I don't know if you'd want to do that. I wouldn't want it to interfere with your studies. What do you think?"

I sat down at the kitchen table and looked at him. The idea terrified me. Working in a public place like that with everyone watching me? I wouldn't know what to do. I'd make a fool of myself. But still, it would be fun to learn how to make all those fancy ice cream concoctions and drinks, and it would mean extra money. And I could still keep doing bottles Saturday and Sunday mornings at the Lees.

"What will they pay me, Pa?" I asked.

"McGrath'll talk that over with you when he sees you. Probably not much to begin with, since you've no experience, but if you treat the customers right you might get some tips."

"I'd like to try it," I said.

"What about your school work?" asked Ma, who had been listening in silence.

By then I'd been at high school almost seven months and knew what was expected there and how to do it.

"Ma, you know I hardly ever bring a book home except for English when I want to read ahead. Every day I have a fifty minute study period and also a thirty minute home room period during the lunch hour because we eat in shifts. I can get everything I have to do done then, and I'll still have the evenings free."

"How do you think you'll get along with McGrath?" Ma asked. "I hear he's a hard driver and expects a lot."

"I'm a hard worker," I said.

"Go talk to him tomorrow, then," said Pa. "I'll phone and tell him you're coming. Then you can decide."

Next day I got off the 2:10 bus at McGraths', as arranged, and went inside. Mrs. McGrath was behind the empty candy display cabinet doing something inside. She smiled at me as I came in.

"Mr. McGrath is out in the back making candy, Peggy. Yuz can go back and see him. I'll talk to yuz afterwards."

I'd never heard the "yuz" form of "you" before. I wondered where she'd picked that up.

I found McGrath seated on a chair, pulling toffee. He shaped the sweet rubbery mass into a long cylinder, put it over a huge steel hook, and pulled it out into a thin rope. Then he folded the rope back into a cylinder and pulled again. Over and over in a set rhythm, his arm muscles bulging. He didn't stop when I came into the room, but nodded at a chair placed at the table. "Sit there," he said.

I sat, and noticed as I did so the metal-lined well in the center of the table. I had no idea what it could be for. It was empty.

"Your father's told you what I want to see you about?"

"Yes," I answered.

"I'll start by saying this. We have high standards here, and anyone we employ will have to live up to them. This is a food-handling business, and absolute cleanliness in your person, your dress and your working habits is essential. The customers do not want to be served in dirty dishes, nor do they wish to see hair in their ice cream. Your uniforms must be spotless at all times, and freshly laundered and pressed each time you appear here."

I nodded.

"Lateness is not permitted. If you start work at 2:30, that means at 2:30 you will be dressed in your uniform and out front, on the floor, doing your job. And you will not leave early. You are on the floor till 5:30."

"Yes, Sir."

"I understand that you have no experience as a waitress?"

"No, Sir."

"That's perhaps just as well, you'll have learned no bad habits. The going rate for the job you will be expected to do is forty cents an hour. Since you have no experience and we will have to train you, I will start you off at one dollar a day. For three hours in the afternoon that comes to how much per hour?" He stared hard at me to see if I could tell him.

"Thirty-three and one third cents."

"Good. We won't have to teach you how to count. When you prove to us that you can do the job to our standard, you will get the going rate."

Wow, I thought—almost twice as much as I'm getting at the Lees! Fifteen hours a week times forty cents will be six bucks a week!

"And any tips you get from satisfied customers will be yours, of course."

"Thank you, Sir," I said, painfully aware of the limited nature of my responses, but not knowing what else to say.

"You'll not only be waiting on tables at this job," McGrath continued, "you will also be making up the orders you receive, either behind the ice cream counter, or out here at the grill if they want hot dogs, hamburgers or sandwiches. I trust that growing up on a farm you have already learned something about preparing food, as well as about driving horses?"

"Yes, Sir," I said. Why did he mention horses? Had he been sounding out the Lees about me?

"You must also learn all the different prices so you can write up the customers' bills," McGrath went on. "We will check the bills for you at first, but we expect you to learn quickly how to do them correctly on your own."

The toffee had apparently reached what McGrath considered the right consistency, so he gave it one final pull into a thin rope. He removed it from the hook, brought it to the table, and spread it out. He took a sharp knife and began cutting the rope into small sections about an inch long.

"There will be slack periods, especially early in the week," he went on. "During those times there will be plenty for you to do. First, make sure the front of the shop is spotless: counter, tables and worktops swabbed down, and everything in order. Then check the candy cabinet to see what needs replacing, and do that. The candy storage room is in there." He waved his arm toward a door in the rear wall of the room. "Mrs. McGrath will show it to you. After you've restocked the cabinet, see what stage we're at in candy making and what you can do to help us."

"Yes, Sir." I felt like a parrot who had learned only two words.

"I'll describe to you the candymaking routine. I make the cream centers for the chocolates, dip them in powdered sugar and arrange them on trays covered with waxed paper. I give the trays to Mrs. McGrath one at a time, and she dips each center into the molten chocolate in that metal well in the table. She'll show you that, as well. Then the dipped chocolates are placed on trays again, taken into the chocolate storage room, and stored in the appropriate boxes. You will be doing a lot of that and keeping track of what we're getting low on.

"You will, of course, have to learn all the prices for the different candies, how to weigh them out accurately for the customers, and calculate quickly and accurately what they owe."

As he talked, I could feel panic fighting to rise within me at the sheer number of things I would have to learn all at once.

"Well, what do you think?" he asked. "Do you think you can handle that?"

I took a deep breath. "I'd like to try," I said.

"Good. Be here tomorrow as soon as that bus lands you here, and we'll get you started. You are to call us 'Mr. McGrath' and 'Mrs. McGrath' in front of the customers, but when they are not present you may call us 'Mr.' and 'Mrs.' Mrs. McGrath will talk with you now. I'll go out front and tell her to come see you."

He hefted up his great bulk and made slow but steady progress toward the front, like a ship under full sail. I heard mumbled conversation, then Mrs. McGrath appeared.

"The Mr. says he thinks yuz'll do. Now I'll see what size uniform yuz'll need—fourteen by the look."

She opened the top of a large wooden chest that stood against the far wall. In it were several stacks of uniforms. She removed one, shook out the folds, and held it up to me. It was crisp and white and had half-inch-wide red and royal blue stripes on the edge of each sleeve.

"That should fit yuz," she said. "And here's the apron and cap."

The apron was small and pert and was also trimmed with red and blue, like the cap. It wasn't really a cap but a rectangular piece of material which stood up at the front of the head to keep the hair out of the way. It had an elastic band attached to secure it.

"Your uniform'll be hanging on the back of the door here in this changing room. She opened a door and showed me a tiny closet-like room with one window high up to let in light. A small mirror hung on the wall. "When yuz get here, change quickly and be out on the floor at 2:30. Then when yuz leave you can change out of it. If it's still clean yuz might need only a fresh apron next day. I send all the uniforms out to the laundry, and I got several 14's, so there'll always be one ready when yuz come."

This was a great relief. I'd inferred from what McGrath had said that I'd have to wash and press my own uniforms, and I couldn't figure out the logistics of having a clean one daily unless I carried it with me to school, which would have been a nuisance and would have wrinkled it badly.

"Yuz won't need a uniform till we open on Wednesday. Tomorrow we'll start showing yuz where everything is," she said. "Yuz can go along now. We'll see yuz tomorrow."

At first it had come as a surprise whenever Mrs. McGrath used the word "yuz," but by the time I left it was already becoming so familiar I hardly noticed it.

I thanked her and left with an odd mixture of apprehension and curiosity churning in my stomach. I got the feeling I was going to have to come to grips with the adult world very fast.

I phoned Kay that evening and told her what had happened. She'd never been to McGraths', nor heard about it, as it had closed for the winter before we became friends. When I told her of my anxieties she just laughed and assured me I'd have no trouble.

"Anyone can wait on tables," she said.

She'd never done it herself, of course, so her reassurance didn't do much to calm my stomach.

74. The Chocolate Dipper

I tried not to let Ma and Pa see my panic after the interview with the McGraths, but they must have sensed how jittery I was. I spent an uncomfortable evening going over and over in my mind what I'd been told and trying to accommodate to it. In my dreams I was still going over it.

By morning I'd had an idea that I thought might help. We'd been taught to take notes on our lessons at school. I liked this way of reinforcing things in my memory and had become a compulsive note-taker. So on my first day at work I came with a small notebook and pencil in my pocket, and as Mr. and Mrs. McGrath showed me what needed to be done and where things were, I made some quick notes.

First, Mrs. took me around the premises. She started with the candy storage room, where rows and rows of black boxes full of candy were stacked on shelves from floor to ceiling. The boxes were arranged alphabetically by flavor. Each box contained layer upon layer of cardboard trays containing the finished candy. Mrs. showed me how to remove a tray, pack the chocolates carefully into a container and take it out to be placed in the display cabinet. She explained the order in which the various kinds were arranged in the cabinet.

Then she took me behind the ice cream counter and showed me where to find the glassware, the dishes, the cutlery, the various syrups and sauces, the nuts, the whipped cream and, in a freezer beneath the counter, the seventeen ten-gallon tubs of ice cream. "Get so yuz can tell the different kinds by the look of 'em, Peggy, so yuz won't be giving the customer cherry instead of raspberry. They all look different even if they're the same color."

She showed me the special scoops for ice cream, one to be used for the large cones, one for the small cones and a still smaller one for the several gobs of ice cream which went, one on top of the other, in the tall thin parfait glasses. She showed me how to scoop properly so the result wasn't full of holes, and how to release the ice cream neatly from scoop into dish. She showed me how to fill half pint, pint and quart ice cream tubs so there were no air holes, but not to jam it in hard. "Give the customer a good fair tub full, but don't try to pack a pint and a half into a pint tub," she explained.

She showed me the lists of ice cream specials and their prices, and told me how to make them, and about the choices of flavor the customers had for each one. I wrote down as much as I could, and wished I'd had a year of shorthand. "It'll come to you as you do it," she assured me. "Don't worry."

Mr. showed me how to weigh out candy, calculate the price, and how to count back change. Then he took me out back and showed me the grill and the cooking equipment while Mrs. was setting up for chocolate dipping. "At first when you get an order you'll come out here and watch me prepare it, if you have time between customers. When you learn how we like it done, you'll be doing it yourself if I'm not available to do it."

Mrs. had filled the heated well in the middle of the table with chocolate, now melted and ready to go. A tub of cherry-flavored soft candy that Mr. had made up earlier was now at the right consistency and ready for action.

Mr. took a spoonful of the mixture, rolled it in powdered sugar and placed it on one corner of a wax-paper covered cardboard tray. In spite of his bulk and the size of his fingers he worked with great speed, rolling centers and placing them in neat, even rows on the tray. When a tray was full, he handed it to Mrs., who had seated herself at the table in front of the heated well. She placed the full tray at one side of the well and an empty tray on the other. Then she picked up a cream center in the fingers of her right hand, dipped it delicately in the melted chocolate, brought it out, and set it down on one corner of the empty tray. She lifted her fingers from it and, so quickly that I hardly saw her, made a crescent on top of the candy with the melted chocolate that remained on her index finger. Then she picked up another center and did the same.

She kept her left hand chocolate-free, while the fingers of her right hand remained covered with chocolate. With a rapidity I couldn't believe, she finished covering the tray with finished chocolates, placing them in immaculate rows. Not a drop of chocolate got on the wax paper between the candies, and each crescent on each chocolate was perfect.

"How do you do that?" I asked. "If I tried it, I'd have chocolate all over my hands and face, all over the table and the floor too."

"Practice," she said, "and patience. I apprenticed a long time. It becomes easy."

"Do you put crescents on all the chocolates?"

"Those are C's—for cherry creams. Maple ones get an M, N is for nougat, T is for toffee, and so forth. When you run out of letters, you can use a number or just make up something, as long as you remember what the something is and use it for that kind every time."

The McGraths had their speeds coordinated so Mr. had the next tray ready by the time Mrs. finished the one before. He did the leg work, giving her the tray of centers and collecting the tray of finished chocolates.

Watching them, I decided that, on balance, work was going to be fun, once I got used to it. It was like going to a new school where everything was different and the world was changed for you because you had suddenly seen another facet of it. Every new job will be like that, I thought—even if I don't like it, it will be showing me something else I'd never dreamed of before.

"Another girl will be starting work tomorrow, Peggy," Mrs. told me when I left that evening. "Her name is Suzy. She'll be coming in at nine so we can show her things before it gets busy. She's had some experience waiting tables at a place in town, so she should catch on pretty fast."

Next day when I arrived at 2:20, Mrs. told me that the morning had been very quiet. "It'll pick up later this afternoon," she predicted, "but meanwhile you can help Suzy wash the outside of the front windows." This pleased me. It was a glorious sunny spring day and I was grateful for the chance to be out in the sun.

Mrs. introduced me to Suzy, a girl of about nineteen who had graduated from high school the year before. She was shorter than I and had what I thought was a rather petulant, though pretty, face.

The McGraths had long-handled window washers with a sponge on one side for washing and a rubber strip for drying on the other. "It's a squeegee," said Mrs. I'd never seen one before and thought it was wonderful. At home we had to stand on a ladder, put ammonia water on with a rag and then dry the windows by rubbing them with crumpled newspapers. The printer's ink was supposed to make them shine.

Suzy and I went outside with a pail of water. The squeegees were easy to use, no ladder was required, and drying was a lot faster than with newspaper. I was enjoying it. "These things are great," I commented to Suzy. She had said nothing since we came outside, and now she turned and glared at me.

"I took this job to wait on tables, not to wash windows," she snapped.

I was quite taken aback. I wasn't used to people who grumbled about working. The only grumbler I had known was Rena. Everyone else did what was needed and didn't complain about it. Mr. had told me there would always be something to do, and I was to keep busy. I assumed he'd told Suzy the same.

We were about half finished when Suzy threw down her squeegee. "I'm not going to do this. It's not the job I was hired for. They had me unpacking boxes of dishes all morning, for God's sake! I've got my period and I've got cramps and I'm not going to do it!"

She stomped back inside and I could see her through the window talking with Mrs. They both went into the back. A few minutes later Suzy reappeared accompanied by Mr. He stepped behind the counter. Suzy came back outside and picked up her fallen squeegee.

Anger was written on her face. "Mr. says if I want this job I'll finish the windows," she said. "I'd like to put this thing through his damn window. I hope I hemorrhage, that'd show him!" and she attacked the scrubbing with a fury that put the lie to her claim of having cramps. I said nothing.

When we'd finished we went back inside, put away the squeegees and washed our hands. I went out front, but Suzy stopped to speak with Mr., and Mrs. joined them. Then Mr. and Suzy came out, went outside and left in his car.

"He's gone to drive her home," said Mrs. She made no further comment. He was back in ten minutes, which was just as well, as no sooner was he back

281

than we began to get busy. A car drew into the parking lot, two couples got out, and headed for the door.

"There's your first customers, Peggy," said Mr. "You know what to do."

I felt my stomach plummet. This was it. I waited behind the counter while they came in and seated themselves at one of the tables. I brought them glasses of ice water, took my green order pad from my pocket, and asked, "May I help you?"

Four faces looked up at me. One of the women spoke first. "I'd like a hot fudge sundae with vanilla ice cream."

"Do you want whipped cream and nuts on that?"

"Um-m-m—just whipped cream. No nuts."

"What's an Augusta Parfait?" asked the other woman.

"Two small scoops of ice cream—vanilla and strawberry unless you want other flavors—in a tall glass with tutti-fruiti syrup between them and hot fudge on top, and whipped cream on top of that. Nuts if you want, and then a cherry on top of everything."

"Sounds good. I'll have that—with nuts."

"I'll have a banana split," said one of the men, rubbing his belly in anticipation.

"What's a Jumbo Yum-Yum?" asked the other.

"That's three large scoops of ice cream—your choice of flavors—hot fudge or hot butterscotch sauce, whipped cream and nuts."

One of the women gasped. "Larry, how can you possibly eat all that?"

"I'll manage," he said, and scanned the ice cream flavors. "I'll have— uh—butter pecan—french vanilla—and—uh—raspberry. With hot butter-scotch sauce."

I scribbled furiously, trying to get everything down.

"What would a Junior Yum-Yum have been if I'd asked for that?" he wanted to know.

"The same, but with small scoops of ice cream instead of large ones."

"Oh, that wouldn't be nearly enough," he said, laughing.

I went back to the counter, got out four glass dishes of the right sizes and shapes, checked my crib sheet which I'd left in view under the counter, and began scooping ice cream.

Mr., who had been watching from the back doorway, came behind the counter. He didn't say anything, just appeared to be checking that the plugs to the frappe mixers were properly in their sockets, but I could tell he had his eye on my reflection in the counter-length mirror. The sweat broke out on my forehead.

To my relief a man came in for candy, and as Mrs. wasn't on the floor Mr. had to go and serve him. I finished making up my four orders and took them over two at a time, serving the women first.

They thanked me and I went back behind the counter. I watched Mr. weighing out chocolates for his customer. As I turned back, I glanced at my customers. To my horror they were all staring at me. Why? What had I done wrong? Did I just look peculiar to them? I glanced away again in confusion.

One of the men cleared his throat loudly. "May we have some spoons with which to eat these delicious concoctions, Miss?"

I could feel the red flood up my face as I dove for the tray of spoons. "I'm sorry," I said as I reached the table with them. "You're my first customers, and I completely forgot!"

The man laughed. "Don't worry about it. We can tell you're new at this."

As I returned to the counter I noticed that Mr. had been observing the incident from the other side of the candy cabinet. As soon as his customer left, he ambled over and joined me.

"Always remember to give your customers the tools with which to eat," he said.

Did he have to say that? I thought. Did he really think I'd ever forget again?

"Luckily the napkins are on the table so you can't forget those," he continued. "Oh, when you serve hot lunches, be sure to check the tables to make sure they have salt and pepper shakers."

"Yes, Sir."

"Now, get the prices of everything onto your order pad and add them up. Then I'll check your arithmetic."

I wasn't used to working with someone hanging over my shoulder, and I could feel the sweat pouring down my back. I gritted my teeth, double checked the posted prices, wrote them onto the orders, checked them again, and added the total twice, once down and once up.

"Lessee," said Mr. He went over everything with great deliberation.

"All correct," he said, and handed the pad back to me.

I waited till the customers were finished, took the bills over, collected their money, and took it back to the till. Mr. watched as I counted out the change, then checked it.

"Right," he said, and I took it back to the table. The man who'd asked for the spoons gave me a ten cent tip. Surprised, I thanked him and they left.

By then it was four o'clock and school children, with or without parents, began coming in for ice cream cones, and a few women came in to get ice cream for supper. By 5:10, the after-work customers started appearing, and at 5:30 I was so busy packing ice cream that Mrs. had to come and tap me on the shoulder.

"It's 5:30, Peggy, you can get out of your uniform now, I'll finish this for you."

I went off and changed and headed up the road toward home. I was glad I had a half mile to walk so I could unscramble my head and unknot my stomach. I'd had my first dose of what seemed to be impossible pressure. And this was a 'slack day'! What would a busy one be like? Thank heavens I wasn't working on weekends!

I was wrong about that. Next day, Thursday, Mrs. confirmed to me what I had already suspected, that Suzy was not coming back. "She's a very spoiled girl, is Suzy. Very spoiled. Will do only what she wants to, and no more. We need someone who is willing to do the whole job, not just the bits she likes. We'll be interviewing more girls today and tomorrow, but if we don't find one by Saturday, would you be willing to come in Saturday and Sunday to help us out? Mr. and I can't handle the weekend alone."

My heart dived into my shoes, but how could I refuse? I didn't want the McGraths to think I was spoiled like Suzy!

75. The Weekend

I sweated it out Thursday and Friday, trying to remember everything I'd been told, sort out prices in my head, recall all the recipes, and cope with the staggering number of special requests from the customers. Meanwhile, several girls came for interviews—and went away again.

Fortunately, it didn't get really busy till after three on Friday, and by then I was beginning to remember what I had to. When it was time for me to go, Mr. and Mrs. were dealing with a crowd that had just arrived. I didn't like to leave them in such a state, but at 5:30 sharp McGrath glanced at his watch and said, "You're off, Peggy."

I went home and phoned Kay to tell her I wouldn't be able to have her out for the weekend.

The McGraths had asked me to come at 3:00 next day. "We'll probably be busy right up till we close at eleven, Peggy, and eight hours is enough," said Mrs. "You'll get an hour off for supper at six."

That Saturday was one I'll never forget. I came down on my bike at ten of three and found the place packed. "We're out straight, Peggy, just out straight!" said Mrs. as I came in. Mr. was in the back, cooking up the orders, and she was trying to cope in the front on her own. With minor fluctuations, we remained "out straight" till closing.

The juke box, which had been relatively quiet during the week, was pouring out the current favorites on the "Hit Parade." I was too busy to pay much attention to it, except when it stopped.

"Not everybody likes to eat with that din in their ears," McGrath explained, "So we got the juke box man to install a 'ten minutes of silence' option. If quiet is worth a nickel to them, they can choose that."

Since I had as yet received little instruction in using the grill, the McGraths decided that till Suzy was replaced Mr. would handle all the back-room food preparation. Mrs. would tend the candy cabinet, and I would work the counter and tables. I was grateful for this arrangement, as it cut considerably the number of things I had to remember all at once. The worst was when parties of five or six came in and all tried to order simultaneously, interrupting each other when they remembered what they'd forgotten to say in the first place, or if they changed their minds.

Mr. and Mrs. helped me whenever they were not busy with their own part of the work. It seemed, to my chagrin, that they were psychic—one or the other of them always had their eye on me whenever I happened to make a mistake.

My worst one that day was when Mr. observed what I did to the chocolate frappe. "'Frap' is a mispronunciation of the French *frappé* which means 'beaten,'" Mrs. had explained when she showed me how to make one. A frappe consisted of one measure of any flavor of syrup the customer wanted, one scoop of ice cream (any flavor and a choice of three sizes of scoop) and a half pint of milk. These ingredients were placed in a quart-size stainless steel container, attached to a mixer, and beaten till they were completely liquidized, creamy and frothy. A milk shake was the same, but without the ice cream.

In this case, the customer, who was sitting at the counter, had ordered a chocolate frappe with vanilla ice cream. I proceeded to make it. As I removed the container from the mixing unit, I became aware that Mr. had come up behind me.

"You've just made a very expensive frappe indeed, my girl," he said. I looked at him blankly, unable to fathom what I'd done wrong.

"You used a half pint of cream instead of a half pint of milk," he informed me, as he picked up the cream bottle from the counter where I had set it.

The milk and cream were next to one another in the refrigerator under the counter, in glass bottles of identical size and shape. Only colorless, slightly raised glass lettering on the bottles distinguished them. The color of the liquid in the bottle should have told me which was the cream, but the light wasn't very good down there. The consistency should also have told me when I poured it out, but I was hurrying to get this order out of the way so I could go out to the tables where several people were waiting.

"What'll I do?" I asked.

"Give it to him. It'll be the best frappe he ever had. Just don't do it again."

The customer was at the far end of the counter and did not hear this exchange. I gave him the frappe and watched as he tasted it. A smile of satisfaction lit his lips, and I hurried off to the tables to get the orders.

McGrath went out back and returned with a red elastic band. When I came back to the counter, he brought out the bottle of cream, put the rubber band around its neck, gave me a significant look, replaced the bottle in the refrigerator, and ambled off without a word.

In spite of being "out straight" all weekend, one thing I noticed was how happy the customers were. A different world existed than the one I knew, and I was being allowed a glimpse into it. Happy people lived there, people who drove out together in their cars on weekends just for fun—just to enjoy themselves. They didn't have cars only for going to work, but for pleasure too—and they didn't feel guilty about it!

They bought treats for themselves just because they wanted to, and they had the money to pay for them. They allowed themselves to have fun. They smiled, they joked. Families existed in this world who could laugh with each other and be glad.

The Lees laughed together, of course, but they were too busy working on weekends to go out just for fun.

Girls not much older than I were coming in with their boyfriends. They weren't shy with one another. They looked into each others eyes and laughed—relaxed, comfortable being together. Not shy and frightened like I was. They stood straight and sure and beautiful. The few that were tall like me didn't bend their knees trying to hide their height.

At six I took my supper break, and biked home with stomach empty and nerves sizzling. Ma had waiting for me a plate of home-baked beans and frankfurter sausages (standard Saturday night supper in Maine before the "hot dog" was ever dreamed of). Beside it was a quart of milk and a glass. This meal revived me remarkably. Refueled, I managed to keep going till closing time.

By ten thirty things had slacked off, and by quarter of eleven the place was empty, the juke box silent.

"Have yuz a sundae, Peggy," Mrs. said to me. "You've earned it!"

I made myself a brandied peach sundae with hot fudge sauce and nuts, took it to one of the tables, and savored it gratefully. It was the most wonderful combination I had ever tasted.

When I biked home, Ma and Pa were both up waiting for me, worried about my bicycling alone up the dark hill at night. Drunken crashes were not unknown on that road. My bicycle had a light, and I knew to be careful, but they never ceased worrying. It was probably the first time either of them had been up till eleven o'clock for many years.

Sunday was largely a repeat of Saturday, except that the afternoon was even busier, and the clientele different. Many people came dressed in their Sunday best, the women in hats and gloves, little girls in flouncy dresses, expensive coats and patent leather shoes, little boys smartly dressed, some even wearing ties and jackets. It was a day for going to church and then taking Granny out for an ice cream—and McGraths' was the place to go. A lot of candy also left the store that day.

Both Saturday and Sunday nights I left with my brain in a hopeless snarl. I was sure I'd never get used to the pressure. Every nerve sizzled, and my stomach was in knots. All night long I kept half waking to find myself scooping ice cream over and over—and asking "Do you want a five or a ten-cent cone? Whipped cream and nuts on that? Vanilla or strawberry ice cream in that strawberry frappe? Mustard and relish on your hot dog? What about onions? Ketchup on your hamburger, Sir? I'm sorry, Ma'am, there won't be any blackberry ice cream till July. If you want a toasted sandwich, it'll be five cents extra. Cream and sugar in your coffee? Did you say a half or a quarter pound of lemon creams? . . ."

Kay'll never believe this when I tell her, I thought.

On the following Tuesday, the McGraths hired Annette Taylor. She was a year ahead of me in high school, and taking the home economics course. She, like Suzy, had experience waiting on tables in town, but there the similarity ended. Annette came from a poor and hard-working family, and had many brothers and sisters. It was clear from the beginning that she was capable. She not only had a knowledge of food preparation, but also was familiar with and at ease with children—which I was not. This made Annette ideal for dealing with unruly kids and remembering to set up the high chair when an infant in arms came in. She was sturdy and unflappable, and we liked each other at once.

By Friday, it was clear that my services would not be required at the weekend, so Kay came out. I took her down to McGraths' on Saturday afternoon, of course, and introduced her to Mr. and Mrs. and the joys of the Jumbo Yum Yum.

76. The Honors List

In the early spring of our freshman year both Kay and I had a shock. At the end of each quarter we took exams, and as a result a quarterly Honors list was read out in assembly and then appeared in the paper. Each time the list had been read that year, Kay and I from the commercial course and Barbara King from the academic course were the only ones in the freshman class who appeared in the High Honors section at the top of the list.

After the spring vacation, at one of the Friday assemblies, four empty chairs were sitting on the stage when Mr. Macomber, the Principal, came out to call the assembly to order. He said that the honor parts for the spring graduation were about to be announced, and gave us a long spiel about academic excellence and brilliant futures for those who succeeded, and read quotations from the Bible to back himself up. One of the quotations declared that:

> To those that hath, shall be given; and from those who hath not, shall be taken away even that which they hath.

Unfair, I thought. Why should the poor always lose out? Was that what people who believed in God thought justice was?

Then Mr. Macomber called out the names of four seniors for valedictorian, salutatorian, and the third and fourth honor parts. The named students, two girls and two boys, came up on the stage and Mr. Macomber explained for the benefit of the ignorant freshmen that these four would be giving the orations at graduation.

I felt my stomach tighten. If Kay and I didn't get off that High Honors list, we'd have to give speeches when we were seniors. I was sure Kay would do fine at that, but the thought of having to get up there myself in front of an assembly hall full of graduating students and parents filled me with horror. I couldn't possibly do that. I would just have to stop doing good work. How else could I get off the High Honors list?

I didn't discuss this with Kay. I was rather ashamed to even be thinking about it, and ashamed of being such a coward. Instead, I thought the matter through and through over the next few days, trying to clarify my thinking and reduce my panic. It boiled down to this:

I was smart enough to get an honor part. The reasons against getting one were:

1. Terror at speaking in public. Reason: The heckling and jeering I'd had to cope with at the country school, of knowing anything I did there, good or bad, would be laughed at or worse. Getting up before the class at the city school hadn't been too bad, the children were friendly and I'd gotten used to it—but giving an oration to the whole graduating class and all their relatives? I felt sick just thinking about it.

2. Boys didn't like clever girls. Several people (all women and girls) including Mrs. Cony had cautioned me with some variant of "Don't let the boys know you're smart, they won't like you—you'll never get married!"

I'd already begun to like the boys, but they showed no sign of reciprocating. I was too tall, too skinny and too shy. Once it sank in with them that I was smart, there would be no hope at all.

But in order not to get an honor part, I'd have to deliberately try to fail, and pretend I was stupid. If I did that, I would hate myself. I didn't want to sell myself short, eliminate any chance of doing anything I wanted to do except get married. Since the boys already didn't like me, it would all be for nothing anyway.

Dick Lee provided the spark that led me out of this dark morass of indecision. He'd noticed the announcement of the Honors list in the *Kennebec Journal*.

"I see you got on the High Honors list," he said, obviously pleased. I hadn't even realized that the list had been published.

"Yes," I said. "So did Kay."

"Your mother'd have been happy about that. I heard her say one day to my mother, 'Someday I'd like to have a child who got all A's in high school.'"

I looked at him in amazement. Though Maisie and Gracie had spoken with me about Mother, Dick never had. He'd been only eight when she died and it hadn't occurred to me that he might be a source of information about her.

Dick's comment about my mother changed everything. If Mother would have been proud of me, and if Dick and his family were pleased, why shouldn't I be proud of being smart? Why should I care if people less clever liked that or not? And why did boys want stupid girls, anyway? If they married a stupid girl, wouldn't that make it more likely that their children would be stupid? Mrs. Lee wasn't stupid. She was the smartest person I'd ever met, and her children were the cleverest. And she'd managed to get married.

Clearly, since Kay and I and Barbara King were the only ones to have been on the High Honors list all year, if this trend continued the three of us couldn't avoid giving a speech. If I couldn't avoid the torture of speaking in pubic, why not aim for giving the best speech? Why settle for a third or fourth honor part if I could be valedictorian? That would have pleased my mother even more than getting all A's. Since I could do nothing else for the woman who birthed me and then died, why not do that?

Having come to that decision, I never looked back. I'd be valedictorian, and I'd give the best possible speech I could, if it killed me.

77. The Visit of Lynde and Winnie

In May, Lynde finished his stint at the Naval Base in Argentia, Newfoundland, and was to be posted to Guam to work on a floating drydock being constructed there. In between, he had a few weeks leave and came with his new wife Winifred to spend a weekend with us. We had no idea what to expect—we'd never even seen a picture of Winnie—knew nothing but her name and that her family lived in Jamestown.

They were coming on Saturday, and I noted with relief that by Friday Pa was already sober. As spring had progressed, I'd noticed, in fact, that he was sober more often. He began to revive as the days lengthened, the sun brightened and warmth began to permeate the earth. He seemed to respond to sun as I did, and to feel the sap of life running through him again.

Lynde and Winnie arrived Saturday about mid-morning in a smart grey Oldsmobile with a trunkful of baggage. I'd been watching from the living room since 9 a.m., and we all went out to meet them.

Though I didn't know what to expect of Winnie, I certainly didn't expect what I saw. She had long, slender legs, and her figure, though lithe, was rounded and voluptuous. Her long, handsome face was framed by rich, dark brown hair which came to her shoulders. She wore it parted in the middle, pulled back at the sides in curves over her forehead, and held just below the temple with barettes. Her mouth was wide and smiling, her eyes blue-green.

Her whole appearance and manner were languid and sensuous, and her voice drawled in what sounded to me like the "southern accent" I had heard on the radio. I didn't know they spoke that way in Rhode Island. She and Lynde kept exchanging long, lingering glances.

Though her face was slender, her features reminded me somewhat of Hazel's, and I commented on this to Lynde. "Guess you're raht at that," he drawled. He'd never drawled before! He seemed to have taken on Winnie's way of speaking. Winnie giggled at this information about Hazel, but the giggle wasn't like giggles I knew, but slow and drawly like she talked. "Sexy" I would call it now, but I didn't understand that then.

We took Lynde and Winnie upstairs with their baggage and installed them in the guest room, which was the front bedroom facing south. The bed had a metal frame painted white and a high bedstead topped by polished brass spheres. Its white cotton spread with a pattern of soft tufts had been worked by Ma years ago.

Winnie's face glowed when she saw the room. "Ah just love antique furniture," she said to Ma. "That bed and the spread are just beautiful—an' Ah noticed that lovely marble-topped table you've got outside in the hall, with that vase of blue larkspurs on it."

Ma, pleased to have one of her enthusiasms appreciated, motioned Winnie out into the hall for a better look at the table.

"I keep it up here where it catches the light from the hall window, and the dark wallpaper behind it sets off the purity of the marble," she explained.

Pa and I took Lynde and Winnie outside and walked around the farm, telling Winnie all about how it used to be when we had animals and big fields of vegetables and fruit. Judy accompanied us. Later, Winnie met Fluff who, as usual, was asleep in Pa's rocker waiting for him to come and offer himself as a cushion.

"Ah see the animals still have the run of the house," Lynde commented in his new accent. I hadn't thought that was unusual. Though the Lees' cats were kept in the barn to catch rats and raise their kittens, their elderly collie was usually sprawled on the kitchen floor to be stepped over.

Meanwhile, Ma had been preparing our noon meal—"dinner," as it was known on the farm. "Supper" was a smaller meal, usually eaten at five. I didn't know town people ate to a different schedule until I visited Winnie a few weeks later.

After dinner, Lynde and Winnie took me in to Augusta to "pick up a few things." Things, as it turned out, meant for me. We'd been poor ever since I could remember, but I think Lynde was shocked by the changes the last two years had brought.

Our first stop was a dress shop, ostensibly to look for something for Winnie, but they had so many attractive clothes for young girls, as Winnie pointed out, that we left with two smart new summer dresses for me, as well as one for her.

We had passed McGraths' on our way to town, and I told them about my job there. When we got back to the farm, Lynde suggested we all go down for an ice cream so they could "look the place over." Ma, who was now very stiff and hobbly, declined to come. Quick to sense Ma's moods, I decided that she was still upset that Lynde had married again so fast after Marge's death. I'd got over my own shock, aided by Pa's understanding answer when I asked him what he thought about it.

Pa joined us, however. He wouldn't eat anything but a raspberry cone— to test the taste of our berries in McGrath's ice cream—but Lynde and Winnie and I made pigs of ourselves with rich and fruity fancy specials. I suggested an Augusta Parfait for Winnie, and Lynde was game to try a Jumbo Yum-Yum. Annette was working the counter and gave us all generous servings. It being Saturday afternoon they were "out straight" of course, but Mr. and Mrs. came over to us briefly to meet my relatives and tell them I was a good worker.

Lynde wanted to take all of us out to the Augusta House for the evening meal to save Ma having to cook. Ma said she didn't feel up to going out, and Pa reneged because of his bad legs.

"I couldn't sit still that long," he said. "My legs would just get cramps, and they're excruciating. I have to keep 'em moving. But you three go. Peggy's never been out to a restaurant."

So the three of us went. Lynde phoned for a reservation.

The Augusta House was the town's only hotel, a big brick affair painted bright yellow. I didn't know people could have dinner there if they weren't staying there.

It was the first time I'd ever had a full meal out, and I couldn't stop staring at the elegant surroundings. The dining room was large, and the royal blue carpet stretched from wall to wall, decorated with exotic red, grey and pale blue medallions in a repeating pattern. Large windows went from floor to ceiling, framed by royal blue velvet drapes. An enormous glass chandelier hung glittering from a long golden cable. On a serving table at one end of the room, covered silver dishes gleamed in the soft light.

I ordered chicken fricassee, Winnie had salmon and Lynde opted for the speckled rainbow trout.

Eager to know the history of their romance, I asked Lynde and Winnie how they had met. They looked at each other languorously.

"I worked at the post office," Winnie drawled, "and Lynde came in every day to pick up his mail. We got to know each other pretty well in two years."

"There I was, alone and lonesome and nothing to do but work," Lynde said. "And there she was, purty as a picture behind that mail window. She was nice and kind to me and always had something pleasant and interesting to say."

Winnie giggled her slow giggle. "He was just the handsomest man I'd ever seen," she said.

"In spite of the bald head?" Lynde asked.

"Because of it, dahlin'."

Lynde laughed his funny laugh backward through his nose.

"That laugh!" said Winnie. "When this man takes me to the movies in Jamestown, the audience stops laughin' at the movie and starts laughin' at him! And someone afterwards is bound to ask me 'who was that bald-headed man I saw you in the movies with?' an' I tell 'em, 'why that's my husband!'"

Lynde grinned at her delightedly. I could see they were crazy about each other.

Later in the meal, Lynde asked me about school. "Your Pa tells me you've been on the High Honors list all year," he said.

I nodded, embarrassed.

"Well, that's some different from your brother. When I went through high school my grades were so bad our mother had fits. I was the disappointment of her life. French was beyond me. I couldn't even pass English."

"But you got A's in math and history," Winnie chimed in.

"That's the only reason they let me out with a diploma," he said. "They weren't supposed to graduate anyone who couldn't pass English, but because of the math they let me squeak through."

"And as soon as you got into Northeastern through the back door, you went to the top of the Honor Roll and stayed there all the way through—and graduated with a Bachelors Degree in Science!" Winnie added.

"That's because you don't have to speak English to build bridges," he said, laughing.

I could hardly believe this. Were they joking? I knew Lynde's letters were misspelled and sometimes ungrammatical, but he didn't talk that way. I'd just thought he was being careless. It was years before I heard of the condition known as dyslexia. Even the medics didn't know about it in the 1940's.

Lynde brought the conversation back to my own schooling.

"Have you thought about going to college, Brenda?" he asked.

"No," I said.

"You should think about it. You've got a good mind."

"There isn't enough money to go to college."

"How do you know?"

"Mrs. Cony says there isn't enough. She told me to take the commercial course and learn to type so I can support myself."

Lynde turned to Winnie. "Our grandfather tied up his estate in such a rat's nest of legalese that no one can get through it. Since I've been over twenty-one I get a little interest from it, and all the heirs are supposed to get a lump sum settlement eventually, but all sorts of conditions have to be met first. Maybe our grandfather knew what he was doing, but I don't think anyone else does, including the lawyers."

Winnie laughed. "The lawyers will end up with the lump sums," she said.

Lynde turned back to me. "Don't give up on college," he said. "Think about what you want to do. Don't let Louise Cony discourage you. See what develops as you go along."

"I will," I said. But to myself I wondered if Lynde realized that I'd have Ma and Pa to support as soon as I graduated from high school and got a full-time job.

Next morning, Ma took Winnie over to her china cupboard to see her collection of pitchers. "I'd like you to have one of them," she said. "Look them over carefully and choose one to take home with you."

Winnie was delighted. She took each pitcher up in turn and examined it, finally choosing a small blue and white Wedgwood piece. Kind Ma, I thought. She's risen above her anger about Marge, and is ready to accept Winnie. I was filled with relief.

Lynde and Winnie left after the noon meal next day, off to Massachusetts to see the Bishops, the family Lynde had lived with after Mother died. They would also call on Aunt Rita and other friends before returning to Jamestown in time for Lynde to leave for Guam on June 15. Winnie would stay with her parents and take back her job at the post office till the war was over and Lynde returned.

Just before they drove away, Winnie said, "I want you to come visit me for a week this summer, Brenda. It'll keep me from bein' so lonely, and you can meet my parents and have some good times on the beach. We've got a marvellous beach. Lyin' on it is my favorite outdoor sport."

"I'd like that," I said.

"Good. I'll write you when I've got the dates sorted out."

78. Decisions

The days grew longer with the approach of summer, and the trees came out in their pale green dresses again. As the beauties of spring unfolded, I felt more and more uneasy about the prospect of not working at the Lees' for the summer. I didn't mind inside work in winter, but by May my whole body was longing for the outdoors. It wasn't only the joys of sun and air I craved, it was the companionship and good humor of the Lees and the hay crew.

As the spring days lengthened and McGraths' got busier, they asked me if I'd be willing to lengthen my three-hour days to eight hours from Friday through the weekend. If I started at three on those days and worked till closing time at eleven, I would have time to go home after school and collect my bike so I wouldn't have to walk home late in the dark. I could compensate somewhat for the increased hours by not coming at all on Mondays and Tuesdays, which the McGraths and Annette could easily handle.

I was pulled in several directions by the McGraths' request. Kay and I had fallen into the habit of doing something together at least one day of the weekend, and starting work at three o'clock on Saturday and Sunday would make doing anything at all very difficult. Monday and Tuesday off was hardly a holiday, either, with school from 8:00 to 1:30. Worse, with all those increased hours I'd have to give up bottle washing at the Lees' on Saturday and Sunday mornings.

On the other hand, after my first six days at McGraths', which included the first hellish weekend, they had upped my wages from thirty-three cents an hour to the going rate of forty cents. Their new proposal would increase my hours to thirty a week. This would mean $12 a week, which seemed a princely sum to me. With family finances what they were, how could I refuse such an offer?

Pa had no income except his Social Security pension, which was only about thirty dollars a month. Since Social Security wasn't introduced until 1935, he'd only been covered for a few years. Ma, after a long process with the authorities, aided by Judge Cony, was receiving $11 a month old age pension. Four weeks work at McGraths' would give me $48, more than both of them got together.

I didn't mention these calculations to Pa, simply told him about the McGraths' offer and said I thought I'd take it.

He and Ma weren't happy with the idea. "That's a thirty-hour week on top of your school work," he said. "It's too much. You won't have the time or energy to get the best out of school."

"Pa," I said, "I've had straight A's all year and I get my homework done at school in the study periods. I've got used to how to do things at McGraths' now, so I don't get as tired. I can do it easy."

And so my lengthened hours began. Though my bedtime had been between eight and nine ever since I could remember, I didn't seem to suffer from the late nights at all, and after the first couple of high-pressure weekends, I stopped dreaming all night about scooping ice cream. I was tired after an eight-hour shift, but by morning I was fully recovered and ready to go again.

As May progressed, I began wondering what Kay was planning to do in the summer.

"Kay, why don't you get a job at McGraths'?" I asked her. They're looking for smart part-timers for the summer. You could do it."

"Uh, uh," she said, shaking her head. "Daddy won't let me get a job till I've graduated from high school."

"Why not?"

"He says it's the last time in my life that I won't have to either work for a living or raise a family. He wants me to enjoy my youth while I can."

This resonated with something I'd heard before. Into my head flashed a vision of Mrs. Sandborg at our kitchen sink washing dishes. She had come in to help us briefly during one of Ma's illnesses, accompanied by two of her children who were too young to go to school. She had several others, was desperately poor, and had to go out to work. She also had a drunk for a husband. I offered to wipe the dishes for her, but she smiled sadly and shook her head. "No, my dear, you go and play while you can. A girl's playing doesn't last."

I couldn't help wondering about Annette, too, who thought she knew exactly what she wanted in life—a husband and children to stay home and take care of. She was already engaged to a boy she'd gone steady with since she was thirteen. She referred to Ed as her "To Be." They would marry as soon as she finished high school.

"Don't you ever want to do anything else?" I asked her one day when we weren't busy and she was chatting away about Ed, her one-and-only topic.

"No, never," she said with absolute assurance.

"Not even when your children are grown up?"

"Then I'll be a grandmother," she said. "If you have lots of kids and they have lots of kids, that's a busy job."

I couldn't understand. It seemed a fate even worse than teaching.

As the end of school drew near, I became more and more uneasy. I'd given up washing bottles at the Lees' when my hours at McGraths' increased, and I missed my daily contact there. And in a month haying would begin.

By the first week of June, with the summer vacation only a week away, I could stand it no longer. I went over on a Saturday morning after Dick had returned from the milk route, and found him mucking out the stable.

"Dick," I said, "Will you take me back on the hay crew this summer?"

He looked at me in astonishment. "I thought you were all set at McGraths'."

"I am, but I don't want to be."

"But why? You must be making decent money and getting all that good experience. And they like you there. McGrath said to me when I was in there the other day, 'I wish all my girls did as good a job as Peg. She's quick and smart and she's a very hard worker.'"

I could feel myself blush.

"Did you know McGrath came to see us before he asked your father about you working for him?"

"No, but I guessed he might have. He said something about my working with horses and I couldn't think where else he would have heard that. Pa said he didn't tell him."

"Why do you want to come back?"

"Because I can't stand being inside on a nice day."

Dick threw back his head and laughed. "That's why I never wanted to be anything but a farmer. How could anyone want an inside job? I'm even happy driving my logging team in the depths of winter. Sure you can come back if you want to. Someone's gotta drive the hayrick."

He paused for a moment. Then, "How much are you making at McGraths', Peggy?"

"Forty cents an hour."

He looked relieved. "Fine," he said. "That's what you'll be getting here. That's the new minimum wage that came in last fall."

So I wouldn't even take a cut in pay! My conscience was clear.

I approached the McGraths about this change of plans with great trepidation. They had been very kind to me, and they'd think I was letting them down. I waited for a slack period when they were both out back and Annette could cover the front.

Their faces went from cheerful to serious in seconds after I opened my mouth. I explained why I wanted to leave.

McGrath shook his head. "I'm sorry to hear that, Peg. You're a good worker and we hoped you'd be with us for a couple of years before you moved on. But you're a country girl, and I guess the farm's in your blood."

I nodded, not trusting myself to say anything.

"What about coming back in September after high school starts? asked Mrs. You could work till we close for the winter."

I shook my head. "Harvest and apple picking won't be finished till the end of October." Then a thought occurred to me. "But look, if you'd be willing to have me, I could come back when you open in April and work till high school is out in mid- June, as I'm doing this year."

"Of course you can, Peggy," said Mrs. "Anytime you want to work for us, you can."

McGrath nodded.

And so on the day that school recessed for the summer, I left the McGraths' employ until the following year.

79. The Showdown

Kay came out to the farm for the weekend to celebrate the end of school. This time she pedaled out on her bicycle rather than being delivered by her father in the car. For some time Kay had been allowed to bike around on the high-school side of the river where she lived, as the streets there were not busy. Now Arthur Moore said she could go out to the farm and back as long as she followed the route he designated.

Pa had also, finally, given me permission to bike on the main roads. How could he refuse? I'd already been biking to work at McGraths' and then back afterwards in the dark.

On Saturday we went out to Sandy Beach at Cobbosseecontee and spent the day swimming and sunning. In the evening we practiced dancing. Kay had brought with her a record of popular dance music. We put it on the graphohone, opened one of the sitting room windows so we could hear it on the veranda, and proceeded to dance out there. I was hopeless at dancing, but Kay was sure I could learn.

When Ma realized what was happening, she was scandalized.

"What are you girls doing?" she demanded, putting her head out the sitting room window.

"Dancing, Ma," I said, resigned to the inevitable lecture.

"But two girls shouldn't be dancing together!"

"How else are we going to learn, Ma? The only time they tried to teach us in the eighth grade most of the boys were too embarrassed to ask anyone to dance, so lots of girls were dancing together."

"That's beside the point. It's time you girls were in bed. It's eight-thirty."

"Ma, even if we stop dancing we are not going to bed at eight-thirty. We are not sleepy. And wouldn't you rather we learn to dance here where you can keep your eye on us than have us go out to Island Park and dance with the boys?"

Ma gave an angry snort and went back to the kitchen where Pa was reading in his rocker. I heard the mumble of voices, then Ma went upstairs, presumably to bed.

"Whew," I said. "Guess she's given up for the night."

"What is the matter with her, Peggy? Why is she like that?"

"I don't know, Kay, but she's getting worse. She objects to everything I do and everything I don't do. Come on, let's dance. I'll try not to step on your feet."

Sunday we tried to sleep late. Ma, of course, was incensed. Dancing the evening before, and now this! Honest hard-working people did not lie abed in the morning.

At eight she knocked on the door and said, "Eight o'clock, girls!" then went back downstairs, expecting immediate compliance. We ignored her. At nine she didn't knock. She came into the room and asked why we weren't up.

"I'm tired, Ma," I said. "I've been working hard all term, and Monday I'll have to get up early to wash bottles." Ma snorted in disgust and went out, slamming the door.

Kay giggled. "Good for you," she said. "I'm glad you stood up to her. Why shouldn't you be allowed to sleep late on a Sunday?" We went back to sleep.

By nine-thirty I heard Ma on the stairs again. By then I was too angry to sleep anyway. I met her at the door and snapped, "All right, we're coming!"

I got Kay and me a hearty breakfast of bacon and eggs, and we enjoyed it in spite of Ma moving around the kitchen with her lips set and a face that would shatter glass. As we got up from the table and started to wash the dishes, I caught Ma's glare. Encouraged by Kay's "Good for you" in the bedroom, I said, "Ma, didn't that God you believe in declare Sunday a day of rest?" Ma straightened as if she'd been shot, and left the kitchen through the dining room door, slamming it behind her.

Pa, of course, was nowhere to be seen. He'd no doubt had an earful from Ma both last night and after we'd failed to surface this morning. He'd taken off to avoid whatever trouble might arise.

I'd realized for some time that Ma was trying to drive Kay away, to stop our friendship by any means she could, and I'd feared she might succeed. Why should Kay want to keep coming out to the farm in the face of Ma's evident dislike? Plenty of girls in town would be glad to pal up with Kay. Why should she bother with me?

I hadn't dared to cross Ma before because her word was law. Pa never resisted her. What she said went. What chance did I have against her?

I'd never talked with Kay about this. I'd just tried to give her as good a time as I could when she came to the farm, and hoped she wouldn't notice that Ma couldn't stand her. Now I realized that shy, quiet Kay had a will of her own, knew what she wanted, and she wanted to keep my friendship. She was willing to persist, against all Ma's venom! I was delighted. It gave me the courage to oppose Ma.

We packed a lunch and spent the morning at a quarry that could be reached from a country road leading off the top of Pelton's Hill. We walked so Judy could come with us. The quarry was much larger than the one in Lees' woods. It had been long out of use, and the water was very deep and green. I was forbidden to go there in the winter, as the ice on a large quarry can be thin and treacherous. In summer, swimming in the stagnant water was neither allowed nor desirable, but the peace and beauty of the scene was worth the trip. We climbed around on the surrounding shelves of granite, ate our picnic lunch and relaxed in the sun. I'd left a note at home so we wouldn't be expected back at noon.

We didn't discuss what had happened with Ma at breakfast. We didn't need to. I knew now that Kay would remain my friend, and she knew that I knew it.

We quietly returned Judy about two o'clock and collected our bikes, without being observed, in time to get to the three o'clock showing of a movie starring Ingrid Bergman. Kay left for home from the theater afterwards.

I got home in time for supper. When I got there, both Ma and Pa were in the kitchen, she getting the meal, he in his chair with the cat sleeping on his shoulders. As soon as I appeared, Ma started in.

"Peggy, I will not allow that girl to come here again," she declared. "You have both been disrespectful to me, and I won't have it!"

This was it. I'd gone too far. What could I do against Ma's wrath?

Before she could go any further, Pa did the totally unexpected. He rose from his chair and did *not* head for the woodshed.

"Peggy," he said, "I want to talk with Ma. You go outside till I call you, please."

I went out and sat on the chopping block in the woodshed, straining my ears to try and hear what was going on. I could catch only a low mumble. Whatever they were saying, they never raised their voices.

I couldn't imagine what was going to happen. Pa had always avoided Ma's displeasure at all costs. Conversation always stopped when she got irritated. Never before had I been sent outside under such circumstances.

In less than ten minutes, Pa came out and found me in the woodshed.

"It's okay, Peggy. I've told Ma that I like Kay, she's a fine girl and your good friend and she can come here any time you want her to. Come on in. Supper's on the table."

Ma's face was white and set rigid. No word passed her lips during the meal. I told Pa about going to the quarry and about the Bergman movie we'd seen.

Ma never again said a word against Kay, but when Kay was present she ignored us.

This sequence of events was a revelation to me. I had stood up to Ma, and the world had not come to an end. Instead, Pa had backed me up. It didn't solve our increasing problems with Ma, but Pa's continued reinforcement, though often silent, helped make them bearable.

I'll never know for sure what passed between her and Pa, but I'd bet my life that Ma said to him, "If that girl comes here again, I shall leave," and that his reply was, "Mother, where will you go? Everyone who would have taken you in is dead."

80. Return to the Lees

Next morning I was back at the bottle-washing sink and rejoicing at my return to the Lee fold. After the bottles, Dick and I discussed the work that would need to be done in the interim before haying started in July, then I went home to get my dungarees on and begin.

I felt reprieved. I knew this might be my last summer working outdoors, and knowledge of the indoor work from which I had just escaped made me ready to savor every minute of it.

Nevertheless, I knew that the job at McGraths' had been an invaluable experience I'd been lucky to have. In fact, I felt that the whole of my first year at high school had changed me profoundly, and not just in matters academic. More important had been my friendship with Kay and working for the McGraths. Friendship and work had helped pry me away from what must have been near pathological shyness. Through them came knowledge of how other people dealt with life, and I stopped fearing the sound of my own voice. I was becoming aware of my increasing competence and ability to cope.

I hadn't stopped being shy, but I was learning to mask it and carry on in spite of it.

The summer's haying was bliss. This year it was Larry I drove on the hayrick. Mollie was now too old to pull a load, and was retired to pasture except for being regularly exercised. This I did when Dick was too busy.

I rejoiced in the sun and the heat, in the sweat trickling down my face on a hot day, in the cold well water and the lick of salt when we got to the barn. Even the tickle of hay chaff down my neck seemed blissful. McGrath was right, farming was in my blood.

Noah and Freddy were still on the hay crew, and a lad who had been too young the year before could be called on when needed, so if I wanted to go off for a day to do something with Kay, that could be arranged. I told the Lees about Winnie's invitation to visit her for a week sometime during the summer, and they said that was fine.

All that summer Pa was sober, or at least not enough under the influence for me to notice. It seemed an amazing piece of luck that with all the weekends she had spent at the farm, Kay hadn't realized Pa had an alcohol problem. His other apparent health problems masked the presence of inebriation, at least for the inexperienced.

Also that summer Pa struck it lucky. An acquaintance named McAusland brought his wife out to look at the lot Pa had on offer. They'd been coming to our farm for berries and jelly in the summer for years, and now that McAusland had retired, they were thinking of living in the country.

The lot Pa showed them lay in the west field, between the apple trees and the grove through which Maude's brook flowed. A stone wall separated it from the road. It hadn't been used for anything but grazing since I could remember. The McAuslands liked what they saw and said they'd think about it.

About a week later they came back with a set of plans and got their heads together with Pa. After several long discussions, to which I was too busy to pay much attention, the deal was closed and we were enough richer to meet a couple of years' mortgage payments and food bills.

81. The Letter

Dick told me that Ma lived in the canning house one winter.

He was talking about the insulation that his mother was thinking of putting in one of their cold upstairs bedrooms and saying what a difference it could make.

"Your canning house is so well insulated that someone could stay out there in the winter," he said.

"Who would want to?" I asked. "No one uses it in the winter."

"Your grandmother lived out there one winter before you were born."

I looked at him in astonishment. "Why, for heaven sakes?"

"Grace and Fred's bungalow was supposed to be finished before winter and she was going to live there with them. But they didn't get the house finished in time, so your Pa insulated the canning house and she stayed there."

I guess Dick didn't expect the intensity of my reaction, which my expression must have made obvious. His face took on a look that indicated he realized this was perhaps something he shouldn't have mentioned.

"But why?" I insisted.

"I don't know, Peggy. Honestly I don't. Nobody ever told me a reason, come to think of it. I guess I was just too young to question it."

What in the world would move Ma out of our farmhouse into the canning house in the depths of a Maine winter? It made no sense. Before I was born? When did Grace and Fred come to live on the farm? I tried to remember what I'd been told. Then I recalled that Pa had said they'd moved into the bungalow the spring after I was born.

So Ma had moved out when my mother was pregnant with me! What had happened between them? I sensed I was getting close to one of those important things I wasn't supposed to know.

It was no use asking Ma, or Pa either, so I approached Maisie Lee about it during our next bottle-washing session, careful not to implicate Dick in my finding out. I had to get this question off my tongue. It had been there too long already:

"Mrs. Lee, there was some trouble between my mother and my grandmother. Do you know anything about it? I know Ma moved out of the farmhouse into the canning house the winter before I was born, and she moved back in to take care of me after Mother died. I can't ask Pa. He'll just shake his head and say he doesn't know."

Maisie regarded me with a look I couldn't interpret—surprise and hesitation, certainly, but mixed with something else. When she spoke, she appeared to be measuring her words carefully.

"I know there was trouble between them, Peggy, but even though your family and ours have been good neighbors and friends for years we've never exchanged personal information of that sort. Farm people are very private people. Your grandmother and your father have had very hard lives, but they don't talk about them."

"I know," I said. "I never knew Ma wasn't my mother till you told me."

Maisie smiled. "Sorry I can't be of more help than that."

I thought that was the end of it. Just another blank wall. But later, when she saw me about to leave after the day's work in the fields, Maisie came out to the driveway with something in her hand.

"Peggy, I want you to have this. You can keep it. It's a letter your mother wrote to me before you were born. It won't answer all your questions, but I think you'd like to have it. Take it home and read it. I can't tell you any more than that."

I took the letter, then almost dropped it as I realized that this was something my mother had held in her hands. That the "Mrs. Merrill Lee" inscribed on the envelope had been written by my mother! The shock went from my hand to my toes and off into the ground, as though I was a channel for lightning.

I was too stunned to do anything but mumble thanks and leave. I crossed the road, entered our farmhouse through the front door so Ma wouldn't see me, and went straight up the front stairs. In my room I took the letter from its envelope and read it:

Dear Mrs. Lee,

I cannot bear to have you and Mr. Lee think that Shirley turned his mother out into a lonely canning house. I have never seen such unfailing kindness and devotion from a son toward a mother—In spite of the fact that I have never seen or heard Mrs. Shaw by word, look or deed, show him the slightest appreciation. He has ever been as generous and dear to her as can be.

I did tell Mrs. Shaw—firmly but courteously day before yesterday—that after Grace came a re-arrangement would have to be made. Her spectacular move over into the canning house was my only reply.

I do not expect any answer to this. Mrs. Shaw is your old neighbor, and I know she has been kind to you in your need. But I cannot bear to have Shirley misjudged, either as a cruel man or a weakling. Every day I think over and over that he is the most wonderful man in the world.

Very cordially yours,

Bess Shaw

P.S. This is my one lone defense, to my nearest neighbor!

What had Ma done to make my mother ask her to leave? The letter gave me a critical bit of the story, a dramatic happening on which to hang things, but still the reason for it all was missing.

82. Rita, 1943

Winnie's letter arrived in mid-July, telling us of Lynde's departure from Norfolk on a Navy aircraft headed for Guam. He had arrived safely and was finding the work on the drydock interesting and challenging, though the heat was fierce. She ended the letter with "I haven't forgotten my invitation, Brenda. How about coming August first?"

I was, of course, now old enough to go by train alone, but Pa, ever fearful, arranged for Rita to meet my train in Boston on July 31. I would stay overnight with her. Next day she would accompany me on the short train trip to Kingston where Winnie would meet us and drive us over the "Bridge Lynde Built" to Jamestown. Rita would stay the day and go back to Boston on the train.

This suited me perfectly. I'd had no contact with Rita since she'd given me Mother's picture the summer before. I was eager for a chance to talk with her alone. Questions I never had time or opportunity to ask her in her brief visits to the farm had been piling up in my mind, and now I also had the mysterious letter Mrs. Lee had given me. I tucked the letter carefully into my handbag before I departed.

Rita met me at North Station and we transferred to the local train for the twelve-mile trip to Melrose. When we reached her home, we lunched on soup and sandwiches, which she had already prepared except for heating the soup.

As I was helping Rita clear up afterwards, she brought up the matter of Mother's picture:

"Brenda, when I visited you last summer I told your father that I'd brought your mother's picture with me to give you, but I didn't mention it to your grandmother. Did either of them talk with you about it afterwards?"

I shook my head, then told her what Ma's reaction had been when she first saw the picture.

Rita nodded. "That's to be expected. But I'd hoped it would spur your father into talking with you about your mother. Didn't he say anything?"

"Not a word. I never saw him even glance at it, but he must have seen it! He must have looked at it when I wasn't there."

Rita sighed, and her forehead twitched. She began piling the dirty dishes in the pan and pouring on soap powder and hot water. I picked up a dish towel, ready to dry as she washed. I decided this would be a good time to start asking some of the questions I'd been saving up.

"Aunt Rita, why won't Ma and Pa ever talk about my mother? I know you said that my mother and grandmother didn't get along, but why not? Something dreadful must have happened to make them never speak of her. Did my mother do something terrible that they couldn't forgive her for?"

Rita swirled the dishwater with her hand to make sure the soap powder dissolved, then began washing the water glasses.

"It was just a clash of wills between two very strong women, Brenda. Your mother tried her best to avoid it, but she couldn't."

I needed more than that, but it obviously wasn't going to be easy. Rita rinsed the water glasses under the faucet, handed them to me to dry, and changed the subject to her rose garden, which lay just outside the kitchen window.

When we'd finished the dishes, we returned to the living room. I picked up my handbag and withdrew Mother's letter from it. I handed it to Rita.

"I heard that Ma spent a winter in our canning house before I was born. I asked Mrs. Lee about it, and she gave me this—but she didn't know why it happened."

Without comment, Rita seated herself on the couch and motioned me to sit beside her. Then she took the letter from its envelope and read it. She sighed and looked over at me. "If you've heard this much, you should hear the rest, Brenda. I haven't wanted to go into detail before, because I hoped your father would talk with you about your mother. It wouldn't have been fair to him, or to your grandmother, for me to interfere before he had the opportunity to do that. But if he can't bear to talk about her I think I understand why. He loved your mother very much. Speaking of her to anyone, even thinking about her, must be very painful for him—he's an extremely shy man and doesn't know how to talk about emotional things like that. Oh, Brenda, your mother was kind and beautiful and very intelligent. If only she'd lived, how different your life would have been!"

Different? Rita had said that to me before, but what did that mean? It might be different, but I wasn't sure it would be better. In my experience, Mothers—Ma and other peoples' except for Mrs. Lee—were oppressive, told you what you couldn't do, and said anything that was any fun was a sin. Would my mother have been any better than Ma?

Rita looked away for a moment, as if collecting her thoughts. "It's hard to know where to start," she said. "Your father's family had been through a terrible two years just before he met your mother. Has anyone told you anything about Florence?"

"Yes. They talk a lot about Florence. She was my father's wife who died of kidney disease."

"Well, they're not totally incapable of speech, then," said Rita. "Florence had a long, wrenching illness for which there was no cure and no relief. Your father and grandmother watched her die by inches, in agony. They loved her dearly, and it was a shattering experience for both of them. Did you know that Florence had been your grandmother's apprentice seamstress before she married your father?"

"Yes, I know," I said. "Ma told me."

"Your grandmother thought the world of her. To her, the marriage of Florence and Shirley was made in heaven. The three of them were a very close, loving unit. Mrs. Shaw and Florence never exchanged a cross word. Very shortly after her death your father had his accident, and about a month after that he met your mother when he went to Melrose to recuperate."

"How long before he married my mother?" I asked, remembering Rita's hesitation when I had asked her that question on my last visit. I sensed there was more to this story than I had been told.

"Bess and Shirley both seemed to know almost as soon as they met that they wanted to marry. But there was a problem. Your father couldn't bring himself to tell Mrs. Shaw—your Grandmother Shaw—that he wanted to re-marry so soon after Florence's death. He knew it would upset her profoundly."

"What did they do?"

"They decided to be married quietly by a justice of the peace with myself as witness. Mrs. Shaw was to know nothing about it until later.

"After the wedding ceremony, I had a small dinner party at my home to introduce your father to friends and relatives he had not met. The poor man, that proved to be very difficult for him. I hadn't realized just how shy he was until then, Brenda. He was terribly uncomfortable. Seated at a long table laid with a damask cloth and the family silver—two knives, two forks and two spoons at each place setting—and he feeling very much under inspection. He didn't know what to do or say."

I could sense how Pa must have felt. It caught me in the stomach. "I wouldn't have known either," I said.

306

"It's hard to come from a quiet, rural background and be suddenly thrust into a world you've never known, with people you've never met before," said Rita. "He was so flustered at one point that when someone passed him the cream for his coffee he poured it into his glass of water. When he realized what he'd done, he drank the water down in one gulp, hoping no one had noticed."

Exactly something I could have done myself, I thought, feeling sick with sympathy for Pa.

"Did everyone laugh?"

"No. Fortunately several people at one end of the table were engaged in conversation and didn't even notice. The few who did showed no sign they'd seen what happened. It's the best way to handle something like that."

"But what did they say about him after he'd gone?"

"Most were sympathetic. There was some curiosity about how the mutual attraction between your mother and father had arisen, and why they had married within two months of their meeting. But except for your mother's sister Alta, who sees little good in anyone, no one held his shyness against him."

Others might have been mystified about the attraction, but I wasn't. I knew what Mother had seen in Pa. He was kind. He was gentle. He was tolerant and meant harm to no one. He loved people deeply. He loved Ma. He'd loved Grace and Barton, and he'd loved both his wives. He had no words, but he knew how to show love without them. He'd shown it to me.

"Where did they go after the dinner party? Did they go back to Augusta to tell Ma?"

"No. They went for a brief honeymoon to our cottage on Megunticook Lake in Camden. Then your mother returned to Melrose where Lynde was in school, and your father went back home to choose the proper time to break the news to your grandmother. But when he got there, he didn't have the nerve to do it."

I could believe that. Pa would never intentionally hurt Ma, or anyone else.

"He went back and forth to Melrose several times to see your mother, telling your grandmother that he was visiting Grace and Fred. This went on all winter. Finally, in June when Lynde's school let out for the summer, your mother gave Shirley an ultimatum: 'Either you tell your mother we are married, and that Lynde and I are coming to live with you, or I'll divorce you.' Your father was caught between the two of them, both of whom he loved. It must have been very difficult for him."

I nodded. "What did they do?"

Rita studied her fingernails carefully, then folded her hands in her lap.

"They worked out a compromise. Shirley would tell his mother that he had met a woman he wanted to marry. He would bring Bess to Augusta for a visit to meet her and get her used to the idea. Then they would have a second wedding ceremony there which your grandmother could attend. No need for his mother to know about the first wedding."

Bizarre as this story was, it rang true. I had never known Pa to go against Ma in any way, except for his unexpected support of my friendship with Kay. I was beginning to understand: It was anger and jealousy and shock at what Ma saw as Pa's betrayal of Florence that had poisoned everything.

"What happened when he told Ma?" I asked.

"The expected reaction. Your grandmother went into hysterics. However, your father stood firm, and said that your mother was arriving to meet her the following week. Luckily, your mother was a brave and determined woman and very much in love with your father. If the bond between them had not been a strong one, it would not have survived."

"So that's why Ma hated my mother and won't tell me anything! She was jealous of her," I said. "How stupid and petty!"

"Try to understand, Brenda. Mrs. Shaw has had an extremely hard life. She was deserted by a drunken husband, who ran off with a hired girl. Your grandmother had to go back to tailoring to support her children while trying to deal with Barton's problems which, I understand, surfaced early, when he was still a child—though I don't know the details. Medical men now suspect that if a child is conceived when the husband is drunk, it can affect the baby's brain—but that's still guesswork. Anyway, your grandmother is a woman of strong loyalties, and the family has been her life. In Florence she had a daughter-in-law who adored her and who gave her a great deal of love and help in a totally selfless manner. She never came to terms with your father's wish to marry someone he had met so soon after Florence's death."

Rita's words gave me not only what I had asked for, but also a completely new and different set of facts, this time about Pa's side of the family. Pa had told me his father had deserted them, but he'd given me no further details.

"So my grandfather was a drunkard," I said.

"Yes, and unfortunately that tendency was passed along to Barton, whom you may or may not know died of acute alcoholism."

I didn't know until then. So that explained the vile temper, the puffy face, and the episode just before he died when he fell off the back steps and then staggered home.

I told Aunt Rita about that incident, then asked, puzzled, "How did you know about Barton?"

"Brenda, your uncle was a drunkard from his thirties on, and though he wasn't living on the farm when your father and mother married, your mother met him several times and knew his background from your father. Since Bess and I had always been the closest of friends, she told me about it."

Again, all these interconnections between people that I had never even guessed! Rita could not only tell me about Mother, but could also fill in things about the Shaws.

So Bart had inherited the tendency toward alcoholism from my grandfather. And Pa must have done the same. I decided not to tell Aunt Rita about Pa's drinking. I just couldn't. It would be a betrayal.

"What happened when Ma and Mother finally met?" I asked.

"The atmosphere was frigid, but a very simple wedding ceremony was arranged at which your grandmother was present. Lynde was not there, he remained in Melrose with his grandparents. Fred stood up with your father as best man. Then your father and mother went to our Camden cottage for a few days, after which she returned once more to Melrose to settle Lynde's affairs there and bring him back with her.

"Ma hadn't met Lynde till then?"

"No, and I'll say this for her, she didn't let her feelings against your mother influence her manner toward Lynde. Bess told me, and Lynde said the same later, that she was always kind to him."

I could understand Ma's kindness. All the time I had known her, she had treated people kindly, fairly and with tolerance. Hadn't she told me for years to always put myself into the shoes of others, to try and understand what each person felt?

During my own lifetime the only exceptions to Ma's tolerant attitude that I'd been aware of were her reactions to Fred's affair with the Widow Beale and, more recently, to my friendship with Kay. I couldn't understand Ma's motives in either of these cases. And now Rita had told me about Ma's reaction to Mother before my birth. This seemed even stranger. Where had Ma's much-valued tolerance gone? That's what I couldn't understand—how she could be such a hypocrite! Why had she acted that way? How could she be so petty, after all the moral talks she'd had with me?

I didn't say any of this to Rita. I was too confused to express it clearly, so I just asked another question:

"So Mother and Lynde moved in?"

"Yes. And for about a year things went on with an icy quietness on your grandmother's part. She said nothing against your mother, but it was clear there could never be any rapport between them. She made Bess feel like an invader. Then something happened which your grandmother took as a slight. Your mother was never quite sure what particular thing she had done to upset her.

"Mrs. Shaw went to Shirley and told him that she could not live any longer under these circumstances and would move all her things upstairs. Her own bedroom, the guest room and what is now your room would serve as her quarters. Lynde could continue to use the other bedroom up there, as before. She would take her meals upstairs from now on."

"And Mother never knew what she'd done to cause this?"

"No. It wouldn't have needed much, Brenda. The situation simply couldn't go on, and they both knew it. I believe they all thought that the new arrangement was for the better. It did keep the two women apart and avoid the worst of the friction. Bess cooked food enough for everyone, and either your father or Lynde would take your grandmother's share up to her. When she came and went from the house, she would do it through the front entrance so she wouldn't have to pass through the rest of the house and encounter your mother."

"But if Ma got the arrangement she wanted, why did she move to the canning house?"

"That final blow-up happened at Thanksgiving, two months before you were born. Because it was a special occasion, Shirley and Bess asked your grandmother if she wouldn't come down and join them for dinner, and she agreed. Your mother was seven months pregnant with you at the time, and not feeling very well. It was quite a load on her to be preparing a turkey dinner without assistance, but she wanted desperately to keep the peace and perhaps improve the atmosphere.

"When everything was ready, your father went up and escorted your grandmother down to the kitchen. They all chatted for a minute or two, then went into the dining room. Bess, Shirley and Lynde had become used to eating by themselves, and no one had remembered to put an extra chair at the table for your grandmother, who noticed at once and was visibly upset. Your father rushed to get another chair from the kitchen, and Bess tried to assure her this was just an oversight, never in the world would she have intended such a thing to happen. But the damage was done. Your grandmother cried out, 'You want to exclude me—you don't want me here at the table at all,' and went storming off back upstairs."

"What did everyone do?"

"Well you can imagine such a scene spoiled their dinner. Your father carved the turkey and served it, then took your grandmother's up to her. No one knows what passed between them when he did.

"A couple of days later, your grandmother came downstairs to get something from the kitchen and found your mother on her hands and knees cleaning up something she'd spilled on the floor. Bess got to her feet, looked directly at her, and said, calmly and politely, 'Mrs. Shaw, after Grace and Fred move into their bungalow in the spring, a different arrangement will have to be made. We cannot go on like this.'

"Your grandmother said nothing and left the kitchen. That evening she got her things together, and next day began moving them over into Grace's vacant and unfinished bungalow. Your father tried to reason with her, to no avail. He did point out to her, however, that it would be very dangerous for her to try and stay in the bungalow—no electricity, no heat, half-done work that could cause her to fall or have an accident. The canning house had a stove and electricity and could be quickly insulated so she could survive the winter there if she insisted on doing that. So that's what was done."

"Wow!" I said.

"Your grandmother never spoke another word to your mother. This did not affect her relationship with Lynde, however. He went over to the canning house every day to make sure she was all right, run errands for her and bring her things. Lynde and your father were always on good terms."

All this was almost too much for me to take in. I must have looked stunned, for Rita got up and said, "I think we both need a cup of tea," and went to the kitchen.

While she was gone, I tried to collect my thoughts. Everything had come at me too fast, and again my world had changed. For one thing, it was becoming clear that there were two Ma's. One was the tolerant Christian who did as she would be done by: the loving mother, good friend and kind neighbor who helped others in time of need. The other Ma acted directly opposite to everything the first Ma claimed to believe in: the denouncer of Fred and my mother, neither of whom had intentionally hurt her; the enemy of Kay, whose only transgression was being my friend. And that second Ma was also the prison guard who wanted to keep me in the strait-jacket of her will and deny me any life she couldn't control.

I was outraged. There was more than one Ma maybe, but there was also more than one me. In fact, there seemed to be several, and all of us wanted out. But angry as I was, I was acutely aware that there was more I must find out from Rita. This might be the last chance I had to get answers to my questions. What if I was never able to visit Rita again? We never had enough time alone to talk when she came to the farm. By the time Rita returned with tea and home-made molasses cookies, I'd formulated what I wanted to ask.

Rita poured me a steaming cupful from the silver teapot and passed the plate of cookies. Then she looked at me quizzically as though to fathom my reaction to what she had told me.

"Please, Aunt Rita, can you tell me about Lynde's father?" I began. "When did he die? What did he die of?"

Rita put down her cup and thought for a minute. "Brenda, we'd better go back even before Lynde's father. Your mother had a very upsetting life. She seemed to attract tragedy.

"In her late teens she became engaged to a very nice Camden boy she knew from the several summers she and Alta spent at our cottage there. His name was Orren Andrews. They planned to marry as soon as they graduated from high school. Your mother herself never finished high school, as she had to drop out in her senior year to care for her mother—your grandmother Sarah Lynde—who was seriously ill, but her relationship with Orren Andrews continued. They would have married in a few months, but in May, just before he would have graduated, Orren died in a drowning accident. He'd gone out alone in a boat, which was later found drifting empty. Then they found his body."

"Couldn't he swim?"

"Yes, but I'm not sure how well. If he'd stood up, overbalanced and fallen in and then tried to swim for shore he might have got a cramp. We just don't know."

"What did Mother do?"

"She was terribly, terribly upset, of course. Everyone was. Her older sister Alta, who was already married by then, was also a good friend of Orren Andrews. When she had her first child some months later, she named the baby Orren."

"How long after that did Mother meet Lynde's father?"

"After Orren's death, your mother went to normal school in Fitchburg to become a teacher. Despite the fact she hadn't graduated from high school, her grades had been so high they accepted her anyway. She graduated from Fitchburg and was teaching in Melrose when she met Lester Russell, who became Lynde's father. He was going to Boston University Law School. They met through friends and fell in love. When he graduated, they married and he took a partnership with a law firm in Derry, New Hampshire. Lester and Bess bought a duplex house there. They lived in one half of it, and Robert Frost and his family rented other half."

"Robert Frost the poet?" I asked incredulously.

"Yes, Robert Frost the poet. A very fine man. I met him several times. Bess and Lester became good friends of his, and after Lester's death the Frosts were very kind and helpful to Bess."

All I knew about Robert Frost were the poems we had read in English class—"Mending Wall," "The Hired Man," "Birches." I liked them all—and my mother had known him!

"Aunt Rita, why did Lynde's father die? That young man?"

"He was a man very unwise about money, Brenda. He invested funds put in his trust by a client in a scheme he thought would bring in a handsome return, but instead the company went bankrupt. In order to cover up the loss of his client's money, Lester embezzled funds from his law firm. He was caught and couldn't face the disgrace. Rather than stand trial, be convicted and jailed, he killed himself."

"My God," I said. "How old was Lynde then?"

"Lynde wasn't even born at the time. Your mother was five months pregnant, and had everything to face on her own—her grief, the disgrace, the birth of her first child. With the Frosts' help she got things settled in Derry and moved back to your grandfather's farm in Melrose. Lynde was born in the Melrose Hospital the following October."

"So Lynde never knew his father."

"No. Your grandfather, Henry Lynde, was the only father he ever knew, and Henry was very fond of Lynde. Bess had always been Henry's favorite, and he did the best he could to soften her trouble and to help her raise her son.

'If only Lester had come to me for money, this would never have happened,' he said over and over.

"Bess's moving back home with Lynde caused considerable strain between your mother and her sister. Alta had always been jealous of her father's love for Bess. Alta and her husband and the child she had named for Orren Andrews were having a struggle financially. She felt that in giving Bess and her child a home and an education Henry was doing much more for Bess than he was for her.

"But your mother was no free-loader, Brenda. She didn't want to remain dependent on your grandfather for support. She wanted to do something to bring in money. She had liked teaching school, but didn't want to spend her life at it. She'd taken piano lessons at the New England Conservatory of Music in her teens. She was very talented, could have made a career in music had she wanted to. . ."

"I didn't know she played the piano!" I interrupted. "Why didn't anyone tell me? Mrs. Cony got me a second-hand piano the year after I began school, and I love playing it. Nobody else in the family has an ear for music. Why didn't they tell me about mother being so good at it?"

"Of course your grandmother would never tell you," said Rita, "and I suspect that your father didn't for fear you'd mention it to your grandmother and cause a scene. I'd have told you before, but it's hard to be sure what you know and what's been kept from you."

"Why didn't mother decide to have a career in music, Aunt Rita?"

"The usual reason. Falling in love and deciding to marry rather than have a career. There aren't many well-known women musicians, Brenda. Most talented women pianists, if they don't stop playing when they marry, become accompanists for men musicians, or teach. It's not easy for a woman to make a living with music, and by the time Lynde's father died, it was too late for Bess to go into it seriously. She went and talked with her former teachers at the Conservatory and they were quite frank with her about that. But your mother was very much interested in social issues, and decided to become a hospital social worker and work with the poor in the Boston slums. Your Grandfather Lynde offered to pay for her training.

"Simmons College had an excellent two-year social work program, but entrance to it required a high school diploma. Bess didn't have one but applied anyway. They were so impressed by her high school and normal school grades, by her teaching references, and by Bess herself at her interview that they told her she could enroll and take the course and the exams. Without a high school diploma, however, they would not be able to award her a degree."

"That's so unfair!" I said. "Couldn't they just give her an examination and use that instead of a high school diploma if she got a high mark?"

"They might do that today, but that sort of examination didn't exist in her time. Very few women went to college at all, and then usually against opposition. But Bess did so well in her courses at Simmons, coming top of her class both years, that when she finished they broke their own rules and allowed her to graduate with a degree in social science."

So Mother had beat the system, against all odds! She had intelligence, spirit and guts.

"Did she get a job in Boston?" I asked.

"Yes. She was hired by the Social Services Department at Boston City Hospital and worked there for a number of years. Then an opening came up for the position of Chief of Services in the Social Work Department at Michael Reese Hospital in Chicago. She applied for it and got it. She and Lynde went out there to live, and she was highly thought of there.

"In the course of her duties she met a Catholic priest with whom she worked closely in the Chicago slums. They fell in love, and he was thinking of renouncing the priesthood so they could marry. His bishop got wind of their relationship, however, and had the priest posted to China. They work very fast when they get wind of something like that. He was out of the country before anyone knew what was happening.

"After he got there he wrote Bess a letter telling her of an opening for a social worker in the town where he'd been sent. He asked her to apply for it and try to join him there."

"Did she go?" I gasped, delighted at the idea.

"She applied and was accepted, but by then she'd had time to reconsider. Lynde, then thirteen and soon to enter high school, was having learning difficulties, and she decided that taking him off to China after all the upheavals he'd been through, would not be in his best interests. She cancelled her acceptance, and Pearl Buck went to China instead."

Robert Frost and now Pearl Buck? Could Rita be making this up?

"Pearl Buck, Aunt Rita? The one who wrote *Dragon Seed*?"

"Yes, the very same."

I'd gone with Kay to see the movie *Dragon Seed*, starring Katharine Hepburn. We were so impressed we'd got the book from the library and read it.

Obviously my mother was a lively personality. I couldn't suppress a smile. "My mother and a priest," I said. "How amazing—how funny!"

"Your mother was a free thinker. She always acted honestly and tried to work for the good of others and never hurt anyone. But she considered that ridiculous rules were things to be gotten around."

"Did she believe in God?," I asked.

Rita hesitated—like Pa, probably wondering whether she should be honest about it. She came down on the side of honesty. "No, I'm afraid she was a non-believer. I tried many times to show her the error of that kind of thinking, but to no avail."

"I'm a non-believer too," I said. "So is Pa."

Rita looked at me in astonishment. "Does your father discuss religion with you, for heaven's sakes, if he won't talk with you about Bess?"

"I never believed in God, Aunt Rita. When I asked Pa if he did, he thought for a minute and then said, 'No, I guess I don't.' I just said 'Good.' That's all. We didn't discuss it."

Rita sighed deeply, and her forehead twitched. I thought she was angry. Instead, she shook her head and smiled.

"You're just like your mother," she said. "I could never win an argument with her, and I don't expect I'll ever win one with you either."

This insight startled and pleased me. So even though I had never known her, Mother and I thought alike! Heredity could account for the way we thought as well as for the color of our eyes and the way we smiled. The question I had asked myself earlier was now answered. Yes, I would have liked Mother better than Ma. Mother was rational and not a hypocrite. She was enthusiastic, free-thinking, adventurous, kind, intelligent, lively, and had a mind of her own. She was just the kind of person I wanted to be.

"Aunt Rita, you told me once that Mother got pneumonia in Chicago. When did that happen?"

"Not long after she decided not to go to China. I think she was exhausted by the combination of the demands of her job and the upset over giving up the priest. She very nearly died. The doctors told her she could never work again, so she had to relinquish her job and return to Melrose with Lynde. At that time her mother, Sarah Lynde, was going through one of her many illnesses, so Bess knew she could at least fill a useful niche helping there while she recuperated."

Now most of the missing pieces had fallen into place. "So that gets us up to the point where my mother and father met," I said.

"That's right," said Rita.

"What an amazing story. Poor Mother, what an upsetting life she had—from one crisis to another."

"And it was in the midst of a crisis that she died," said Rita.

I nodded. Then remembered: "Aunt Rita, is my Aunt Alta still alive?"

"Oh yes, she's very much alive and living in Melrose."

"And her son Orren—he'd be my first cousin, wouldn't he?"

"Yes, and he's very much still alive—and living with his mother."

"Aunt Rita, could I meet them? I never realized I had an aunt and a cousin till you mentioned them."

Rita's face clouded. "I would not recommend that you meet her, or Orren—or that you ever try to."

"But why?"

"Possibly your mother phrased it best, Brenda. She once said to me, 'The kindest thing I can say about my sister Alta is that she is mentally deranged.'"

"Is she crazy?"

"I think she is crazy, though as far as I know she has never been hospitalized for it. She had a 'nervous illness' which caused her to drop out of Wellesley College after eight months. Neither Bess nor I knew exactly what it was, but it wasn't serious enough to prevent her marrying John Walsh a few months later. No, I wouldn't say she is insane, but she meant your mother no good, nor would she mean you and Lynde any good. She is a poison pen letter writer and inflicts her considerable talent in that line onto those she dislikes. I've received a few of her letters, believe me!"

Was anyone on either side of my family normal? I wondered. I surely wasn't. How could I expect anyone else to be?

"You know what we shall do, Brenda?   We've got just enough time before we need to think about supper."

"What?"

"I shall drive you by your Aunt Alta's house. It's something you should see. It's one of the oldest houses in Melrose, and it's on the Historic Register. Then after that, I shall take you to Wyoming Cemetery and show you your mother's grave. Come on, let's go."

Rita drove to within a block of Alta's house and parked the car. "You get out and walk past it, up around the corner to see the side and back, and then come back here. I'll wait in the car. She won't know who you are even if she happens to be looking out the window. It wouldn't do for her to catch sight of me. She'd think I was plotting all sorts of dire things. It's the white house right on the corner."

I got out and did as she told me, walking slowly and with a relaxed, rather vacant air. It was a large white clapboarded "salt box" with the roof sloping down nearly to the ground in the rear. A small rectangular sign mounted next to the front door proclaimed, "Joseph Lynde House, 1702." There was no sign of life behind the windows.

I returned to Rita's car. "It's a beautiful house," I said. "And so old! 1702! I'd love to see inside it."

"It's a historic specimen, if you like historic specimens," said Rita. "I think it's ugly myself—I wouldn't want to live in it. Now I'll take you up to the cemetery. It's just up the road from here."

I didn't want to see her grave. I wouldn't be seeing her. A cold stone with her name on it and buried beneath it a skeleton and what was left of skin. And I'd be expected to say something to show how I felt, or cry like I'd been expected to when we visited Grace's grave after she died. The dead were dead and couldn't be brought back, no matter how we cried or what we did or said.

I didn't want to look at a grave. I'd rather look at her picture, with her smile and warm eyes and her hair falling curly onto her shoulders.

I didn't tell Aunt Rita this, of course. I sat docile beside her as she drove the paths of Wyoming Cemetery looking for the right place. When she found it among the other rows and rows of graves, I stood respectfully as she pointed out the inscription:

Bess Lynde Shaw
1884-1928

It didn't impress me then that it was a tall stone with four polished sides, each inscribed with several names, nor was I aware that around this stone were others with the names of Lyndes engraved on them. Rita didn't call my attention to them. She didn't mention, either (perhaps she didn't know), that there was also another, older cemetery where even earlier Lyndes had come to rest. Even if she had told me, it wouldn't have meant anything to me then. I was simply anxious to fulfill Rita's wish that I see Mother's last resting place, and then get away as soon as possible.

But I knew one thing before I left Melrose. Some day, somehow, I would find my way into that beautiful old house and meet my mysterious Aunt Alta and her son Orren. I would see for myself.

83. Jamestown

Next day Winnie met Rita and me at Kingston station, at the foot of "Lynde's Bridge." I'd never seen a bridge like it. It rose up before the car in a steep hill to a peak high above Naragansett Bay, with a massive structure above it to hold it up, and then we went down the other side of the hill-that-was-a-bridge and we were in Jamestown. That bridge must have been a good two miles long. Rita, too, was impressed. She hadn't seen it before either. Winnie laughed at our exclamations of surprise. "He didn't build it all himself, you know," she said.

Jamestown was a tiny island, and Winnie's parents, the Clarkes, lived on a quiet tree-lined street in a rambling old white house with lots of rooms and a big back yard with a doghouse in it. An elderly shaggy dog called Nero, who was not allowed to enter the family home, occupied the doghouse.

Winnie's mother, Mrs. Clarke, was a large, pale woman in a loose, soft dress of fine dark printed muslin. Her plump face, framed loosely with white hair, was round and serene, her movements slow and languid. She'd birthed and raised six children, and now, said Winnie, she'd done her bit and could relax. Her face gave off a calm that soothed whoever was near her. She never raised her voice. She greeted me kindly.

I didn't see much of Mr. Clarke while I was there except at mealtimes. That dark and sinewy old man was retired and kept largely to his desk indoors or his gardening shed in the back yard. On fine afternoons he was off fishing with his retired cronies.

Winnie's two sisters, both in their early thirties, were living at home. Penny, plump and dark like her father, tense and smoking one cigarette after another, was single. Ida, slender, light-haired and blue-eyed, had recently married. She and her husband Jack were looking for a house in Jamestown to buy.

Russ, the youngest son, a couple of years older than I, also lived at home but was only around that day long enough to say hello and leave.

I noted with interest that none of the Clarkes drawled like Winnie when they talked.

A massive lunch had been prepared by the two sisters while Winnie was fetching us: roast beef, baked potatoes and carrots, and a salad of lettuce, cucumber, onion and other raw vegetables.

I'd never had a salad of raw vegetables before, though I liked to munch on them straight from the garden when I was weeding. What Ma called salad was cold cooked vegetables with home-made salad dressing on them—an unpleasant, sour stuff made of vinegar and eggs that I detested. I never ate it if I could avoid it.

This salad Ida had made looked tempting and fresh, but I noticed it had on it what I assumed to be salad dressing, although it was a pale ivory instead of the vile yellow stuff Ma made. Not wanting to be impolite, I took a very small amount onto my plate when the salad was passed to me. After getting up my courage while I munched several delicious bits of roast beef, I tasted the salad gingerly. What delight! The ivory dressing was nothing like Ma's. It was creamy and smooth, tangy but not vinegary, and it did wonderful things to the raw vegetables. "This salad dressing is good," I exclaimed.

"That's mayonnaise, Brenda," said Ida. "Haven't you ever had it before?" I shook my head. Ida rose from the table, went to the refrigerator and brought back a glass bottle half full of the ivory colored substance. She put it down in front of me so I could read the label, "So you'll know what to look for in the shops." I vowed I'd get some as soon as I got home.

After we'd eaten our fill, Ida and Penny, assisted by Jack, did the washing up while Winnie took Aunt Rita and me for a drive around Jamestown. The small island was directly across from Newport, and was served by an hourly ferry to that town. A long strip of sandy beach stretched between a concrete jetty, from the far end of which people were diving, to a pier which extended out about the same distance and contained shops: groceries, drug stores, and candy shops.

"We'll come down here tomorrow and soak up some sun, Brenda," Winnie said.

When we'd done a circuit of the island, it was time to drive Rita to her train, and she went off, back to Melrose.

318

Sunday was relaxed and sun-filled. Winnie, Penny, Ida and Jack took me to the beach. They spent most of their time sunning and chatting, but lots of young people my own age were in the water, and they were friendly.

After hearing me speak, one girl said to me "You sound like a Mainiac." Another girl, seeing my startled expression, explained. "A 'Mainiac' is what we call someone from Maine. Are you from Maine?"

"Yes," I said, "but how did you know?"

Everyone laughed. "We just listened to you talk," one said. It was the first time I realized that I must sound just as peculiar to strangers as they did to me.

The three sisters and Jack all worked, so next day and for the rest of the week I didn't have their company till after five. They had planned things well, however. They produced Alvin, a young lad a couple of years younger and half a head shorter than I, who was visiting relatives in Jamestown and was at loose ends and bored.

Since there was no hint of physical attraction between us, we relaxed and hit it off at once. We swam, hiked about the island, dug clams, went to the movies, ate ice cream, and compared our totally different lives—the Maine farm girl and the city boy from New York.

In the evenings the sisters taught me bridge and canasta, and gossiped about their friends and local scandals.

Ida was good with hair, and showed me how to put my shoulder-length tresses up in pincurls and then brush it under into a page-boy. "You look absolutely glamorous, Sugarpuss," she declared, and everyone agreed.

Friday night Winnie arranged for her brother Russ to take me to a movie. I'm sure she must have bribed him to do it, and we were as stiff with each other as two cranes. There was a great fussing over me before this event. The sisters were going to dress me up in proper dating attire, like the town gals, Winnie said. Ida, who was my size, provided the dress—a pale orange-yellow mid-calf muslin with a flared skirt and puffed sleeves. Penny, who had feet as long and slender as mine, provided sandals, and Winnie a suitable shoulder bag.

"Hey, Glamorpuss," Winnie cried when they were finished. "You look tee-riffic!"

To tell the truth, I felt pretty silly. I liked my hair in the page boy, but I was uncomfortable in fancy clothes and was not used to sandals with heels. I was also worried about getting the curse. I'd had my first period two months before—three days of spotting which didn't amount to much—then nothing since. I was cross at even having to think about it. Thirty years of nuisance ahead of me! On the other hand, I had a sense of relief. In the eighth grade Rena and I had been the only girls in the class who hadn't had the curse yet. Rena had started lying and saying she had so she could get out of gym once a month.

319

The girls in the commercial course didn't mention such things—either they were too well brought up and prim, or they'd had it so long they just took it for granted. There was no other way of telling, because gym wasn't an option in the commercial course.

At Winnie's I learned the interesting terms 'Falling off the roof' and 'Grandma's coming to visit' for getting the curse.

Now I was worried about the pale pristine unprinted yellow-orange of the dress Ida had lent me. What if—what if, horror of horrors, I got the curse in the movies and it came through on my skirt? I didn't say anything about my anxiety, however—I was too embarrassed.

When it was time to go I felt conspicuous and too tall, but when I stood up beside Russ before we left, he was a good six inches taller, and I found myself actually standing up straight.

The sisters waved us off, and we walked awkwardly along to the movie house with no idea what to say to each other. Luckily, the movie was funny, but as soon as we left, the awkwardness returned. We managed a few sentences, but bade each other a polite goodnight at arms length as soon as he got me home. Then Russ buzzed off, presumably to meet his friends. I told everybody how good the movie was and how much I'd enjoyed the evening. If they didn't believe me, they didn't let on. And, blissful relief, I had not got the curse.

Next day, Saturday, Winnie took me on the ferry to Newport to go shopping, again ostensibly to look for something for herself, but when we got back on the ferry I clutched two large bags full of clothes for myself. I protested at the expense, but Winnie just said, "Sugarpuss, Lynde's out there in the Pacific with nothin' to spend his money on, so why shouldn't he do something nice for his little sister? You'll need those duds for school."

She'd bought me two soft wool pleated skirts: one in a large plaid of ivory and pale blue with dark brown lines through it, and a brown and a blue sweater to match; the other, a beige- and-grey tweed, with a beige cardigan and a forest green sweater to go with it.

"Brenda," she said on our way back on the ferry, "You don't wanna go to college. Don't listen to Lynde. That's no life for a girl. You wanna get married."

I'd heard that before and cringed inside.

"You're a good lookin' girl with your hair all done nice and good clothes on, an' you're gonna have a good figure when you fill out a bit. You'll wow the boys."

"Fat chance," I said glumly.

"You listen to me, Brenda, there's nothing wrong with your looks. But for heaven's sake, don't let the boys know you're smart. They won't like you."

320

My face must have carried some expression she couldn't interpret, for she laughed suddenly and tousled my hair. "You just listen to your big sister Winnie," she said. "She knows what she's talkin' about."

I couldn't interpret my feelings just then any more than she could interpret my expression. Winnie had been wonderfully kind to me and I was grateful, but I felt resentment flooding through me. She was trying to change me. Trying to tell me what to do with my life. I wasn't good enough the way I was. A quick mind was a disadvantage—a handicap I mustn't let anyone know about. Love and having babies was all that mattered, and you didn't need brains for that.

Ma, on the other hand, was trying to change me too, trying to make me into someone I wasn't and never could be. To her, sex was a sin and men were an evil to avoid. The only reason for marriage was to have children. I liked men, and I was sure when the time came I would like sex. But I wasn't going to ruin my life for it. I didn't like babies, and I'd seen too many girls and women trapped by them. If I didn't want babies, I wouldn't have them.

That night, the three sisters and Jack and I were invited to a cookout given by friends who had a house and a large yard overlooking the water. Hot dogs and hamburgers were roasted on a grill above an open fireplace, and beer was served in cans. I'd never had beer before. I only drank one, and at first taste I didn't like it, but soon concluded it went remarkably well with cook-out food.

The others didn't stop with one, and after a few beers the jokes began. They weren't like the "dirty jokes" the Allens told; they were much more subtle and didn't include obscenities. The ones I could understand were risque and very funny, but most of them were over my head. The people present were all young marrieds, and they howled with laughter at these jokes. Obviously a whole sexual language of which I was unaware, as well as the age difference, separated me from these people. One man said to Winnie, "I'm afraid we're shocking your sister-in-law." I laughed and said, "Don't worry, I don't get most of them."

Next day was Sunday and the holiday was over. Winnie drove me to Kingston to pick up the Boston train. Aunt Rita met me at South Station and took me by subway to North Station where the one o'clock train left for Maine. We had just time to lunch at the station cafeteria, and then I was off. I'd be home by five, in time for supper.

84. Perspectives

The visit to Jamestown changed my perspective radically. I tried to sort things out in my mind coming back on the train. I was beginning to see that the three women of influence in my life wanted different things for me.

Ma wanted me to stay at home, have nothing to do with men, have no interest in clothes, and be a good plain little girl of twelve forever.

Mrs. Cony wanted me to be a successful secretary. This could lead, in her view, to two possible desirable outcomes. The most desirable: attracting a well-heeled professional man to marry and support me. The less desirable: being able to support myself, and Ma and Pa, and be a burden to no one.

Mrs. Cony's scheme allowed me to be modestly attractive, to dress well, and to have enough brains to be a good secretary—but I mustn't let the boys know I'm smart.

Winnie also cautioned me against having brains, but gave me the unqualified go-ahead to be as feminine and seductive as possible, as long as I remained pure and untouched till the "right man" came along. Then I would be madly in love, blissfully happy, and faithful forever.

None of these options appealed to me. They all closed doors that I wanted to leave open. I didn't know what lay behind these doors, but I wanted the freedom to find out.

They were all saying to me, "Don't do what you want to do, do what I tell you to do, and don't ask why."

These opinions, I noted, all came from women.

What were the men's opinions?

Only three had expressed any.

Pa had asked me what I wanted to do—presumably because he wanted me to do it. I told him my three ambitions, but before we could discuss it Mrs. Cony had ended the conversation with, "Don't be silly. . . go and learn to type."

Dick had done two things: He had expressed his faith in me to do what was usually considered men's work, and do it well. Later he'd been pleased that I was on the High Honors list and had taken the opportunity to tell me my mother had wanted a child who got all A's in high school.

Lynde had suggested college and told me not to let Mrs. Cony discourage me.

Why were the women and the men so different?

I'd hardly got back from Jamestown when Ma started in on me. She didn't like my new pageboy hairdo or the pair of earrings Winnie had given me when I left.

"That hair style is too old for you," she snapped. "And those earrings—they're silly baubles meant to attract men's attention. It's a blessing she didn't try to get you to pierce your ears!"

That's all I needed.

"Ma," I said, "if men and sex are so dirty, why did you get married?"

I had said the unsayable. She opened her eyes wide in shock, then spat out, "I wish I hadn't!"

Then suddenly her eyes filled with tears. "But then I couldn't have had my little babies," she said, and turned away.

That silenced me. The possession of babies was all that mattered to her. Sex was just an unpleasant but necessary means of getting them. And once she'd had them, she'd been deserted.

Snatches of a folk song I'd heard came back to me:

> Don't sing love's songs,
> You'll wake my mother.
> She's sleeping here
> right by my side. . .
>
> All men are false
> Says my mother
> They'll tell you wicked
> Lovin' lies
> And then the next thing
> They'll court another
> Leave you alone
> to pine and sigh . . .

How many years had I slept beside Ma? How much could I have learned from her if she'd only been willing to speak, to explain what had happened to her and the reasons behind it? Why did she expect me to live my life on the basis of things she wouldn't tell me?

The situation with Ma seemed hopeless, and it was getting steadily worse. I could do nothing to please her.

I didn't want to hate Ma, who had been so kind and loving when I was little. I could see that she still loved that child who had been me—meek, compliant, so like my father. I wanted to love Ma, but I was no longer that child and never could be again. The girl I was becoming, the girl who was so like my mother, Ma could never love, so she would continue to deny that I existed.

85. The Trunk

I don't know why I overlooked the trunk for so long. Probably it was fear of looking into dark spaces, of seeing phantom hands waving at me from the gloom of the attic gables. It was only after my fear of the attic had lessened that I realized there were objects out on some floorboards near the east gable where the roof never leaked.

It had rained heavily the night before, and I came up with a flashlight and bucket to empty the water that had accumulated in the pails near the west gable. I don't know why it was that day rather than any other that I shone my light over into the opposite gable. Perhaps I sensed that the attic held secrets it had never revealed to me.

The thin pencil of light swept into the blackness, illuminating nothing but the beams and timbers of the house. Then it fell lower and disclosed that in this one area the central planking extended outward from the long axis of the attic, forming a narrow path right to the margin of the gable. And something was sitting out there. Not a ghost, a trunk.

Surprised, I made my way out to it, careful not to stumble off the planking. It was not a large trunk, and not heavy. I could easily drag it back to the central catwalk. The trunk was thick with dust, I could feel its softness when I touched the handles.

I got it out to the center, then dragged it along to the stairwell where the sun was pouring in through the window. Luckily the trunk was not locked. I undid the large metal clasp in front and the smaller ones at the sides and tried to open it. It resisted at first, but then the glue of dust fell away and I raised the lid.

A pile of papers clipped together in several bundles occupied one side. The other side contained a small packet of letters tied with string, a notebook, and a number of photographs. Most were unframed, but some were in old-fashioned hinged cases which held two pictures and folded together to form little closed boxes. The cases were dark brownish grey, decorated with raised floral patterns of the same color, and had fancy brass clasps to hold the two halves closed. The pictures they contained were printed on metal instead of on paper. Tintypes like the ones in Ma's album!

In one picture a solid, well-built man of about fifty, dressed in an old-fashioned black suit, sat with hands in lap, looking thoughtfully past the camera. He appeared serious but content, as if he had attained a longed-for dream and was looking ahead in reverie toward the future. His features were strong, eyes deep-set under straight brows. A dark beard adorned his chin and fell about six inches below it.

Beside him stood a woman, younger than he, her arm falling in a graceful line to rest lightly on his shoulder. Her long dress was full-skirted with a tight bodice, and the light color suggested ivory. Her face was oval, cheek bones high. Her mouth turned down slightly at the corners, her nose was neat and slightly upturned. She, too, gazed thoughtfully past the camera, her expression serene but with a hint of sadness, as if she saw things in the future that had not occurred to the man. There were no names to tell me who they were.

The other pictures were of children and young adults, separately or in groups. One depicted a young boy in a Lord Fauntleroy suit. Who could they be? I didn't know enough about clothes to date the photos, but from the little I knew, some of these had to be pre-Civil War. Could they be Ma and Pa's relatives? Perhaps my great-grandparents?

I turned to the pile of papers and picked up the first bundle. It was a manuscript. The sheet on top said

The Nameless Brat
by
Bess Lynde Russell Shaw

I felt the shock travel from my fingers to my neck and up to the top of my head. I almost dropped the page.

Bess—my mother's name. Lynde—her maiden name. Russell—the name of my brother's father. Shaw—my father's name. This was Mother's trunk, and all my mother's names! Those pictures must be of my mother's family, not my father's! Why had no one ever shown me this trunk?

I examined the page carefully, trying to keep my hands from shaking. It had been typewritten except for the 'Shaw', which had been added in pen in neat Spencerian script. She'd written this story before she married my father, then.

Beneath this bundle were four others, all manuscripts, all neatly typewritten, all by Bess Lynde Russell with "Shaw" added in pen. My mother had written all these stories!

I began reading the first one—a story about a social worker in a large Boston hospital who helped poor people and immigrants living in the Boston slums. It told of an Italian family whose unmarried daughter had become pregnant. The social worker was trying to calm the girl's father, who had declared that his daughter was a sinner damned to hell. "I'll throttle the nameless brat," he shouted.

I finished reading the story, then continued on through the other four. They were all about poor people having a hard time in the Boston slums.

The fact that my mother had written all these stories amazed and thrilled me. And yet the stories themselves did not satisfy me. The stilted Victorian language, the cliches and the sentimental flavor bothered me. I was sure I wouldn't have written them that way. The characters didn't seem real. Though Mother had worked with people like this, I sensed that she had never lived with the poor. But the stories were Mother's, and they were precious to me. Had she published them? I wondered.

Next, I untied the packet of letters. I read them through carefully, but they were from people I'd never heard of, about things that had no meaning for me. I tied them up again and put them beside the stories.

Finally, the notebook. It smelled musty and had a grey-and-ivory marbled cover and a dark grey binding. Inside on the yellowing pages were entries in Mother's handwriting, obviously written hurredly as the thoughts had come to her.

It seemed to be a sort of diary, but the entries were undated, and initials were used instead of names. They were fragmentary and not in a context I could understand. Did I know any of these people?

Then I found an entry that was all too clearly about someone I knew:

> I can do nothing to turn away her wrath. Though she seldom speaks to me, the anger is always there under the silence. . . Nothing I do or say, or refrain from doing or saying helps . . . I am grateful that her hatred does not extend to Lynde. She is always kind to him and treats him well. I'm sure he senses the tension and animosity, but he has no idea how deep it runs or how it is affecting us all . . . Grace, of course, when she is here, sides with Mrs. Shaw and will not speak to me, though Fred is always courteous. . . There seems nothing I can do to stem Mrs. Shaw's hatred. My only solace is that Shirley says he is still in love with me.

Stunned, I put the diary down. Everything Rita had told me about my grandmother was true! There really were two Ma's, neither of whom I understood, and one of them hated my mother. And I was also two people: one who came from my father, and one who came from my mother. Did Ma hate the half of me that was my mother? Is that why she tried to control me as she did, to keep the half which was Mother from coming out? I knew, even through my anger, that she loved the part of me who was my father.

Obviously I couldn't approach Ma about the trunk. Surely if she'd known it was there she would have destroyed its contents long ago.

Did Pa know about the trunk? There was no use asking him. I was sure he wouldn't talk about it. He'd never say anything against Ma, or against Grace—or against Mother—or against anyone.

If only I'd found the trunk before visiting Rita! I could have asked her about the pictures and the letters—could have taken them with me.

I arranged the papers and photographs carefully, closed the lid, and dragged the trunk back toward the gable end. Ma and Pa never came up to the attic any more because they had difficulty climbing stairs. The trunk was safe enough where it had been all these years—yet I didn't want to risk leaving it there. What if it disappeared? My sixth sense told me I'd better conceal it if I could.

I shone my flashlight over into the space between the gable and the finished room. It showed that the planking extended to the corner where the room had been completed, and continued on around it. After carefully checking the width and solidity of the planking, I pushed the trunk out along it and guided it around the corner. No flashlight could pick it out there. It would be safe, and no one would know where it was but me.

86. Sophomore Year

That autumn, 1943, I went into my sophomore year at Cony High.

Because so many male teachers had gone off to war, I was in for an unexpected delight at the beginning of that year. The law against married women teaching school had been relaxed, and Mrs. Weaver replaced the sour and boring Miss Purse as my teacher of English. Mrs. Weaver was kind, warm and seemed to understand young people instinctively. She gave us a strong foundation for business English. More important, she had us read Dickens' *A Tale of Two Cities*, followed by *Great Expectations*, both of which I found totally absorbing.

Mrs. Weaver, Mrs. Varney who taught us typing, and the shorthand teacher Miss Jackson are the only instructors I remember from that year. Kay and I were already aware of Nora Jackson's reputation for toughness and her demands for perfection. She was the bête noire of the commercial course—the unyielding sieve that sorted out competence from incompetence.

At the end of our freshman year she had administered the aptitude test for shorthand, which divided our class into those who would be allowed to take shorthand and those who would not. Kay and I both did exceptionally well in the test, and, like the others who passed, we were automatically elected to the Cony Commercial Club which met on Wednesday evenings once a month. On these occasions, Kay arranged for me to stay overnight with her. Her parents agreed to her suggestion at once, and appeared delighted that their daughter had found a friend.

I remember little of those meals at the Moores' and the meetings afterward, but I do recall helping Kay out about the liver. The Moores' doctor had taken a sample of her blood and declared her to be anemic. He advised her mother to feed her liver once a week.

Kay was a picky eater at the best of times, and liver was her special hate. With my acquiescence she told her mother I liked liver and seldom had it at home, so the Wednesday evenings when the Commercial Club met, liver was always served at the Moores'. By a bit of accomplished sleight-of-hand, Kay managed to get the liver off her plate and onto mine without being observed. I was always famished by the time Mrs. Moore served supper at six, an hour later than I was used to eating, and liver was a favorite of mine. I had no trouble at all doing away with my double portion.

The only other memory of those occasions was the matter of the girdle. We had to appear at the Commercial Club meetings in the sort of clothing that proper young secretaries should wear to an office. That meant a conservative dress or a blouse and skirt, silk stockings and Cuban heels. In high school girls were allowed to wear slacks to school in winter because of the cold, so I brought my skirt, stockings, garter belt and shoes with me on Commercial Club days. One Wednesday I forgot my garter belt and asked Kay if she had an extra one I could borrow.

"I haven't worn a garter belt since my mother let me get a girdle when I was twelve!" she announced with a superior air. "I'll lend you my spare girdle. You should have been wearing one for the past three years, for heaven's sake!"

"Why?" I asked.

"To keep your figure in trim, of course."

I glanced at plump Kay, then down at my own bony frame.

"If my figure was any trimmer it wouldn't be there," I said. "Besides, girdles look horribly uncomfortable."

"Well they're not," insisted Kay. "Here. Wear this tonight. You'll see."

I'd never put in a more constrained and uncomfortable evening in my life. I vowed then that I'd never, ever, wear a girdle again—a vow that I've kept!

Shorthand is a challenge. I love it.

Nora Jackson stands in front of the shorthand class, feet far apart, ramrod straight, gripping the time clock in her hand: "Feet flat on the floor, arms all on the desk, and get something on the paper for every word I say!"

She is a sturdy woman in her forties with scarcely visible breasts. She reminds me of a tightly packed sausage in the skin of her dark blue dress. Her hair is almost white with only flecks of grey and is cut in a severe short shingle. Her dark blue eyes match her dress, and they flash. She expects the best.

We sit like athletes poised for the starting gun, feet pressed to the floor, arms completely supported by desk, shorthand pens in fingers that grip them like tight springs.

Nora Jackson starts the time clock and begins to dictate.

She is giving us a timed test, 100 words per minute for ten minutes. Then we must transcribe the dictated material into typewritten copy in a set period of time. We are allowed only five errors or we flunk. No A, B, or C-type grades. It's pass or fail.

Just before the test Nora Jackson has limbered us up by dictating to us at 110 words per minute. This gets the adrenalin going with the stress of trying to keep up, gets us primed. After that, the 100 words per minute seems slow.

Nora Jackson's technique is the inverse of Vera Varney's. Mrs. Varney has us type to a metronome which she gradually increases in speed. "Keep the rhythm even, so the keys won't pile up on you, girls, and make those fingers fly," she'll say. Then she'll stop the metronome and time us while we type an assigned passage as fast as we can.

Nora Jackson is even more of a perfectionist than Vera Varney. Secretaries must be completely trained when they leave the commercial course. No half-way measures.

She regularly gives us three types of shorthand test: The timed dictation test, the shorthand form test, and the brief form test.

Gregg shorthand forms are based on a phonetics of flowing lines and curlicues that can be put together at speed. A symbol represents each letter and each different sound. We must also learn "brief forms" for the common words that occur over and over in ordinary speech. These are usually represented by the form for a single letter. For example, the word "have" is represented by the symbol for "v" which is a long downward curve. "Be," "but" or "by" are represented by the symbol for "b" which is simply a curve in the opposite direction.

There are 180 brief forms, and for these the pass mark is 100 percent, or we will fail the course at the end of the year. We can take the brief form test as often as we wish until time runs out in June. When it runs out, so do our chances.

Miss Jackson also lectures us on office techniques and comportment. We are always on time. We are always polite. We are always impeccably clean, neat, well pressed and never attired in anything frilly. We never paint our fingernails or let them grow into claws. We never wear bright red lipstick. Only pale pink or peach is suitable. We do not wear spike heels and party frocks to the office. We must always address our boss as "Sir" or "Mr." We must always ensure that we are in before our boss and that his desk and papers are neatly arranged. Know what he needs to have easily at hand and have it there. Make sure we know his appointments for the day and have the files ready for him. Anticipate what he will ask us to do, and if possible do it before he asks. Don't do things tomorrow, do them yesterday.

We all like and respect Nora Jackson. We know we can't get away with a thing, and we don't try.

87. The Medicine Man

Pa, who had been sober most of the preceding summer, hit the bottle again with the onset of winter. I hoped things would improve in spring as they had before, but they didn't.

Ma, too, had continued to slide down hill. She had no appetite and we could get her to eat little but tea and toast. The flesh hung slack from her face and the bones of her arms.

One morning in early January she stepped out onto the back porch to get some fresh air—told me later she'd been feeling a bit faint. I wasn't paying attention to what she was doing out there, but happened to glance through the window just as she fell. I saw her slide down the outside wall of the house, on which she must have been leaning, and collapse like a sack. I dashed out, shouting for Pa, who was somewhere in the outbuildings.

It was another of her open-eye attacks. She was on her back, shoulders against the wall of the house, staring and senseless. I could tell by the smell that her bowels and bladder had let go.

Pa banged in through the shed door faster than he'd moved for months and joined me on the porch.

"Go phone the doctor," he said.

Dr. Murdoch had retired and another doctor, Kelsey, had taken over his practice. I told him what had happened and asked him to come out.

"She's just fainted, obviously," he said. "She'll snap out of it. I can't come running out into the country every time some old lady faints. They do it all the time."

"But what if she's dying?" I cried. He didn't answer, just hung up.

I headed for the porch, shouting, "Pa, he won't come out."

"The bastard," said Pa.

"Who shall I call?"

"Wait, I think she's coming out of it."

Ma was blinking, shaking her head, apparently trying to focus. We managed to get her sitting up, and by then she was insisting she could walk. She remembered nothing about the attack, but was mortally embarrassed about her loss of bowel control.

"Oh God, let me die," she moaned. "I don't want to end up like this."

It was not the first time I'd heard her pray for death, nor would it be the last. She refused to let us help her clean up, said she'd do it herself.

"Pa, can a doctor just refuse to come?" I asked while we waited to escort her from the bathroom. "What if she'd been dying?"

"Doctors can refuse anything they want to the likes of us," he said. "We'd been paying what we could when we could to Murdoch. He knew he'd get it eventually. But after Kelsey took over it got around that he wasn't catering to slow payers. We don't owe him a goddam cent, because I settled our account as soon as I got the money from McAusland. But the account shows a history of slow pay, so Kelsey won't risk making a house call. We'll have to make an appointment for Ma and have the money in hand when we get there."

As soon as Ma was clean and resting in bed, Pa got on the phone to Kelsey and made an appointment for that afternoon. Ma couldn't have got on and off a bus, so we went with her in a taxi.

After Kelsey examined Ma, he declared there was nothing wrong but extreme old age and lack of interest in food.

"What do you expect at eighty-eight? Give her a glass of port wine before lunch and dinner to stimulate her appetite."

We got the port on our way home, but Ma was dead set against drink—hardly surprising with three alcoholic men in her life—so the bottle remained in the cupboard, open but untouched, until I got into it one night after Pa had gone to bed. I was doing the washing in the old electric machine in the kitchen, and got slap happy on it. When I finished it several days later it was never replaced. We just continued in our nearly hopeless efforts to get Ma to eat what we cooked for her.

88. The Down Staircase

In March, 1944, I returned to McGraths' as promised. Mr. informed me at once that since I was now sixteen I must apply for a Social Security card. Mr. would regularly withhold a small amount from my pay to be sent, with an equal amount from him as my employer, to the federal government. This would build up over all the years I worked, he told me, and when I retired I'd have a pension.

"You young people are lucky," he said. "When you're my age, you'll be sitting pretty."

Pa agreed when I told him. "If the government keeps its promises, the chances of the next generation will be a lot better than ours."

On my first day back, I found Annette sporting a wedding ring as well as her engagement ring. She and Ed had married in February. She was only seventeen.

"How come?" I asked.

"We decided we'd waited long enough," she said.

It was soon obvious why, and she left in June when high school let out to become a full time homemaker and await the first birth.

Meanwhile she talked all spring of nothing but babies and fixing up the apartment she and Ed had rented. It was an obsession I knew I would never have.

Little else had changed at McGraths'. Weekends were still busy, although gasoline rationing lessened the rush somewhat. Other than that, the routine went on much as usual. The juke box still ground out its repetitive hit parade numbers:

> Gonna take a sentimental journey
> Gonna set my heart at ease
> Gonna take a sentimental journey
> To renew old memories

and other lyrics which affixed themselves to my brain so I heard them in my sleep.

Pa was drunk most of that spring. I never knew where he got his liquor, or how much it cost. He probably went to town after it on the bus while I was at school.

One day in May, while high school was still in session, he showed up at the bus station to get the 2:10 back to the farm. I was waiting for it as well. Guess he'd forgotten I took that bus after school to go to McGraths', because he looked shocked when he saw me. He was teetering on his feet and clearly sloshed. Why the hell did he have to take this bus, I thought. All the farm kids from Manchester took it, and everybody on board knew me. But they didn't know him, come to think of it. No one there had ever seen my father, as far as I knew. Perhaps they'd think he was just an acquaintance.

I went up to him. "What are you doing in town, Pa?" I asked. He tried to answer, but his words were slurred and illogical.

I got him on board and into a seat. The bus was crowded so I couldn't sit beside him. I stood hanging onto a strap a ways behind him. I was due at McGraths' at 2:30, and when I pushed my way past his seat to get off I said, "See you later" into his good ear. He looked up with eyes unfocused but filled with what looked like remorse, regret and love. I got off the bus fighting tears.

When I got home at 5:15 for supper he was passed out on the bed. If Ma had noted his condition, she didn't say, nor had she made any attempt to start supper. She seemed vague and disconnected. I quickly got something together for Ma and me to eat. Then I made sure Pa was all right, covered him up and took my bike back to work.

By the time I left McGraths' at eleven, the temperature had dropped and the fog had come down. As I rode my bike across the parking area, the gravel grated under the tires. Not like it did in daytime with the sun on it—then it clicked with a sharp, hot ring as if it were alive. Tonight it had a smooth, muffled sound, faded and greyed like old cotton.

I reached the road and the sound changed abruptly as I went onto the moist concrete. The fog ahead of me billowed up like smoke. It reached out its fingers and beckoned, then receded, eluding me. A car approached from behind, and for a moment the white fog was sliced sharply with two yellow beams of light. A muffled roar moved by me, leaving only a golden blur receding into the night.

The fog thinned and shredded itself for a moment; gauzy wisps threaded across the road in front of me. It swirled in little eddies and lay in pools in the ditches.

I was passing the Lees' orchard now—how grotesque the trees were, crouching there, waiting. The fog writhed around their roots, long, luminous, crawling, and crept up the trunks to clutch at the foliage.

As quickly as it had thinned, the fog started to billow back again and suddenly it was all around me—soft, seductive, pale. Then out of the vapor a figure appeared: pale grey, hardly differentiated at first from the fog. I felt my skin wrinkle all along my spine. A wraithe, a specter, waiting to clutch at me as I passed.

Then in a flash I knew who it was. It was Ma with a shawl over her head, out looking for me.

"Peggy," she said, relieved as I stopped beside her. "I was worried, you out in this fog. I came to find you."

"Where's Pa?" I asked.

"In bed," she said.

Still drunk, I thought. A sudden warmth suffused me as I realized the courage of what Ma had done. In spite of her mental state she knew I might be in danger and that Pa was not fit to get out of bed. She had risked her own safety to go out on her tottery legs into the fog to look for me.

I could see nothing ahead for us now but disaster. Ma had been failing fast that winter. Time had stopped for her when I was twelve, but for a while that was the only symptom that seemed out of the ordinary. She was often cranky and unreasonable, but that was nothing new. It was just getting harder to take.

I didn't understand about old age and what could happen to people when it overtook them. I was angry instead of being sympathetic. No wonder Pa was drinking, I thought. Facing financial ruin, bedevilled with ill health, unable to work, and now having to deal with a totally unreasonable mother and a daughter he didn't know how to talk with. No wonder all the men on Pa's side of the family were drunks, with someone like Ma on their tails all the time. Ma had made Pa's life hell. She'd made him miserable about my mother, and now she was making him miserable about everything else—especially about me. I could do nothing to please her. That's why Pa had retreated more and more into the woodshed and spoke only when he had to. It was Ma's fault. I was convinced she could stop her insufferable nagging if she wanted to.

But now other symptoms were starting to surface. Ma began hunting for things. Things she hadn't had for years, like her Potts irons. They were the kind of "flatiron," made of cast iron and heavy as lead, which were placed on the back of the stove to keep hot. The handle was kept separately on a cool shelf, ready at any moment to be clipped on so the iron could be lifted over to the ironing board. Farm wives must have had the arms of Atlas to use them, and Ma, who had become so frail, couldn't have lifted one now if she tried. She'd have to go back before my birth to find those irons. We'd had an electric iron ever since I could remember.

Ma also began accusing Pa of things he'd done years ago, thinking he'd done them yesterday. But, strangely, she didn't try to bring the dead alive again. She never spoke of Grace or Barton in the present tense, or went hunting for them in their bungalows. Though she got the past mixed up with the present in other unpredictable ways, that was an error I never knew her to make. She seemed able to remember those things that had occurred during my lifetime, as long as they preceded the cut-off point of twelve.

And Pa—what was he thinking of, retreating into the family affliction, drink? He knew what had happened to Barton well enough, and to his father and grandfather before him, but it made no difference to him.

Drink was his only solace for pain and grief, and the money for food was going down the drain with it. Damn good thing I was working.

In mid-May Mrs. McGrath told me that a lawyer who practiced in town had come in and asked about me. Wanted to know what kind of worker I was. It wasn't hard to guess what was going on. I knew Nora Jackson placed her pupils in part-time jobs when suitable ones became available. I'd heard the name Taylor Garvin from Gracie. He was a crony of her boss Judge Cony, but I knew nothing else about him.

Sure enough, next day after shorthand class Miss Jackson called me aside. "Taylor Garvin is looking for a girl to work for him during the summer, and I recommended you. I told him you'd been working at McGraths', and Mr. Garvin went out and saw them. He liked what they said about you and wonders if you could come in to his office after school today and see him."

"I have to catch a bus at 2:10," I said.

"I told him that. He says if you come straight down at 1:30 he'll see you quickly so you won't miss your bus."

I felt three things all at once: fear, pleasure, and regret. Fear of an unknown job, pleasure at being asked, and regret as I saw my precious summer at the Lees' slipping away from me. I said I'd go and talk with him.

"Good," said Miss Jackson. "The job will give you the opportunity to use your shorthand. He'll be dictating letters to you. You've passed your 120 words per minute test, so you'll have no trouble. You'll have to get used to the legal vocabulary, but I think you'll enjoy it." She gave me his address.

Taylor Garvin's establishment was on Water Street on the second floor above a shop. I went up the stairs and entered a large area divided into a waiting room and offices. Two young women were working there behind a low railing. I approached the one at the desk nearest the stairs. She looked up from her typewriter and smiled. Her eyes were a startling sea green which surprised me. I didn't know eyes came in that color.

I told her who I was.

"Oh, yes, he's expecting you. Just have a seat, and I'll tell him you're here." A row of chairs ran along one side of the waiting room, and I sat down while she went off toward the back of the building. As I did so I caught the eye of the other girl behind the railing. She was slender with long dark hair hanging loose onto her shoulders. Her face was very pale, but lit up and seemed to glow as she smiled at me.

The girl with green eyes returned at once followed by Taylor Garvin, a large man in his late fifties, over six feet, slightly stooped but muscular and well built. He introduced himself and ushered me into his office, which was at the back with a view over the river. He indicated a chair in front of his desk and I sat down.

"Miss Jackson has recommended you to me as a good student and a quick learner," he began. "I had a word with Mr. and Mrs. McGrath yesterday and they say they are pleased with your work. I'm looking for a girl who would work for me during the summer taking letters, doing general typing and filing and working on insurance reports. The hours would be eight to five Monday through Friday and eight to twelve on Saturdays. The salary would be sixteen dollars a week. Would that sort of thing appeal to you?"

"I think so," I said, ice forming in my stomach at the thought of being imprisoned indoors forty-four hours a week during the summer.

"I wonder if you could start coming in part time after school the first of June? That will let you give McGraths two weeks' notice and get a week's part-time experience here before school lets out."

"Yes, I could do that," I said.

"Good. If you came in from two to five that first week we could get you started."

He took me out and introduced me to the two secretaries, Gladys of the green eyes and Crystal. A young man emerged from an office near Gladys' desk and was introduced as Mr. Garvin's son, Clifford.

Then Mr. Garvin shook hands with me, and I left.

It had been almost too easy. I was glad I hadn't known the day before about the interview, it would only have given me time to get nervous. But what was I going to say to the McGraths?

I told Mrs. first, and her face fell. "I'm sorry to hear that, Peggy. I was hoping to keep yuz another year. In fact I was going to ask if you'd like to apprentice with me to be a chocolate dipper. I think you have the speed and coordination to do it."

It was the nicest compliment Mrs. could have paid me. I had never ceased to admire her skill, and very much doubted that I could ever equal it. Also I knew that dipping chocolates would soon drive me crazy, but I thanked her for the offer.

Mr. had joined us in time to pick up our conversation. "I figured when Mr. Garvin came asking about you that our time together would be limited," he said. "We both wish you well. You've done a good job for us."

Incredible as it seems, Kay still didn't realize what condition Pa was in, any more than I had before the Allens clued me in. She'd just assumed he was ill, and I didn't enlighten her. But the Saturday after my first week at Garvin's, I could hide it from her no longer.

She met me at Garvin's office at twelve noon on Saturday, when I finished for the week. We caught the twelve ten bus out to the farm together. She would stay for the rest of the weekend.

After lunch we took a walk up to Lees' Quarry with Judy, and I told her all about the ins and outs of my week at Garvin's. There was nothing yet which, with our two years of typing and one of shorthand, we both couldn't easily handle, I assured her. It was mostly getting to know where things were and what should be done when. I'd been tense and nervous at first, but was already relaxing. The office atmosphere was cheerful, and no one had expected the impossible.

After our walk, we had an early supper and took the bus back into town to go to the six o'clock movie. We got the nine o'clock bus home.

When we got back Ma had gone to bed, but we found Pa in a pool of blood on the kitchen floor, dead drunk. He reeked of booze. Even Kay couldn't miss that. I got him into a sitting position and tried to assess the damage.

"What the hell have you done to yourself?" I asked him.

"Fell down and hit my nose on a chair," he muttered. His nose and under his eyes were black. Looked like he'd really smashed his face.

336

I called Dr. Kelsey's office and said there'd been an accident, could he come? Luckily, Dr. Kelsey was on vacation, and a substitute was on duty. He didn't seem to realize he could refuse to answer calls from the country, so he said he'd be right out.

"Help me get him into bed, will you?" I asked Kay. She recoiled. I hadn't been noticing her reaction to all this, but now I saw she had a look of horror, fear and disbelief on her face.

"Forget it, I'll do it myself," I said. Pa was a bit more conscious now. "Come on, push with your legs," I told him as I pulled on his arms. He got to his feet and I led him off to bed and sponged off the blood.

"I'm going to call Daddy," said Kay as I emerged.

"There's nothing he can do," I said.

She got on the phone anyway, and I heard her say, "Daddy, come and get me. I want to come home."

Rats leave a sinking ship, I thought, my gut contracting. I hadn't thought Kay would do that to me. There was talk at the other end of the line, then:

"Mr. Shaw fell and broke his nose and there's blood all over the floor."

Pause.

"He was drunk. That's why he fell."

I winced. Did she have to tell him that?

"But Daddy, I don't want to stay out here all night with someone drunk!"

Fairly lengthy pause. I could hear the sharp but undecipherable grating of Arthur Moore's voice leaking from the receiver.

"All right."

Kay hung up. "He won't come and get me. Says I should stay with you."

Good for Arthur Moore, I thought. He must have told her she couldn't leave me in the lurch.

The doctor arrived and sized up the situation. Pa was slap-happy and trying to be funny. With considerable aplomb and good humor the doctor went along with it.

"You must have had a lallapalooza of an evening," he said to Pa. "You're feeling no pain now, but you will. I'll give these pills to your daughter, and when you start to hurt ask her for one."

He turned to me. "His nose is broken, but by the look it's been broken before and not set. I don't think this bang he's had will make it much worse. Now if he were a pretty young girl like yourself I'd suggest getting it set, but he's not, and doing it would cost a lot of money. After the pain and swelling go away if it doesn't bother him or interfere with his breathing, I'd just leave it."

"Okay," I said.

The doctor packed his bag. "Do you want to pay me now?" he asked.

"Have Kelsey send us a bill," I said. "He knows us, and I haven't got enough on me right now."

Won't Kelsey be creamed when he finds out his fill-in doctor went out into the sticks and saw the likes of us, I thought as the doctor left.

Though I didn't tell her so, I was furious with Kay for wanting to run out on me. Fair weather friend! If this had happened to her, I'd have helped her get the old man up and sponged off.

That night I dreamed about a staircase. It resembled our front stairs with its elegant, highly polished banister and worn carpeting, but it didn't go straight from top to bottom. At the top, a sweeping curve fell gracefully into a half-spiral. I was standing in the chill half light near the bottom, terrified because I couldn't go back up, and there was no way to get off at the hall floor. The stair didn't end there, but continued down, disappearing into a dark, undulating fog. I could see nowhere ahead to put my feet.

89. The Talk with Pa

Following the incident when Pa broke his nose, I feared my friendship with Kay was over. Next morning when Kay and I arose, Pa was still sleeping it off. I checked that he was breathing regularly and in no need of another pain-killer. His entire face was one large bruise, and it hurt me to look at it.

Ma had eaten before we got up and, as was her custom now, ignored us completely. She made no mention of Pa, nor did I. I got the usual breakfast of grapefruit, bacon and eggs for Kay and myself.

Kay did not refer to the happenings of the night before either. Instead, we talked about the 140 word per minute shorthand test that we'd be facing on Tuesday. Kay and I and a girl named Marilyn were running neck and neck in shorthand competence and were the only serious contenders for being first to attain the 140. Marilyn had been off sick for a week.

"It's not fair to Marilyn for us to sit that test if she's not back by Tuesday," Kay commented.

"No, it isn't," I agreed. "It won't be as much fun, and less of a challenge without her."

"If she's not back tomorrow, I'm going to ask Miss Jackson if she'll put off the test till she is," said Kay.

"Do you think she'll be willing to do that?"

"We'll see."

That was so like Kay. Fair and generous and willing to act on it. Except in exceptional circumstances. I felt a stab of agony at thought of losing such a friend, even though she'd tried to abandon me last night.

Shortly after 10 a.m. Arthur Moore appeared to take Kay home. He normally came for her late in the afternoon. Although he'd insisted she stay with me overnight, he must have known that, under the circumstances, she'd appreciate being picked up early.

When Kay left, I figured it was the last time she'd ever come to the farm. After all, she was a nice girl from a sober and hard-working family. She wouldn't want to know me now. I dreaded having to see her tomorrow at school. What would she say to me then? Would she speak to me at all?

To my surprise, there seemed no change next day in Kay's cheerful and friendly attitude toward me. She never mentioned the nose incident again.

Marilyn was still absent on Monday, and Kay did approach Nora Jackson about postponing the 140. Miss Jackson agreed to put it off till Friday, but when Marylin still had not returned by then she insisted that the test must go on. No one in the class passed it. The "pass" requirement was five errors or less during the ten-minute take. I had nine and Kay seven. Though we hadn't deliberately set out to "throw"the test, we were both relieved by the result.

After class, Kay asked, "Shall I meet you at Garvin's tomorrow noon? We could take a hike with Judy, and then Sunday if it's nice we can bike out to Cobbosseecontee again."

"Sure," I said, several tons of worry sliding from my shoulders.

I decided that Kay was in some ways like Pa. She didn't verbalize problems. She just encouraged them to fade away by silence and good will. We never talked about Ma and Pa after that, only about our own concerns. It didn't leave us short of things to say. A look passing between us over some new development in Ma's exasperating behavior was enough to fill in any gap.

The summer of Pa's broken nose was the first summer I missed Aunt Rita's annual visit. She showed up unheralded on a Saturday afternoon in early July, and I was not at home. Kay had again come for the weekend, and we had gone off on our bicycles.

When we returned, Pa told us Rita was very sorry not to have seen me.

My first reaction was one of relief because Pa was sober that day. I'd been dreading Rita finding out he was drinking—like his father, his grandfather and his brother. He'd been sober more often since the broken nose incident. I think he was profoundly embarrassed by it, and took special pains to abstain when he knew Kay was coming to the farm. Also, he felt better in warm weather when the days were longer and the evenings lighter.

My second reaction to missing Rita's visit was disappointment and frustration. Why did she never let us know when she was coming? I wanted to talk with her about mother's trunk—perhaps get her up to the attic to see it, if I could. That might not be too difficult if Ma was going through a confused period, but the clarity of her mind varied greatly from day to day and could never be predicted. She could still be unnervingly sharp when one least wanted her to be, and in spite of her mental decline, she was always extra vigilant when Rita called. It was a small miracle that Rita had got me off into a field long enough to give me Mother's picture last year.

Pa was still sober the day after Rita's visit, and after Kay left I came across him as I was passing through the woodshed on my way to the stable. He was sitting on the chopping block smoking. He looked up and said:

"Rita says I should talk to you about your mother."

Shock and disbelief went through me. Had the impossible happened? Had Rita finally induced him to speak? What could she have said to him? I looked at him intently. The lines on his face were deep and strained.

"She says I don't talk to you enough, or tell you about things. Trouble is, I don't know how."

I didn't "know how" either. This had never happened before. I didn't know what to do, all the things I'd wanted to say left my head. "What was Mother like?" was the only question I could manage to blurt out.

"Nice woman. She could play the piano."

"What did she play?"

"She didn't play here. We didn't have a piano."

"What did she look like?"

"Gray hair, curly. Rita was her best friend."

The shadowy Mother was no clearer. Pa leaned forward, elbows on knees, rough farmer's hands pressed awkwardly together. The lines in his face were taut. We had always understood each other without words. Now he wasn't like Pa at all. I wished he would stop. Yet there was so much I wanted to know. In desperation I said, "Which did you like best, my mother or Florence?"

"I liked the one who gave me you," he said, and choked up. I was hot with embarrassment.

Pa fished in his pocket, brought out a small leather folder and handed it to me. I opened it. The photograph of a woman looked out at me. She was probably in her late thirties, with clear smooth skin, large eyes under full brows, neat well-sculpted nose and mouth. Her gray curly hair was worn short and high and formed a cloud about her head. She smiled thoughtfully out of the faded sepia photograph. Only head and shoulders were visible. She was dressed in summer white—what appeared to be a plain but elegant jacket over a square-necked low-cut dress. A slender chain, probably gold from the way the light caught it, disappeared into her bosom. She was lovely. She looked nothing like me.

"She put a note on the back," Pa said, "and there's a poem."

I took the photograph out of its case and turned it over. The neat Spencerian hand, the hand I had now come to recognize as Mother's, had written, "I love you Shirley. It's only for you." There were also clippings about their wedding, and the poem:

Two shall be born, the whole wide world apart,
And speak in different tongues and have no thought
Each of the other's being, and no heed.
And these, o'er unknown seas, to unknown lands,
Shall cross, escaping wreck, defying death;
And all unconsciously shape every act
And bend each wandering step to this one end—
That, one day, out of darkness they shall meet
And read life's meaning in each other's eyes.

I replaced the clippings and the poem behind the picture and handed the case back to Pa, speechless.

"Some day," he said, "You'll meet someone. Then you'll know what I can't tell you."

He subsided into silence. The lines in his face loosened. It was over. I relaxed. He was Pa again.

Eliza Ridley Pratt, 1828-1896 (my great-grandmother)

Ma (Emma Mentora Pratt Shaw) as a young woman

Ma and Henry Barton Pratt ("Uncle Bit"), about 1920

Aunt Grace (Grace Shaw, later Gordon) as a young woman

Left, Uncle Bart (William Barton Shaw); right, Pa (Shirley Woodman Shaw)

The Shaw farmhouse

Pa, shovelling snow

Peggy (Brenda Shaw), age 11

Lynde Russell, about age 23

Bess Marguerite Lynde, about 1904

Alta Lynde Walsh

Orren Lynde Walsh and Miriam Houdlette

Henry Lynde, about 1870

Sarah Johnston Lynde, about 1870

Henry Lynde, about 1925

Warren Lynde

Warren Lynde and Nancy Scarlett Lynde, 1848

90. Of Toni Waves and Love Letters

Gladys had been with Taylor Garvin for five years, since she was twenty, and her air of complete poise and quiet confidence set the tone for the office. She knew all the clients, the ins and outs of their cases, and was a willing fund of information which Crystal and I could draw on whenever we needed. Crystal, who was nineteen, had been there only a year and clearly admired and looked up to Gladys.

It soon became apparent that Gladys' life outside the office revolved around the dance pavillion at Island Park. The pavillion was on a tiny island just off shore in Cobbosseecontee and was connected to the mainland by a short wooden bridge. On Saturday nights the young swingers of Augusta went there to jitterbug or "cut a rug."

Gladys went every Saturday with her friend "Sharky"—short for Charlene—who worked at another Augusta law office. The two were on the phone to each other daily, ostensibly about clients of mutual interest to the two law firms, but the calls were at least fifty per cent concerned with a rehash of last Saturday's dance and speculations about the ones to come.

"Gladys is very popular," Crystal confided to me. "She's a wonderful dancer and the boys just crowd around her. Some people say she's 'fast,' but she isn't. She just loves to dance, and she can keep the boys in order. She's a really good, generous person under that flippant humor."

Her generosity showed up in many ways, not least when the Toni Wave hit town. The marcel wave had been introduced by a French hairdresser in the late 1800s and required only a hot curling iron and a comb to produce a soft, flattering wave. The effect didn't last, though, and had to be renewed daily. By the 1930s, the marcel had been replaced by the "permanent wave," which was said to last six months and was much more complicated. A solution that reeked of ammonia and other strong chemicals was swabbed onto the hair, which was then rolled up tightly on small metal cylinders. These were clamped into the permanent wave machine. This instrument of torture consisted of a tall metal pedestal at the top of which was a round hollow metal ball. From holes in the ball sprang many long electric wires with clamps on the ends. The clamps fit over the hair-covered cylinders. When the machine was turned on, electric current heated the cylinders and the hair rolled upon them. The same principle as the electric chair, but unless something went drastically wrong the results were not as final.

The amount and duration of the heat was critical. Too little and too short meant no curl. Too long and too hot meant the burned hair stuck to the cylinders. The permanent wave was "permanent" in that the hair never recovered from it, and when it went wrong one had to wait until one's hair had grown out and been cut off.

The Toni Wave was the beginning of the end for that old method of permanent waving. The Toni Company developed a cold process with which a permanent wave could be done at home. The wave was only guaranteed to last three months instead of six, but it was supposed to be less damaging to the hair.

The Toni fad had just hit town when I began work at Garvin's, and Gladys had given herself two with great success. Her hair looked every bit as good after the Toni as it had when done the old way in a beauty shop. She was eager to spread her expertise among us.

Crystal refused to participate on religious grounds. Permanent waves were an assault on nature and a sign of vanity. Me? I was eager to try the Toni. My stubbornly straight, fine hair was impossible to do anything with.

Gladys arranged for me to come home with her after work to do the deed. I could stay overnight and go from there to work next morning. Gladys' parents were away for a few days, so we'd have the place to ourselves.

We feasted on beans and hot dogs for supper and then adjourned to the bathroom to get on with the Toni wave. The bathroom was large and impressive with gleaming white porcelain fixtures and a shower at one end of the tub. On the shower curtain brightly colored fish swam between clumps of coral. Deep blue linoleum covered the floor. Thick padding beneath it made it luxuriously soft and springy to step on.

Gladys opened the Toni Wave packet and mixed the ingredients according to the instructions enclosed. When combined, the chemicals reeked every bit as much as the ones in the beauty shop, so we kept all the bathroom windows open. Gladys swabbed my hair with the stuff and then expertly rolled it up for me in tight little pin curls.

Timing of the process was critical. For Gladys' thick, luxuriant mane it took an hour, but for my thin, wispy locks forty minutes was suggested.

While I was undergoing this cold cooking, we cleaned up the mess in the bathroom. Gladys, in the one clumsy move I ever saw her make, upset one of the bottles and the remaining chemical spilled out onto the beautiful blue floor. Where it landed, the floor immediately turned brilliant pink. I was horrified. "Your parents'll kill us both!" I gasped.

Gladys just laughed. I was astounded. How could she just laugh? She'd ruined her parents floor!

"Nothing in the world will get that stain out," I said. "They'll raise hell when they see it!"

Gladys laughed even harder at my consternation. "Don't be a goose," she exclaimed when she got her breath back. "They'll know it was just an accident. Wow, look at the color of that pink! It's hilarious!" and she went off into another spasm of laughter.

It was my first encounter with someone who could laugh at disaster. That episode taught me a great deal about survival.

The most immediate fall-out from the Toni Wave, however, was my hair. It started to come out in handfuls after a few days. Gladys regarded my head with what I suspect was alarm, but her first comment was, "The inspectors must have been asleep when that batch of Toni Wave was made."

Being a woman of action, Gladys took things in hand at once and did for me what was probably the best possible thing under the circumstances. She shortened what was left of my hair and instructed me in the fine art of the pin curl. "That'll fluff out your hair and give it body," she said.

She was right. When the dried pin curls were brushed out, the hair loss was hardly noticeable, and I liked the shorter length. It was only a few weeks before the missing hair had grown back in again.

As time went by, watching and listening to Gladys taught me a great deal. I observed her diplomacy with Garvin's clients, her ability to calm troubled waters, and saw her turn the light of her smile onto situations that had been dark and ominous.

Her generosity also extended to telling Crystal and me some of the inside stories of what went on in Garvin's law practice—and in his personal life as well. Crystal and I were only the takers of dictation for routine letters and the makers of boring phone calls to follow up on insurance claims. It was Gladys who took the crucial letters on big cases.

And it was Gladys who every Friday night mailed a fat handwritten envelope that Garvin always handed to her as she left at five.

"That's his weekly love letter to his girlfriend in Boothbay Harbor," Gladys confided to us. "She and her husband have a summer villa next to the Garvins' house there. Every Friday at four o'clock he shuts himself up in his office and writes her ten pages or so. He gives it to me to mail so he won't forget to do it."

Crystal and I looked at each other in mutual shock. A reputable lawyer like Garvin with a handsome wife and three grown children giving his secretary love letters to mail for him?

"Are you kidding?" I asked Gladys.

"Girls," she said, "This is the way the world works. The rich and powerful can do anything they please, and always have. You'd better get used to it."

"Does his wife know?" I asked.

"Who knows what Stella Garvin knows? Not I," said Gladys.

It wasn't many months before I realized that Garvin must know that Gladys had enlightened us about his affair. He did and said things in front of us without embarrassment, obviously not overly concerned with secrecy. Indeed, he seemed to take a certain pride in our knowing that he was a man of the world and made his own rules.

The first example of this occurred when Garvin's wife Stella happened to be passing the office and dropped in on the chance that Garvin was there. He wasn't, but she stayed a few minutes to chat with us. She was a charming woman and we all liked her. While she was there, the afternoon mail arrived. The postman put it on Gladys' desk, as was his habit. A small square box was in among the letters, and to my surprise Mrs. Garvin picked it up, turned it over and over, and proceeded to open it.

I saw Gladys go white and make what I thought was going to be a restraining gesture with her arm, but she stopped before completing it.

Mrs. Garvin calmly took off the outer wrapping paper. The box beneath was gift wrapped, and a card was attached. Mrs. Garvin opened the card and read it. Without the least change of expression, she commented, "Oh, it's a birthday present for Taylor from Mr. and Mrs. McIver. He'll be so pleased." She did not open the box, and left the card beside it.

"Well, nice talking with you girls," she said. "I must be off. Sorry I missed him."

And she was gone.

"Oh, my God," Gladys said. "I should have stopped her—but how? I couldn't just snatch the box out of her hands." She picked up the card and read it to us:

"Happy Birthday my Darling. Wish I could share it with you. Can't wait for our weekend. Yours always, always. Phoebe."

"That's his girlfriend Phoebe McIver," Gladys said.

A few minutes later Garvin returned to the office. Gladys told him at once what had happened.

"I'm sorry, Mr. Garvin. I just didn't know how to stop her," she said.

We watched as Garvin picked up the card and read it. He looked up and smirked at us, obviously delighted at the message. He showed not the slightest sign of consternation.

"It's a habit of Stella's to check my mail," he said. "Don't worry about it, Gladys." He picked up the box and took it and the card into his office.

Much later, Phoebe McIver had occasion to visit Augusta and came by the office. She lived up to our expectations: Dark, sultry, beautifully dressed, delicately scented, and with a subtly sensual air. Presumably she was expected, as Garvin came out before Gladys even had time to announce her and ushered her into his office. Half an hour later he ushered her out, their eyes meeting in a long, langorous look as they shook hands at the office door.

Garvin turned back with a smug look and glanced at us.

"Not bad, Mr. Garvin!" I said. I didn't intend to say it—it simply came out because I knew in my gut it was what he wanted. I was right. He winked at me like a fellow conspirator.

"Old lecher," I thought as I watched his retreating back. Gladys and Crystal suppressed giggles with difficulty.

I think Gladys relished enlightening me and Crystal about the ways of the world, especially de-mythologizing the rich for us. When Garvin asked me to attend a luncheon conference with him at the Augusta House to take notes on the proceedings, I worried that my ignornace of etiquette would be my downfall. "Don't worry your head about that," Gladys said. "Just watch them. They eat like pigs, and drink like them too."

Drink was one of Crystal's bugaboos. A strictly religious girl brought up in one of the fringe Protestant sects, she could not reconcile her principles with Taylor Garvin's stand on prohibition. In Maine local options were in force. Each town voted on whether to be "Wet" or "Dry." Taylor Garvin worked hard to make sure Augusta remained "Wet."

Crystal, with more zeal than sense, shyly but persistently tried to make him see the error of his ways. At first he was amused at this, but now Gladys warned Crystal that she was beginning to irritate him—so she'd better knock it off. She couldn't afford to lose her job, so she agreed, reluctantly, to drop it. For the time being. I'd already convinced her that it was hopeless to continue trying to help me find God.

Unfortunately, she didn't stick to her resolve. It was an election year, and as campaigning on alcohol legislation got under way, she could contain herself no longer. Again, she approached Taylor Garvin about his immortal, but immoral, soul. She spoke to him about this in the main office area, near the door, and in such a low tone that neither Gladys nor I caught her exact words, though the import was clear.

Garvin stared at her for a moment, then said, "Come into my office please, Miss Bronson."

As their backs disappeared through the door, Gladys looked at me and said, "I reckon she's had it."

"Really, Gladys? Would he fire her?"

"Peggy, he told me if she ever said another word to him about alcohol, she'd be out."

She was. By the end of the afternoon, Crystal had cleaned out her desk and gone.

91. Latin

By the close of my sophomore year, I'd become increasingly aware of a lack in my high school education. I was becoming restless, dissatisfied and hungry for information other than shorthand, typing and filing. I was sure more interesting things were available in the academic course, though I had little idea what they were. I knew foreign languages were taught there, and I overheard someone say they liked ancient history, which I thought must be about stone-age man.

The only foreign language I'd ever heard was the French-Canadian spoken by some of my classmates. Most French-Canadian children went to parochial primary schools, but now that I was in high school, a sizeable proportion of our commercial course was French-Canadian. I couldn't understand a word but *oui* and *non*, and wished I knew enough to try and speak French with them.

During the last week before summer vacation I went to the office and asked if there was any way I could take either French or ancient history as an extra subject in the fall. Miss Cooper checked my schedule and said no. My commercial classes conflicted with both.

"If you're seriously interested in taking French, why don't you go talk with Miss Peacock, the French teacher. Perhaps she could help you. She occasonally does outside tutoring."

Miss Peacock didn't have time to tutor me, but she lent me a first year French book to take home over the summer and read through.

"Perhaps you can get a feel for the language and then take it in a later year," she suggested.

I took the book home and read the rules of grammar and pronunciation and the vocabularies. It was both enlightening and frustrating. I learned a lot of words I had no idea how to pronounce, and none of them seemed to have any relation to what came out of the mouths of my French classmates.

That fall, after my first summer at Garvin's, I went back to school as a junior. I decided to try again to see if I couldn't somehow fit French into my schedule. Maybe Miss Cooper had made a mistake. I went to the office the first day of school, and luckily found Mr. Macomber behind the counter. I told him of my desire to take French and about the frustrations of my summer struggle with the textbook. He checked the schedules and confirmed that there was indeed a conflict.

"Have you thought about taking Latin?" he asked.

"No," I said. "Isn't that called a 'dead language' because no one speaks it any more?" I was remembering my conversation years before with Mrs. Lee about the names of body parts which came from Greek and Latin.

Mr. Macomber smiled. "That's what some people call it," he said, "but it's anything but dead. It's the basis for French, Spanish and Italian, and it has made a profound contribution to English. If you have a general interest in languages and how they evolve, Latin would do you more good than French."

That word "evolve." It resonated in my head. It smacked of both the development of life and of history. I hadn't thought of languages evolving or having a history.

"I note," said Mr. Macomber, "that you have a study period at the time that one of the first-year Latin classes meets. If you felt it wouldn't interfere with doing your homework, you could give up a study period and take Latin."

"Yes," I said, "I'd like that."

I had some extra study periods that year, and my hours at Taylor Garvin's would be considerably less than my hours at McGraths' had been.

Mr. Macomber's suggestion opened up a whole new world of meaning and gave me an ongoing love of language. I had not imagined how different in all aspects another language would be—the declensions of nouns and the forms of the verbs, the backward way the sentences were put together, how adjectives changed forms with the gender of the nouns, that sex and gender were not equivalent. Though difficult at first, these concepts yielded to patience and effort.

To my delight, my teacher was Mrs. Weaver, whom I'd had for English the year before. She taught with great energy and imagination and made Latin come alive. She asked us each to make a scrapbook containing all the words derived from Latin that we came across in our general reading.

I began devouring the daily newspaper, cutting out words, sentences, paragraphs and advertisements to use in my scrapbook. I kept seeing Latin derivatives everywhere: on billboards, on movie marquees, in ads, along the road on Burma Shave signs.

The worst upset I had all that winter was when I had collected a large amount of material to paste into my scrapbook. I was working stretched out on the dining room floor near the fireplace, and the cuttings were on a spread-out newspaper, sorted out, arranged, and ready for pasting in. The phone rang, and I left things where they were to go and answer it.

Ma, who had been in her disconnected mode all day, came into the dining room, saw the paper on the floor with the cut up bits on it, decided I couldn't be bothered to pick up after myself, and threw the whole lot into the fire.

I could have killed her. I, who never cried, burst into tears of impotent rage. I had to start the whole thing over again.

An even greater disappointment, however, was that I could not go on to second year Latin because of a conflict of schedules. None of my study periods happened at the right time in my senior year. I was deeply disappointed, but nevertheless the enlightenment I'd gained from my one year of Latin could never be taken away from me.

92. Alta

In spite of my last visit to Rita in Melrose, most of my questions about my mysterious Aunt Alta remained unanswered. The information Rita had given me had no substance, when I came to examine it. All I was really left with was the conviction that something wicked, something forbidden, something unmentionable remained beyond my ken—lurking behind the dark windows of that beautiful old house.

All I'd gotten from my father was "Alta's a strange woman." He would say nothing against her. And nothing more about her.

Ma, when approached, was really past giving a reliable account of anything. She said contemptuously "I never met her," and set her lips hard.

Rita's warning to keep away from Alta guaranteed, of course, that I would do whatever it took to meet my aunt and her son, and Rita should have known it. Come to think of it, maybe she did know. Perhaps I have more to thank her for than I thought.

My cousin Orren would be much older than I, of course, as he had been the son of Alta's early (and only) marriage, and I the daughter of my mother's second, late one. He would be in his late thirties now, and Rita had said he was still a bachelor, living with his mother.

I tried to find out more about Aunt Alta and Orren from Lynde, but he knew even less than I. He couldn't really remember Alta, and only vaguely recalled Orren, with whom he'd played when they were both very young and living in Melrose. At that time whatever had gone wrong in the family had not yet occurred. Lynde and Mother had left Melrose for Chicago when Lynde was five, and he had not seen his aunt or his cousin since. He knew nothing whatever about what had happened. Was not, in fact, even aware that anything had happened until I told him. Our mother had said nothing to him about it, nor had Rita. I couldn't imagine why grown-ups were so tight-lipped with the young.

Come to think of it, if Rita had told Lynde nothing—why had she told me as much as she had?

Unfortunately Lynde, in addition to his ignorance, had a near total lack of interest in the details of other people's lives, and no desire whatever to rake up past trouble.

"Forget it," he said.

My chance to meet Alta came quite unexpectedly the fall when I was seventeen. Gracie had been invited to Boston for the weekend to see a friend. She didn't want to make the four-hour drive alone, and asked if I'd like to go with her. I couldn't believe my luck, and agreed at once. I was keen for any chance to get out of Augusta.

365

"Gracie," I asked her, "could we possibly go through Melrose on the way? I've got an aunt and a cousin there I've never met, and I'd love to drop in and see what they're like. We wouldn't stay long."

"Sure," said Gracie. "That'd be fun."

I had to slake my curiosity. If Alta and Orren were there, we'd find them!

We reached Melrose early in the afternoon. I wasn't sure of Alta's address, even though I'd visited the site with Rita. All I could recall was that it was on the corner of Grove and Lebanon Streets. We found a public telephone in a drug store, and looked up "Walsh." There were several of them, but only one, A. E. Walsh, was on Lebanon Street. This was easier than I'd thought. We asked the pharmacist for directions, and he told us that the intersection of Grove and Lebanon Streets was only a block away.

I recognized the house as soon as I saw it. Narrow white clapboarding, roof sloping nearly to the ground in the rear. We parked beside it and got out of the car. As we walked up the path to the door, I noted that the windows were leaded and set with small squares of glass of irregular thickness. These showed the various hues of violet characteristic of glass which has counted centuries.

The sign near the front door still proclaimed "Joseph Lynde House, built 1702." So at last I had tracked Alta down! I felt utterly brazen. No Aunt Alta was going to frighten me. "Come on, Gracie," I said, "Let's ring the bell."

We went up the steps, and I rang. There was a long pause, then we heard footsteps. The door was opened by a woman of quite imposing height. Her dark green velvet dress fell in soft folds from its yoke, and was held in at the waist by a jewelled belt. Her hair was greying chestnut and fluffy around a long, rectangular face. She must have been in her sixties, but could easily have passed for ten years younger. Her eyes were over-large, set far apart, and slatey blue, flecked with green. Her left lid flickered ever so slightly. She looked at me inquiringly.

"Are you Mrs. Alta Walsh?" I asked.

"I am Alta Lynde. My husband's name was Walsh."

"I'm your sister Bess's daughter, Brenda. I was passing through town, and since we've never met I thought I'd come by. I hope it's not inconvenient?"

The slate-blue eyes seemed to darken and the pupils diminished in size.

"Bess's daughter. Well!" Her sharp glance took me in with care and precision. "You have Bess's eyes," she said. At least that was one thing upon which everyone seemed to agree.

"This is my friend Grace Lee," I said.

Alta nodded. "Will you come in?"

We entered a small hallway with doors opening off and a stair straight ahead. The hall was half-panelled in dark wood, with the widest boards I'd ever seen. The floor boards were wider still, and decorated with curious repeating designs in black, partly obscured by hand-made scatter rugs in traditional patterns, some hooked, others braided. A wall hanging of two peacocks and the portrait of a young woman in nineteenth century dress adorned the walls. The carpet on the stair had obviously been hand-crafted for this particular staircase.

Alta said nothing, but her penetrating eyes seemed to see through me to my bones. Her look suggested that it was I who should speak. Not knowing what else to say, I commented,

"You have a beautiful house. I see by the plaque outside that it was built in 1702. I never dreamed the family came here so early!"

My comment relaxed her stare and loosened her tongue.

"Oh, much earlier than that," she said. "The original settler came in 1631, eleven years after the Mayflower. He was Thomas Lynde, great-grandfather of the Joseph Lynde who built this house. The first Lynde house, which Thomas built in 1638, was just a low farmhouse with a cellar and ground floor and a shallow loft above."

"Is that house still standing?" I asked.

"No, that burned down in the early 1700's. There's an interesting story attached to it. One particularly severe winter during a long blizzard the house was completely buried in snow. Relatives and neighbors came to the rescue on snowshoes and passed food down the chimney to keep them going till they could be dug out. That's why this house was built high, so the upper windows would always be clear of the snow. And the long slope on the roof at the back allows easy slide-off—of people and of snow."

This information was so unusual and unexpected that I was quite carried away with it. I assumed Alta's lecture on the house was only a prelude to what would be a longer visit, so I not only listened with rapt attention, but asked for more:

"I was noticing the designs on the hall floor," I said. "I've never seen anything like them."

"Stenciling. Very rare. Only two or three other examples of stenciled floors remain in New England. And the boards themselves have quite a history. When this house was built, a law was in force prohibiting the cutting of trees more than one and a half feet in diameter. If you measure these boards you'll see that some are quite illegal—over two feet in width. Since you're interested I'll give you this pamphlet."

Alta removed a folded piece of paper from a pile on the entry table and handed it to me.

"This was put out by the Historical Society and gives some details of the house and the family. I keep some here in the hall for interested visitors."

"Oh, thank you," I said as she handed it to me.

"I noticed you looking at the stair carpet," she went on.

367

She was right. It fascinated me. It had been designed so that the portions covering the treads were in an irregular pattern of roughly parallel lines of varied and subtle coloring. The portions that covered the risers formed a sequence of scenes and emblems. The topmost scene was a recognizable portrayal of Alta's house.

"I've never seen anything like it, Aunt Alta," I said. "That scene at the top with the house in it—that's this house, isn't it?".

"Yes, indeed. And on the panel below it is the family coat of arms, below that the horse and plow my father used when I was a child."

"Who made the carpet, Aunt Alta?"

"I did. I designed and worked it myself, incorporating family history and personal history. The panel below the horse and plow is a ship of the type that brought our ancestor Thomas to Massachusetts. The dog with the spiked collar was a family pet. The heraldic badges are of early settlers who intermarried with the Lyndes."

Alta did not mention the tombstone with no name on it shown on the very bottom panel, and I felt it was perhaps better not to ask.

"It's fascinating," I said. "It must have taken you years to work it. And you designed it yourself!"

"Oh, yes. And all these rugs as well, and the wall hangings. The idea of a stair runner isn't original, it's an old New England tradition, but the designs are, of course, unique to each family."

"And the portrait?"

"That was done by our ancestor Hannah Lynde, who was an artist. It is presumably a portrait of someone in the family: She has the Lynde nose and dimple in her chin. I inherited the Lynde artistic ability. Those pieces of china on the hall table were painted by me."

The china was exquisite: a set of small covered dishes decorated with bachelor's buttons of several shades of blue on a subtly changing background. The covers of the dishes were edged in gold. Aunt Alta was obviously very talented.

"Well, it was nice of you to call in," she said, her tone changing abruptly.

The change was so sudden I was startled. Did she want us to leave? We'd hardly got there, and all we'd done was talk about the house. My chance to find out more about Mother and to meet my cousin Orren was evaporating before my eyes. Gracie and I exchanged surprised glances.

Alta drew herself up to her full regal height. Clearly the interview was drawing to a close. And we hadn't even been asked into the living room!

Desperate to remain longer, I said:

"Is my cousin Orren at home? I've always wanted to meet him."

Alta's brows lowered slightly and the slate-blue eyes again darkened. She hesitated. Then: "I'll go and see." She disappeared up her hand-made stair carpet, and was gone at least five minutes. This we put to good use, examining everything in the hall in minute detail, and even stretching our necks through the open living-room and study doors, which only whetted our desire to see more.

I heard Alta returning above, and we quickly went back to the middle of the hallway.

"Orren has locked himself into the bathroom," she said as she descended. "He won't come out." The information was matter-of-fact, her face showed no sign of emotion.

I was struck dumb. How does one reply to something like that? She obviously desired our presence no longer, so we took our leave as politely as our astonishment would allow.

As soon as we were in the car, Gracie and I exploded into laughter. "Why in heaven's name would your cousin lock himself in the bathroom?" she asked as soon as she could speak.

"More likely Alta locked him in," I gasped.

"If that isn't the funniest thing I've ever seen, Peggy! She didn't ask one thing about you, or about your Ma and Pa, or what you were doing, or how you managed to find her! She never even asked us to sit down. It's incredible!"

"I guess Aunt Rita was right," I said. "The woman is crackers!"

It was only after we'd driven off and were several miles further on our way to Boston that I realized I'd left behind the pamphlet Aunt Alta had given me. I'd put it down on the hall table to examine one of the bits of china while she was upstairs, and hadn't had the wit to pick it up again. I cursed myself, but neither dared to go back for it nor wanted to further delay Gracie.

It wasn't so much the loss of the pamphlet that chagrinned me—it was acute teenage embarrassment. My aunt would at best think me a fool; at worst, rude and callous. Then I realized how ridiculous I was being. My stupidity in leaving the pamphlet couldn't hold a candle to my aunt's strange behavior.

93. Stovetop Coffee

As Ma sank further into senility, she became unable to cope with cooking. Burned food and forgotten meals became common. Pa and I, neither of whom knew how to cook, took over. Though Aunt Grace had shown me in early childhood how to make pies, turnovers and omelettes, she became ill before she could take my culinary education further. Ma had shown me nothing in that line. She hadn't the patience or the energy left to train me. She had a reputation in the neighborhood of being an excellent cook, and I remembered her wonderful baking-powder biscuits, breads, raised rolls, shortcakes, fricassees, stews and roasts—but they'd been things of the past for quite a while. In spite of her expertise, I suspect she'd always hated cooking. Certainly, convincing Ma not to cook now was not difficult.

Pa's stomach had been bothering him for some time. The result, I'm sure, of the New England farm habit of keeping the used coffee grounds hot in a pan on the back of the stove and just adding water as needed. Waste not, want not. The local doctors warned their patients about this, as they did about smoking. Said poisons leached out from coffee grounds and attacked the lining of the stomach. Almost guaranteed to result in chronic indigestion—and possibly cancer if one didn't die of something else first. But who ever listened to doctors? Most people couldn't afford one to listen to.

Pa's idea of cooking was very much like making coffee—keep the water hot on the back of the stove and add vegetables as needed.

"I can't chew tough vegetables, not with my teeth," he said. "If they disintegrate in the water, so much the better, it makes a nice nourishing brew that I can drink."

Of course the vitamins were killed before we got to ingest them, and the salts from the metal pan leached out into the fluid and did who knows what damage. But we didn't know that. How ignorant we were.

Luckily I didn't drink coffee, and I got one meal a day at the high school cafeteria during the week. That and drinking lots of milk and enjoying raw or nearly raw vegetables in summer saved me. I was a lazy cook, and impatient for quick results. If I gathered fresh vegetables for supper, I just threw them into boiling water and fished them out as soon as the fork would penetrate. Pa told me to just leave his in to get soft.

"I wish you'd get those teeth out, Pa," I said. "I know you hate the idea of getting used to false teeth, but at least you could chew with them."

He just shook his head. "Too much money."

Pa faded almost as fast as Ma. He got thinner, sicker, less mentally able to cope.   Bedevilled by Ma's continual irrational diatribes, he'd retreat to the woodshed or sleep in his rocking chair in the kitchen with his cap pulled over his eyes. He used a lot of handkerchiefs, snuffling and barking from the long-term effects of cigarettes, and from the whiskey.

Ever since I could remember, everyone at the farm had always seemed to be suffering from continuous colds, even Ma, Grace, and Edith—the non-smoking females. Probably suffering from the effects of inhaling the smoke from Pa's, Fred's and Barton's endless self-rolled fags. And from the bacteria and viruses spread around by washing the endless piles of phlegmy handkerchiefs with no attempt at sterilization.

From the time of Barton's death onward there had been continuous illness: First Grace's, and then Ma's and Pa's, repeating endlessly, alternately or together. Pa's stint at the shipyard in Bath had nearly killed him and was followed by an even longer stint in bed. Both before and during that, and afterwards, Ma was never well. The deaths of Grace and Barton had nearly killed her. She was consumed by exhaustion, grief, hopelessness and the wish to die.

Physically strong and basically healthy, she could have lived to be a hundred in better circumstances. Instead, she told me she'd never wanted to reach seventy—to grow decrepit and senile and unable to cope with all the never-ending problems and trials of her life. She'd had enough and too much of that already, but the all-too-stubborn flesh—which had been made for better things—was too strong to let her go, despite the dissolution of her mind. In spite of our efforts to get other food into her, she was eating only tea and toast, and that with difficulty.

I was angry at everyone and everything, sick of living with illness and impending death, tired of feeling guilty that we were in this predicament and being told by Mrs. Cony that I was the one who would have to get us out of it.

My friendship with Kay and the Lees and my easy successes at high school and on the job sustained me, but there seemed to be nothing to look ahead to but illness and death.

Ma might live another ten or fifteen years. By then it would be too late. At thirty no one would want me, and as far as I could see, marriage to a good man was the only road I was likely to find to a bearable life. After the initial challenge and fun of learning typing and shorthand, I was beginning to realize I didn't want to spend my life at it, yet it was all I was being trained for.

All the faults for which I thought I had forgiven Ma came back to obsess me. I could no longer admit to myself that I still loved her, it was too painful. She had deceived me, betrayed me, embarrassed me, hated my mother. And Ma would go on forever. There was no escape.

94. The Seventeenth Summer

"It's not fun anymore, Kay."

"What's not fun any more?"

"Shorthand. Typing."

"Why not?"

"It was only fun as long as I was learning—when it was still a challenge. But now that I've found out how to do everything and have to do it over and over again all the time at work, it's become maddening."

"I thought you liked working at Garvin's."

"Oh, at first I did. For the first six months it was wonderful, even though I was scared to death of making mistakes. I found out I could take dictation from an absent-minded employer who is completely ungrammatical and never says quite what he means. I could get it all down verbatim and then make a proper letter out of it. It was fun keeping a check on the mail, and on who comes in and out. It's still fun finding out what kind of trouble the clients are in to make them need a lawyer. And phoning up people to snoop for the insurance company."

"So what's the matter, Peggy? I don't understand."

"It's the ever-lasting shorthand and typing. It's deadly. And legal documents are deadly—written to be as obscure as possible so you need a lawyer to figure them out. I get so bored, Kay, especially on bright sunny days when I'd rather be back haying at the Lees. I keep making stupid mistakes because I can't keep my mind on what I'm doing. I could never spend my life at it, Kay, never!"

"But what else could you do?"

"I don't know. But something. Anything."

"You'd get sick of that, too."

"Not if it was a job I was doing for the love of it—like writing or painting or playing an instrument."

"Oh, don't be silly. Only brilliant people with a lot of talent and money and free time can be writers or painters or musicians."

"Kay, don't you want to do anything but be a secretary?"

"Well—I wanted to be an opera singer once. But Daddy couldn't afford to send me for lessons. I don't think about it any more. I'll be perfectly happy being a secretary. As long as I do a good job that I can take pride in."

"But never doing anything for yourself? Always for some man who's getting rich and eating like a pig and sailing around in his yacht and enjoying his summer home and his mistress while you go home to your parents and go to a movie on the weekend and maybe a concert once a month if some visiting orchestra comes to town? Never going anywhere or seeing anything new?"

Kay shook her head in disbelief. "Gosh, you're hard to please, Peg!"

"Yes, I am hard to please! I want to see Europe. I want to speak French. I want to go to China. And climb mountains, and see pyramids and learn everything! I want to do it all, Kay. We've each got only one life. Don't you realize it? We couldn't do it all if we had a thousand years, and we've got only one lifetime!"

"I can save my money and travel on my vacations."

"Two weeks a year? It takes two weeks to get to some of the places I want to see, let alone see them and come back again. And you couldn't afford the fare on a secretary's salary."

"You're not going to be very happy, Peg. You're too discontented with what you've got."

"Are you contented with what you've got—honestly?"

372

Kay thought a moment. "Well, no, I'm not. But it's not going to help me one bit to fret about what I can't have. My father is never going to be rich, and neither am I. And neither are you. Anyway, you couldn't leave your Ma and Pa."

"If it wasn't for that, you know what I'd do? I'd go to Boston and get a job after I get out of high school. We could go together, Kay. Share an apartment. Explore the city, go to concerts, meet interesting people, go to dances. And after we'd "done" Boston for a couple of years we could do the same in New York or San Francisco. Or maybe we could join the Diplomatic Service and see the world!"

Kay smiled and shook her head. "You're a dreamer, Peggy. Where do you think we'd get the money for the train fare to Boston, let alone a month's rent for an apartment before we even started looking for a job?"

"We'd save up."

"How much money have you ever been able to save up?"

I didn't answer. It was clear that whatever I suggested, Kay would say it couldn't be done. But it could be done. Somehow, if one cared enough and worked hard enough one could find a way out.

Not long after that conversation with Kay, I wrote a story about a girl who lost control at her place of work and flailed her fellow employees with a broom. The men in white coats came and took her away.

Her brother came to see her in the insane asylum and found her in a straight jacket.

"Why have they put you into this?" he asked.

"Because I broke a mop over the nurse's head," the girl replied.

"Why are you like this? Why?" he asked, shocked and shaking at her behavior.

"Because I can't get out," she screamed—"because wherever I am, I can't get out."

Then I had the dream. I was in an old house with a group of people I didn't know. It was night and we were frightened because the house was haunted, and the ghost was dangerous. We tried never to be alone, always to move about the house with at least one other person because we didn't know where the ghost was, or how it would attack. One of the people in the house was a young girl in a pale yellow chiffon dress with a full skirt. Her hair was dark, and in it she wore a band of yellow roses.

An elderly grey-haired woman had the room next to mine—a strange woman who spoke to no one, and whom nobody knew.

The house was laid out just like the farmhouse. I'm sure it was the farmhouse, though it didn't seem to be my home. I can't remember all the scenes in this dream, but everyone grew increasingly frightened. The next-to-

373

last scene occurred at night. I was trying to make my way down the dark stairs to find something precious that I had lost. I was alone and terrified, but somehow my predicament resolved itself and I was back in my bedroom safely. I "awakened" (still in my dream) to the screaming of the old woman in the room next door. In the dim light I saw the girl in yellow come out of the woman's room. She had a knife in her hand. I knew at once that the old woman was dead. The girl in yellow was the evil ghost, and she had killed her.

Then I really awoke. I was in my own bedroom at the farm. It was morning, and sunlight was streaming through the window, making a yellow rectangle of light on the bedroom floor—the same color as the ghost's yellow dress, as if she'd dropped a piece of it when she left. Outside, the day was warm and beautiful.

With the force of revelation the meaning of the dream came upon me. The old woman in the dream was Ma, and if I stayed in the same house with her much longer I would kill her.

95. The Way Out

With the passing of summer and the return to school, some of my anger left me. Since I couldn't take second year Latin, Mr. Macomber suggested I peruse the academic course syllabus and choose any extra subject I wished, as long as it fit into my schedule.

An art class coincided with one of my study periods, so I chose that. It was a small class of six girls, and we spent the fall term trying to do quick portraits of one another in pencil or pastel. Then we did self portraits using mirrors. I loved that class, and came away from it each week happy and excited. It relieved to some extent the boredom of my other classes.

At the beginning of December, Mr. Macomber announced that the following week the entire senior class, all courses, would be given examinations conducted by Boston University. The examinations would last three days and would test our abilities, aptitudes and general knowledge. We couldn't study for these examinations, but it was extremely important that we attend. No excuses were valid except serious illness.

This sounded interesting. I'd like to know what my aptitudes were. I didn't worry about the exams, and the following week when I took them, they seemed easy. I'd never had exams like them before. The questions were contained in a printed booklet. Each of us was given one, and an answer sheet. For every question, the answer sheet gave five possible answers with five matching slots. Using a special pencil, we had to fill in the slot that corresponded to the correct answer. The completed answer sheets were to be taken to Boston and run through a special machine that would grade our answers automatically. We'd be told how we did after the Christmas vacation.

When we returned to school in early January, Mr. Macomber announced at morning assembly that the following week a man from Boston University would be at the high school from Monday through Friday. He would see each member of the senior class and discuss with us the results of the tests. Our home room teacher would give us our appointment times, and we should report to the office ten minutes early.

My appointment was the last one on the last day, scheduled for 1:00. I got there at 12:50 as instructed, and waited. At 1:30 Miss Cooper told me things were running behind and I'd have to wait a little longer. At quarter of two she allowed me to phone Taylor Garvin's office to say I'd be late.

It was 2:15 before I was called in. A pleasant-looking gray-haired man ushered me in and introduced himself. He indicated a chair to me and seated himself behind the desk.

"I'm sorry to have kept you waiting for so long, Peggy," he said, "but I left you till last because I wanted plenty of time to talk with you, and things got a bit behind."

"That's all right," I said.

"I'm happy to tell you that you did extremely well in the examinations. Your verbal and mathematical abilities are very high, and you also show high mechanical aptitude."

I was surprised, and showed it. "But I've never had any math," I protested. "Only bookkeeping."

"That doesn't matter," he explained. "The tests do not measure how you have done in your course work, they measure your innate ability. Had you decided to major in mathematics, you would have done very well in it. The same goes for the other things we test for. They are meant to show potential."

"I see."

"Were you planning to go to college, Peggy?"

"No. There isn't enough money."

"Would you like to go?"

"Oh, yes," I said. "I'd love to go."

Anywhere, anything to get away from home, I thought.

"Mr. Macomber and your teachers speak very well of you, Peggy, and believe you would make good use of a scholarship. One of the missions of Boston University is to find and educate young people of high intelligence who would not otherwise be able to attend college. Our catchment area includes Maine, which used to be part of Massachusetts. Another mission of Boston University is to serve as wide a spectrum of the community as possible. We wish to make meaningful education available in many directions, and so we have many separate colleges with different emphases and objectives."

He paused, perhaps to allow me to assimilate what he had said, then continued:

"Peggy, if you were granted a scholarship that paid your tuition, would you be able to provide for your own room and board?"

I hesitated, not having any idea how much that would be.

"You could live in the dormitory and eat there for $460 for each academic year," he said.

"I work as a legal stenographer after school and full time in the summer. I could save part of it," I said.

"Well, we can discuss that in more detail later," he said. "The main problem is that instead of taking the academic course you took the commercial course. Why did you do that?"

"My legal guardian insisted on it. She said I had to learn to support myself in case no one wanted to marry me."

An odd look crossed his face, but all he said was, "That's unfortunate. It means you lack sufficient credits to get into Boston University's College of Liberal Arts, which is where you belong. However, I have worked out a compromise to get you there in the end if you're not afraid of some extra work."

"I know how to work hard," I said.

"Good. My suggestion is this: You have already been through four years of an excellent commercial course, and have had on-the-job experience. You could, with no difficulty whatever, be enrolled in the College of Practical Arts and Letters. You could enroll for the absolute minimum number of commercial subjects. You are already thoroughly familiar with the subject matter and could get A grades without further study. At the same time, you could take an overload of such subjects as English Literature, European History, a foreign language—there are various options available to you. Spend your study time on these and get the best grades you can. At the end of two years' study you will have an Associates Degree in Commercial Science and enough credits to transfer to the College of Liberal Arts, where in a further two years you will have the degree of Bachelor of Arts."

I had two simultaneous reactions to this sugggestion: Horror at the thought of ever setting foot in another commercial class, and a great flare of hope as a shining, threadlike path spooled out before me with freedom at the far end.

"Yes," I said. "Yes. I know I could do it."

"All right. Now I'll go over with you the details of how we may be able to manage this and discuss the possible ways of financing it. Then I want you to go home and discuss it with your guardian and the rest of your family. After that, you can write to me and we'll take it from there."

I left the office with a peculiar feeling of detachment. I knew I had put my feet firmly on the path to freedom, even though I didn't dare trust it. Things were never as expected. High school hadn't been, and college might be no better. I was certain the road would be difficult and full of unforeseen trials and hazards. But I was equally certain that I would go, and would shirk none of them.

"You can't possibly go to college, you know."

Louise Cony and I were seated in her living room. She had asked me to come and see her when I phoned about the scholarship. I was surprised—I'd assumed she would come out to the farm so we could discuss it with Pa.

I looked at Mrs. Cony's accusing face. "But why?" I asked. "Lynde went to college, and he almost flunked out of high school. He couldn't even pass English. He told me they let him squeak through because he was so good at math. I've had a straight A average, and I've won a scholarship that will pay my tuition."

"That's beside the point. Lynde is a man, and he didn't have parents to care for. He went to college so he could make a good living and support a wife and children comfortably."

"What if he'd had parents to take care of like I have?"

"Your mother's side of the family was well off. It wouldn't have been a problem. Your Grandfather Lynde would have seen to that."

"My grandfather left me money, Mrs. Cony. That, together with my tuition scholarship, will be enough to get me through college, Pa says."

"Your grandfather left a trust fund for his heirs, and you only get a small amount of interest from that. You must conserve that carefully to help you with any emergencies you may face later if you don't have a husband. What you do with it when you are twenty-one is your business, but meanwhile I'm here to see that you don't spend it foolishly."

"Are you saying I can't go to college because I'm a girl?"

Mrs. Cony looked a bit taken aback at this, hesitated, and tried to side-step the question. "I'm saying that it's your duty to stay with your people."

"And if I were a boy it wouldn't be?"

"That's different. I repeat: Boys must learn to make a good living so they can support their wives, children and also their aging parents."

I thought about the implications of this for a minute. Then: "But if a man is out there earning the money, who takes care of his parents?"

"His wife, of course."

"And who takes care of her parents?"

"Why, she does, unless she has a sister to share it with her."

I saw a succession of traps opening in front of me, extending further and further into the future.

I didn't pursue the conversation any further. Let her think she'd won.

That night I said to Pa, who was, for the moment, sober: "Pa, do you object to my taking up my scholarship and going to college?"

"No, of course not. I want you to go."

"What will you and Ma do when I'm gone?"

"I'll take care of us," said Pa.

"Mrs. Cony says I can't leave you. She won't release the money."

"I'll tell her different," he said. "I'll go see her tomorrow."

I just looked at him. What could he possibly say to change her mind? She had the money, and she had the power to stop me. She was my legal guardian. There was nothing he could do.

I don't know what Pa said to her, but when I got home from Garvin's next day he was waiting for me with a glowing face.

"It's O.K., Peggy. You can go."

I couldn't believe it. "Pa, whatever did you say to her to change her mind?"

His seamed face displayed the broadest grin I'd ever seen on it.

"What she needed to hear," he said.

Louise Cony said nothing more about my not going to college. In fact, she hardly spoke to me at all. She made the necessary financial arrangements to pay my dormitory fee and to give me a small food allowance, but she set her lips in a hard line of disapproval whenever she saw me.

What could Pa have said to her? She didn't have to listen to him. The money was in the bank, and if she hadn't released it I wouldn't have had a penny. I couldn't possibly have gone to Boston—not until I was twenty-one, and by then it would be too late to take up the scholarship.

My gratitude to Pa for what he did was profound. I was sure his powers of persuasion, against his own interests, had saved my sanity.

The day I had dreaded for three years finally came. When we appeared for assembly the Friday morning after the end of Spring vacation, four empty chairs sat waiting on the stage. Mr. Macomber was going to announce the honor parts for graduation. I was sitting next to Kay, of course, and we glanced at each other in apprehension.

Mr. Macomber came out on stage and gave approximately the same speech he'd made each year for this occasion—even to the final quotation:

> To those who hath shall be given,
> and from those who hath not, shall be
> taken away even that which they hath.

Then he put down his Bible and announced: "The Valedictorian of the senior class, with a grade point average for her four years' work of ninety-five and thirty-eight one hundredths percent, is . . .

. . Peggy Shaw."

I was sure I was going to faint, but Kay grabbed me and kissed me. "Congratulations!" she whispered. "Oh, I'm so happy for you!"

"Peggy, will you come up and sit here on the stage, please?" said Mr. Macomber.

Somehow I got my legs under me and covered the distance to the stage in the midst of the clapping, but I can't remember actually doing it. Mr. Macomber shook my hand and I sat down.

"The Salutatorian, with a grade point average for her four years' work, of ninety-four and forty-six one hundredths percent, is . . .

. . Barbara King."

Barbara and Kay had been neck and neck for that second part, and I'd hoped Kay would get it.

Barbara came up, shook Mr. Macomber's hand, and sat down beside me. She looked disappointed. I'd heard she'd set her heart on the Valedictory. I felt a twinge of guilt for depriving her of it.

The awarding of the third honor part stunned me. It went to Paul Wendell, with a grade point average of 91.3 percent. He was a bright boy, but he'd missed out on High Honors several times, putting him out of the running, surely. Kay should have had that part. There must be some mistake.

The fourth part stunned me still further. Ted Leland, with 88.78 percent was announced.

What had happened? Kay and Barbara and I must have all been within a couple of points of each other, and yet Kay had received nothing! Not even a word of congratulation for her high grades!

I was sure there had been a mistake. From the stage I couldn't see Kay's face, and I couldn't find her afterwards, so instead of going to my first class I headed for the High School office. Miss Cooper was behind the counter. I told her what had happened about the honor parts. "I'm sure Mr. Macomber has made a mistake," I said. "Kay Moore should have had that third honor part."

"Why no, of course not," Miss Cooper said. "Every year there are two honor parts for boys and two for girls. It wouldn't be fair to the boys if they never got to give a speech at graduation, would it? It's always been done that way."

"But that's not fair to the girls," I said.

"Well, that's the way it is," she said and turned away to answer the phone.

Obviously there was no point arguing, so I left; but I was beside myself. Did this mean that every spring two girls like Kay who had worked hard and got High Honors for four years were passed over for some boy who might never have received High Honors once? High Honors started at 90 per cent, and Ted didn't even have that!

It had been clear to me right through grammar school that girls knew their lessons better than the boys did. When a girl in eighth grade had mentioned this to our teacher, Miss Perkins had told her it was because girls were willing to work harder than the boys, but that the boys were actually brighter.

This had made me so angry that I had asked another teacher about it: "Why are girls better at their lessons and get higher grades on their report cards than boys, Miss Pratt?"

Miss Pratt used this fact, which she did not deny, as an example of the boys' innate superiority. "The boys have the creative intellect to be leaders," she told me. "They could get high marks if they wished, but they don't want to work that hard, and no woman teacher is going to tell them what to do. And that's the way it should be."

The way it should be? First, I was shocked that a woman teacher could say such a thing. Then I could feel anger rising in me till my head throbbed with it.

When I told Kay of my rage at her being denied an honor part, she just laughed. "It doesn't matter," she said. "That's just the way it's done. I know what my grade point average is, and that's good enough for me." She must have been deeply disappointed, but she certainly didn't let it show.

Mr. Macomber's repeated quotation flashed back into my mind. It had disturbed me both times I had heard it. Now I understood why.

The unfairness of the honor part distribution added to my already increasing resentment of school. It had never been what I'd hoped it would be, and I'd become aware when looking through the academic course syllabus that the well-to-do children in that course, though no brighter than I, had been given opportunities I would never have.

For some time I'd been getting twitchier and twitchier about being assigned homework in transcription class. Transcription was really an extention of the shorthand class, and followed directly after it. We sat at our typewriters and transcribed the material Miss Jackson had dictated to us the hour before. According to the class description it was a two-credit course and required no homework, yet every day we were given an assignment to do for the next day.

With my job at Taylor Garvin's and my extra class in Art, I felt I had plenty to do without homework that should never have been given. On top of that, Mr. Macomber told me I must have extracurricular sessions with the public speaking teacher because I'd be giving the Valedictory at graduation.

An undercurrent about the transcription homework had been circulating around the class for some time, particularly among students like myself who worked after school. Margie mentioned our discomfiture to Miss Jackson, who then gave us a lecture about laziness not belonging in an office. We would do whatever homework she assigned us.

After class, as soon as Miss Jackson left the room, I said to my dispersing classmates, "Let's not do the transcription homework. She can't make us."

Marilyn, with whom I was running neck and neck on shorthand speed and who was ahead of me in typing speed, agreed. "Great idea," she said. "Miss Jackson can't very well complain about us to the Principal, because it's right in the catalogue that there's no homework requirement for the class."

Kay tried to talk us out of it. She liked Miss Jackson and didn't want any trouble. "It won't hurt us to do a little extra," she said.

"You can say that, you don't work after school," I pointed out to her.

Next morning when Miss Jackson asked for our transcription homework no one moved to comply, and no one said a word. We didn't have to. She realized in a flash what we were doing. I'd never seen Jackson so angry.

"Girls, if that homework is not on my desk before you leave the building at 1:30, you will all be graded F for the day and I will report the class to the Principal for insubordination!"

As we left the classroom I saw Kay and two other girls go up and hand Jackson their homework, which they had done "just in case."

"Come on," Marilyn said to me, "We'll get to the Principal first."

Mr. Macomber was out in the front office and spoke with us over the counter. We told him about the strike and why we did it, and explained that it was particularly hard on those of us who worked after school. Mr. Macomber heard us out and thanked us for coming, but did not comment on the rights and wrongs of the matter.

Next day in transcription class, Miss Jackson blew the roof off. Mr. Macomber had seen her and told her she was not to give us transcription homework. She didn't say a word to Marilyn, but she did to me, as if I were the only one who had gone to Macomber. "You are disloyal and a trouble-maker and I am disappointed in you," she said to me. Clearly she was sure I was the ringleader. She was right, of course.

Then she turned to the rest of the class: "This has been the worst senior class I have ever had," she declared. "What's got into you girls? Is it the effects of the war, or what?"

We all sat in numbed silence while she told us off.

The matter was never alluded to again, and there was no more transcription homework.

Instead of feeling upset at the telling off, I was elated, surprised by a sense of my own power to change events.

Kay told me she felt terrible for Miss Jackson, who was such a good teacher and had been so kind and helpful to everyone. "I went up to her afterwards and apologized for all of us," she said.

I wasn't angry with Kay. She was doing what she thought was right, and she hadn't tried to hide it. She was no coward. She was risking everyone else's wrath by doing it, and I respected her for it. Some of the others in the class were not as forgiving.

96. The Valedictory

By the end of my second year with Taylor Garvin, I knew more about him and about the legal profession than I really wanted to. His depressed wife, his extramarital affair, his drunken son and his incredible vanity.

But Taylor Garvin was how the real world worked. It was run by men of power who did what they pleased and hurt whom they pleased and made lots of money in the process. The others got along as best they could in the interstices of the network.

And yet, men like Garvin could be benevolent to those they liked, and do kindnesses that were neither asked for nor expected. When he heard I was going to college, Garvin told me I could work for him during the summers if that would suit me—which of course it did. I was planning to spend the summers with Pa anyway, and would need to work, so fitting back in at Garvin's would be ideal.

Also, Taylor Garvin wrote my valedictory speech.

I'd been at a total loss what to do. The topic Mr. Macomber had assigned me was "Education." No other details. Just "Education." I didn't know anything about "Education." I just thought a lot of what I'd been through the past four years was a waste of my life. Interesting in part while it was being learned, but eventually a dead end. A trap with no way forward. If I let it, it would stick me with typing and taking shorthand for a living for the rest of my life. Latin, art, and parts of the English curriculum were the only things I felt would sustain me in a meaningful way.

I didn't know how to express this in words, I could only feel it in my gut. I did a draft of the speech, but was not happy with it. It was an inarticulate attempt to say what I meant but had no words for. The only phrase I can remember is "We must educate 'Education.'" What I wanted to express was roughly: "Let's teach the teachers to give us hope of getting out of poverty with something to do that won't trap us in routine servitude forever," but I didn't know how to say that.

I was supposed to show the draft to Miss Pickering, a sour, remote elderly teacher of English in the academic course who was to edit the honors speeches. She understood none of it. She made a lot of corrections which were meaningless and beside the point, possibly to avoid telling me I didn't know what I was talking about.

Time was passing and I couldn't bring myself to look at that draft again.

Toward the end of April, Taylor Garvin, full of good will and self-satisfied bluster, asked me what my speech was going to be about and how I was doing on it.

I told him I didn't know a thing about "Education" and that was what I was supposed to write about.

"Ah," said Taylor Garvin. "I often give speeches—to the Rotary Club, the Kiwanis Club, the Elks, and the Law Society. I'll write you a speech."

"Great," I said.

He didn't ask me what slant I'd like him to take, which was probably just as well.

I didn't think he'd really do it, but next morning he brought in a yellow legal pad containing several pages of his inscrutable scrawl and handed it to me. "There it is," he said. "I'm sure you'll find that most suitable."

I thanked him and read it over quickly at my desk. It was about the right length, and included the phrase "In this Atomic Age," which he said education had to live up to.

I typed it up, thought about it and rewrote it in my own words so it wouldn't sound like Taylor Garvin. Then I gave it to Miss Pickering, who read it and passed it back with very minor alterations in sentence structure, and no comments about the content at all. She sent me to rehearse it with Miss Ripley, the teacher of public speaking. I constituted a class of one, once a week for the rest of the year, and Mr. Macomber said I was getting credit for it.

By the time I was sent to Miss Ripley, I was paralytic at the thought of making the speech, so she taught me how to do diaphragmatic breathing to calm my nerves and get oxygen into my blood so I wouldn't pass out on stage.

Nearer the time, Kay, knowing the flat panic I was in, rehearsed me, over and over. On graduation day we went up to Lees' Quarry and rehearsed in the sun and fresh air for the last time, then went down to McGraths' for a sundae. I was chewing Aspergum for a sore throat and was sure I'd lose my voice.

Ma and Pa didn't attend the graduation ceremonies. Ma by that time wouldn't have known where she was or why, and Pa said he couldn't sit still that long without his legs cramping. Gracie offered to go with me and give me a ride in. Dick had something that had to be done in the back field and couldn't come, she said.

Mrs. Cony met us there; and Kay, who had been keeping an eye out for me, joined us. "Where is your brother Dick?" she asked pointedly of Gracie.

"Doing what farmers have to do on summer evenings," Gracie replied.

She and Mrs. Cony went off together to find seats, and Kay and I went to join our classmates.

By then, I'd stopped being scared and was getting angry. I've worked like hell for four years trying to get an education and Gracie and Mrs. Cony are the only ones who'll come to see me graduate, I thought.

I sat through the opening ceremonies and the first three Honors speeches with my head clear and a feeling of seeing everything in extra sharp focus. Then it was my turn.

My anger served me well. I got up there and faced that sea of faces without a tremor and spoke my bit clearly, firmly and with the expression Miss Ripley had drilled into me. Kay, who by now knew the speech as well as I did, told me afterwards that I had left out one short sentence of little significance, but I'm sure that no one but she noticed. Toward the end of the speech, I remembered to step forward and directly address my farewell paragraphs to my fellow graduates, as I'd been coached.

Then it was over and the applause began.

After that the prizes were given. I got the something-or-other prize for the highest grade point average and was voted Most Likely to Succeed. Kay got the prize for Excellence in Commercial Studies, and we were both initiated into the National Honor Society along with a dozen or so others. The general mood during the prize-giving was relaxed and upbeat, and I joked with a boy on my left whom I'd never dared speak to before.

When the ceremonies were over, I went in search of Gracie and Mrs. Cony. As I passed two women who were standing together, I heard one of them say to the other as they looked at me, "Her parents must be so proud of her!" I turned to them and said, "They weren't even here tonight," then swept off before they could recover from their shock.

Ma and Pa had gone to bed when I got home, so I crept upstairs in the dark and cried into my pillow for a while. Exhaustion was a good opiate, however, and I was soon asleep.

Next day I went to clean out my desk and take back my graduation gown the school had provided. Miss Kingsley, a teacher of English for secretarial students who had been particularly nice to me, saw me and congratulated me on my speech.

"Don't congratulate me, congratulate Taylor Garvin, he wrote it," I said.

Shock spread over her face. "But—but why?" she asked.

"Because after four years in the commercial course I have nothing to say about education that is worth saying," I said, and left.

Let that rumble around in the teachers' room for a while, I thought.

97. Fall Fashions, City Water and Delusions

Three weeks before I left for college, Lynde and Winnie came for the weekend on what was to be their last visit to the farm. They'd left their year-old son—Stephen Lynde Russell, born while Lynde was in the Navy—with his grandparents in Jamestown for a few days.

Though they didn't say so, I think they came at that time especially to make sure I had suitable clothes to take with me. The shops were full of fall and winter fashions, and they took me to Chernowsky's because "Winnie just wanted to have a look around."

When we left the store, I had a fall jacket, a raincoat and a stylish warm winter coat in soft moss green with a scarf and gloves to go with it. Also a smart wool dress in plain royal blue which, as Winnie put it, could be "dressed either up or down." My protests because of the expense were unavailing.

During the weekend Pa brought out his plan of the farm showing how it could be divided up into houselots. He told Lynde his plans for doing this if he could talk City Hall into bringing water out.

Lynde and Winnie listened politely, but I could tell Lynde wasn't impressed. Pa'd had a few and sounded like it. Lynde must have thought he was just a deluded old man who figured he could save himself and his family with a bright idea that wasn't so bright and couldn't work.

"They'll put water out here some day," Lynde said to me later, "but not in time to help your father, I'm afraid."

I didn't argue with Lynde, I knew he was right. But I was also sure Pa's idea was perfectly sound. Pa was no dreamer, and I longed to defend him. If City Hall had been willing to cooperate, we would have been all right. But what could I say? Someday, somebody we didn't know would buy the farm and make a packet from this land. Unfortunately, it wouldn't be us.

Part Six: Escape

98. The Boston and Maine

You can't get to Maine by train anymore. The old Boston and Maine run closed in the late fifties, and now you have to fly or go by road. For people like me who don't like to drive, it's kind of sad. It used to be four hours from Boston to Augusta on the train, time to do my college homework, or read the better part of a novel, or write letters, or even write a poem or two. You can't do that on a bus—at least I can't. Makes me queasy.

When I was going to Boston University in the late forties and vacations came, the five or six "Maine-iacs" from our dormitory would go north on the train together, telling yarns and jokes, gossiping about our love lives, and singing songs like

> Coming down from Bangor
> On the Boston train
> After weeks of hunting
> In the woods of Maine

on and on through all the verses. Or we'd take seats in the coaches that had tables so we could play cards: poker, gin rummy, black jack, bridge, canasta.

On one trip home, though, I didn't go with the others. It was a trip that I forgot about for years. I didn't want to remember it. Occasionally, however, one particular scene would flash through my mind, but I'd quickly put it out of my head. It was something I couldn't believe I'd done, and I didn't know why I'd done it.

Part of my first year at Boston University, that which involved family problems at home, was mostly too terrible to remember, and I can't recall much of it. Sometimes I try to dredge it all up again, but only bits of it will come.

For a long time I couldn't even remember what time of year it was on that occasion when I had to go home but didn't want to—nor how it was that I found myself in a room in the Hotel Manger with a man who'd picked me up in North Station.

Finally, however, by the process of elimination, I realized it couldn't have been the three-day Armistice Day break in November. That weekend the dorm had stayed open for those girls who couldn't go home. I'd decided not to go either, because I never wanted to see home again, or what awaited me there. But in the Thursday assembly, just before the long weekend began, I'd heard a voice in my head saying, "You've got to go home, Peggy. You've got to go home." I don't know who or what was speaking, but I knew that something was very wrong and I had no choice but to go.

When I got to the farm I found Pa blotto from drink and Ma, now age 93, wandering out in the back field in the cold without even a sweater on. She didn't know where she was, nor who I was.

I found and threw out the whiskey bottle Pa was working on and pumped him full of black coffee. Then I got on the phone to Mrs. Cony, who was the only one who could do anything about anything. She came out to the farm at once and sized things up. She never wasted time—she arranged for Ma to go into a nursing home next day. It was run by somebody she knew would be kind to Ma.

She told Pa he'd just have to sell off more of the farm for house lots to pay for it.

"Isn't there any way I can use some of my inheritance money to help pay the nursing home?" I asked. "Can't I borrow from it and pay it back after I finish college?"

She looked at me scathingly. "No. You know very well, and I've told you repeatedly, you cannot touch that money until you're twenty-one. And a good thing, too. If I hadn't been managing it, you wouldn't have a red cent now. That money is for your well-being and your emergencies, not your family's. But what are you doing in Boston going to college while your people are in this condition? You're a girl, it's your duty to be here taking care of them and earning money for their support."

"Don't, Louise, please don't say things like that to her," said Pa.

She'd said that sort of thing to me all my life which, as she had continually pointed out, was to be one of duty. And until September, when I'd gone off to college in spite of everyone, it had been.

So the Hotel Manger incident couldn't have been that weekend. And it wasn't the long weekend at Thanksgiving, or the two-week Christmas break, either. I left for home with everybody else on those occasions. It was definitely after Ma had gone into the nursing home and Pa was living at the farm all alone, except for his bottle and the dog.

At Thanksgiving and Christmas Pa stayed sober while I was there, and we went every couple of days to see Ma at the nursing home. Sometimes she remembered who we were; sometimes she didn't. On her better days she'd be sitting up in bed against a mound of pillows, and when she saw us she'd look at Pa and beg him, "Take me home, Shirley. Take me home."

"I can't, Ma" he'd say, "I can't," and he'd sit there and cry, and she'd cry too, and so would I. She'd forgotten all about the college business. She thought I was still twelve years old, and living at home with Pa.

Pa never asked me to quit school and come back home. Everyone else did, but he said to me, "Live your life, Peggy, none of this is your fault."

So the vacation I don't want to remember must have been the week-long spring break. That must be right. By then I'd been in college long enough to begin to know the ropes and to find out where the college men went to dance.

I was living at Merlin House, the women's dormitory at 84 St. Botolph Street, which paralleled Huntington Avenue. It was before the various scattered colleges of Boston University all came together at the new campus on the Charles River.

Across the street, at 89 St. Botolph, was a whorehouse. Sometimes sailors with their legs full of rum would get the two buildings confused and come to the dorm. They thought the housemother was the Madam. Sometimes in spring and autumn the girls and the Madam would come out and sit on their front steps in the sun. They'd wave and smile at us, and we'd wave and smile back.

The dorm was in a bad area, and we girls were never allowed out at night unless two or more of us went together, and then only from 9:45 to 10:30 after we had finished the compulsory two-hour evening study period. Then we could go get coffee and a snack around the corner on Huntington Avenue at a place called Syd's.

The dangers so evident to our elders did not seem to perturb us. We thought the whores and the flashers and the drunks were all very funny. None of us admitted to fear of being attacked. In those days the papers weren't filled with stories of rape, murder, dismemberment, necrophilia, harrassment, beatings and abuse. And there was no TV.

Most of us had been shielded from the extremes of human evil. On the farm we never locked a door, and few people in the town nearby did either. At the dorm it was different. We had to sign in and out and had to be let in when we returned by whoever was on the desk. Nevertheless, we took the idea of rape pretty casually. We'd all heard that bit of sophisticated wisdom "If rape is inevitable, you might as well lie back and enjoy it." The Boston Strangler hadn't started operating yet, and we were still safe enough going anywhere in Boston alone in the daytime. We hadn't learned yet to be afraid of men.

It was also a time when most young college girls were still virgins, or if they weren't they didn't tell. If you were a nice girl you never let a boy kiss you on the first date, or even on the second. By the third it was considered okay. No one I knew admitted to ever having been French kissed—that was disgusting. How could you ever let anyone's filthy tongue in your mouth?

At the spring break, as during Christmas vacation, the dorm closed. Most of the girls would leave on Friday, but if that were not possible we could stay on until five p.m. on Saturday. On that particular Friday night only one other girl and I remained along with the housemother and her husband, who had a separate apartment on the third floor. The other girl, Clare, would be leaving first thing in the morning. We went out for an early supper, getting back before dark. I wasn't put off by the idea of staying overnight in the nearly deserted dorm, but Clare was jumpy. Her room was on the ground floor, and several times during the year she or her roommate had been drawn to the window of their room by pebbles thrown up by a flasher who was standing outside exposing himself. It was generally believed in those days that that sort of nut was harmless, all he wanted to do was be looked at—but Clare didn't believe it. I suggested she come up and sleep in the vacant twin bed in my room, which she did with great relief.

I spent most of next day going to museums and walking along the Esplanade beside the Charles River in the early spring sunshine. Then just before five I returned to the dorm, picked up my suitcase and signed out with the housemother. I told her I was catching the 6:30 train to Maine, and she had no reason to doubt me.

I took the subway to North Station and checked my bag, then retraced my route as far as Copley Square. I had a hot pastrami sandwich at Schraffts', then went into the Boston Public Library. I stayed there until eight o'clock, when the Saturday dance at the nearby Y.W.C.A. began. I was in the habit of going to it on Saturday nights if I didn't have a date. I would go with my roommate or with two or three other girls from the dorm. It was ideal. No alcohol was allowed, and it was well chaperoned. Parents couldn't have complained about a thing. We were almost always escorted back to the dorm by likeable lads with cars, who would then suggest we meet again for double dates. Tonight, of course, I went alone, and left alone, which was against dorm rules but who was to know?

The dance wasn't as crowded as usual because of the vacation, but there were the college students who lived locally. The band played the customary tangos, rhumbas, fox trots and waltzes. During the second set, a John-Paul-Jones made sure everyone got to dance. Later they played the game where all the girls throw a shoe into the middle of the floor and all the men scramble to get one. I always wore my black suede pumps with the gold clips on the side because they were easy for the men to match up.

It was an all right dance, but I hadn't met anyone I wanted to leave with when it ended at eleven. The night train for Maine left at 12:45 a.m. and there was nowhere else to go, so I took the subway back to North Station. I got there by 11:30, and had an hour and a quarter to kill before the train left. I was too depressed to read. I wished I could just sleep through the next week and not have to cope with things at home again and remember how hopeless it all was. Yet I couldn't not go home.

I didn't notice the man who sat down on the bench beside me at first. Not until he spoke. "Catching a late train?" he asked. I looked at him. He was middle-aged, and his hair was gray with yellow streaks and a slight curl. His long face had good lines, but it was covered with skin that had started to wattle at the chin line. His mouth was well-formed and slightly bowed. Twenty years ago he might have been handsome, now he looked worn, tired and none too clean. His mouse-colored raincoat hung limply from his shoulders.

"Yes," I said. There seemed no reason not to talk with him. I was sick of my solitude and of my thoughts. Perhaps he was as depressed as I was. I told him I was a college student going home to Maine for a week.

"Got time for a drink before your train goes?" he asked. My better judgment had vanished long since, and the idea appealed to me. His offer seemed kind, not dangerous. I glanced at my watch. It was 11:40.

"Just a quick one, maybe. My train goes at quarter to one. What about yours?"

"Plenty of time," he said. "There's a bar just across the street."

By the time we got there, however, the barman was just locking up. "You closing early?" asked my companion, irritated.

"Yeah," said the barman, offering no explanation.

"Too bad," I said. "I need a drink."

"Come on, then, we'll get one at the Manger."

"Okay. Will their bar still be open by the time we get there?"

"If not they'll sell us a bottle and let us take it to one of the rooms."

I'd never been in a hotel in my life, except the Augusta House when Lynde or Taylor Garvin took me there for dinner. I was too ignorant to realize the implications of what he was saying. At the Manger I waited in the lobby while he went up to the desk. He returned with a bottle, two shot glasses and a room key.

"No problem," he said. "Standard procedure."

We went up in the elevator to the fifth floor, found the room, and he unlocked the door. It was a bare, brown room with a dresser, table, two chairs and a bed. He put the two shot glasses on the table, opened the bottle and poured some out. He handed me a glass. "To our respective journeys," he said, and drained his glass. I did the same. The whiskey was strong stuff, but I managed not to choke on it. It felt warm and good all the way down.

"Downed like a professional," he said.

We were still standing. He took off his coat and helped me out of mine. Then he took me in his arms, fastened his open mouth onto mine, and tried to lead me over to the bed. In a flash I realized what a total and utter fool I was. I clamped my jaw, kept my lips closed and tried to push him away. His tongue on my lips and cheek was slimy and his breath smelled metallic and sour under the whiskey.

I'd done farm labor for years and was strong for a girl. I very nearly broke away from him. He was clearly surprised at my strength, and stopped trying to kiss me.

"No!" I said to him. "All I wanted was a drink! I've got a train to catch."

I can't imagine what he must have seen in my face, what combination of distress, fear, confusion, anger and shock was playing on it. I felt all those things, but the worst was the shock at my own incredible stupidity.

He held me at arm's length and just looked at me for a moment.   Then, "What in hell is an innocent kid like you doing here with the likes of me in the Hotel Manger in the middle of the night?" he asked. He dropped his arms, turned, picked up the bottle and put it in his left coat pocket. Then he picked up the two shot glasses and put them in his right pocket. He took my hand and said, "Come on, I'll take you to your train."

The night clerk glanced up when we reached the lobby. "We didn't like the room," said my companion. The clerk shrugged and turned back to what he was reading without a word.

Back in the station I got my suitcase out of check, and we found the right track by 12:30. We stood by the engine, talking and drinking the rest of the whiskey. Neither of us mentioned what had happened at the Manger. He spoke of his sister and her kids. It seemed odd that he was part of a family, had ordinary connections and relationships. What would his sister have made of his activities that evening? Did he come to North Station every night looking for women? "Are you married?" I asked. "Not any more," he said. He didn't elaborate.

At twenty to one he walked me down to the passsenger cars, kissed me gently on the cheek, with his mouth closed, and handed up my suitcase as I climbed aboard. By the time I found a seat and looked out the window, he was gone.

The few passengers were mostly young service men, going home on leave, trying to sleep. We ignored one another. I was too addled from the whiskey to read, but too strung up to doze off. It was quarter of five when the train wheezed into Augusta and stood hissing in the dark. Only three or four other people got off. Being Sunday, there would be no bus going past our farm till noon, so I checked my bag and went out into the pre-dawn chill. Water

Street was deserted, and I encountered no one along the quarter mile to the bridge over the Kennebec. I went out onto the bridge and kept walking. The water swirled black and deep below me, but in the sky a barely discernible flush suggested that the world continued to turn. I reached the other end of the bridge and started uphill toward the High School.

Half way up, Spruce Street went off to the right, and I turned onto it. Kay lived at No. 12. I'd go there and wait till time to catch the noon bus. She and her family lived in a duplex, and I went down the side to their entrance. It was locked. So accustomed was I to our farm habits that this possibility had not occurred to me. I went back out to the street and surveyed the front of the house. There was a door on each side of the dividing line of the duplex. The one on my friend's side was locked. I tried the one on the neighbors' side. It came open in my hand. I'd never met the neighbors, never even seen them, but I stepped inside. The door had opened directly into a bedroom. A young man and woman lay profoundly asleep on a big double bed, and never moved as I stepped quietly across the carpet to the door opposite, which was ajar. I slipped out, passed through two other rooms, and found the door that let me out into the common entrance corridor. The door into Kay's half of the house was next to it. It was unlocked, and I went in. I helped myself to milk from the refrigerator, went into the living room and lay down on the couch, fully clothed, pulling my coat over me.

Kay's father discovered me, deeply asleep, when he got up at nine to tend to the furnace. He left me in peace until the rest of the family arose. I told them how I got in and they just laughed. They weren't ones to make a mountain out of things. As far as I know, the neighbors never found out.

I can't remember how I got through that next week. Nothing comes back to me except a visit—and there must have been more than one—to the nursing home. Ma showed no sign that she recognized either Pa or me. She lay staring blankly at the ceiling.

Was that visit the last time I saw her alive? No, that must have been later—in the summer. Why is it so hard to remember? I would have been home that summer, working at Taylor Garvin's again to earn the money for Pa and for school in the fall.

The nursing home called Pa—that was it—said my grandmother was going. When we got there she was lying on her back, breathing hard, and her head kept turning on the pillow, turning, turning. Her eyes were only half closed but she was seeing nothing. Then suddenly her eyes came full open and she looked directly at me. She cried out—not in words, for she was beyond them then. I don't know if it was me that she saw, or if it was Death.

Three days later she lay in Plummer's Funeral home like a life-sized sleeping doll in her dark blue dress and silver hair, surrounded by flowers.

Now the trains don't run to Maine anymore, and the farmhouse where we lived has been torn down and the land covered over with streets and shopping malls. The trains didn't outlast Ma by very long. She died in 1947, and within a dozen years the Boston and Maine Line had closed.

Ma's life encompassed most of that line's existence. She was born in 1854. In 1860 when Lincoln's train came electioneering through Maine, town and countryside turned out to meet it. Ma's parents brought her into town by horse and carriage to see the President. She once told me she remembered the train because she had never seen one before, and it terrified her. She didn't remember Lincoln at all.

It was summer when we buried Ma. Summer when the fresh, warm clods of earth filled her grave, and Pa was with me. His tears mingled with mine and we knew in our common grief what she had meant to us, she who had been Mother to us both.

99. Fifty-three Bridge Street

Deaths come in threes. I'd heard that for years. It had been true in the year of my birth: First, my grandmother Sarah Lynde—two weeks later my grandfather and my mother. Later, it had been first Barton, then Grace, then Marge.

Now Ma was dead, and not long after I returned to Boston University for my second year, Mel Lee died.

His death had been a long time coming. He'd been ill ever since I could remember, yet he had remained the center of his family, much loved, cherished and cared for with cheerfulness and good will. If Mel was the center of the family, Maisie was its heart, and she'd never faltered.

Pa wrote me and I wrote Maisie, clumsily trying to say how sorry I was. Yet Mel's death must have been a great release for her. For them all.

Two deaths.

Who would be next?

I wasn't superstitious, but I was afraid for Pa. All my life my loved ones had been only one step ahead of death.

All the time I was in Boston Pa wrote me a post card a week, always on a Friday—and I wrote him a card a week, too. It was an immutable habit for both of us. You can say a lot on a post card if you write small. Pa couldn't get as much on one as I could. His hands were so shaky he had to hold the right one steady with the left in order to write at all. Every time I went home, Pa would give me a bunch of stamped post cards so I wouldn't forget to write.

So when no post card showed up one Monday morning in April, I was worried, but figured it had probably been held up in the mail. This was toward the end of my second year at Boston University, nine months after Ma had died, and five months after Mel Lee's death. When the post card hadn't come on Tuesday, I knew something was wrong. I walked around the corner to Syd's for change when classes were over, then went down to the college basement where the pay phones were. I asked the operator for a station-to-station call to Augusta Maine 896-W.

After a series of clickings the Augusta operator answered. She tried the line to the farm. Unfamiliar buzzings and cracklings assaulted my ear. "That line has been disconected," the operator said.

I looked at the receiver in my hand in disbelief. How could this be? What had happened? Had Pa been unable to pay the phone bill and got cut off? Wouldn't he have told me?

"Please try 'M' on that line," I said to the operator. That was the Lee's number. Gracie answered.

"It's Peggy," I said. "I just tried to phone Pa and the operator says the phone's been disconnected."

"Your farm's been sold," she said. "Your Pa's moved out."

Stung with shock, I could only try to get my breath for a minute.

"But where is he? Where did he go?"

"I don't know, Peggy. He never said a word to anyone. He'd had the 'For Sale' sign up on the lawn for weeks, and then two days ago a piece of card was pasted over the 'For Sale' which said 'Sold', and we saw strangers in the yard. My mother went over to find out what was happening. One of the men in the yard said he was the new owner and your father had moved out."

"Didn't he leave any message for me?"

"Not with us."

I felt panic rising up from my toes. I don't even remember hanging up the phone. He'd gone—somewhere—where? He hadn't told me. He'd sold our home and hadn't told me! I didn't even know he'd advertised it for sale—I thought he was just selling off house lots as usual.

My people had never told me anything. None of them. And they never would!

Wherever Pa was, was Judy with him? What had happened to my dog?

My head hummed. I realized that I wasn't breathing and gulped air. Who would know? Who would he have told?

Louise Cony's face condensed out of the chaos that was my brain. I got her number from Information.

"Oh, you've finally got around to calling, have you?"

So she knew! The bitch! Why hadn't she let me know?

394

"Where is he?"

"In an apartment at 53 Bridge Street—second floor. A real estate friend of mine had one vacant. He sold the farm and the buyer wanted to go in at once to start working on the property. Your father phoned me to see if I knew of anything for rent in town."

"Is he all right?"

"Hadn't you better come home and see?" Her voice rang with contempt and, it seemed to me, with triumph at my obvious discomfiture.

I told the housemother there was a family emergency and got on the 6:30 p.m. train.

It was 10:30 when I reached Augusta. Bridge Street was what its name implied, going straight up the hill from the bridge on the west side of the Kennebec. I was out of breath by the time I'd climbed up to No. 53. It, and all the houses surrounding it, were slum property. Mrs. Cony had said second floor. No lights were on. I went around to the side where a rickety wooden stair went up the outside of the house. The door at the top was locked. It had a small glass pane in the top half, but it was too dark to see anything inside. He must be in bed. I heard a yelp on the other side of the door followed by snuffling and whining—it was Judy! She knew who it was. At least she was safe.

I knocked on the door. No answer. I banged on it. "Pa!" I shouted. I was looking for something with which to break the glass panel, when I heard a rustling inside and a light switched on. I saw Pa's silhouette appear on the other side of the door. He opened it, and Judy burst out to greet me. Pa and I hugged and kissed each other. He reeked of whiskey, but he wasn't drunk.

"I was sound asleep," he said. "You been knocking long?"

"I was getting ready to break the door down. Why the hell didn't you tell me you'd sold the farm and moved out?"

"Everything happened so fast I didn't have time. What with passing the papers, I was late getting a post card off to you. You won't have got it yet."

"This place is a dump! What are you doing here? What's that awful sour smell?"

"The place is filthy, haven't had the chance to clean it yet. It's cheap and it was available. It'll do till I can find something to buy that I can afford."

"Did you get a decent price for the farm?"

"Not bad. The house and land brought me $9,000. I orta be able to get a small place in town for $5,000 and still have enough to eat on for a while."

I began to relax. Things weren't as bad as I'd feared. He'd got enough for the farm to keep him going till I was out of college, with luck. We might be all right yet.

I spent the rest of the week and the weekend helping him clean up the place. By Sunday we'd got rid of the smell. The apartment had a tiny kitchen with an old cast-iron wood stove, a chipped enamelled sink sitting on pipe legs, an ancient refrigerator, and a table and two chairs Pa'd brought from the farm. Our old Morris chair adorned the living room, along with our couch, which served as Pa's bed. My room was off the living room, a tiny box about eight by eight. A large mattress lay on the floor, almost covering it. No bathroom, just a closet with a toilet, no room for a wash basin.

"It's not fancy, but we can camp out here this summer okay," Pa said. "You'll be home in six weeks, Peggy. I'm countin' the days."

He was right, we could cope here for a while if we had to.

The biggest problem was the cockroaches. They were everywhere, lying low, but they'd come out at the smell of food. You could see them just on the edge of your vision, and hear a scuttling that was easy to miss, that you thought at first you were imagining. They'd come out at night, too. If you got up and turned on the light, you'd hear them scrambling for cover.

I went to the hardware store and bought a pair of rubber gloves, some sponges and a bug bomb—the kind with a button on the top that you press open with your thumb. I made sure everything edible was in the refrigerator where it wouldn't get tainted.

"Come on, Pa, you and I and Judy are going to a movie," I said. "Gene Autry's at the Capitol. You haven't been to a movie for a hundred years."

"I can't sit still that long," he complained.

"We'll get you an aisle seat so you can walk up and down every fifteen minutes if you need to. Or take Judy out and walk her around the block and come back in again. Keep your ticket stub and they'll let you in."

I got Pa and Judy out the door and downstairs, then went back, put the bug bomb down in the middle of the living room, jammed the sprayer button open with a match stick, and ran for the door.

By the time we got back from the movie and re-entered the apartment, the bomb had exhausted itself. We threw open the windows and the door and aired out thoroughly. Then I put on the rubber gloves and went around with broom, brush and dustpan and swept up the piles of dead roaches that were all over the floor and on every surface, and flushed them down the toilet. I washed the floor and sponged off all the surfaces so we wouldn't get the bomb poison on our hands and feet, being especially careful in the kitchen so it wouldn't contaminate our food.

By the time I left for Boston on Sunday, Pa was settled in as clean and comfortable as possible in that hovel. By the time I was back in the summer, maybe he'd have found something else. If not, we'd get along somehow. At least we'd be together.

The third death wasn't Pa after all. It was Judge Cony. It happened suddenly, no warning. Got up in the morning looking forward to an important case on the circuit court. Ate a good breakfast. Rose from the table. Dropped dead. Pa wrote me a special extra post card about it. Ridiculously, the first thing I thought of was Rena. Had she stabbed him through the heart?

The next card Pa sent told me that Louise Cony had gone into a severe depression and was in the Augusta State Hospital. Cony's death had been followed a week later by that of her beloved old dog Pete. It had been too much.

When I came back for the summer at the end of May, Pa had not found a house to buy which suited him. "What's on the market in the range I can afford has got so much wrong with it I wouldn't dare touch it. I gotta wait till the right one comes up, Peggy. I'll know it when I see it."

It seemed odd not being on the farm, not having the fields and woods around me, nor seeing the Lees every day. I went out to see them occasionally—usually on a Saturday afternoon after finishing at Garvin's. Just to make contact, see how they were, what they were doing. I'd go out on the bus, maybe walk back, careful to leave before they'd feel obliged to ask me for supper.

They always greeted me kindly, and if anything was going on that I could lend a hand with, I'd do it. But I wasn't part of it anymore. Dick, Gracie and Maisie were their usual open, friendly selves, but I was no longer involved in their lives.

Gracie was still working in Judge Cony's office, helping Louise Cony settle up his affairs. Mrs. Cony had come out of her depression, converted to the Catholic faith and taken up her life again. By the end of the summer, Gracie took a job in Washington, D. C., for a Maine Congressman who had been one of Judge Cony's friends. She was escaping, as I had. Her departure left a second gaping void at the heart of the Lee family, though Maisie and Dick did not allude to this.

Everything, everything was changing, even with the horses on the farm. My old friend Mollie had died—at age thirty, something of a record for a horse—and Dick had sold Ricky and bought a tractor. He was raising a Morgan filly to be a saddle horse and thinking seriously about giving up the milk route and breeding horses for a living.

It wasn't the same farm anymore. I hated the tractor on sight—hard, metallic, unyielding, cold. There was something foreign and threatening about it, as if it held the power to negate everything I had held dear. Farming as I'd known it had vanished with Mollie and Ricky. I seemed to be looking at everything through glass, not really touching things. I'd gone elsewhere and couldn't come back.

And yet because of Pa and my love for him, I had to come back. I lived in two worlds now, and wasn't really part of either. Luckily, my ability to keep my mind in compartments served me well now. When in Boston I threw myself totally into that life, with all its opening doors. But when I came home, I became part of that context again, and dealt with it however I could.

I retreated further and further behind my wall of glass and didn't go out to the Lees as often. The farm I had known was gone forever. Except for coming back temporarily to see Pa, the only direction I could go now was forward.

100. The Unravelling

"Pa, I know it wasn't easy living with Ma. There wasn't much you could do but try and dull the pain. But now that she's gone, will you stop drinking?"

I asked him this not long after my summer at 53 Bridge Street began. He looked up at me with rheumy eyes suddenly filled with tears. "I'll try," he said. "Bart tried to stop and he couldn't. My father tried and he couldn't. But I'll do what I can."

"Promise me you'll *stop*, Pa."

He hesitated for a long moment, staring down into the corner of the room. I figured he didn't want to make me a promise that he couldn't keep. Then he looked up at me and said:

"I promise. Let's make a pledge. Neither one of us will have another drink unless we have it together."

"Done," I said. "I pledge."

He was sober for the rest of the summer. I kept my nose on the alert for the smell of whiskey and checked all the cupboards, closets and drawers regularly for hidden bottles, but smelt nothing and found nothing.

I was encouraged, but I hardly dared hope. He could keep it up while I was at home, perhaps, but what about after I left in the fall? I'd long since stopped believing in happy endings.

The summer was unexpectedly wonderful. It wasn't so much that I had come home, but that he had come home. Now that he was sober, he became again the Pa I'd known when I was little, before Ma's mind had gone. He'd been away in a dimension I couldn't enter, but now he'd come back. My gut feeling, which I'd almost forgotten, that we knew each other completely and sufficiently without words, returned.

And now came an added bonus. Maybe it was the absense of Ma that freed his tongue, or perhaps it was just that I was now old enough to talk with him as an adult. Slowly he began to express himself more. Never much at a time, just bits here and there.

Like the fact that after Bart died he'd asked Edith to marry him, and she had refused.

I couldn't imagine why Pa would want to marry Edith, but the full implications did not hit me until later. Edith could have been my stepmother! It would have been a disaster. Sometimes I hated Ma, but I also loved her. I never could have loved Edith.

Another time Pa told me a bit about Bart, too:

"He was odd from the time he was a child, and the kids at school picked on him. Kids'll pick on anyone who's different. Bart had a hernia, so he wasn't supposed to go in for rough and tumble stuff. I had to keep an eye on him at school to make sure he didn't get beaten up. But he was a charmer with the ladies when he got older. Big man, handsome, loved to dance. Used to go to the dances in New Sweden and the girls loved him."

"Pa, I remember Ma telling me a story about a Ouija board. She and some other people were playing with one, and Bart was late coming home. Ma asked the Ouija where Bart was, and it spelled out, "He's in Sweden, dancing with the foolish Swedes.""

"Yeah," said Pa. "I remember that."

"Why did he take to drink, Pa?"

"I dunno. But nothing we could do would stop him. By the time he was forty he was drinking anything he could get his hands on. Even vanilla extract—that's what they call 'baking a cake' in Maine. Then he fell off a ladder and hurt his back. It was very painful and he took a long time to mend. He got hooked on the morphine they prescribed for the pain."

"What did Edith do?"

"She and the rest of us managed to talk him into going into the state mental hospital where they had a unit for drug addicts. He was in there five months. They got him off the morphine, but when he got out he went right back on the bottle. Then one night he must have got onto some funny stuff, because he went on a rampage and tried to burn down a store in Hallowell. Instead of putting him in jail, they put him back into the lunatic asylum. That's why he wasn't around much for a while. He was in and out of there. When they let him out, he'd just go back at the drink again. It finally killed him."

So now I knew. Poor Edith. No wonder she decided to stay single.

Pa totally spoiled me that summer. He'd always be up before me, and when he came to wake me at 7:30, my eggs, bacon, grapefruit and coffee would be ready for me. When I got home from work ravening at 5:30, supper was on the table, and he insisted on doing the dishes afterwards. My presence clearly made him a happy man, and he couldn't do enough for me. I felt ashamed and guilty that I'd soon be deserting him again.

As September approached, my eagerness to return to school, to my new friends and the wonders of Boston was tempered by a feeling of dread. Would Pa's determination evaporate as soon as my train pulled out?

"Are you sure you'll be all right after I leave?" I asked him the last evening I was home. He knew exactly what I meant.

"We pledged," he reminded me.

In October he wrote me that Louise Cony had told him about a house. It was on Cony Street (which was named for Judge Cony's grandfather) and was just across from the high school. The house was coming on the market. The elderly owner's wife had died after a long illness, and he was moving in with one of his daughters. The place hadn't been kept up, and the price was low. Pa had looked it over and decided to buy it. The money from the sale of the farm would cover it, with a few thousand left over. There was an apartment upstairs that was already rented, and a room in back of that with a separate entrance suitable for letting to a single person.

Pa said he could live on the rent and do the repairs himself when he felt up to it.

The weight of the world rose from my shoulders and floated off. He might still be able to cope on his own for a while, and fixing up the house would give him something to do. Again I was reprieved.

When I came back for the November 11th long weekend, the sale had gone through and he'd moved in. It was a long rectangular Victorian style house with elegant proportions, painted white with dark grey shutters. The ceilings were not as high as in the farmhouse, so it would be easier to heat. A small front porch meant we could sit outside on hot evenings. Pa had the downstairs back bedroom off the kitchen, and he'd made up the front bedroom ready for me when I got back.

In spite of its relative decrepitude, the house was a comfortable place and had been left basically clean by the former owner. I met the upstairs tenants, a quiet middle-aged couple with strict religious beliefs, who, Pa said, always paid their rent on the day it was due. I figured we were lucky.

Our "bathroom" was a dark little closet-like room with a toilet and wash basin but no tub. The house had been built as a one-family dwelling, and the proper bathroom put in at that time was now part of the upstairs apartment.

The first time I went into our bathroom, I got a fright. I didn't know where the light switch was but, though it was near evening, some light was filtering in through a small clerestory window. I sat down on the toilet in the half-light. A faint glow caused me to glance into the dark corner to my left. A shining figure was standing there.

"Jesus Christ!" I said.

That's who it turned out to be. Pa told me when I came out that the former owner's wife had died of cancer. She was a deeply religious woman and kept a luminescent statue of Jesus in the bathroom to comfort her.

Over the weekend I did some fine tuning on the cleaning and helped Pa cover the grey and faded wallpaper in the living room with a fresh coat of ivory emulsion. I enjoyed decorating. It would be fun fixing the place up bit by bit as we could.

By the time I returned for Thanksgiving, he'd rented the back room on the top floor to Bertha, a young woman who had a motorcycling boyfriend. She was a warm and friendly girl, and he'd given her kitchen privileges. Since she was cooking for herself and frequently for the boyfriend too, she'd started cooking for Pa as well. He chipped in on the ingredients and ate with them.

I was delighted that he'd found a place where he could feel comfortable and cared for. He was smiling more, carrying himself better, had more energy. Yet, though I felt an immediate warmth and kinship for Bertha, I was (and this shocked me) acutely jealous. She had taken my role of daughter and I felt almost redundant. This was nonsense, of course and I knew it, but the feeling was there.

My reprieve lasted that year and part of the next. As far as I know, Pa didn't drink during that time. Certainly he was sober every time I came home.

In May I got my Associate's Degree in Commercial Science. As predicted, the overload of classes I'd taken had enabled me to make up my academic deficiencies, and Boston University had accepted me into the College of Liberal Arts to study for a Bachelor's Degree. I'd be able to enroll in the fall as a junior.

As I had attained a two-year degree, I was no longer eligible for scholarship aid. However, now that Pa had a home and a small but stable income, I could save most of my summer wages toward my tuition. And in January I'd be twenty-one and in control of my own finances. Louise Cony could do nothing to stop me now. I could spend my meager inheritance on tuition and books if it pleased me to do so.

I thought Pa was basically okay and I could get on with my life. He was still terribly thin, but he'd always been thin. We'd eaten well while I was home. Once I was gone he would start eating with Bertha again, so he wouldn't be neglecting himself, as I knew he'd done the last year or two at the farm and at Bridge Street.

The fall term began well. I was now old enough to escape from dorm life, and found a small apartment in Cambridge at a rent I could afford. I was able to select classes that appealed to me fitted into the core curriculum I would need to graduate: Music Appreciation, Anthropology, Physics, Philosophy, and German.

I'd also signed on at the Boston University Employment Service for part-time work to help pay my expenses. They sent me out to several short-term jobs, then got me regular work typing up research papers for Dr. Robert Lincoln, a physician in Medford who was working on a treatment for cancer. The research interested me immediately. I'd had no experience with medical terminology, but its Latin and Greek roots intrigued me, and I was learning fast.

As usual, I went home on all the long weekends and holidays. Pa seemed to be doing well and was looking happy. He'd regained some of his strength and was getting on well with repairing and redecorating the house. He was still very thin, but I thought that this was normal for him.

In the one-week spring vacation, however, I noted that he was having difficulty eating. I'd tried many times before to get him to a dentist, but he'd always refused, insisted his teeth didn't bother him. Ostensibly he feared the inevitable expense, but more, I suspect, the trauma of having his teeth out. This time, however, I insisted. I made the appointment and went with him to the examination and the extraction.

The dentist was appalled at the condition of Pa's mouth. "Good God," he said to me after the examination, "why has he let this go so long?"

"No money," I said.

"He's got a mouthful of abscessed teeth. I don't know why the pain hasn't killed him! I can only guess that he's one of those rare individuals who don't register pain. I'll get them out, but it won't be easy. It'll be at least a month before his mouth will heal so I can fit teeth. Meanwhile, get some good food into him. He's not in good shape." He went over with me the combination of tinned baby foods, cereals and freshly pureed vegetables, meat, fruits and vitamin pills that would be suitable.

I took Pa back to Cambridge to stay in my apartment while he recuperated. I wanted to keep an eye on him. I'd take him back in a month for the fitting. From what the dentist told me, I was beginning to see the diet he'd been getting from Bertha hadn't been doing him much good. I was also beginning to see that my own knowledge of what constituted a balanced diet was less than minimal. I had, in my ignorance, not been doing what I should for him.

In Cambridge, I got him going on the new regimen. He seemed to be thriving on this and certainly seemed happy. Now that Ma was gone, he always seemed to be happy when we were together. Love and regular doses of good food were paying off. He'd be all right now.

He wasn't, of course. Everything had been going wrong for too long, been let go too long because of no money and ignorance.

Three weeks after he came to Cambridge, he got a pain in his abdomen. It started late one afternoon, beginning slowly. He took a couple of aspirins. They didn't help. By bedtime I could tell he was worse, though he didn't say so. I didn't have a doctor of my own, so I phoned Dr. Lincoln and told him Pa's symptoms. Lincoln couldn't come himself, but gave me the number to ring for the doctor on call that night. "Use it if he feels worse," he said, "otherwise I'll see him in the morning."

Pa went to bed and managed to get to sleep. I checked on him before I turned in an hour later, and all was quiet. About one a.m. he called out to me and I went in. He'd got up and gotten a pail and was sitting on the bed, vomiting into it. "Pain's worse," he said.

I got on the phone. The doctor on call said he'd come right away. He didn't. Forty-five minutes later I phoned him again. He apologized. He'd fallen back to sleep. He was there ten minutes later.

Pa was lying on the bed in his pajamas. The doctor asked him to remove them. I'd never seen Pa naked before, and I'm sure he was as excruciatingly embarrassed as I, but I didn't want to leave him. Pa's skin was dull white, his penis lying flaccid between his legs. The doctor spotted at once a lump in his groin.

"What's this, Dad?" he asked, putting a finger on it.

Pa winced. "Hernia, he said. "Had it for years."

I didn't even know what a hernia was, and never having seen Pa undressed before, I'd never even known he had a lump.

"Why have you had it for years, man? Why didn't you get it fixed?"

"Couldn't afford it. It's never bothered me."

"Well, it's bothering you now. Hernias should never be let go. They can strangulate, and then you're in big trouble. They're perfectly treatable if you get them early."

The doctor turned to me. "Tomorrow morning I want you to take him to his regular doctor and get something done about this. Meanwhile, I'll give him something to ease the pain and help him sleep."

I lay down on the living room couch so I could hear the minute Pa moved or made a sound. I knew things were bad and didn't even try to sleep.

I waited till seven a.m. when I figured Dr. Lincoln should be up and phoned him.

"Don't fool around with this," he said. "A strangulated hernia is serious, especially at your father's age. Call a cab and take him to the Emergency Department at Cambridge City Hospital immediately. They'll have to see him, and it'll save time."

I got Pa up and dressed and into the cab and we were at Cambridge City in twenty minutes. He looked terrible and couldn't stop vomiting. We took a pail in the cab, and I tried to stop gagging.

Fortunately there was no one ahead of us at that time in the morning, and they took him in at once. They asked me about his symptoms. I told them all I knew, and they told me not to worry.

They prodded his hernia and made the same comments as the doctor on call had: Why had he let it go so long?—It should have been fixed years ago.

They said they'd need to do tests, I should come back tomorrow. Not to worry, they'd take good care of him.

Next day when I went back he was sitting on the edge of the bed puking dark brown liquid into a pan. He said the doctors were doing tests—"As if what I got ain't obvious," he said.

What could I say? What could I do? He kept puking up the brown stuff. I didn't have the guts to stay long. I was never good with people vomiting. The fruit I'd brought him wasn't going to do him any good, obviously.

As I went out through the swinging double doors, someone who looked like a doctor was going in. "He can't stop throwing up," I said, pointing to Pa.

"Oh, are you the daughter?" he asked. "I'd like a word with you, if I may." He took me to his office.

"Your father's hernia will have to be taken care of surgically, and soon," he said. "But he's not in good condition. He's skin and bones. What's he been doing to himself?"

"He hasn't been well for years," I said. "Heart trouble, bad circulation in his legs. He started drinking heavily when I was about twelve, but as far as I know he's been on the wagon for nearly two years. But his teeth were so bad he was having trouble eating. He had them out three weeks ago, and he's waiting for his gums to heal before he gets fitted for teeth."

"He's one of the worse cases of malnutrition I've seen," the doctor said. "If there's a history of alcoholism, that's a contributing factor. Alcohol prevents proper absorption of food. Bad teeth and poor diet have no doubt contributed as well. And now he's dehydrated from the vomiting. I'm having a drip set up for him. We must get some fluid and protein and sugar into him before we can operate. But we can't wait too long. I'll put him on the list for surgery tomorrow morning."

Malnutrition? Pa was always skinny, ever since I could remember, but I hadn't thought it was malnutrition. The farm diet was good until we had to give up the vegetable garden. I thought malnutrition only happened in places like Ethiopia.

My face must have shown what I was feeling, for the doctor said, "Try not to worry. We're watching him carefully. We'll do our best for him. By the time you come for afternoon visiting hours tomorrow, we should know how he's doing."

I tried to believe him. What else could I have done? Or asked? Or said? I still don't know.

I went back to the ward to see Pa.

"They'll get you fixed up tomorrow," I reassured him. "The doctor said you're on the list for surgery in the morning. I'll come see you in the afternoon. You'll be okay."

As I said it, I knew I didn't believe it. Worse, I didn't think he did either. I kissed him and left, a feeling of hopelessness pressing down on me. I knew Pa was slipping away from me. What could anyone do for him now? It was too late. It was the last time I saw him alive.

I didn't have morning classes next day and was scheduled to go to Medford to type for Dr. Lincoln. Then I'd cut my afternoon classes and see Pa. I'd left Lincoln's number at the hospital in case they wanted to reach me.

The phone call came mid-morning. It was the hospital. Come as soon as possible, they said.

I knew why they'd called, and I didn't want to go. I didn't hurry. I finished the letter I was typing, made a phone call the boss had asked me to make.

My delay upset Marguerite, Dr. Lincoln's nurse. "Aren't you going?" she asked. "You'd better get over there. They don't call you for nothing."

But I couldn't do anything about death. And I knew he was dead.

And so it had come to this.

At the hospital the doctor confirmed what I already knew. They hadn't even had time to operate.

All I could feel then was relief.

Epilogue

101. Knitting it Back Together

It's taken years to knit the past back together, to try and develop a more complete pattern.

After Ma had gone to the nursing home, when I found Pa at 53 Bridge Street, nothing remained but the clothes on his back and what furniture would fit into those three miserable rooms. I'd come out of my childhood with only the clothes on my back, too, and my life had moved south to Boston. I knew I'd never live permanently in Maine again.

Pa had kept Mother's photograph on him till he died. Then I put it beside my own photograph of her at fourteen and kept them where I could see them wherever I went, through many moves and changes.

After Pa's death, I sold the house on Cony Street and didn't go back to Augusta for years. Kay had moved to Boston, so I had no need to return to visit her, and the thought of seeing our old farm was too painful to contemplate, even to visit the Lees. The past was over and I wanted to forget it. I thought then that it wasn't important. I was free at last, and my mind was already projected into the future. The people I'd met in Boston were the ones who counted, who knew and liked what I was becoming, who had chosen me as a friend or as a colleague without questioning where I'd come from.

To one of these people, my part-time employer Dr. Robert Lincoln, I owe my career in science. He recognized and encouraged my interest in scientific research, and showed me the route to take in getting the necessary training to make it my career.

I didn't allow myself to think about the loss of our farm and its contents until the late 1960s when I was doing research in Scotland, married to an Englishman, and mother of two children. Maisie Lee sent me a letter across the sea to tell me about the destruction of our farmhouse and outbuildings. The owner, she said, after finally getting the City of Augusta to have a water main run out to the Manchester line, had sold off all the remaining lots of land at a handsome profit, as Pa had once hoped to do. Then he tore down everything that remained standing except Bart's bungalow.

Our barn came down first, Maisie said, then the connecting sheds and stable, then the house. The last recognizable thing visible was the front staircase with its elegant banister. The floors at top and bottom had collapsed, and for a few minutes the naked staircase stood alone amidst the rubble, leading upward toward open sky. Maisie said their view across the street was strange and bleak without our house and buildings. Hard to get used to.

It was only then, faced with that finality, that I allowed myself to think about my past and all the things I still didn't know or understand about it. The questions came slowly, but once they'd come they wouldn't go away.

What had happened to the contents of our home when Pa sold out? The antique marble-topped table and the cedar chests antique dealers had been trying to buy from Ma for years? The corner what-nots and their knick-knacks, the china closet with Ma's collection of pitchers, the picture in the living room of a younger Ma in her best organdie dress, and the larger one of my great-grandmother Eliza in its oval wooden frame which hung in the dining room? And the one of Lynde at age three, dressed in a little Victorian dress as was the custom then for boys under five? Where had Ma's old album of tintypes gone, the one that she would never talk about? What about the kitchen utensils—some of them very old, like the blue-and-white buttermilk-ware pitcher, the Willow-ware plates, the wooden churn?

And what had happened to my piano?

Had Pa auctioned everything off—just left it to the auctioneer to get rid of? Or had he tried to sort it out? Agonized and cried over it? While he was alive, I never could bring myself to ask him. I didn't want to upset him over what he'd done. There was no way to undo it. I just wanted to forget.

And Mother's trunk! I hadn't thought about it since before I went away to college. Blanked it out completely. Her trunk, filled with her manuscripts, the letters I never understood, and pictures of people never identified. How could I have forgotten? Why hadn't I taken its contents to Rita for explanation and identification? She would have known, of course, but now Rita was dead and beyond all questioning. I was filled with consternation and guilt that I hadn't done all I could to save that trunk and its contents.

407

What had Pa done with it? Burnt it and everything in it? Why hadn't he saved it for me? Ma was dead and gone and could no longer have been hurt by it, or have stopped him. I couldn't bring myself to be angry with him. He'd probably done all he could in an impossibly difficult situation. I should have been there to help him.

Suddenly I knew what had happened. Of course! The trunk had been sitting at the edge of the east gable when I had found it, and would be seen by anyone who bothered to flash a light in there. But I'd moved it—dragged it over the planking around the finished room—pushed it around the external corner of the room, under the slope of the roof, where it couldn't be seen from the catwalk. Pa wouldn't have known where to find it even if he'd remembered it. The trunk would have gone down with the house and been taken to a dump someplace where demolished houses go. The anonymous end of a dead woman's trunk, the pictures, letters and manuscripts scattered and lost.

It was my own fault. Pa wasn't to blame after all.

After Pa's death it was thirty years before I went back and saw the Nissan salesroom planted over the site where our farm house had been. By then, Maisie was dead, and Dick and his wife Ruth, and Gracie, now retired, had moved further out to a farm in Manchester at the end of a dirt road. They were raising Morgan horses and selling vegetables and Ruth's home-made fruit pies. They'd be safe there from the blight spreading outward from Augusta.

Across the road from the site of our farm, a shopping mall called "Lee Farm Mall' sprawled over what had been the Lees' land, obliterating that part of my past, too.

In writing this account of my childhood and adolescence in Maine, I've come to realize that everything I am I owe to those kind, gentle people who brought me up, and to my mother who, if she couldn't give me her care, gave me her genes.

Pa, Ma and Aunt Grace tried to live good lives against all odds, and gave me what love and shelter they could. In a fairer world they would not have fallen into the twin traps of poverty and illness.

I like to think Pa gave me his gentleness, his honesty and his basic fairness. His willingness to do unto others as he would be done by. His love of nature and his respect and care for living things. He taught me the art of communication without words, with both humans and animals. Most important, he let me know by example that some men can be trusted.

Ma shared with Pa in giving me a love of animals and of nature. But she also gave me her guts and will: If at first you don't succeed, try, try again. Never-give-up stubborn grit. Grin and bear it, even this shall pass away. Waste not, want not. I like to think she gave me her generosity too, her willingness to share what she had with those who had less.

And her tolerance. Yes, tolerance. She *was* a tolerant woman, except about my mother, Fred and Kay. They were too close to home, and symbolic to her of betrayal. She blamed my mother for tempting Pa into "betrayal" of Florence, Fred for "betrayal" of Grace, and Kay for abetting my desire to grow up and leave.

Having herself been abandoned for another woman, Ma had become obsessed by the notion of betrayal. Faithfulness was sacred to her, till death and even after. The depth of her continued hatred for her husband Henry Meader Shaw suggests that she had loved and been faithful to him in spite of his alcoholism, and that his desertion had been the unkindest cut of all.

And what did my mother give me? I'll never know for certain, but I like to think that her genes underlie the workings of my brain, and that I got my enthusiasm, energy and love of life from her. And her intelligence, her skepticism, and her iconoclasm. Her spirit, her verve and her creative abilities. Where did my love of writing, painting and music come from if not from her, and from her mother Sarah Lynde?

I've had three compulsions all my life: To write, to play music, and to paint. It's largely through these that I know my mother. My brain is wired up the same way hers was. These three talents have been her enduring legacy, my pleasure and my salvation.

102. The Making of a Scientist

I went to work for Dr. Robert E. Lincoln of Medford, Masssachusetts, as a part-time stenographer while studying for a liberal arts degree. Within a few months of meeting him, I'd decided to take a leave of absence from Boston University to help him full time in his fight for approval of a controversial cancer treatment. I divided my time between working at his clinic and reading up on anatomy, physiology and microbiology at the Harvard Medical School Library.

When I left Dr. Lincoln's employ three years later to return to Boston University, it was with the determination to become a scientist and do medical research.

When I asked Dr. Lincoln if he thought I could get into medical school, he looked at me sadly and shook his head.

"You haven't a hope in hell of getting into medical school. You've got the brains all right, but you're female, and there's a quota for women. Since you haven't been dedicated to doing medicine since you were six, you wouldn't stand a chance. You haven't had the background in science, and you're already twenty-four, with another two years of undergraduate college to do. They'd just laugh at you."

He then went on to encourage me to switch to a biology major and aim for a Ph.D. "If you're serious about wanting to do research, that's the way to go. The Ph.D's the union card. With that, you can get in the back door of some medical research establishment and go as far as your brains and tenacity will take you."

I liked this idea. I'd learned on the farm that if you want something and seemingly impossible obstacles are preventing you from getting it, there's always a way around them, over them, under them or through them, if you can only find it.

This unlikely switch in the direction of my life after I met Dr. Lincoln is not as unlikely as it seems. It arose naturally out of my childhood experiences on the farm.

From my first realization at five that I had been deceived about my mother, I was determined to learn the truth. The continued deceptions about the nature of Barton's and Grace's deaths added to this. My investigative powers were sparked early on when I discovered that if I asked the same question of five different people I would get five different answers. This meant I had to decide which answer to believe, or to look further for one. I learned never to accept at face value anything I was told. People can be honestly mistaken, innocent or ignorant. They can also be purposely misleading if it suits them.

I also discovered quite early that unanimity of opinion does not always indicate truth. Thus the skeptical frame of mind necessary for a scientist had already been established by the time I left home. So had the work ethic. I'd found out that the best way to get not only the needed results but also approval, respect—and to some extent affection—was to work hard.

From the time I first entered Boston University at eighteen, it took another eighteen years and many interruptions before I got that Ph.D. This led to a National Institutes of Health Post-doctoral Fellowship to work for two years at the University of Dundee Medical School in Scotland. That commitment unexpectedly lasted twenty years, resulting in my publishing thirty-eight research papers in scientific journals, and two editions of a textbook in my field of inquiry.

As Dr. Lincoln had predicted, I had found a back door, and all I had to do was walk through it.

410

Appendix

This Appendix summarizes a few of the many bits of information that bear on the story but did not fit chronologically into the memoir. Most of this information came to light within the past few years as a result of my determined search for family records.

It was the right time to do such a search. Some things you can't fully understand till you've had children, grown older and known tragedy as an adult instead of as a child. Only then do certain facts, rumors and suppositions about individuals, places and events start fitting together into some approximation of truth.

Mother's Side of the Family

My mother was my first concern because of the wall of silence Ma erected around her. Her side of the family tree proved not too hard to fill in. In the early 1980's I fulfilled my vow to find my cousin Orren. He and his wife Miriam not only accepted me into the family but gave me their friendship and trust. Between them, they answered some of my questions and pointed the way to finding out more. They told me of a manuscript written in 1930 by Orren's mother (my Aunt Alta). She based it on her own genealogical researches, and a copy was available at the Melrose Public Library. This thirty-page document gave details of our branch of the Lynde family.

In brief, our ancestor, Deacon Thomas Lynde, was born in Dunstable, England, in 1593 or 1594 to a family thought to have emigrated there from Holland. He came to America in 1631 or 1632 and settled in Charlestown, Massachusetts, near where the Bunker Hill monument stands today. He is buried almost in its shadow.

In 1636 Deacon Thomas was granted a large tract of land by the Crown in what is now Melrose (then part of Charlestown), and built the first Lynde house there in 1638 for his son, Ensign Thomas Lynde. Deacon Thomas

Lynde and his descendants were all farmers, and from 1638 on, Lyndes continued to live in Melrose and to be buried there.

Another Lynde, Simon (1624-1684), came to Boston in 1650. His son Benjamin (1666-1745) was Chief Justice of the Province of Massachusetts Bay. He resided in Salem, where both he and his son Benjamin, Jr. were judges of the Superior Court. Family tradition says that Simon Lynde's father Enoch (1585-1636) and Deacon Thomas Lynde were cousins, but I have discovered no written record of this relationship.

Orren Lynde Walsh's wife Miriam had not known my mother, as she and Orren were married after Mother's death. Orren said little about Bess, and gave the impression that he either knew nothing of, or at any rate did not wish to talk about, the feud between his mother and mine. He did mention that Bess had been her father's favorite. I feared I might never learn more about Mother herself than the few facts Rita and Lynde had told me.

Orren died in 1986. In 1993 I visited Miriam who, then in her late eighties and very frail, was still living in the Joseph Lynde house on Lebanon Street. She told me that I was the only one left in the family who had any interest in it. Would I like to have the Lynde family Bible? Would I also like to borrow family pictures from which I could get negatives and prints made? I accepted these offers with the deepest gratitude.

I don't know whether Miriam knew what was contained in the section of the family Bible where the Lynde family births, deaths and marriages were recorded. If she did, she left me to find out for myself.

The records started with the birth of my great-grandfather Warren Lynde in 1799, and ended with the deaths of my mother Bess Lynde and grandfather Henry Lynde on August 14, 1928. My grandmother Sarah Lynde and Alta's husband John Walsh also died in 1928. Not a good year for the Lyndes.

More interesting than the records themselves are the additions made to them in the hand of my Aunt Alta dated 1930, the same year she dated her genealogical manuscript. Alta had written in the margins of the Births and Deaths pages, completely filling them with a venomous attack on her father and my mother:

> A few notes on my father, Henry Lynde & sister, Bess Lynde Shaw—No worse sister or father pretending to be decent ever lived.
>
> My father charged me $3.00 board for Orren when born and I bought the milk & hired some one to tend him & paid my board, John's board & the nurse's board as well as the baby's—Dear Father—It was every cent John earned. He even refused to let me bury John in the family lot at the cemetery & never came to his funeral.

My father was so m[ean] that he wouldn't give me a head of lettuce while it rotte[d] on the ground. The only good recollection I have of hi[m] is my mother taking him by the neck and throwing him o[ut] the bed—he treated her rotten. Never spoke to her for yea[rs] unless someone was present.

Bess Russell Shaw in[flu]enced my father Henry Lynde to leave her the family hom[e] & all in it, writing lies against me & Ren [Frank Warren [Ly]nde, Alta and Bess's brother]. See her [Bess's] own letters[,] my father laying [sic] in my box at Melrose Trust Co[.] [w]ritten in May 1927 from Augusta, Me. My father was [u]nnatural father—a skunk.

My father spent $2800 i[n] [Ju]ne & July [1928] fixing up 391 Pleasant St. for Bess & S[haw] to come & live there. Pa[...] & Bess died 2 weeks before [...] to move in and 2 hours before the auto arrived that h[e] just bought them. God works in curious ways. He judg[ed] [th]em alright!

Shaw told me at their funer[al] soon as they got in the house they were going to restra[...] father but they were willing to accept nearly $4000 [...] man not o.k. Some Christian social worker Bess!

d, Alta Walsh

Next to the entry of Lynde's father's d[eath] [Al]ta had scrawled "a thief," and opposite death entries for both Bess an[d] Lynde she had entered, "Dirty Skunk." She also decorated the ma[...] [e]ntry of my mother and father, Bess and Shirley, with "Two dirty skun[ks...]" [Wa]s "dirty skunk" the only epithet she knew?

Although Alta herself had recorded the ma[...] my mother and father and the death of my mother, she did not record[...]. She appears to have decided that I did not exist.

I asked Miriam about the letters Alta claime[d...] a safe deposit box. She had no knowledge of them, but did tell me a[bout...] [corres]pondence between Alta and the Wyoming Cemetery Director regar[ding the Ly]nde family plot. Miriam, as Orren's widow, was now holder of the[...] arranged for me, as next of kin, to receive copies of these letters.

The letters told me that Alta, to whom control [...] [h]ad passed after her father's death, had refused to let Lynde's first w[ife...] [b]e buried there. Poor Marge was buried alone in another graveyard.

The letters also told me of Alta's attempt to pre[vent...] [o]f my mother in the family plot. Failing that, she refused to have m[y...] [n]ame put on

413

the gravestone. Aunt Rita hired a stone mason to engrave it on the stone against Alta's wishes, without her knowledge.

Pa's Side of the Family

Once I'd partially settled the matter of Mother, my thoughts turned to Pa and Ma, his mother. Though I'd lived the first twenty years of my life with them, I now knew more facts about Mother's people than I did about theirs. All I had to go on were my memories of the few visitors we had when I was a child, and the names of people and places I had heard repeatedly during my childhood in conversations between adults. If anyone explained to me who these people were, I don't recall it. I don't think this was deliberate deception. More likely, I was simply not interested in what they were willing to freely mention in front of me.

First, Ma: What had motivated her? Even now, she continues to elude me.

The following is a patchwork formed of memories, bits of information Ma did give me, correspondence with city clerks, offices of vital statistics, graveyard superintendents and War Records Offices in Washington, DC), and genealogical records found through the Latter Day Saints Family History Center. This information enabled me to locate two second cousins once removed with interest in genealogy, and to visit places in Aroostook County, Maine such as Caribou and Woodland, Presque Isle, and New Sweden—places I heard Ma speak of when I was a child. Town clerks, local librarians and historical societies in those towns were immensely helpful.

Slowly a picture of the younger Ma began to take shape.

Ma—Emma M Pratt, born 1854—was a tough and courageous woman, forged in the War, which began when she was six. Conscription hit the poor hard: she told me the story of a young farmer neighbor with several children who to keep from leaving his family was notified that he must go to war, cut off his left hand with a The wealthy had an easier way: If they could either pay a fee or hire a substitute.

Ma's father Pratt, wasn't conscripted, he volunteered—a decision hard for me to understand, since he was thirty-eight and had a wife and six children. In and his family had made the long, difficult trek over nearly impassable from Oxford County in central Maine to Aroostook County near the Canadian Border. En route they broke their journey in the Molunkus area long enough for Eliza to deliver their sixth child, Henry B Then they continued on to the pioneer township of Lyndon, as Caribou, where they settled on a small farm.

Ar He became the January first, 1864, and was sent to the First District of Colum assistant to the company surgeon in March,

414

and served in this capacity until June 29, when he was declared missing in action. He was captured at Stony Creek, Virginia, July 19, and imprisoned.

The existing records disagree: one lists Artson as a prisoner in the infamous Andersonville Prison, another reports he was in Libby Prison. He was not a strong man, and the wretched prison food and the confinement rapidly eroded his health. He weighed seventy-nine pounds when he was paroled on August 22, and he died thirteen days later on September 4, 1864, in an Annapolis hospital. The death certificate reads "Scorbutus (scurvy) and chronic diarrhea." He was buried in Annapolis, Maryland.

Ma was nine when her father went off to war. Although old enough to remember him clearly, she never mentioned him to me. I learned his first name, Artson, only through the Latter Day Saints, and later through his war records.

I can't imagine what my great-grandmother Eliza must have gone through after Artson's death—six children to raise alone, hard times. I remember Ma speaking often of someone she called "Stover." Who was he? Eliza's lover, husband, platonic dear friend? Ma never mentioned his first name, but I learned later that he was Nathan Stover, born in Lovel, Maine, in 1842. Ma said he made a great deal of her when she was a child, called her "Tola" and admired her long thick blond braids and her tiny waist. He would put his two hands around her waist and marvel because she was so slender that they went all the way around.

When Stover came back from an absence (probably from the War) and saw Ma again he cried out in distress, "Tola, what's happened to your yellow hair?" As often happens with children, her blonde hair had darkened to light brown. Ma said it brought tears to Stover's eyes to find her so changed.

Ma must have found him changed too. Records I discovered show that he lost an arm in the war. The Army surgeon was about to amputate it when they had to flee with the retreating Union Army from the battle of Gains Mill, Virginia, to avoid being taken prisoner or killed. After the retreat, off came his arm. Strangely, Ma never mentioned this, which seems odd. He certainly could no longer put his two hands around her waist to measure it.

What was the relationship betweeen Stover and Eliza? Ma implied he was just a friend of the family, but the Caribou records show that Nathan Stover married Eliza not once but twice. No record of a divorce was found. However, between Artson Pratt's death and Eliza's first marriage to Stover in 1877 she was briefly wed to a man named William I. Brown. Who Brown was and what happened to him remains a mystery, with no one left alive to supply the answer.

There is nothing to tell us of Eliza's second marriage to Stover, except a brief entry in the diary of her youngest son Henry Barton Pratt, who was, among other things, a justice of the peace. The entry is dated December 23, 1890, six years before Eliza's death:

> I hauled a load of shingles to Caribou 9 m borrowed $35 from Lufkin and Holmes. Married Mother and Stover per Order.

Whose order? Eliza's? Stover's? A legal directive of some sort?

Pa had told me that toward the end of her life Eliza suffered from "softening of the brain" and went insane—whatever that layman's term meant. The town records state only that Eliza died at age sixty-eight, in 1896. No cause of death is given.

Could her mental deterioration have brought family pressure on Stover to remarry her and take care of her in her last years? Or did the deranged Eliza demand a second ceremony as reaffirmation of their existing marriage?

Henry Barton Pratt, who performed the ceremony, was not only a justice of the peace, but also a town councillor, a game warden, a sheriff, and a one-time partner with Stover in a grocery store, besides being a potato farmer and a woodsman. He was also an amateur surgeon, who found plenty of work to do in this pioneer community a hundred miles from the nearest doctor. His diary mentions, among other operations he performed, amputations and the opening of an accident victim's skull. People in towns like Caribou could and did turn their hand to anything.

In the fall of 1994 I made my first visit to Caribou. The Evergreen Cemetery held rich finds for me. I not only located the grave of my grandfather Henry Meader Shaw and his second wife Hilma Spongberg, but I found a gravestone that commemorated Artson Pratt.

Artson was initially buried in Maryland, but he was later brought back and laid to rest in the Pratt lot. His name is carved on the Pratt family stone. He was given a tight little space on one narrow side of that stone:

Artson K. Pratt
1st P C Cav
died in
Annapolis, MD
Sept 5 1864
Æ 38 yrs

Artson was joined eight years later by his son David. The inscription below Artson's reads:

David L. son of
Artson K &
Eliza H Pratt
died
Nov 18 1872
Æ 16 yrs

In 1896 Artson was joined by Eliza, who now lies between two of her three husbands, Artson and Nathan.

The front of the stone records the family of Artson and Eliza's son Henry Barton Pratt. The broad back of the stone proclaims in large letters the name of Artson's successor, Nathan Stover:

Nathan W. Stover
Co D 5th Regt, ME vols
b. Nov 29, 1842

Eliza H. his wife
Aug 23, 1828 - July 13, 1896

The difference in the dates of birth of Eliza and Stover is striking: Stover was fourteen years younger than Eliza, only twelve years older than Ma.

Returning to Ma: whatever she had to go through when she was growing up, it made her the indomitable woman she was, and allowed her to cope with repeated disasters until she, like her mother before her, lost her mind to age and illness.

If Ma became a strong and dominant matriarch, it was because she had to. She had no father to soften and protect her early years. She and Henry Meader Shaw married when she was twenty, and he deserted her and their children after fourteen years of marriage.

Married at twenty, divorced at thirty-four. Not a common thing in those days. Divorce was condemned, and divorcees suspect. When I knew Ma, she gave the impression that she lived a celibate life forever after, and implied that she found single life a blessed relief from clumsy and importunate male demands.

But did she live celibate? The diaries of her brother Henry Barton Pratt mention her dropping by often on Sundays with "Parker." Who was Parker? A possible candidate is Parker Hardison, young brother of Ai Hardison who married Ma's sister Josephine. Parker was several years Ma's junior, but by thirty-four, who was counting? Parker was already married to a woman named

Tirza, and remained so till he died. But why assume that human affairs were any less complex in our forebears' time than in ours?

Whatever liaisons Ma may have had, she wanted to make sure I avoided any of my own—that I avoided men altogether, if possible.

Both of the two sons she bore to Henry Meader Shaw ended in alcoholics' graves. The popular medical lore at the time held that alcoholism was transmitted from father to son if intercourse took place when the father was drunk. Now, in the day of DNA, medical scientists invoke "genetic pre-disposition," which is not the same thing, but might lead to the same end. Does alcoholism slide down the generations on the chromosomes? Did the women not succumb because "nice girls don't drink" and so they never were allowed the opportunity?

And what about my grandfather Henry Meader Shaw?

Nothing but a gravestone in Evergreen Cemetery, Caribou. All the LDS records have given me is the Shaw line of descent from Deacon John Shaw, born in Weymouth, Massachusetts, about 1730. He migrated north to Buckfield, Oxford County, Maine, where his son Jotham was born in 1764.

The record is incomplete, but Jotham, it is said, was one of eighteen children. He married in 1786 and produced ten children of his own. The Buckfield graveyard is full of Shaws, none of whom, if the *History of Buckfield* (Cole & Whitman, 1915) is complete, appears to have done anything worthy of note.

The record goes from Jotham down the generations in Buckfield to Francis Cushing Shaw, who, before he was killed by being run over by an ox cart, sired Henry Meader Shaw. Henry was named for his uncle Henry Meader Shaw, who had died young.

Some time in his youth, Henry moved from Buckfield to Lyndon, now Caribou, where presumably he met Ma.

Death Certificates

I've learned how misleading death certificates can be. Frequently they give only the final reason for the stopping of the heart. I thought one might solve the mystery of Aunt Grace, who died slowly over a two-year period from an undiagnosed illness. The certificate lists her cause of death as "stroke."

Bart, my terrifying uncle who died of his long love affair with alcohol and morphine, was certified to have died of "sudden heart failure." Furthermore, his date of death was given as August 1934, which would make him dead when he found me in the cornfield after I ran away from school.

Pa died of "inguinal hernia with intussusception and strangulation," which says nothing of the years of neglected health, smoking, alcohol, malnutrition and septic teeth.

On the Lynde side, things were more accurate. Grandfather Lynde: "stroke." Mother: "grave hysteria with heart block." Sarah Lynde: "carcinoma of the colon."

And poor Marge. Half a century later, writing this memoir and still haunted by her death, I obtained her death certificate from the Melrose City Clerk. I'd always suspected suicide, but the certificate read: "pneumonia; carbuncle, left chest." This didn't answer the question about suicide, of course, or why this twenty-five-year-old woman died in a mental hospital. Pneumonia can be secondary to many things. Had she made an attempt on her life, been saved, but, weakened by loss of blood or infection from a wound, contracted pneumonia?

The story on both sides of the family still goes on. Endless clues remain to follow, each of which will no doubt lead to a cluster of other clues. I am constantly amazed by how much a persistent sleuth can turn up. As Pasteur said, "Where observation is concerned, chance favors the prepared mind."

Credits

"Don't sing love songs . . ."
   Snippets from an old folk song.

First stanza from the poem "Fate," by Susan Marr Spalding
   In : *An American Anthology 1787 - 1900.* Houghton Mifflin: 1900.

Reference for Chapter 92

Early American Stencils by Janet Waring, Dover Publications, Inc., New York, 1968, pages 81-82; Figures 93 and 94.

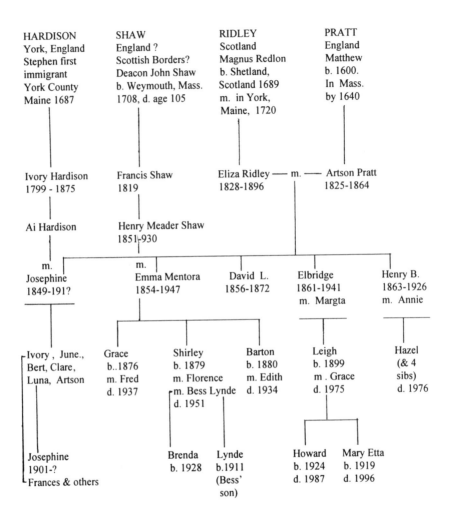

HARDISON
York, England
Stephen first
immigrant
York County
Maine 1687

SHAW
England ?
Scottish Borders?
Deacon John Shaw
b. Weymouth, Mass.
1708, d. age 105

RIDLEY
Scotland
Magnus Redlon
b. Shetland,
Scotland 1689
m. in York,
Maine, 1720

PRATT
England
Matthew
b. 1600.
In Mass.
by 1640

Ivory Hardison
1799 - 1875

Francis Shaw
1819

Eliza Ridley —— m. —— Artson Pratt
1828-1896   1825-1864

Ai Hardison

Henry Meader Shaw
1851-930

m.
Josephine
1849-191?

m.
Emma Mentora
1854-1947

David L.
1856-1872

Elbridge
1861-1941
m. Margta

Henry B.
1863-1926
m. Annie

Ivory , June.,
Bert, Clare,
Luna, Artson

Grace
b..1876
m. Fred
d. 1937

Shirley
b. 1879
m. Florence
m. Bess Lynde
d. 1951

Barton
b. 1880
m. Edith
d. 1934

Leigh
b. 1899
m . Grace
d. 1975

Hazel
(& 4
sibs)
d. 1976

Josephine
1901-?
Frances & others

Brenda
b. 1928

Lynde
b.1911
(Bess'
son)

Howard
b. 1924
d. 1987

Mary Etta
b. 1919
d. 1996

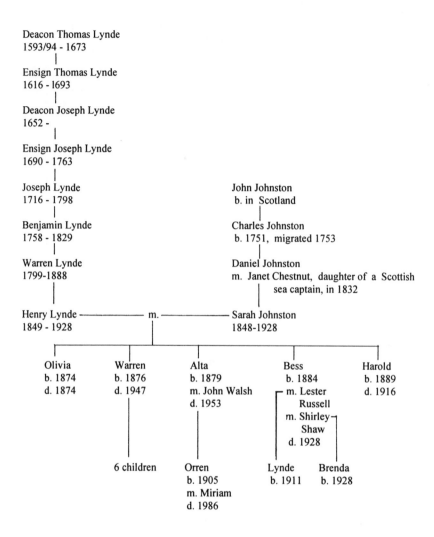

Deacon Thomas Lynde
1593/94 - 1673

Ensign Thomas Lynde
1616 - 1693

Deacon Joseph Lynde
1652 -

Ensign Joseph Lynde
1690 - 1763

Joseph Lynde   John Johnston
1716 - 1798   b. in Scotland

Benjamin Lynde   Charles Johnston
1758 - 1829   b. 1751, migrated 1753

Warren Lynde   Daniel Johnston
1799-1888   m. Janet Chestnut, daughter of a Scottish
                            sea captain, in 1832

Henry Lynde ———————— m. ———————— Sarah Johnston
1849 - 1928   1848-1928

Olivia	Warren	Alta	Bess	Harold
b. 1874	b. 1876	b. 1879	b. 1884	b. 1889
d. 1874	d. 1947	m. John Walsh	m. Lester	d. 1916
		d. 1953	Russell	
			m. Shirley	
			Shaw	
			d. 1928	
	6 children	Orren	Lynde Brenda	
		b. 1905	b. 1911 b. 1928	
		m. Miriam		
		d. 1986		

ORDER FORM

Please send:

____copies of *The Dark Well* @ $14.95   _____

Shipping - $2.50 first book; $1.00 each
    additional book. Priority shipping:
    $4 first book.   _____

Sales tax (Maine only) 0.90   _____

                         TOTAL $_____

Send check or money order to:

Audenreed Press
P. O. Box 1305 #103
Brunswick, ME 04011

or order by phone: (207) 833-5016

Please **print** your name and address:

Name_____

Street/P.O. Box_____

City_____State_____Zip_____

Phone_____